The Indo-Pacific: Trump, China, and the New Struggle for Global Mastery

"Richard Heydarian's splendid new book is a wide-ranging, creative, informative, thoughtful, and venturesome antidote to complacency regarding the future of the Indo-Pacific region. Well worth reading for its scope, ideas, and verve."
—Don Emmerson, *Senior Fellow Emeritus, Stanford University*

"Richard Heydarian's new book deals front and center with the two great geo-strategic issues of our time: the rise of the Indo Pacific, and the strategic competition between a Donald Trump led US and a Xi Jinping dominated China…. Richard weaves these themes through his book, importantly, including from the perspectives of middle and small powers in the Indo Pacific."
—Stephen Francis Smith, *Former Australian Defense and Foreign Minister*

"This is an ambitious effort, a survey of global strategic risks and diplomatic opportunities from one of Southeast Asia's most authentic and articulate policy voices."
—Rory Medcalf, *Professor and Head of the National Security College (NSC), Australian National University*

"Richard Heydarian is part of a thinning line-up of young dynamic Asian strategic thinkers. Coming from a country still grappling with major powers rivalry, Richard's views brings credible insights to the dilemmas faced by many countries in the Indo-Pacific. I have always found Richard's strategic analyses to be original, thoughtful and most importantly, honest. He does not compromise when it comes to intellectual integrity. Richard's thoughts on the evolving IndoPacific, as well as US and China competition, deserves the attention of policy-makers, many of whom are still searching for the right path forward for the region."
—Dino Patti Djalal, *Former Vice Minister for Foreign Affairs of Indonesia, and Founder of Foreign Policy Community of Indonesia (FPCI)*

"Heydarian examines the shifting landscape of the Indo-Pacific, the Sino-American competition that will define the region for decades to come, and the efforts of small and middle powers seeking to hold the line against both Chinese revisionism and potential American decline. His project is ambitious, undeniably necessary, and offers important insights on topics that will likely dominate international relations for much of this century."
—Gregory B. Poling, *is director of the Asia M Center for Strategic a*

"Heydarian's book is an ideal read for those who want an informative account with a panoramic view and in-depth analysis of the emerging Indo-Pacific. This region is the main theater of the century's contest—the strategic competition between the United States and China. Heydarian incisively examines the competing visions and approaches of the two great powers, but he also shows how several other regional states can shape the strategic environment."
—Alexander L. Vuving, *Professor at the Asia-Pacific Center for Security Studies (APCSS)*

"Richard Javad Heydarian, a leading voice among a new generation of Asian strategic thinkers, has composed a wide-ranging, timely, and thought-provoking illustration of a region of immense importance. He draws upon an astonishingly broad range of intellectual sources and covers many of the dominant strategic issues of our times, including the impact of the Trump presidency, the motivations behind China's Belt and Road Initiative, and Japan's ambitious reengagement with the world."
—Dhruva Jaishankar, *Fellow in Foreign Policy Studies, Brookings India*

"In the plethora of literature on the Indo-Pacific, this is a rare insightful account. Richard artfully parses the paradoxes surrounding the construct, and examines its many competing versions. Through a careful study of theoretical frameworks—old and new—he explains why regional states interpret the idea differently; how the concept's natural evolution is impacted by the innate impulses of key actors; and why its eventual form might depend on the outcome of the contest for supremacy between powerful states."
—Abhijit Singh, *Senior Fellow, Observer Research Foundation (ORF), India*

Richard Javad Heydarian

The Indo-Pacific: Trump, China, and the New Struggle for Global Mastery

palgrave
macmillan

Richard Javad Heydarian
Visiting Research Fellow
National Chengchi University
Taipei, Taiwan

ISBN 978-981-13-9798-1   ISBN 978-981-13-9799-8   (eBook)
https://doi.org/10.1007/978-981-13-9799-8

Cover image: © Pool/Pool/Getty Images

This Palgrave Macmillan imprint is published by the registered company Springer Nature
Singapore Pte Ltd.
The registered company address is: 152 Beach Road, #21-01/04 Gateway East, Singapore
189721, Singapore

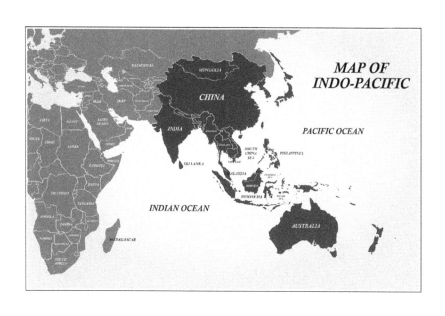

MAP OF INDO-PACIFIC

To my loving father, Nasser, who introduced me to the world of global politics in my younger years; and N. for pushing me to evolve beyond myself.

ACKNOWLEDGEMENTS

This book marks the culmination of almost a decade of research, which, incidentally, coincides with the beginning of my career as a writer and geopolitical analyst. It all started in Cairo in December 2009, when I began, with focused intention and analytic obsession, to reflect on the intimations of a revolutionary upheaval in the Near East, a region that I was quite familiar with. As I wrote in an article entitled "Egypt's impending political earthquake" (March 31, 2010) shortly after my visit, the North African nation faced a "potential watershed…and a fierce [political] battle for Egypt's soul" in the coming months, especially ahead of crucial elections that could determine the post-Hosni Mubarak era. Apparently, what was on the horizon was nothing short of a total revolution, which toppled the Mubarak regime the following year. Soon after, I found myself writing my first book, still in my early 20s then, on the Arab uprisings, its roots, and its long-term implications for Asia and beyond. Afterwards, I never looked back again, deciding to devote myself fully to a newfound calling as a dispassionate, yet committed, analyst of geopolitics, from Cairo to California and beyond.

Over the next decade, I traveled, in my capacity as an academic, policy adviser, and writer, across the world, meeting senior officials and leading experts from Perth to Pyongyang, Brussels to Beijing, New Delhi to New York, and Tehran to Tokyo, as well as giving talks and lectures on geopolitics in the world's leading universities. During this period, I also had the pleasure of having exchanges, some longer and on the record, with various heads of state and world leaders, including the Malaysian Prime Minister Mahathir Mohamad, Presidents of the Republic of China (Taiwan) Ma Ying-jeou and Tsai Ing-wen, Australian Prime Minister Malcolm Turnbull, and Philippine President Rodrigo Duterte. I also had the pleasure of meeting, interviewing and/or exchanging views with former world leaders, who appeared as world-weary yet cosmopolitan and hopeful, such as President Fidel Ramos, a pillar of regional integration in post-Cold War Asia, and Prime Minister Helen Clark, a pillar of global peace and development in recent decades, not to mention other former leaders such as President Gloria Macapagal Arroyo. Not to mention meeting foreign and defense ministers as well as a plethora of senior officials from nations across the Indo-Pacific, who eagerly and earnestly shared, with unabashed candor and sincere puzzlement, their personal, bureaucratic, and strategic dilemmas to me. Each leader, bearing his/her own idiosyncrasies and eloquent tryst with destiny, not only revealed a new layer of psychology of leadership, but also, and more importantly, the depth of challenges faced by nations across the Indo-Pacific. This book is precisely about revealing, through my own eyes and based on my decade-long research and exchanges with senior policy-makers, the existential challenges haunting the world's most promising yet also beleaguered nations.

This book is also very personal to me, a form of vindication even. My father wanted me to be a doctor, following his (and my sister's) footsteps in the medical field. My mother, herself an academic and university professor, wanted me instead to become a lawyer, the first in our family. I eventually became neither, striking my own direction by carving out an improbable niche at the intersection of academe, media, and policy-making realms—fixing my gaze on the world and trying to capture its many nuances with more than 1000 articles over the past decade and millions of published words. This book is dedicated to my loving father, who helped me hone my linguistic skills (I grew up with multiple languages and in multiple countries) and, from a very young age, encouraged me to listen to BBC Radio and remain constantly interested in international news to keep abreast with global geopolitics. Thus, before reaching the age of 10, I already developed some familiarity with the intersection of petro-politics, capitalism, and the American empire. Never had a fully "normal" childhood, yet I'm eternally grateful to my loving parents, who introduced me to world culture and global politics with patience, tenderness, and all-out support throughout my developmental years.

This is also my longest book yet, taking more than three years to write, and drawing on a decade of scholarly and journalistic material. It also brings together my perspective as someone who spent years in both ends of the Eurasian landmass—my father hailing from the Caspian Sea, while my mother is from the city of pines in the Cordillera Mountains, with a large chunk of my extended family residents and citizens of the United States. The book is a mélange of the melancholy sweet contemplation of my father's folks—who told me about the Soviet invasion during the First World War and the horrors of conflict and confrontation that bedeviled the Near East for the next hundred years—as well as the Latin-Asiatic dynamism of my mother's clan, who have spread across the world with an inscrutable tenacity and irrepressible yearning for the many permutations of the American dream.

This book is also about my personal advocacy and convictions. Once settled back in East Asia, having had to leave my birthplace in the Philippine for few years following a horrific earthquake that devastated our home town (Baguio) in 1990, I devoted much of my early adulthood to making sure that, at least in my own little capacity, the South and East China Seas don't turn into another Persian Gulf, a theater of war where many of my loved ones spent their golden years fighting, though under different flags, against the brutal Saddam regime. The Indo-Pacific, therefore, is something personal to me; it represents the broad landscape of my mixed identity, heritage, and psycho-emotional horizons. In phenomenological lexicon, the geopolitics of the Indo-Pacific has constituted my "life world" of meaning and purpose and geopolitical imagination.

This book wouldn't have been possible without the support of countless family members, friends, and colleagues, who helped me better understand the internal politics and strategic orientation of a plethora of complex nations across the mega-region. Let me begin by thanking my aunt Rodelisa Foronda, who has always been by my side throughout very trying moments in my life and even accompanying me in some of my foreign visits. I would like to thank my mentor Professor Walden Bello, who arranged my visit to Cairo back in 2009 and, throughout the years, encouraged me to write, develop my own voice, and helped me connect with a global network of thinkers. I am also very grateful to long-time friends and colleagues such as Ambassador Dino Djalal, and the Foreign Policy Community Indonesia folks, who have helped me understand Indonesian politics and foreign policy, not to mention arranging our trip to North Korea in 2018. And same goes to Indonesian colleagues in the University of Indonesia and Center for Strategic and International Studies (CSIS), especially Andrew Mantong and Evan Laksamana, as well as many newfound friends in Kompas, Jakarta Post and the broader Indonesian media and civil society. Exchanges with former Indonesian Foreign Minister Marty Marty Natalegawa, especially ahead and during our ASEAN-Australia Dialogue panel in 2018, was also very helpful. I'm also profoundly thankful to Professor Gordon Flake and friends in the Perth USAsia Centre, who helped me develop a better understanding of Western Australia and the country's Indo-Pacific orientation. I'm also grateful to former Australian defense and foreign minister Stephen Smith, who was arguably the first leader to embed the Indo-Pacific paradigm into high-level strategic discourse and policy-making. Folks at the Australia National University, especially professors William Tow, Rory Medcalf, and John Blaxland, have also provided invaluable insights for the book. Surely Dr. David Capie, Director of the Centre for Strategic Studies at Victoria University in Wellington, was a precious source of knowledge on New Zealand's foreign policy. Colleagues in India, particularly Abhijit Singh (Observer Foundation), Dhruva Jaishankar (Brookings), Raja Mohan (National University of Singapore), and Brahma Chellaney provided a profoundly analytic look into India's gigantic ambitions and challenges. I have also been blessed to have had the friendship, and back-and-forth exchanges, with the indefatigable Donald Emmerson, who always encouraged my heterodox thinking with his own—and has been kind enough to host me in Stanford. Not to mention colleagues and friends from the Washington DC think tank world, including Amy Searight and Greg Poling of the Center for Strategic and International Studies (CSIS), Joshua Kurlantzick of Council on Foreign Relations (CFR), and colleagues from Hudson Institute, including Dr. Saturo Nagao and Dr. Patrick Cronin, as well as the Brookings Institution, Carnegie, RAND corporation, and the Heritage Foundation. I'm also grateful to friends from Southeast Asian think tanks, including the S. Rajaratnam School of International Studies (RSIS), Institute of Security and International Studies (ISIS), Thailand, the Institute of Southeast Asian Studies (ISEAS), and Diplomatic Academy of Vietnam, among many others, who hosted me for lectures throughout the years. Exchanges with regional diplomats such as Ambassador Bilahari Kausikan and Ambassador Wilfrido Villacorta were surely refreshing. I would also like to thank European colleagues, particularly the European Institute for

Asian Studies (EIAS) in Brussels and Koc University in Istanbul, for hosting my talks and sharing their views with me. This book wouldn't have been possible without the insights of countless senior policy-makers, who shared their views with the author, ranging from the European External Action Service (EAS) of the European Union, who hosted me twice in late 2016 and late 2017 for consultations; the Japanese government, including foreign and defense ministries, as well as senior officials such as Nobukatsu Kanehara, Deputy Secretary-General of National Security Secretariat and Assistant Chief Cabinet Secretary in the Prime Minister's Shinzo Abe's office in 2017; North Korea's government, including Kim Yong-dae, vice president of the Presidium of Supreme People's Assembly, and Vice Minister for Foreign Affairs Ri Gil-song, in addition to various officials from other organs of the state; and senior officials from Australia's Department of Foreign Affairs and Trade (DFA), Canada's Global Affairs department, and senior officials from China, South Korea, New Zealand, India, and Singapore, among many other Indo-Pacific nations. I am also grateful to senior officials in the Barack Obama and Donald Trump administrations, including Indo-Pacific chief commanders Admiral Harry Harris and Philip Davidson, for providing the view from the perspective of a global empire. In my own home country, the Philippines, I was also privileged to have extensive exchanges with senior policy-makers such as Defense Secretary Delfin Lorenzana, former Foreign Secretary Albert Del Rosario, Associate Supreme Court Justice Antonio Carpio, and the late former National Security Adviser Roilo Golez—all patriots who have done their best to protect peace and prosperity in the region. I'm also grateful to colleagues such as Jay Batongbacal, Director of the University of the Philippines' Institute for Maritime Affairs and Law of the Sea (IMLOS); Professor Aileen Baviera, UP Asian Center, and Ambassador to China, Chito Sta. Romana, who provided the perfect soundboard for my ideas on Philippine foreign policy and candidly shared their views with me. I also like to thank senior commanders and officers from the Philippine Navy, Philippine Airforce, Philippine Marines, Philippine Army, and Philippine Coast Guard, who shared their invaluable operational views with me throughout the years. Thanks to an International Visitor Leadership Program (IVLP) in 2014, I also had the chance to exchange views with leading experts on South China Sea and international law, including Professor Anthony C. Arend (Georgetown University), Professor John Norton Moore and Professor Myron H. Nordquist (Virginia University), Professor Mathew Waxman

(Columbia University), Professor James Hsiung (New York University) and several law-of-the-sea experts at the United Nations (UN) and the Asia-Pacific Center for Security Studies (APCSS), among other legal scholars. Trained as a political scientist, their legal analyses were hugely complementary to mine. The list is long, yet I hope they all know how grateful I am to them.

I would like to thank my editors and publishers, who allowed me to use some excerpts from my previous works, including Harry Kazianis from the National Interest and Shawn Crispin from the Asia Times Online as well as editors from The Diplomat, Carnegie-Tsingua Centre, South China Morning Post, Nikkei Asian Review, Brookings Institution, CFR, CSIS, and, of course, Dindo Manhit, my former colleague at De La Salle University and director of the Stratbase-**ADR Institute** for Strategic and International Studies (ADRi), who kindly allowed me to use my special study on China's Belt and Road Initiative for this book. Above all, let me thank my research assistant Stephanie Serapio, among my brightest students ever, who helped me pull off this increasingly expanded and ambitious book. I sincerely hope that this book will mark a pioneering effort for a systematic analysis of the Indo-Pacific, and the many opportunities and challenges that this new geopolitical center of gravity presents in the coming years and decades.

CONTENTS

LIST OF FIGURES

CHAPTER 1

The New Cartography of Power

Whoever is lord of Malacca has his hands on the throat of Venice… Who understands this will favour Malacca. —Tomé Pires[1]

International politics, like all politics, is a struggle for power.[2] —Hans J. Morgenthau, *Politics Among Nations*

[The Indo-Pacific is] a beautiful constellation of nations, each its own bright star, satellites to none…. —President Donald Trump, Da Nang, Vietnam[3]

Reflecting on the future of the global order, the late Singaporean Prime Minister Lee Kuan Yew warned that the rise of China is so consequential that it won't only require tactical adjustment by its neighbors, but instead an overhaul in the global security architecture.[4] As the former Asian leader bluntly put it, though "[t]he Chinese will [initially] want to share this century as co-equals with the U.S.," they ultimately have the "intention to be the greatest power in the world" eventually.[5] According to this paradigm, this century will increasingly replicate the bipolar system in the preceding one, except this time China will be taking the Soviet

[1] Kaplan (2010).
[2] Korab-Karpowicz (2010).
[3] Trump (2017b).
[4] Allison et al. (2013).
[5] Khong (2015).

© The Author(s) 2020
R. J. Heydarian, *The Indo-Pacific: Trump, China, and the New Struggle for Global Mastery*, https://doi.org/10.1007/978-981-13-9799-8_1

Union's place and, likely, even dislodge the West from atop the global "Peking order."

Not long after the demise of the Singaporean leader, his prophetic insights are congealing into an indubitable geopolitical reality. Today, China is the world's largest exporting nation, largest consumer of basic goods, and increasingly also the leading source of investments, particularly in strategic infrastructure, especially in Asia and across the developing world (see Chapter 4). Meanwhile, economic vigor has translated into strategic assertiveness and military muscle, as China opens up overseas bases, beginning in Djibouti but more stealthily across the Indian Ocean, expands its blue water navy, and coercively transforms adjacent waters into its "blue national soil."[6] Above all, China's new paramount leader, Xi Jinping, has completely discarded the low-key diplomacy of his predecessors in favor of an all-out bid for global primacy, going so far as promoting a "uniquely Chinese model" of development overseas[7] and gradually establishing an "Asia for Asians"[8] order across the Eurasian landmass to the exclusion of Western powers and Japan. Though packaged as ostensibly a trillion-dollar connectivity initiative, the Belt and Road Initiative (BRI) is, above all, about laying the foundation of a "Chinese world order."[9]

And this is precisely the backdrop against which the contemporary discourse vis-à-vis the "Indo-Pacific" should be understood: In a sense, it's a fundamentally new geopolitical construct that reflects the strategic sensibilities of great powers as well as the ineluctable geo-economic integration spanning from Canada to Cairo over decades of relentless globalization. The mega-region is also where the next World War could be ignited. The Harvard academic Graham Allison, who carefully studied the Cuban Missile Crisis,[10] foresees five possible areas of conflict between the United States and China, namely a war over the South China Sea, Taiwan, North Korea, East China Sea involving Japan, or a prolonged and devastating trade war.[11] The Indo-Pacific is both a cauldron of

[6]Holmes (2013).

[7]Bloomberg (2018).

[8]Jakobson (2016).

[9]Maçães (2019).

[10]Allison and Zelikow (1999).

[11]Allison (2017a).

geopolitical competition as well as economic dynamism. It's where the future of the world will be determined.

REVENGE OF HISTORY

In the twilight years of the fifteenth century, Portugal and Spain, the first Western superpowers, divided the world into two spheres. The Treaty of Tordesillas (1494) left vast portions of the Indian Ocean at the mercy of an expansive Portugal, which built naval strongholds from the Persian Gulf to Goa and Malacca Strait, while Imperial Spain dominated the Pacific and much of the Americas.[12] The upshot was a new geopolitical fault line, which artificially divided an ancient and coherent Sino-Islamic episteme anchored by monsoon-driven maritime trade stretching from the Western Pacific to East Africa.[13] Though far from hegemonic, the Chinese came closest to ruling the high seas before the advent of European imperialism. The dual-ocean voyages of Zheng He, a Muslim admiral from the Ming Dynasty who extensively relied on the expertise of co-religionist seafarers, underscored the inherent inseparability and thick networks of commercial and cultural interdependence across the Pacific and Indian Oceans. By the nineteenth century, there was a renewed recognition of the "Indo-Pacific" mega-sphere. This was especially the case in the Anglo-American world, including the very British Empire, which oversaw a vast pan-Asiatic dominion from Suez to Singapore, as well as among eminent Anglo-American strategists such as Alfred Thayer Mahan and Halford Mackinder. The following century saw the further crystallization of this trend, as Imperial Japan began to build its own Indo-Pacific empire, stretching from the Pacific Islands to the borders of British India, while the German strategist Karl Haushofer deeply influenced Nazi Germany's conception of the centrality of the mega-region.[14] During the early decades of the Cold War, British and Australian defense agencies routinely discussed the Indo-Pacific Basin.[15]

---

[12] Sue (2014).

[13] Kaplan (2011).

[14] See for instance Weigert, Hans W. "Haushofer and the Pacific." Foreign Affairs 20, no. 4 (1942): 732–742. https://doi.org/10.2307/20029189; Sempa, Francis. 2015. "Karl Haushofer and the Rise of the Monsoon Countries", The Diplomat. March 10. https://thediplomat.com/2015/03/karl-haushofer-and-the-rise-of-the-monsoon-countries/.

[15] Medcalf (2013).

So what makes the contemporary discussion of the Indo-Pacific anymore unique? Is this just a reassertion of an old geopolitical reality?

The Indo-Pacific, as it's conceptualized and understood by regional powers today, is at once about and beyond the China question: It's geopolitical as well as geo-economic; synthetic and spontaneous; and ineluctable (structural) as well as policy-driven (agential). On one hand, it's all about the Asian behemoth, and how other powers and regional actors seek to respond to its rise. Or, to put it in more stark terms, it's about "constrainment"[16] of China's ambitions in ways that give greater voice to rising powers while discouraging coercively disruptive revisionism. The influential American scholar Michael Mendelbaum has even suggested that a "new containment" strategy, which draws on Cold War tactics against the Soviet Union, "offers the best chance to defend American interests in the twenty-first century."[17]

Naturally, Beijing has not lost sight of this dimension of the Indo-Pacific paradigm. No wonder then, the Chinese Foreign Minister Wang Yi derisively characterized it as an "attention-grabbing idea" that will "dissipate like ocean foam."[18] Yet, major powers have embraced the new geopolitical concept wholeheartedly.[19] The Indo-Pacific now constitutes what historian Yuval Harari termed as an "inter-subjective truth."[20] Beginning with the Manmohan Singh administration, India, the heartland of the Indian Ocean realm, facilitated the establishment of "a stable, secure and prosperous Indo-Pacific region." Australia became the first country to officially name its region as the Indo-Pacific, with former Foreign Minister Stephen Smith spearheading the effort. After all, the continent-nation is home to the famed saltwater crocodile (*Crocodylus porosus*), also known as the Indo-Pacific crocodile. Under President Susilo Bambang, Yudhoyono Indonesia, the world's largest Muslim-majority nation, began discussing the "*Indo-Pasifik*"—a dynamic region, which, in the words of former Foreign Minister Marty Natalegawa, has turned into the "engine of global growth."

During her tenure as arguably the most high-profile American Secretary of State, Hillary Clinton often talked about Washington as

[16]Segal (1996).
[17]Mandelbaum (2019).
[18]Birtles (2018).
[19]Medcalf (2013).
[20]Harari (2015).

the anchor of peace and stability in the "Pacific Century," though she often also discussed, along with her Assistant Secretary for East Asia Kurt Campbell, the broader Indo-Pacific theater as the main strategic focus of the America. While reaching out to Indo-Chinese nations, Hillary's successor, John Kerry, described Burma, then a liberalizing nation, as part of a crucial "Indo-Pacific economic corridor." But it was the US Navy Pacific Command, later renamed as the Indo-Pacific Command, which played a central role in operationalizing the concept and, subsequently, embedding it in Washington's strategic lexicon. Former commander of the US Pacific Command, Admiral Samuel Locklear, discussed the "Indo-Asia-Pacific," while his successor, Harry Harris, incessantly mentioned the growing importance of a vast yet internally coherent geostrategic space from Alaska to Zanzibar. Even some Chinese strategists have reluctantly embraced the concept, transliterating it as *Yin Tai*.[21] As Australian strategist Rory Medcalf explains, the Indo-Pacific reflects "a conscious shift among thinkers and policy makers in multiple places, from Washington to New Delhi, Canberra to Jakarta,"[22] and the need to[23] "dilute China's profile" and its "impact in a larger ocean, in a wider regional context." As China aggressively pursues Mackinderean dominance in the Eurasian landmass—namely, the heartland stretching from the Indo-China and South Asia to Central Asia, the Middle East and Eastern Europe—the United States and its allies still maintain Mahanian superiority in the Indian and Pacific Oceans.

The Japanese Connection

If there is a single figure, who has played the greatest role in bringing about the "Indo-Pacific" age, arguably that distinction should go to Japanese Prime Minister Shinzo Abe. Since his return to power in 2012, Abe has, with unmatched single-mindedness, dedicated himself to revamping not only his country's post-World War II foreign policy, but also the emerging post-American world order. In an influential ope-ed in 2012, entitled.... he laid down of the most compelling... singular geopolitical united, [where he argued:] "Peace, stability, and freedom of navigation in the Pacific Ocean are inseparable from peace,

---

[21] Medcalf (2013).

[22] Ibid.

[23] Nelson (2017).

stability, and freedom of navigation in the Indian Ocean." This was in fact a reiteration of his 2007 speech[24] at the Indian Parliament, titled, "Confluence of the Two Seas," where he spoke of a "broader Asia" and the "dynamic coupling" between the two vast oceans as "seas of freedom and of prosperity." Under his leadership, he vowed that Japan will "play a greater role in preserving the common good in both regions."[25] Less than a decade later, almost all relevant players across Asia, North America, and Oceana, have now embraced Abe's vision as a geopolitical truism. Former US Adm. Harry Harris, who is partially of Japanese descent through his mother and is currently the US Ambassador to South Korea, generated great buzz by memorably speaking of the Indo-Pacific as an indivisible strategic system extending from the "Hollywood to Bollywood."[26] Crucially, the Trump administration wholeheartedly embraced[27] the ideological and normative underpinnings of Abe's vision, which called for a concert of democratic powers, namely Australia, India, Japan, and the United States, amid the rise of China, the preeminent revisionist power of the twenty-first century. What Abe has vigorously advocated[28] for is the establishment of a robust, yet nimble, Quadrilateral Alliance, the so-called "Quad," of like-minded powers to keep Chinese ambitions in check. It's fundamentally a "coalition of deterrence" against China. With Singapore thrown into the mix, the "SQUAD" has become another potential geopolitical grouping. In many ways, it has become almost impossible[29] to separate the Indo-Pacific from the QUAD, or SQUAD, and the Trump administration's "Free and Open Indo-Pacific" order (FOIP). What brings these[30] "like-minded" countries (or the SQUAD) together are their capability (i.e., a robust naval force) as well as shared interests and norms, namely upholding a rules-based international order that ensures free access to Sea Lines of Communications through battling threats from non-state actors as well as constraining the revisionist tendencies of rising naval powers across the Indo-Pacific realm, China in particular, but to a lesser degree

[24] Abe (2007).
[25] Abe (2012).
[26] Rajghatta (2018).
[27] Pence (2018).
[28] Madan (2017).
[29] Smith (2018).
[30] Medcalf (2013).

also Russia and Iran. But as Medcalf observes,[31] "The Indo-Pacific is not simply a new term for the Asia-Pacific," but rather, "it reflects changes in economics, strategic behavior and diplomatic institutions that are having real consequences regardless of who utters the words." In former Foreign Minister Stephen Smith's words, "I was persuaded that the rise of India as a great power and the rise of Indonesia ... would cause the geo-strategic design [of the future regional order] to be more than simply [about] the US, China, the Pacific and North Asia."[32]

THE GLOBAL TINDERBOX

The Indo-Pacific's internal coherence and global significance is almost self-evident. Despite rapid advances in technology, much of the world's trade is still conducted through the seas. Rising powers, ranging from Iran to India and China, are located across the Eurasian "Rimland,"[33] where there is precious access to the Indian and Pacific oceans. Today, 90% of global trade and up to two-thirds of hydrocarbon shipments transit through oceans. Much of the activity is taking place in the Indian and Pacific Oceans, where the bulk of global population, nuclear powers, and booming economies reside. The Indian Ocean alone is responsible for almost half of the world's total container traffic, and hosts about 70% of hydrocarbon transshipments. Smallest of the three oceans, it's a tinderbox of geopolitical tensions, economic vibrancy, and unremitting insecurity, hosting the major navigational chokepoints of global trade, namely the Straits of Hormuz, Bab el Mandeb, and Malacca. The Strait of Hormuz, which narrows down to only 21 miles at the precipice of US-Iranian geopolitical fault lines, hosts up to 40% of global seaborne oil shipments. The Strait of Malacca, squeezed among Singapore, Indonesia, and Malaysia, hosts half of the world's merchant fleet capacity, half of world oil shipment, and about a quarter of world trade.[34] And Southeast Asia, home to one of the world's fastest-growing economies and populations, lies squarely at the intersection of the Indian and Pacific Oceans,

---

[31] Ibid.

[32] Interview with author, December 2018.

[33] Garrity (2013).

[34] Kaplan (2011).

further accentuating the growing influence of Indonesia, the other emerging giant of the 21st century.

Of course, the Indo-Pacific gained greater pungency in light of the growing dependence of East Asian industrial giants, namely China, Japan, and South Korea, on Middle Eastern hydrocarbon resources in the past two decades. The two Gulf Wars as well as the Global War on Terror only accentuated this geopolitical reality, with East Asian economies fretting over their energy security while the United States assisting counter-terror operations from lush jungles of Mindanao all the way to the deserts of Marrakech. The period saw East Asian countries such as Japan not only providing financial and development assistance, but also taking the unprecedented decision to deploy troops, though unarmed and for engineering operations, to assist American post-conflict stabilization efforts in the Middle East. It also saw China playing an increasingly prominent role in arming Middle Eastern powers; negotiating major oil deals with the likes of Saudi Arabia; as well as mediating the nuclear negotiations between the West and Tehran.[35] In 2004, the United States launched the Proliferation Security Initiative (PSI), the brain-child of current National Security Adviser and former UN Ambassador John Bolton, which sought to disrupt and degrade seaborne proliferation of Weapons of Mass Destruction (WMD) from the Red Sea to the East China Sea. As Indian strategist Grupeet Khurana notes, "[s]uch interconnectedness led analysts…[towards] the search for a suitable regional nomenclature," since "'Asia' was too broad and continental. 'Asia-Pacific'—which traditionally stood for 'the Asian littoral of the Pacific'—was inadequate," thus the term ["Indo-Pacific,"] pertaining to the confluence of the Indian Ocean and Pacific Oceans, "seemed more appropriate."[36] Thus, the Indo-Pacific, as a strategic framework as well as geopolitical sphere, is at once about China but also a new and broader security architecture that far exceeds the whims and wherewithal of a single power. The emerging post-American order in the mega-region, Zbigniew Brzezinski warned, is important because "[i]f America falters, the world is unlikely to be dominated by a single preeminent successor, such as China….more probable would be a protracted phase of rather inconclusive and somewhat chaotic realignments of both global and

---

[35] Yergin (2008).
[36] Kuo (2018).

regional power…"[37] The prospect of anarchy lurks over the horizon. The scramble for post-American Indo-Pacific, meanwhile, is now fully in motion.

COMPETING VISIONS FOR THE INDO-PACIFIC

There are times when global conferences are not only talk shops and Vanity Fairs for the security wonks, but also serve as a bellwether of the emerging geopolitical fault lines. This was particularly the case during the 2018 edition of the Shangri-La Dialogue (SLD), which brought together defense officials and experts from across the globe, and where participating nations advocated for competing visions of an ideal order across the Asia-Pacific. In particular, Indian Prime Minister Narendra Modi, the event's keynote speaker, effectively inaugurated the arrival of the "Indo-Pacific" era. In a well-composed speech, he confidently marked the emergence of India as a global power and, crucially, a pillar of the Indo-Pacific theater, which straddles the vast Indian and Pacific oceans. The Indian leader presented India as a transcontinental "pivot state," committed to free-market economics and political freedom at home, while deploying its naval prowess to preserve freedom across international waters. In his quasi-Nehruvian speech, Modi touted India's long tradition of strategic nonalignment by underscoring New Delhi's deft ability to navigate geopolitical fault lines and transcend superpower competition. He celebrated[38] the "extraordinary breadth" of US–Indian relations, the "maturity and wisdom" of Sino-Indian relations, and India's "special and privileged" strategic partnership with Moscow. The Indian leader advocated a vision whereby the middle powers of the Association of Southeast Asian Nations (ASEAN)—Australia, India, Japan, and South Korea—collectively preserve a "free and open" Indo-Pacific order in the region. In Modi's strategic paradigm, despite the vicissitudes of American influence in the region, liberal values of openness and freedom will continue to prevail, thanks to the existence of likeminded democratic partners. Even the ASEAN, which is composed of mostly authoritarian regimes, is founded on the liberal principles of dialogue, consensus, free trade, and political openness. Thus, the world may be entering a post-American era, but the Indo-Pacific region won't

[37] Brzezinski (2013, 75).

[38] The International Institute for Strategic Studies (2018, June "Shangri-La Dialogue 2018 Highlights: Day One").

necessarily be dominated and defined by the other global superpower: China. Modi's middle powers-driven vision of shared order and collective prosperity, however, is just one of the three main narratives which are competing for political currency in the Indo-Pacific.

As for Indonesia, it has introduced some twist to the Indo-Pacific concept, putting forward an ASEAN-centric vision that recognizes China as a pillar of the emerging security architecture. This is in contrast to Modi's vision (likely shared by Australia and, to a lesser degree, Japan), which favors selective and cautious engagement with China, or rather "congagement" (simultaneous constrainment and engagement). For Indonesia, a perennially nonaligned nation, the ASEAN values of consultation, consensus, and peaceful exchanges of ideas and goods should continue to guide relations among regional states, including the great powers. Indonesian Foreign Minister Retno Marsudi recently unveiled a more inclusive version of the "Indo-Pacific," which promotes an "open, transparent and inclusive" order based on "the habit of dialogue, promoting cooperation and friendship, and upholding international law."[39] For Indonesia, and much of the ASEAN, China is simply too big and important to be realistically excluded from any regional order. In short, the ASEAN views China as an integral element of the Indo-Pacific security architecture.

The maritime element of the Indo-Pacific paradigm, however, makes it a perfect counterpoise to China's land-based march and dominance across Eurasia; a campaign that has been boosted by President Xi Jinping's ambitious BRI. To the Trump administration, the heart of the Indo-Pacific paradigm is a US-led Quadrilateral Alliance, also known as the "Quad"[40]; a group composed of the United States, India, Australia, and Japan, to balance against China. Harry Harris, former chief of the United States Pacific Command (PACOM), has been a key advocate[41] of this strategy. According to this more muscular conception of the Indo-Pacific, China is "dividing and conquering" the ASEAN using a mixture of coercion and diplomatic "carrots," and major regional powers should step into [the fray and] check Beijing's revisionist ambitions in the Indian Ocean and the Western Pacific overall, but particularly in the East and South China Seas. In both the National Security Strategy (NSS)[42]

[39] Anya (2018).
[40] Heydarian (2018a).
[41] Larter (2017).
[42] Trump (2017a).

and National Defense Strategy (NDS) papers,[43] the Trump administration embraced this second narrative for the Indo-Pacific. The mega-region is precisely where all four of America's adversaries are perched, namely China, Iran, North Korea, and Russia. As the US government currently sees it, we are lurching into a new Cold War, with China as the US' chief geopolitical rival. During the SLD, then US Defense Secretary James Mattis painted[44] China as the main threat to the Indo-Pacific order. He criticized "China's militarization of artificial features in the South China Sea" through the "deployment of anti-ship missiles, surface-to-air missiles, electronic jammers and, more recently, the landing of bomber aircraft at Woody Island [in the Paracels]."

He also reiterated America's indispensable role as the anchor of stability and prosperity in the region, particularly through ensuring "freedom of navigation for all nations" across the Pacific and Indian Oceans by leveraging US naval might. Though divergent in many ways, Modi's and the Trump administration's conceptions of the Indo-Pacific have one crucial thing in common: they both view China as a threat to a "free and open" regional order. New Delhi would prefer to rely on democratic middle powers to ensure collective security, while keeping a wary eye on China without turning down economic engagement with its giant neighbor. Meanwhile, Washington is keen on assembling an anti-China alliance of regional powers to preserve its maritime primacy in the region. What drives Washington's Indo-Pacific strategy, however, is the Trump doctrine, which is the subject of the following chapter.

And this brings us to the key arguments of the book. Nowadays, it's fashionable to talk about the "Chinese Century." Yet, there are at least four reasons to be skeptical. First of all, China's bid for strategic primacy is taking place within a period of American strategic resurgence,[45] particularly under the Donald Trump administration, which has shown far less self-restraint[46] in challenging China. Conventional views on the Trump administration portray a picture of American strategic retreat, especially given the American president's unpopularity in the region as well as his decision to nix the TPP deal, a pillar of the Obama administration's Pivot to Asia

---

[43] U.S. Department of Defense (2018).

[44] The International Institute for Strategic Studies (2018, June "Shangri-La Dialogue 2018 Highlights: Day Two").

[45] Autry (2018).

[46] Heydarian (2018b).

(P2A) policy. A more nuanced analysis, however, reveals a more complex, if not contrary, picture. On one hand, Washington has stepped up its Freedom of Navigation Operations (FONOPs) and nuclear bomber aerial patrols across the South China Sea,[47] openly defying China's excessive territorial claims in the contested maritime space. The Trump administration has given greater leeway to Pentagon to check China's maritime assertiveness, including on decisions concerning FONOPs.[48] It has also doubled Foreign Military Financing (FMF) to key regional allies,[49] including the Philippines, openly called on China to remove advanced military assets in the disputed South China Sea, and even treated China's paramilitary forces operating in the area as de facto extensions of the PLA Navy. In fact, the Trump administration also made the unprecedented decision to openly suggest that it will come to the Philippines' rescue in an event of a conflict with China in the South China Sea.[50] With the support of the US Congress, the Trump administration has also expanded its strategic engagement with the region through the multi-billion dollar Asia Reassurance Initiative Act (ARIA),[51] which augments American defense and military footprint and diplomacy in the Indo-Pacific, as well as the $60-billion Better Utilization of Investments Leading to Development (BUILD) initiative,[52] which aims to mobilize high-quality American investments across strategic markets in the region, particularly in East Asia. Thus, one could argue that the P2A policy, which was fundamentally meant to constrain China's assertiveness, has truly begun under the Trump administration. On the trade front, the United States has openly sought fundamental changes in China's trade and industrial policies,[53] questioned the viability of the BRI,[54] and pressured allies and partners to shun Chinese high-tech investments,[55] particularly in strategic sectors. While the relative gap between Beijing's and Washington's economies and military capabilities has dramatically narrowed

---

[47] Ibid.

[48] Based on conversations with former senior Pentagon officials under the Obama administration; also see Lubold and Page (2017) and Gordon (2017).

[49] Esmaquel II (2018).

[50] Ranada (2019).

[51] Panda (2019).

[52] Zumbrun and Hughes (2018).

[53] Wu (2018).

[54] Lu (2019).

[55] Lee (2019).

in the past decade,[56] China still lags far behind the United States[57] in terms of net stock of resources including soft power, technology, manpower, military hardware, economic resources, and natural endowments and precious minerals, which can be mobilized in periods of conflict.[58] As perspicacious scholars such as Michael Beckley have noted, "a nation's power stems not from its gross resources but from its net resources—the resources left over after subtracting the costs of making them."[59] China also faces massive internal structural challenges, including an impending demographic winter, rising social unrest, a growing environmental crisis, and imbalances in the real estate and banking sector.[60] This doesn't mean that China is on the verge of collapse necessarily, but the Asian powerhouse has serious structural vulnerabilities that can't be discounted. To be fair, the US "resurgence" has been mostly in the realm of military pushback against China, and there are deep concerns over the predictability of American policy under the populist in the White House.[61] America's political paralysis at home is also a major source of concern. As Josef Joffe notes in the *Myth of American Decline*, which traces several waves of erroneous "declinism" discourse throughout the second half of the twentieth century amid the initial rise of the Soviet Union and Japan: "Only the United States can bring down the United States."[62] Yet, the latest surveys show that most of the world still prefers the United States to China as the global leader.[63]

And this brings us to the other important issue, namely how America's allies and like-minded partners are filling in the developmental vacuum amid Trump's protectionist policies. What augments America's edge over China is its broad and durable network of regional alliances,[64] particularly with middle powers of Japan, Australia, and, increasingly, India, which share common, though not identical, concerns over China's rising assertiveness.[65] In fact, other regional powers, namely Japan and

[56] Allison (2017).
[57] Beckley (2011) and Joffe (2014).
[58] Lange et al. (2018).
[59] Beckley (2018).
[60] Sharma (2012).
[61] Bialik (2018).
[62] Joffe (2014, 221).
[63] Wike et al. (2018).
[64] Ikenberry (2011).
[65] Madan (2017).

Australia, which are committed to a "free and open" Indo-Pacific, support the US-led pushback against China. It's within this context that one should understand Japan's successful efforts,[66] in tandem with Australia, in resuscitating the TPP agreement, which Trump perfunctorily ditched. In contrast, China hardly has a single reliable ally to promote its vision and values for the region. Both North Korea and Pakistan, considered as Beijing's closest strategic partners, have sought to diversify their external relations in recent years. While Pyongyang has sought direct negotiations with Washington,[67] largely for the removal of punitive sanctions on its flailing economy, Islamabad, in turn, has pivoted to Saudi Arabia, not to mention that it continually relies on the International Monetary Fund (IMF) for financing, to reduce its excessive dependence on and ballooning debt to China, partly due to the BRI.[68] China simply has no capable and reliable allies to count on, at least not like the US.

The US partners, by contrast, are quite capable in their own right. Japan, a US treaty ally, already has its own multi-billion dollar connectivity initiative, which is powering a plethora of critical infrastructure projects across Southeast Asia. Australia and the ASEAN have also signed an investment agreement, which aims to "develop a pipeline of high-quality infrastructure projects, to attract private and public investment."[69] India is separately expanding its developmental assistance to and strategic cooperation with ASEAN countries.[70] Rather than relying on American instructions or initiatives, each of these middle powers is engaging ASEAN nations either together or individually to help build a "rules-based" order in the Indo-Pacific. The ongoing strategic battle is not fought primarily through matching China's initiatives dollar-by-dollar, but instead, and more crucially, over the rules and regulations that will govern the global development and strategic infrastructure investment landscape. It's still too early to talk about a "Quad" alliance against China, but each of these four powers has shown increasing interest in aiding Southeast Asian nations' developmental and security needs and aspirations.

But what about smaller powers? This is where we should look at sustained efforts by Southeast Asian nations to diversify their strategic partners

---

[66] Fujioka and Miller (2018).

[67] Heydarian (2018c).

[68] Aamir (2019).

[69] Westbrook (2018).

[70] Pant (2018).

and sources of foreign investment. Though known for their historical tensions with the West, the leaders of Malaysia (Mahathir) and the Philippines (Duterte), not to mention the communist leadership in Vietnam, have welcomed closer strategic cooperation with and investments from the United States and, most importantly, Japan. Even poorer Southeast Asian nations such as Myanmar, Cambodia, and Laos have proactively sought Japanese developmental and infrastructure investments to reduce their reliance on China.[71] Southeast Asian nations, both small and larger, have jealously guarded their postcolonial quest for strategic autonomy, playing one great power against the other while seeking to avoid overreliance on a single foreign power.[72] Thus, one should not underestimate smaller nations' omni-balancing capabilities and strategic impulses. Overall, both low- and middle-income Southeast Asian countries have assiduously sought, whether on a bilateral or multilateral (via the ASEAN mechanism) basis, diversified strategic relations with Indo-Pacific powers, from India and Russia to Japan, China, and the United States, as well as sources of investment and aid, with Japan still serving as a leading regional partner. In fact, Japan by far remains as the leading source of infrastructure investment in Southeast Asia.[73] Nonetheless, the post-Cold War era mostly saw the United States serving as the prime security guarantor in Southeast Asia, while Japan has served as the prime economic player since World War II. China's emergence as a new pole has only expanded the pool of Southeast Asia's strategic partners, though with the United States and Japan playing a less decisive role in recent years. This only shows that Southeast Asian nations aren't pawns on a geopolitical chessboard, but instead active players with considerable agency in shaping their own strategic destiny. The upshot of this highly dynamic and contested strategic landscape is the emergence of multiple centers of power and varying degrees of strategic freedom accorded to each state, thus no single power can fully shape the regional security, economic, and diplomatic agenda of Southeast Asia.

The biggest challenge for China's bid for regional hegemony, however, is its own unsophisticated approach to regional diplomacy, which has been plagued by alienating "we are big, you are small" hubris,[74]

---

[71] Furuoka (2019).

[72] See for instance Weatherbee (2010) and Shambaugh (2018).

[73] Jamrisko, Michelle. "China No Match for Japan in Southeast Asian Infrastructrue Race." Bloomberg. June 23, 2019.

[74] Kurtlantzick (2011).

massive infrastructure projects that lack transparency and sustainability, open disregard for smaller nations' search for autonomy, as well as its increased assertiveness amid the ongoing disputes in the South China Sea. No wonder why authoritative surveys across Southeast Asian nations show that 7 out of 10 respondents hold negative views of China's BRI, while less than half expressed confidence in China's ability to play a constructive leadership role in the region.[75] The most trusted nation in the eyes of Southeast Asian nations remains Japan. China is undoubtedly a major player in the region, but far from its inevitable hegemon.

The final, and arguably most important, argument of the book concerns the future of the Indo-Pacific. With the impending non-security challenges of climate change, technological disruption, and transnational terrorism, no single power will be capable of dictating the regional agenda. Instead, what's needed, and will likely be the case, is the emergence of new patterns of cooperation among regional powers, which will involve both China and the United States. The advent of spoke-to-spoke cooperation among US allies and strategic partners, which have acted increasingly autonomous of Trump's dictates, portends the fluid, horizontal, flexible networks of cooperation emerging in the Indo-Pacific. Thus, the book is, accordingly, divided along these four key arguments.

The next chapter looks at Trump's neo-isolationist foreign policy, and his emphasis on an "America First" doctrine. It examines his lifelong obsession with America's real and imagined trade deficit with Asian economies, particularly Japan, South Korea, and China, but also, to a lesser degree, other export-oriented Southeast Asian countries. The chapter situates Trump's foreign policy outlook, which was further enunciated in the National Security Strategy (NSS) and National Defense Strategy (NDS) of 2018, within a broader isolationist, populist, and unilateralist traditions in American history, which have at times shaped, if not directed, the country's relations with the Asian region.

The chapter argues that Trump's foreign policy outlook is at once novel, reflecting the president's unique character and the contemporary circumstances that paved the way for his ascent to power, as well as old, drawing on a combination of nativist conservatism, traditional exceptionalism and militaristic unilateralism that are deeply rooted in the psyche of sections of American elite and broader populace.

---

[75] Tang et al. (2019).

Meanwhile, the succeeding chapter, "The Great Distraction," looks at how the Middle East and North Africa (MENA), perched at the western edge of the Indo-Pacific, continues to sap and chip away at American strategic resources and attention span, undermining efforts by multiple administrations, including the Obama presidency, to pivot to Indo-Pacific theater. It briefly looks at post-Cold War administrations' prolonged military interventions in the Middle East, South and Southeast Asia, and Africa, beginning with the First Gulf War and reaching a new phase of warfare with the rise (and fall) of the so-called Islamic State (IS). More contemporarily, it argues that despite the best efforts of the Obama administration to disengage from the region, the Middle East has continuously exhausted a disproportionate share of American foreign policy energy.

It covers, albiet briefly, more recent developments, specifically the implications of Trump administration's embrace of the Israeli-Saudi axis against Iran. It assesses the implications of his unilateral withdrawal, in defiance of international law, from Obama's landmark nuclear deal with the Islamic Republic. The chapter shows that Trump's decision effectively torpedos the Joint Comprehensive Plan of Action (JCPOA), which only exacerbates an already fragile geopolitical situation in the region—threatening to revive military brinkmanship between Tehran and Washington. It also looks at the rollercoaster geopolitical showdown at the eastern edge of the Eurasian landmass, specifically the back-and-forth exchanges of threats and affection between Trump and the North Korean supreme leader Kim Jung-un, and how this represents both a great distraction as well as a potential diplomatic breakthrough that could end the longest interstate conflict in East Asia.

The next three chapters, meanwhile, look into the brewing New Cold War between the United States and China, and how the Asian powerhouse is carving out a new sphere of influence at the heart of the Indo-Pacific, stretching from the warm waters of Southwest Asia to the tropical jungles of Southeast Asia and the Pacific Islands. It digs deeper into the evolving dynamics of Sino-American rivalry in East Asia. After three decades of rapid economic expansion, and successfully maintaining robust growth amidst an economic meltdown in the West (and Japan), China rapidly closed its economic gap with the United States. In the process, China managed to amass up to $4 trillion in exchange reserves, making it a primary global creditor and a source of much-needed investments across Asia and beyond. China's rising economic fortunes also went hand in hand with a rapid expansion in its naval fleet and accelerated innovations in its military technology. Soon,

China began to expand its defensive perimeter by gobbling up disputed features in the South China Sea, jostling with Japan over the Senkaku/ Diaoyu islands, and placing restrictions on American naval presence in Western Pacific. In response, the United States has increased its military footprint in Asia, pushing for greater access to bases in Australia, the Philippines, and Singapore, and mobilizing its resources and allies against a domineering China. Economically, China also pushed for major initiatives such as the Asian Infrastructure Investment Bank (AIIB) and Maritime Silk Road project, which stand in competition with Bretton Woods institutions led by the West—and are poised to revamp the infrastructure and development landscape in Asia. The chapters look at how China sought to rapidly fill up the vacuum of American economic leadership in the region, building a new geopolitical order in its own image.

Yet, the book also argues that China's bid for hegemony is ultimately inchoate, as the Asian powerhouse struggles with internal structural contradictions, backlash among neighboring countries and beyond, and a resurgent West that has embraced confrontation rather than engagement with Beijing. The book contends that the relative decline of the United States will not automatically lead to a *Pax Sinica* order in the Indo-Pacific. Instead, what we are likely to witness is the growing role of middle powers, particularly Japan, India, Australia, Indonesia, as well as resident European powers such as Britain and France, in shaping the regional security architecture. At the minimum, these powers want to maintain a "free and open" Indo-Pacific, where free trade as well as freedom of navigation and overflight in high seas is preserved. They want to ensure that no single power, especially a revanchist China, exercises sole control over sea lines of communications in the area, particularly in the all-important South China Sea. These middle powers have sought to ameliorate American retrenchment by tightening interoperability and military cooperation among themselves, proposing alternative regional trading regimes, offering alternative development initiatives, and stepping up infrastructure investments across South and Southeast Asia. Japan has emerged as the fulcrum of such efforts. This will be the subject of Chapter 7.

The following chapter, meanwhile, looks at the role of smaller powers, particularly Malaysia, the Philippines, and Vietnam, in mediating great power rivalry as well as shaping their own strategic fate amid a rapidly shifting geopolitical landscape. It will focus directly on the personal role of strongmen figures such as Rodrigo Duterte in the Philippines and

Mahathir Mohamad in Malaysia in amplifying as well as exploiting new strategic spaces created for smaller powers and their struggle for autonomy. The final chapter looks at the prospects for a Pax Indo-Pacific, a regional order that is neither dominated by the United States nor China, but instead anchored by what Gilles Deleuze and Félix Guattari would term as a "rhizomatic" order (as opposed to an arboreal-hierarchical order),[76] where a network of relatively autonomous and highly interdependent powers, with varying degrees of strategic freedom and geopolitical influence, collectively shape geopolitics from Cairo in the west to Canada in the east as well as Alaska in the north to Australia in the south. The post-American world, therefore, doesn't necessarily belong to China, but instead an uneasy, fluid network of interlocking alliances, partnerships, and rivalries, which will cope with the twin challenges of climate change and disruptive technical innovation in the age of Fourth Industrial Revolution—exacerbating already existing socioeconomic faultiness and civilization tensions among rapidly growing economies in the region.

The Indo-Pacific is where the world's leaders in green technology and Artificial Intelligence (AI) are emerging; but it's also where the greatest contributors to global warming,[77] oceanic pollution,[78] and illegal, unreported, and unregulated (IUU) fishing reside.[79] In fact, China is the greatest contributor, by far, on all fronts. The mega-region is also where hundreds of millions of people may lose their jobs as a result of technological disruption, while billions more will be at severe risk due to the deleterious impact of climate change (see Chapter 9). As Brzezinski warns, the post-American era will likely have "no grand winners and many more losers, in a setting of international uncertainty and even of potentially fatal risks to global well-being [of human species]."[80] Given the depth and gravity of challenges on the horizon, soon talks of a Sino-American rivalry for global mastery could seem both misplaced and misguided, as an ineluctable coalition of powers struggle to collectively hold the line against the coming anarchy that will sweep the Indo-Pacific mega-region.

[76] Deleuze and Guattari (2009).

[77] Friedrich et al. (2017).

[78] Li (2015).

[79] Hosch (2019).

[80] Brzezinski (2013, 75).

REFERENCES

Aamir, Adnan. "China's Disappointing Aid Offer Dashes Pakistan's Hope of Debt Rescue." *Nikkei Asian Review.* February 11, 2019. https://asia. nikkei.com/Politics/International-relations/China-s-disappointing-aid-offer-dashes-Pakistan-s-hope-of-debt-rescue.

Abe, Shinzo. "Asia's Democratic Security Diamond." *Project Syndicate.* December 27, 2012. https://www.project-syndicate.org/commentary/a-strategic-alliance-for-japan-and-india-by-shinzo-abe.

Abe, Shinzo. "Confluence of the Two Seas." Speech, India. August 22, 2007. *Ministry of Foreign Affairs of Japan.* https://www.mofa.go.jp/region/asia-paci/pmv0708/speech-2.html.

Allison, Graham. *Destined for War: Can America and China Escape Thucydides's Trap.* Boston: Houghton Mifflin Harcourt, 2017a.

Allison, Graham. "The Thucydides Trap." *Foreign Policy.* June 9, 2017b. https://foreignpolicy.com/2017/06/09/the-thucydides-trap/.

Allison, Graham, and Philip Zelikow. *Essence of Decision: Explaining the Cuban Missile Crisis.* London: Pearson, 1999.

Allison, Graham, Robert Blackwill, and Ali Wyne. *Lee Kuan Yew: The Grand Master's Insights on China, the United States and the World.* Cambridge: The MIT Press, 2013.

Anya, Agnes. "East Asia to Hear About Indo-Pacific idea." *The Jakarta Post.* May 9, 2018. https://www.thejakartapost.com/news/2018/05/09/east-asia-hear-about-indo-pacificidea.html.

Autry, Greg. "Trump's China Policy Is a Triumph." *Foreign Policy.* November 28, 2018. https://foreignpolicy.com/2018/11/28/trumps-china-policy-is-a-triumph-wto-trump-gdp/.

Beckley, Michael. "China's Century? Why America's Edge Will Endure." *International Security* 36, no. 3 (2011): 41–78. https://www.mitpressjournals.org/doi/pdf/10.1162/ISEC_a_00066.

Beckley, Michael. "Stop Obsessing About China." *Foreign Affairs.* September 21, 2018. https://www.foreignaffairs.com/articles/china/2018-09-21/stop-obsessing-about-china.

Bialik, Kristen. "How the World Views the U.S. and Its President in 9 Charts." *Pew Research Center.* October 9, 2018. http://www.pewresearch.org/fact-tank/2018/10/09/how-the-world-views-the-u-s-and-its-president-in-9-charts/.

Birtles, Bill. "China Mocks Australia Over 'Indo-Pacific' Concept It Says Will 'Dissipate'." *ABC News.* March 8, 2018. https://www.abc.net.au/news/2018-03-08/china-mocks-australia-over-indo-pacific-concept/9529548.

Bloomberg. "Here's a Peek at Xi Jinping's 'Uniquely Chinese Model' for World Domination." *Business Standard*. December 29, 2018. https://www.business-standard.com/article/international/here-s-a-peek-at-xi-jinping-s-uniquely-chinese-model-for-world-domination-118122900386_1.html.

Brzezinski, Zbigniew. *Strategic Vision: America and the Crisis of Global Power.* New York: Basic Books, 2013.

Deleuze, Gilles, and Felix Guattari. *Anti-Oedipus: Capitalism and Schizophrenia (Penguin Classics)*. London: Penguin Classics, 2009.

Esmaquel II, Paterno. "PH to Get Lion's Share of U.S. Security Aid in Indo-Pacific." *Rappler*. August 29, 2018. https://www.rappler.com/nation/210699-philippines-get-biggest-chunk-us-security-aid-indo-pacific-region.

Friedrich, Johannes, Mengpin Ge, and Andrew Pickens. "This Interactive Chart Explains World's Top 10 Emitters, and How They've Changed." *World Resource Institute*. April 11, 2017. https://www.wri.org/blog/2017/04/interactive-chart-explains-worlds-top-10-emitters-and-how-theyve-changed.

Fujioka, Toru, and Brett Miller. "Japan Pushes on with TPP-11 With U.S., China at Odds." *Bloomberg*. December 6, 2018. https://www.bloomberg.com/news/articles/2018-12-06/japan-pushes-on-with-tpp-11-as-u-s-and-china-remain-at-odds.

Furuoka, Fumitaka. "Can Japan Contribute to Equitable Development in ASEAN?" *East Asia Forum*. March 16, 2019. https://www.eastasiaforum.org/2019/03/16/can-japan-contribute-to-equitable-development-in-asean/.

Garrity, Patrick. "Defending the Rimland." *Claremont.org*. October 28, 2013. http://www.claremont.org/crb/basicpage/defending-the-rimland/.

Gordon, Michael. "Trump Shifting Authority Over Military Operations Back to Pentagon." *The New York Times*. March 19, 2017. https://www.nytimes.com/2017/03/19/us/trump-shifting-authority-over-military-operations-back-to-pentagon.html.

Harari, Yuval Noah. *Sapiens: A Brief History of Humankind*. New York: Harper, 2015.

Heydarian, Richard Javad. "Revived 'QUAD' Alliance Eggs on China's Response." *Asia Times*. March 1, 2018a. https://www.asiatimes.com/article/revived-quad-alliance-eggs-chinas-response/.

Heydarian, Richard Javad. "Trump Is Forcing China to Reassess Its Strategy." *The National Interest*. October 20, 2018b.

Heydarian, Richard Javad. "Why North Korea's Change of Heart on Peace Negotiations?" *China-US Focus*. April 24, 2018c. https://www.chinausfocus.com/foreign-policy/why-north-koreas-change-of-heart-on-peace-negotiations.

Holmes, James. "The Commons: Beijing's 'Blue National Soil'." *The Diplomat*. January 3, 2013. https://thediplomat.com/2013/01/a-threat-to-the-commons-blue-national-soil/.

Hosch, Gilles. "Report: China Ranks Worst on Global Illegal Fishing Index." *The Maritime Executive*. May 2, 2019. https://www.maritime-executive.com/editorials/report-china-ranks-worst-on-global-illegal-fishing-index.

Ikenberry, G. John. "The Future of the Liberal World Order." *Foreign Affairs*. May 1, 2011. https://www.foreignaffairs.com/articles/2011-05-01/future-liberal-world-order.

Jakobson, Linda. "Reflections from China on Xi Jinping's 'Asia for Asians'." *Asian Politics & Policy* 8 (2016): 219–223. https://doi.org/10.1111/aspp.12230.

Joffe, Josef. *The Myth of America's Decline: Politics, Economics, and a Half Century of False Prophecies*. New York: W. W. Norton, 2014.

Kaplan, Robert. "Monsoon." *The New York Times*. November 19, 2010. https://www.nytimes.com/2010/11/21/books/review/excerpt-monsoon.html.

Kaplan, Robert. *Monsoon: The Indian Ocean and the Future of American Power*. New York: Random House Trade Paperbacks, 2011.

Khong, Yuen Foong. "The Reality of US-China Competition." *The Straits Times*. December 30, 2015. https://www.straitstimes.com/opinion/the-reality-of-us-china-competition.

Korab-Karpowicz, W.J. "Political Realism in International Relations." *Stanford Encyclopedia of Philosophy*. July 26, 2010. https://plato.stanford.edu/entries/realism-intl-relations/.

Kuo, Mercy. "The Origin of 'Indo-Pacific' as Geopolitical Construct." *The Diplomat*. January 25, 2018. https://thediplomat.com/2018/01/the-origin-of-indo-pacific-as-geopolitical-construct/.

Kurlantzick, Joshua. "The Belligerents." *The New Republic*. January 27, 2011. https://newrepublic.com/article/82211/china-foreign-policy.

Lange, Glenn-Marie, Quentin Wodon, and Kevin Carey. "The Changing Wealth of Nations 2018: Building a Sustainable Future." *World Bank*. 2018. https://openknowledge.worldbank.org/bitstream/handle/10986/29001/9781464810466.pdf.

Larter, David. "Adm. Harry Harris, the Military's Hard-Line Commander in the Pacific, Comes to Capitol Hill." *Navy Times*. April 25, 2017. https://www.navytimes.com/news/your-navy/2017/04/25/adm-harry-harris-the-military-s-hard-line-commander-in-the-pacific-comes-to-capitol-hill/.

Lee, Jeong-Ho. "China, US Trade Barbs Over Huawei and South China Sea at Munich Conference." *South China Morning Post*. February 16, 2019. https://www.scmp.com/news/china/diplomacy/article/2186473/china-us-trade-barbs-over-huawei-and-south-china-sea-munich.

Li, Jing. "China Produces About a Third of Plastic Polluting the World's Oceans, Says Reports." *South China Morning Post.* February 13, 2015. https://www.scmp.com/article/1711744/china-produces-about-third-plastic-waste-polluting-worlds-oceans-says-report.

Lu, Zhenhua. "Mike Pompeo's 'Irresponsible' South China Sea Energy Claims." *South China Morning Post.* March 13, 2019. https://www.scmp.com/news/china/diplomacy/article/3001491/mike-pompeo-accuses-beijing-creating-debt-traps-and-energy.

Lubold, Gordon, and Jeremy Page. "U.S. to Challenge China with More Patrols in Disputed Waters." *The Wall Street Journal.* September 1, 2017. https://www.wsj.com/articles/u-s-readies-plan-to-increase-patrols-in-south-china-sea-1504299067.

Maçães, Bruno. *Belt and Road: A Chinese World Order.* London: Hurst, 2019.

Madan, Tanvi. "The Rise, Fall, and Rebirth of the 'Quad'." *War on the Rocks.* November 16, 2017. https://warontherocks.com/2017/11/rise-fall-rebirth-quad/.

Mandelbaum, Michael. "The New Containment." *Foreign Affairs.* March/April 2019 Issue. https://www.foreignaffairs.com/articles/china/2019-02-12/new-containment.

Medcalf, Rory. "The Indo-Pacific: What's in a Name?" *The American Interest.* October 10, 2013. https://www.the-american-interest.com/2013/10/10/the-indo-pacific-whats-in-a-name/.

Nelson, Louis. "In Asia, Trump Keeps Talking About Indo-Pacific." *Politico.* November 7, 2017. https://www.politico.com/story/2017/11/07/trump-asia-indo-pacific-244657.

Panda, Ankit. "What ARIA Will and Won't Do for the US in Asia." *The Diplomat.* January 14, 2019. https://thediplomat.com/2019/01/what-aria-will-and-wont-do-for-the-us-in-asia/.

Pant, Harsh. "The Future of India's Ties with ASEAN." *The Diplomat.* January 26, 2018. https://thediplomat.com/2018/01/the-future-of-indias-ties-with-asean/.

Pence, Mike. "Mike Pence: The United States Seeks Collaboration, Not Control, in the Indo-Pacific." *The Washington Post.* November 9, 2018. https://www.washingtonpost.com/opinions/mike-pence-the-united-states-seeks-collaboration-not-control-in-the-indo-pacific.

Rajghatta, Chidanand. "Invoking 'Hollywood to Bollywood', US Renames Pacom as Indo-Pacific Command." *The Times of India.* May 31, 2018. https://timesofindia.indiatimes.com/world/us/invoking-hollywood-to-bollywood-us-renames-pacom-as-indo-pacific-command/articleshow/64403933.cms.

Ranada, Pia. "South China Sea Covered by PH-U.S. Mutual Defense Treaty—Pompeo." *Rappler.* March 2, 2019. https://www.rappler.com/nation/224668-pompeo-says-south-china-sea-covered-philippines-us-mutual-defense-treaty.

Segal, Gerald. "East Asia and the 'Constrainment' of China." *International Security* 20, no. 4 (1996): 107–135. https://doi.org/10.2307/2539044.

Shambaugh, David. "U.S.-China Rivalry in Southeast Asia: Power Shift or Competitive Coexistence?" *International Security* 42, no. 4 (2018). https://doi.org/10.1162/isec_a_00314.

"Shangri-La Dialogue 2018 Highlights: Day One." *The International Institute for Strategic Studies.* June 1, 2018. https://www.iiss.org/blogs/analysis/2018/06/shangri-la-dialogue-2018-day-one-highlights.

"Shangri-La Dialogue 2018 Highlights: Day Two." *The International Institute for Strategic Studies.* June 2, 2018. https://www.iiss.org/blogs/analysis/2018/06/shangri-la-dialogue-2018-day-two-highlights.

Sharma, Ruchir. "10 Reasons to Believe in China Slowdown Story." *The Economic Times.* July 9, 2012. https://economictimes.indiatimes.com/opinion/et-commentary/10-reasons-to-believe-in-china-slowdown-story/articleshow/14753357.cms.

Smith, Jeff. "Unpacking the Free and Open Indo-Pacific." *War on the Rocks.* March 14, 2018. https://warontherocks.com/2018/03/unpacking-the-free-and-open-indo-pacific/.

Sue, Caryl. "Jun 7, 1494 CE: Treaty of Tordesillas." *National Geographic.* May 15, 2014. https://www.nationalgeographic.org/thisday/jun7/treaty-tordesillas/.

Tang, Siew Mun, Moe Thuzar, Hoang Thi Ha, Termsak Chalermpalanupap, Pham Thi Phuong Thao, and Anuthida Saelaow Qian. "The State of Southeast Asia: 2018 Survey Report." *Yusof Ishak Institute.* January 29, 2019. https://www.iseas.edu.sg/images/pdf/TheStateofSEASurveyReport_2019.pdf.

Trump, Donald. *National Security Strategy of the United States of America.* 2017a. https://www.whitehouse.gov/wp-content/uploads/2017/12/NSS-Final-12-18-2017-0905.pdf.

Trump, Donald. "Remarks by President Trump at APEC Summit." Speech, Da Nang, Vietnam. November 10, 2017b. *White House.* https://www.whitehouse.gov/briefings-statements/remarks-president-trump-apec-ceo-summit-da-nang-vietnam/.

U.S. Department of Defense. *Summary of the 2018 National Defense Strategy of the United States of America.* 2018. https://dod.defense.gov/Portals/1/Documents/pubs/2018-National-Defense-Strategy-Summary.pdf.

Weatherbee, Donald. *International Relations in Southeast Asia: The Struggle for Autonomy*, 2nd edition. Lanham: Rowman & Littlefield, 2010.

Westbrook, Tom. "Australia, ASEAN Agree to Start Regional Infrastructure Cooperation." *Reuters.* March 19, 2018. https://www.reuters.com/article/

us-asean-australia-infrastructure/australia-asean-agree-to-start-regional-infra-structure-cooperation-idUSKBN1GV09V.

Wike, Richard, Bruce Stokes, Jacob Pushter, Laura Silver, Janell Fetterolf, and Kat Delvin. "4. Most Prefer That U.S., Not China, Be the World's Leading Power" in "Trump's International Ratings Remain Low, Especially Among Key Allies." *Pew Research Center.* October 1, 2018. https://www.pewglobal.org/2018/10/01/most-prefer-that-u-s-not-china-be-the-worlds-leading-power/.

Wu, Wendy. "To End the Trade War, 'China Must Deliver Its Promises to Reform and Open Up." *South China Morning Post.* November 19, 2018. https://www.scmp.com/news/china/diplomacy/article/2173858/end-trade-war-china-must-deliver-its-promises-reform-open.

Yergin, Daniel. *The Prize: The Epic Quest for Oil, Money & Power.* New York: Free Press, 2008.

Zumbrun, Josh, and Siobhan Hughes. "To Counter China, U.S. Looks to Invest Billions More Overseas." *The Wall Street Journal.* August 31, 2018. https://www.wsj.com/articles/to-counter-china-u-s-looks-to-invest-billions-more-overseas-1535728206.

CHAPTER 2

The Trump Doctrine: The Art of Creative Disruption

Is this how a superpower commits suicide!?[1]—An ambassador from a major Indo-Pacific nation on Trump presidency

The counsels of impatience and hatred can always be supported by the crudest and cheapest symbols…[2] —George Kennan, *American Diplomacy*

The fox knows many things, but the hedgehog knows one big thing. —Ancient Greek poet Archilochus[3]

Shortly before unleashing his million-strong army on European soil, the Persian Emperor Xerxes, "the king of kings" (*Shahanshah*), confidently rebuffed the misgivings of his cautious adviser, Artabanus, who seemed unsure about the viability of the (ultimately ill-fated) second Persian invasion of Greece.[4] Overcome by the fire of megalomaniac ambition, the Persian emperor emphasized the value[5] of decisiveness, arguing, "if you were to take account of everything," you would end up "never do[ing] anything," since it's always "better to have a brave heart and endure one half of the terrors we dread than to [anticipate] all of the terrors and suffer nothing [in actual world] at all." Extolling the virtues

[1] Heydarian (2018d).
[2] Kennan (1951, 56).
[3] Berlin (1953).
[4] Chua (2009).
[5] Gaddis (2018).

© The Author(s) 2020
R. J. Heydarian, *The Indo-Pacific: Trump, China, and the New Struggle for Global Mastery*, https://doi.org/10.1007/978-981-13-9799-8_2

of bold leadership, Xerxes, the most powerful man of his time, fervently believed that ultimately "[b]ig things are won by big dangers." Confronting increasingly unified and strategically nimble Greek city-states, however, he later finds out that there was more of danger than victory in the biggest gamble of his political life. For ancient historians, Xerxes' failed invasion of Greece, which led to a humiliating retreat for the Persians and the subsequent rise of the Delian League led by Athens, marked the beginning of the end for the world's first global empire.[6]

Much of contemporary writings on the US President Donald Trump tend to portray him as essentially the modern Xerxes, who would spell the end of American primacy by embarking on misguided foreign policy campaigns based on a hubristic belief in the self-styled "stable genius" of his negotiation instinct. In "Art of the Deal,"[7] Trump nonchalantly boasts: "My style of deal-making is quite simple and straightforward. I aim very high, and then I just keep pushing and pushing and pushing to get what I'm after. Sometimes I settle for less than I sought, but in most cases I still end up with what I want." To him, it's more about instincts you're born with than intelligence and judgment: "More than anything else, I think deal-making is an ability you're born with… It's not about being brilliant. It does take a certain intelligence, but mostly it's about instincts." Like Xerxes, Trump is in charge of a declining "hyperpower." According to Amy Chua, a hyperpower is a centralized political authority that "clearly surpasses that of all its known contemporaneous rivals; it is not clearly inferior in economic or military strength to any other power in the planet, known to it or not; and it projects its power over so immense an area of the globe and over so immense a population that it breaks definition of mere local or even regional preeminence."[8] Trump also perfectly fits German Sociologist Max Weber's typology of "charismatic" leaders, who are, at least in the eyes of their devoted supporters, "endowed with supernatural, superhuman, or at least specifically exceptional powers or qualities."[9] In this sense, the American president harkens back to a more ancient understanding of leaders. But many around the world remain unconvinced by Trump's grandiose claims and self-perception.

[6]Holland (2007).

[7]Trump (2015).

[8]Chua (2009, xxii).

[9]Tucker (1968).

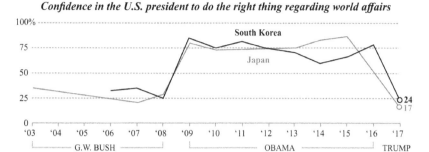

Confidence in the U.S. president to do the right thing regarding world affairs

Source: Spring 2017 Global Attitudes Survey. Q30a.

Fig. 2.1 Confidence in the US presidency among key Asian allies (*Source* Pew Research Center)

Authoritative surveys have consistently shown a virtual collapse[10] in American soft power under Trump's presidency (see Fig. 2.1), with majority of citizens among key allied nations in Europe and Asia questioning the judgment and competence of the man in the White House. According to the Pew Research Center, international confidence in American leadership declined significantly in 2017.[11] This has been most acutely felt in the Asia-Pacific region, the new center of gravity in global geopolitics. Among America's Asian allies, such as South Korea and Japan, confidence in the American president's ability to make the right judgment dropped by as much as 71% and 54%, respectively.[12] In Indonesia, the world's largest Muslim-majority nation, it dropped by 41%. This is nothing short of a disaster for American soft power. According to an authoritative survey by the Singapore-based Institute of Southeast Asian Studies (ISEAS), which solicited the views of leading strategic thinkers in Asia, as many as 72% of respondents believe that Trump's presidency has chipped away at the country's reliability as an anchor of stability in the region.[13] Up to 51% of respondents expressed "little confidence" in the Trump administration to do the right thing, leaving China as the biggest beneficiary with 73% of respondents

[10] Bialik (2018).

[11] Wike et al. (2017a).

[12] Wike et al. (2017b).

[13] ISEAS-Yusof Ishak Institute (2017).

identifying the Asian powerhouse as the most influential actor in the region. The downward trend in American soft power broadly held up during Trump's second year in office.[14]

In this light, today's America and its strategic rivalry with China supposedly echoes the declining Achaemenid Persia's against a rising Greece two millennia earlier. To be fair, there are striking parallels between Xerxes and Trump. Both leaders, the most powerful men of their times, belong to what British philosopher Isaiah Berlin characterized[15] as the "hedgehog" personality type (as opposed to the "fox"), who "relate everything to a single central vision, one system, less or more coherent or articulate, in terms of which they understand, think and feel – a single, universal, organizing principle in terms of which alone all that they are and say has significance." (Berlin's immortal "animal kingdom" analogy was inspired by a line among the fragments of the Greek poet Archilochus' works, which says: "The fox knows many things, but the hedgehog knows one big thing."). In Trump's case, that "single central vision" is all about winning and domination of rivals and opponents. In the acerbic wisdom of Gore Vidal, "It is not enough to succeed. Others must fail."[16] For Trump, the putative leader of the world's most powerful nation, in an anarchic world without a central authority, this means nothing short of indisputable global hegemony. But the problem with Hedgehogs in charge of empires is that, as John Gaddis pithily warned, "with great power comes great responsibility...but also the danger of doing dumb things."[17] Trump's zero-sum understanding of global affairs also contradicts the fundamental understanding of the concept of strategy. As the prominent British strategist Sir Lawrence David Freedman notes in his magisterial *Strategy*, "the realm of strategy is [also] one of bargaining and persuasion," since "conflicts can be resolved through building on shared interests or forging a winning coalition with the next available partner."[18]

To many experts, Trump is indeed one that is prone to "doing dumb things." Writing for Politco magazine, Thomas Wright of The Brookings Institution, described Trump as an anachronistic figure with

[14] Bialik (2018).
[15] Berlin (1953).
[16] *The Guardian* (2012).
[17] Gaddis (2018).
[18] Freedman (2015, xii).

a "19th century foreign policy," which "seeks nothing less than ending the U.S.-led liberal order and freeing America from its international commitments."[19] The American president, over the span of three decades, has remained broadly consistent on three key grievances, namely deep "unhapp[iness] with America's military alliances and feels the United States is overcommitted around the world…that America is disadvantaged by the global economy…[and his] sympathetic [attitude] to authoritarian strongmen [overseas]."

Wright's Brookings colleague Robert Kagan, a leading neoconservative thinker, is even more uncharitable. He has described Trump[20] as a "television huckster, a phony billionaire,[21] a textbook egomaniac," who will bring fascism to America by exploiting "popular resentments and insecurities, and with an entire national political party — out of ambition or blind party loyalty, or simply out of fear — falling into line behind him." Years later, writing for *The New York Times*, Kagan warned about the dangers of Trump's neo-isolationism, which represents a "new direction in American foreign policy, or rather a return to older traditions — the kind that kept us on the sidelines while fascism and militarism almost conquered the world." To Kagan, Trump is either a fascist or fascist enabler, who, in either case, spells moral and strategic doom for America. On the other side of the political spectrum, eminent liberal thinker John Ikenberry discussed the Trump-led "plot against American foreign policy," which relies on "dark narrative of national decline" and "transactional view of international relations"[22] He criticized Trump for "miss[ing] the larger, interdependent logic of the U.S.-led system"[23] and how American isolationism means that the whole "architecture of bargains and commitments" that underpin the global system "will [eventually] give way." He accused the American president of "sabotage[ing] the order it [America] created" throughout the post-World War II era.[24] Paul Krugman, in his essay "Fall of the American Empire," echoed a similar sense of dreadful dismay, arguing that, "[w]hat we're witnessing is a systematic rejection of longstanding American values — the values that

---

[19] Wright (2016).
[20] Kagan (2016).
[21] Farhi (2016).
[22] Ikenberry (2017).
[23] Rose (2017).
[24] Nye (2016).

actually made America great."[25] He accused the American president of "trashing the things that made [US] great, turning us into just another bully — one whose bullying will be far less effective than he imagines." Reflecting on whether the Liberal International Order (LIO) will survive, Harvard scholar and former senior Pentagon official Joseph Nye lamented how, for the first time in recent memory, "the [very] desirability and sustainability of the [international liberal] order have been called into question" with Trump interrogating whether the "costs of maintaining the order outweigh its benefits," while favoring a zero-sum outlook that sees "interactions with other countries on a case-by-case transactional basis," where there are only two groups, winners and losers. Thus, Nye warns how he is "much more worried about the rise of Trump than the rise of China."[26] For him, there is an impending tragedy, where "Americans and others may not notice the security and prosperity that the liberal order provides until they are gone—but by then, it may be too late."

FROM "AMERICA FIRST" TO "AMERICA ALONE"

On the other side of the Atlantic, Kori Schake of the International Institute for Strategic Studies reflected on Trump's visit to Europe for the NATO summit in mid-2018, where the American leader found himself at loggerheads with transatlantic allies over burden-sharing and alliance commitments. Perturbed by the open confrontation among the allies, Schake warned, "[d]ecades from now, we may look back at the first weeks of June 2018 as a turning point in world history: the end of the liberal order."[27] For Schake, we "are entering a new, terrifying era," where Trump and "his closest advisers would pull down the liberal order…"

She questions the factual basis of Trump's complaints against allies, noting that the number of American military forces stationed in Europe declined by 85% since the end of Cold War, that American defense spending went from 40% of the GDP during World War II to less than 4% in recent years. To Schake, Trump's foreign policy vision

---

[25] Krugman (2018).

[26] Allison (2018).

[27] Schake (2018).

is essentially a "bare-knuckled assertion of unilateral power" couched in the triumphant "America First" slogan. As The Atlantic's Jeffrey Goldberg reports, senior Trump administration officials described the Trump Doctrine as essentially: "We're America, Bitch," where "[p]ermanent destabilization creates American advantage" and others will "see over time that it doesn't pay to argue with us."[28] For Niall Ferguson[29] practically the whole scholarly and think tank establishment, whom he described as people with at least two university degrees (PALTUDs), has portrayed Trump, in varying shades, as an unhinged populist, who is overseeing the destruction[30] of the American-built LIO with gusto. "To the foreign policy experts, he is a bull in a china shop, trampling the 'rules-based international order' underfoot," Ferguson explains, while "[t]o the economics establishment, he is a human wrecking ball, smashing more than a half-century of consensus that free trade really works better than protectionism."

In an article entitled *Is America Still Safe for Democracy?*, Robert Mickey, Steven Levitsky, and Lucan Ahmad Way warn about the reversal of President Woodrow Wilson's vision of "making the world safe for democracy,"[31] as expressed in his April 2, 1917 speech before a joint session of Congress to seek Declaration of War against Germany, under Trump's leadership. To them, "the Trump presidency could push the United States into a mild form of what we call 'competitive authoritarianism'—a system in which meaningful democratic institutions exist yet the government abuses state power to disadvantage its opponents."[32] And the conventional wisdom is that Trump is not only a disaster for American soft power and the broader LIO, but also a boon for authoritarian powers such as China. As China expert Yadong Liu explains, Trump's "withdrawal from the Trans-Pacific Partnership, his tough approach to trade with Japan, and his talk of removing U.S. troops from South Korea" have, collectively, "served China's interests by accelerating the decline of U.S. influence in Asia, opening space for China to expand its influence even faster than it had ever thought possible."[33] In short,

---

[28] Goldberg (2018).

[29] Ferguson (2018a).

[30] Rose (2017).

[31] Ellwood (1918).

[32] Mickey et al. (2017).

[33] Liu (2018).

Liu argues, "China could hardly hope for a more cooperative occupant of the White House." What's taking place, according to conventional wisdom, is an "imperial unraveling," where Trump can be "best seen as a culmination, a product of the United States' steady defection from the very order it was essential in establishing and sustaining." As Asli Bali and Aziz Rana write in The *Boston Review*, the Trump Doctrine is anchored by "the boldness with which a declared reliance on coercion and conquest now sits uncomfortably beside America's professed moral authority; and the implications of Trump's ethno-nationalism for how global allies and enemies are conceived."[34]

In his latest book,[35] arguably the first authoritative account of the White House under Trump, veteran journalist Bob Woodward has characterized the White House as dominated by uncouth nationalists, who are "trying to make policy on a string of one-sentence clichés," while the senior members in Trump's cabinet, who would all later resign or get fired, reportedly see him either as a "moron," "fifth or six grader," or "an idiot." For Marxist philosopher Slavoj Zizek, Trump is an unparalleled force of disruption, who is corrosively emaciating the thick networks of informal rules and norms, which have undergirded laws governing proper behavior and conduct, including for the highest elected office in America—and the most powerful presidency in the planet.[36] In this way, he is shaking up the system unlike any of his predecessors since, at least, the Nixon era. Scratch the surface a bit, however, and a more nuanced picture emerges.

First of all, charges of illiberalism against Trump are hypocratical at best and factually in correct: as Graham Allison points out, Washington "never promoted liberalism abroad when it believed that doing so would pose a significant threat to its vital interests at home. Nor has it ever refrained from using military force to protect its interests when the use of force violated international rules."[37] In the words of Indian strategist C. Raja Mohan, the United States has acted "exceptional," meaning it has shown little restraint in defying international norms and laws, whenever it saw it fit. From America's unilateral invasion of Iraq in 2003 and institutionalized

---

[34] Bali and Rana (2017).

[35] Woodward (2018).

[36] Zizek (2019).

[37] Allison (2018); Also see for greater overview of the evolution and structure of American foreign policy Wittkopf et al. (2007).

torture of prisoners in Guantanamo and Abu Ghraib to perpetual kinetic actions, including usage of Special Forces and lethal drones, against enemy combatants and civilians across the Greater Middle East (often with minimal regard for sovereignty of host nations and lives of innocent civilians), even the most liberal of American presidencies have engaged in "exceptionalist" behavior.[38] Meanwhile, much of the mid-twentieth century right until the collapse of the Soviet Union saw American covert actions, including toppling of democratically elected regimes in Iran and Chile, as well as all-out armed interventions across the so-called "Third World."[39] Since 1945, the United States has been involved in 211 conflicts across 67 countries. As Daniel Immerwahr explains, "clearly this is not a country that has kept its hands to itself."[40] Comparing the concept of the LIO to the age-old quip about the Holy Roman Empire, scholars such as Ferguson have questioned if there were ever a truly "liberal order" on the "international" level in recent history. As the British historian notes,[41]

> For one thing, there was nothing very liberal about the economic order that was established in 1945. It was devised by people - notably John Maynard Keynes - who had repudiated classical liberal economics and believed that international trade should be limited and capital movements controlled. It was also not a truly international order. After 1945, it very quickly became a bipolar order that divided the world. There was nothing international about the Cold War. It was a battle between two empires and two ideologies, and the rest of the world's nations had to choose sides. In short, the notion of a liberal international order, born in 1945, is a historical fantasy.

Charles Kupchan of the influential Council on Foreign Relations,[42] meanwhile, argues that Trump's "America first" policy is "not so much abandoning" Washington's commitment to the LIO in as much as he "tapping into an earlier incarnation" of longstanding trope of American skepticism vis-à-vis global entanglements. For much of its history, Kupchan writes, American leaders were focused on "insulating the American experiment from foreign threats, shunning international entanglements, spreading

---

[38] Savage (2017).
[39] Ferguson (2005).
[40] Immerwahr (2019).
[41] Ferguson (2018b).
[42] Kupchan (2018a).

democracy through example rather than intrusion, embracing protection-ism and fair (not free) trade, and preserving a relatively homogeneous cit-izenry through racist and anti-immigrant policies. In short, it was about America first."

In the words of the first American President George Washington in his Farewell Address, "The great rule of conduct for us in regard to for-eign nations is in extending our commercial relations, to have with them as little political connection as possible."[43] And to be fair, America's decline is partially the structural byproduct of the rapid rise of China, which has openly called[44] for a twenty-first century new regional order of "Asia for Asians."[45] Since 2013, the Asian powerhouse has rolled out an alluring package of development initiatives,[46] which could poten-tially redraw the economic landscape of the region and beyond. With China emerging as the world's economic engine, it is proactively reclaim-ing its historical place in the sun (see Chapters 4 and 5)[47] But it is also the byproduct of the tempestuous Trump presidency's devastating impact on American standing in Asia.

But is Trump alone to be blamed for America's declining standing across the world? Is he a historical aberration, or simply reinforcing a sec-ular trend in the trajectory of American global power? Is he an unmit-igated disaster for American power? As frightening as the image of a vindictive American unilateralism under Trump may look like, the US president, however, has had, so far, three unexpectedly positive effects in the context of East Asia, where China has embarked on an irrepressible march for global mastery.

The first positive impact of Trump's unorthodox "hedgehog" approach to global politics, particularly in Asia, has to do with China. So far, Trump has created an optimal margin of unpredictability, which has thrown off[48] the leadership in Beijing. In fact, the Chinese leadership has openly bemoaned "confusing"[49] signals from the White House, reflecting their growing sense of vulnerability and desperation to get things right.

[43] Kupchan (2018b).

[44] Chin (2014).

[45] Yoon (2015).

[46] Heydarian (2014).

[47] Allison (2017).

[48] Bloomberg (2018, September).

[49] Agence France-Presse (2018).

While predictability matters in terms of long-term strategy, and is central to credible global leadership, a certain dose of unpredictability, if properly deployed, can bring about significant tactical advantages (see Chapter 7). This is better known as the Madman Theory,[50] or as Obama put it, the "crazy Nixon" approach,[51] given the former American president's risky strategic gambles in Southeast Asia and vis-à-vis China and the Soviet Union, which ultimately strengthened Washington's hand by reshuffling the regional strategic configuration to Moscow's utter shock. With Trump throwing in an unexpected level of unpredictability into the picture, the Chinese leadership has been forced to go back to the drawing table. Long accustomed to "fox" type of American leadership, particularly in the case of the cerebral Obama[52] who was known for long pondering his every move[53] often to the verge of paralyzing indecision, China managed to correctly guess the coordinates of Washington's strategic resolve.

This was particularly the case in South China Sea, where Chinese President Xi Jinping moved ahead, beginning in late 2013, with massive reclamation and militarization of disputed land features based on the correct assumption[54] that the ever-cautious and calculating Obama administration wouldn't risk a military escalation to draw the line in the waters (see Chapter 6). A year earlier, China also anticipated inaction[55] by Washington when it moved ahead with ejecting the Philippines, an American treaty ally, from the Scarborough Shoal after a months-long naval standoff between Manila and Beijing. Under the Trump administration, however, Washington has shown growing resolve to confront China in adjacent waters, empowering the Pentagon to conduct more aggressive and frequent Freedom of Navigation Operations (FONOPs) in the South China Sea. Openly characterizing Beijing as a revisionist power[56] in its National Security Strategy, Washington is also contemplating major war games[57] in the area in a show of force against

[50] Carroll (2005).

[51] Goldberg (2016).

[52] Chollet (2016).

[53] Nasr (2013).

[54] Greenert (2018).

[55] Pascual Jr. (2016).

[56] Trump (2017).

[57] Starr (2018).

a revanchist China, while expanding defense assistance[58] to and strategic infrastructure investment initiatives in the Indo-Pacific region. What the Trump administration has brought to the table, so far, is a combination of (seeming) resolve and unpredictability, two missing elements that China was able to fully exploit in previous years. As a result, Washington is in a better position to pursue Reagan-like "peace through strength" approach vis-à-vis Chinese maritime assertiveness.

THE ART OF WAR

The Trump administration hasn't only stepped up military countermeasures against China, but it has also, despite the supposed Trump–Xi personal rapport, escalated its trade war[59] with the Asian powerhouse in ways that few could have anticipated only a year earlier. In his second year in office, the Trump administration imposed punitive tariffs on up to $250 billion[60] of Chinese products while greater restrictions have been placed on Chinese investments in America as well as technology exports to China. Some experts believe that the Trump administration is seeking nothing less[61] than decoupling China from the global supply-chains, forcing Western companies to relocate operations to friendlier Asian territories such as Vietnam or/and onshore their overseas productions. Trump's seeming unpredictability, and penchant for a muscular showdown, has dramatically altered China's risk calculations, forcing Beijing to constantly revisit its strategic assumptions. China's leadership, as Henry Kissinger observed,[62] broadly focuses on the element of *Shi,* which can be roughly translated as momentum or, in Soviet-Marxist lingo, the "overall correlation of forces" in its strategic planning. Right until Trump's presidency, Beijing calculated that history was on its side, since time will only make it stronger relative to Washington, which, following Nixon's China visit, seemed more intent on preserving vital economic ties than checking China's revanchist ambitions. In fact, for a long time, the American business community and the Wall Street elite

---

[58] Yong (2018).

[59] Bloomberg (2018, August).

[60] Blumberg (2018).

[61] Friedman (2018).

[62] Kissinger (2012).

were seen as big advocates[63] of stronger Sino–American relations. Under Trump's presidency, however, the table has turned. No less than former Goldman Sachs chief executive officer (CEO) and US Treasury Secretary Henry Paulson, long regarded by Chinese elite as an "old friend," has warned of "the prospect of an Economic Iron Curtain—one that throws up new walls on each side and unmakes the global economy, as we have known it."[64] Along with other influential intermediaries and business elites, he has called for meaningful concessions, including structural economic reforms that put an end to China's mercantilist trade practices and predatory policies toward foreign companies and their technology. The upshot is an emerging bipartisan consensus[65] in Washington, where Trump's toughening stance on China is largely welcomed as a long overdue policy recalibration[66] between the world's two superpowers. In addition, the Trump administration has pushed for major infrastructure-focused initiatives in strategic nations, particularly in the Indo-Pacific, in order to counter China's economic initiatives.[67]

Some countries seem to be intent on exploiting the growing Sino–American rift. In particular, North Korea, long seen as China's all-weather ally, has sought direct communication channels with Washington, which has led to two unprecedented summits between Trump and the North Korean Supreme Leader Kim Jung-un. As one North Korean official told the author during a semi-official visit[68] to Pyongyang in April 2018, "With some American presidents, you have to make decisions quickly." In fact, the Trump administrations' direct and unprecedented engagement with the North Korean leadership has placed it in an optimal position, whereby it doesn't have to trade strategic concessions in exchange for Chinese cooperation on the Korean Peninsula issue. If anything, Trump doesn't seem to have even bothered to engage in "issue-linkage" strategic bargains[69] with China over North Korea, though he initially was mindful of it.[70] More broadly, North Korea's renewed openness to peace negotiations holds the

---

[63] Anderlini (2018).

[64] Ip (2018).

[65] Politico (2019).

[66] Kampbell and Ratner (2018).

[67] Hughes and Zumbrun (2018); Zumbrun and Hughes (2018).

[68] Heydarian (2018a).

[69] Poast (2013).

[70] Woodward (2018).

promise of altering the regional geopolitical landscape, potentially allowing Washington and its allies to divert vital yet finite strategic capital to other key flashpoints, particularly in the East and South China Sea down the road. As one senior South Korean journalist, who has deep connections in the Blue House told the author in November 2018, the Moon Jae-in administration is convinced that the Kim regime is willing to give up its nuclear weapons, albeit not overnight, in exchange for economic revival, a cornerstone of Kim Jung-un's modernization program (see Chapter 3).[71]

Crucially, however, Trump's seemingly unhinged leadership has forced other middle powers to step up to the plate. In the past years, all major naval powers, from Japan and South Korea to Australia, Britain, and France, have taken a more proactive stance and expanded[72] their strategic presence across vital sea lines of communications across the Indo-Pacific, even conducting their own versions of FONOPs close to Chinese occupied islands in the South China Sea. On its part, India, formally defined by its "non-alignment" strategic doctrine, has upgraded naval cooperation with like-minded nations, which have been perturbed by China's rapidly expanding naval capabilities and maritime ambitions. As Indian Prime Minister Narendra Modi made it clear[73] in the 2018 Shangri-La Dialogue in Singapore, Asia's strategic future is post-American, but not necessarily dominated by China, since middle powers are ready to contribute to preserving a "free and open" order in the Indo-Pacific (see Chapter 7).

In fact, the middle powers have also been pushing back against Trump's trade protectionism and China's predatory economics, including through "debt-trap" diplomacy, by pushing for sustainable and quality infrastructure investment initiatives as well as major multilateral free trade deals, particularly the TPP-11,[74] which is led by Japan, Regional Comprehensive Economic Partnership (RCEP) agreement, which is facilitated by Indonesia[75] and the Association of Southeast Asian Nations. Japan and the European Union also concluded the world's biggest bilateral free trading agreement[76] in hopes to dent the

---

[71] Discussions during a briefing by the author to a delegation of senior South Korean journalists organized by the US State Department in early November 2018.

[72] Heydarian (2018b).

[73] Heydarian (2018c).

[74] Hurst (2018).

[75] Hermansyah (2018).

[76] BBC News (2018).

fallout from Trump's protectionism (see Chapter 7). Yet, a major obstacle to American leadership in the Indo-Pacific is its misguided policies and debilitating entanglements in the Greater Middle East. This constitutes the "Great Distraction," which undermines Washington's ability to retain primacy in the world's most dynamic region, namely East Asia, where China seeks to create a neo-tributary system. And the Trump administration is heading toward a disaster in that region with far-reaching consequences for the Indo-Pacific.

REFERENCES

Agence France-Presse. "China Bemoans 'Confusing' Us Signals but Holds Hope for a Trump-Xi Meet." *Manila Bulletin.* October 15, 2018. https://news.mb.com.ph/2018/10/15/china-bemoans-confusing-us-signals-but-holds-hope-for-a-trump-xi-meet/.

Allison, Graham. "The Myth of the Liberal Order." *Foreign Affairs.* June 14, 2018. https://www.foreignaffairs.com/articles/2018-06-14/myth-liberal-order.

Allison, Graham. "The Thucydides Trap." *Foreign Policy.* June 9, 2017. https://foreignpolicy.com/2017/06/09/the-thucydides-trap/.

Anderlini, Jamil. "American Executives Are Becoming China Sceptics." *Financial Times.* November 14, 2018. https://www.ft.com/content/389a92c2-e738-11e8-8a85-04b8afea6ea3.

BBC News. "EU Signs Its Biggest Free Trade Deal with Japan." *BBC News.* July 17, 2018. https://www.bbc.com/news/business-44857317.

Bali, Asli, and Aziz Rana. "America's Imperial Unraveling." *Boston Review.* October 16, 2017. http://bostonreview.net/politics/asli-bali-aziz-rana-americas-imperial-unraveling.

Berlin, Isaiah. *The Hedgehog and the Fox.* London: Weidenfeld & Nicolson, 1953.

Bialik, Kristen. "How the World Views the U.S. and Its President in 9 Charts." *Pew Research Center.* October 9, 2018. http://www.pewresearch.org/fact-tank/2018/10/09/how-the-world-views-the-u-s-and-its-president-in-9-charts/.

Blumberg, Yoni. "Trump's $250 Billion in China Tariffs Are Now in Effect—Here's What Could Get More Expensive." *CNBC News.* September 25, 2018. https://www.cnbc.com/2018/09/25/with-trumps-250-billion-in-china-tariffs-heres-what-will-cost-more.html.

Carroll, James. "Nixon's Madman Strategy." *Boston.com.* June 14, 2005. http://archive.boston.com/news/globe/editorial_opinion/oped/articles/2005/06/14/nixons_madmanstrategy/.

Chin, Curtis. "Xi Jinping's 'Asia for Asians' Mantra Evokes Imperial Japan." *The South China Morning Post.* July 14, 2014. https://www.scmp.com/comment/insight-opinion/article/1553414/xi-jinpings-asia-asians-mantra-evokes-imperial-japan.

"China, Unsure of How to Handle Trump, Braces for 'New Cold War'." *Bloomberg*. August 17, 2018. https://www.bloomberg.com/news/articles/2018-08-17/china-unsure-of-how-to-handle-trump-braces-for-new-cold-war.

Chollet, Derek. *The Long Game: How Obama Defied Washington and Redefined America's Role in the World*. New York: PublicAffairs, 2016.

Chua, Amy. *Day of Empire: How Hyperpowers Rise to Global Dominance—And Why They Fall*, p. XXII. New York: Anchor, 2009.

Ellwood, Charles A. "Making the World Safe for Democracy." *The Scientific Monthly 7*, no. 6 (1918): 511–524. http://www.jstor.org/stable/7088.

Farhi, Paul. "What Really Gets Under Trump's Skin? A Reporter Questioning His Net Worth." *The Washington Post*. March 8, 2016. https://www.washingtonpost.com/lifestyle/style/that-time-trump-sued-over-the-size-of-hiswallet.

Ferguson, Niall. "A Terrible, Horrible, No Good, Very Bad President Builds an Empire." *Boston Globe*. June 11, 2018a. https://www.bostonglobe.com/opinion/2018/06/11/terrible-horrible-good-very-bad-president-builds-empire.

Ferguson, Niall. "The Myth of the Liberal International Order." *Belfer Center*. January 11, 2018b. https://www.belfercenter.org/publication/myth-liberal-international-order.

Ferguson, Niall. *Colossus: The Rise and Fall of the American Empire*. Westminster: Penguin Books, 2005.

Freedman, Lawrence. *Strategy: A History*. Oxford: Oxford University Press, 2015.

Friedman, Uri. "Donald Trump's Real Endgame with China." *The Atlantic*. October 4, 2018. https://www.theatlantic.com/international/archive/2018/10/trump-china-trade/572122/.

Gaddis, John Lewis. *On Grand Strategy*. Westminster: Penguin Press, 2018.

Goldberg, Jeffrey. "A Senior White House Official Defines the Trump Doctrine: 'We're America, Bitch'." *The Atlantic*. June 11, 2018. https://www.theatlantic.com/politics/archive/2018/06/a-senior-white-house-official-defines-the-trump-doctrine-were-america-bitch/562511/.

Goldberg, Jeffrey. "The Obama Doctrine." *The Atlantic*. April 2016. https://www.theatlantic.com/magazine/archive/2016/04/the-obama-doctrine/471525/.

"Gore Vidal Quotes: 26 of the Best." *The Guardian*. August 1, 2012. https://www.theguardian.com/books/2012/aug/01/gore-vidal-best-quotes.

Greenert, Jonathan. "Tenets of a Regional Defense Strategy: Considerations for the Indo-Pacific." *The National Bureau of Asian Research*, no. 72. August 21, 2018. https://www.nbr.org/publication/tenets-of-a-regional-defense-strategy-considerations-for-the-indo-pacific/.

Hermansyah, Anton. "Indonesia Targets to Conclude RCEP Negotiations This Year." *The Jakarta Post*. April 24, 2018. https://www.thejakartapost.com/news/2018/04/24/indonesia-targets-to-conclude-rcep-negotiations-this-year.html.

Heydarian, Richard Javad. "I Just Visited North Korea: Here Is What the World Needs to Know." *The National Interest.* May 5, 2018a. https://nationalinterest. org/feature/i-just-visited-north-korea-here-what-the-world-needs-know-25708.

Heydarian, Richard Javad. "Middle Powers Step Up in Asia." *China-US Focus.* October 24, 2018b. https://www.chinausfocus.com/foreign-policy/ middle-powers-step-up-in-asia.

Heydarian, Richard Javad. "The Shangri-La Dialogue Takeaway: China's Rapid Rise Is Redefining the Asian Order Like Never Before." *South China Morning Post.* June 9, 2018c. https://www.scmp.com/news/china/diplomacy-defence/ article/2150001/shangri-la-dialogue-takeaway-chinas-rapid-rise.

Heydarian, Richard Javad. "This Is How a Superpower Commits Suicide." *New Perspectives Quarterly* 35, no. 1 (2018d). https://doi.org/10.1111/ npqu.12115.

Heydarian, Richard Javad. "The BRICS Bank: Multipolarity or Beijing Consensus?" *Aljazeera.* July 21, 2014. https://www.aljazeera.com/indepth/ opinion/2014/07/brics-bank-beijing-consensus-201472183428811634.html.

Holland, Tom. *Persian Fire: The First World Empire and the Battle for the West.* New York: Anchor, 2007.

Hughes, Siobhan, and Josh Zumbrun. "Senate Approves Plan to Double Funding for Global Infrastructure Projects." *The Wall Street Journal.* October 3, 2018. https://www.wsj.com/articles/senate-approves-plan-to-double-funding-for-global-infrastructure-projects-1538595889.

Hurst, Daniel. "Amid US Trade Tensions, Japan Formally Completes TPP-11 Entry." *The Diplomat.* July 13, 2018. https://thediplomat.com/2018/07/ amid-us-trade-tensions-japan-formally-completes-tpp-11-entry/.

Ikenberry, G. John. "The Plot Against American Foreign Policy." *Foreign Affairs.* April 17, 2017. https://www.foreignaffairs.com/articles/ united-states/2017-04-17/plot-against-american-foreign-policy.

Immerwahr, Daniel. "How the US Has Hidden Its Empire." *The Guardian.* May 8, 2019. https://www.theguardian.com/news/2019/feb/15/the-us-hidden-empire-overseas-territories-united-states-guam-puerto-rico-american-samoa.

"In New Trump Tariffs, China Sees Master Plan to Thwart Its Rise." *Bloomberg.* September 18, 2018. https://www.bloomberg.com/news/arti-cles/2018-09-18/in-new-trump-tariffs-china-sees-master-plan-to-thwart-its-rise.

Ip, Greg. "Once an Optimist on U.S.–China Relations, Henry Paulson Delivers a Sobering Message." *The Wall Street Journal.* November 6, 2018. https://www. wsj.com/articles/once-an-optimist-on-u-s-china-relations-henry-paulson-delivers-a-sobering-message-1541548800.

ISEAS-Yusof Ishak Institute. "How Do Southeast Asians View the Trump Administration?" *ASEAN Studies Centre.* April 5, 2017. https://www.iseas. edu.sg/images/centres/asc/pdf/ASCSurvey40517.pdf.

Kagan, Robert. "This Is How Fascism Comes to America." *The Washington Post.* May 18, 2016. https://www.washingtonpost.com/opinions/this-is-how-fascism-comes-toamerica/2016/05/17/.

Kampbell, Kurt, and Ely Ratner. "The China Reckoning." *Foreign Affairs.* February 13, 2018. https://www.foreignaffairs.com/articles/china/2018-02-13/china-reckoning.

Kennan, George. *American Diplomacy: 1900–1950.* Chicago: University of Chicago, 1951.

Kissinger, Henry. *On China.* Westminster: Penguin Books, 2012.

Krugman, Paul. "Fall of the American Empire." *The New York Times.* June 18, 2018. https://www.nytimes.com/2018/06/18/opinion/immigration-trump-children-american-empire.html.

Kupchan, Charles. "The Clash of Exceptionalisms." *Foreign Affairs.* February 13, 2018a. https://www.foreignaffairs.com/articles/united-states/2018-02-13/clash-exceptionalisms.

Kupchan, Charles. "Trump's Nineteenth-Century Grand Strategy." *Foreign Affairs.* September 26, 2018b. https://www.foreignaffairs.com/articles/2018-09-26/trumps-nineteenth-century-grand-strategy.

Liu, Yadong. "How Trump's Policies Are Helping China." *Foreign Affairs.* September 28, 2018. https://www.foreignaffairs.com/articles/china/2018-09-28/how-trumps-policies-are-helping-china.

Mickey, Robert, Steven Levistsky, and Lucan Ahmad Way. "Is America Still Safe for Democracy?" *Foreign Affairs.* May/June 2017 Issue.

Nasr, Vali. "The Inside Story of How the White House Let Diplomacy Fail in Afghanistan." *Foreign Policy.* March 4, 2013. https://foreignpolicy.com/2013/03/04/the-inside-story-of-how-the-white-house-let-diplomacy-fail-in-afghanistan/.

Nye, Joseph. "Will the Liberal Order Survive?" *Foreign Affairs.* December 12, 2016. https://www.foreignaffairs.com/articles/2016-12-12/will-liberal-order-survive.

Pascual Jr., Federico. "Aquino: US Brokered Failed Panatag Deal." *Philstar Global.* May 31, 2016. https://www.philstar.com/opinion/2016/05/31/1588604/aquino-us-brokered-failed-panatag-deal.

Poast, Paul. "Issue Linkage and International Cooperation: An Empirical Investigation." *Conflict Management and Peace Science* 30, no. 3. (2013): 286–303. https://doi.org/10.1177/0738894213484030.

Politico. "Bipartisan US Bill Seeks to Toughen Donald Trump's Approach to China." *South China Morning Post.* January 5, 2019. https://www.scmp.com/news/world/united-states-canada/article/2180794/bipartisan-bill-seeks-toughen-trump-approach-china.

Rose, Gideon. "Present at the Destruction?" *Foreign Affairs.* May/June 2017. https://www.foreignaffairs.com/articles/2017-04-17/present-destruction.

Savage, Charlie. *Power Wars: The Relentless Rise of Presidential Authority and Secrecy.* New York: Back Bay Books, 2017.

Schake, Kori. "The Trump Doctrine Is Winning and the World Is Losing." *The New York Times.* June 15, 2018. https://www.nytimes.com/2018/06/15/opinion/sunday/trump-china-america-first.

Starr, Barbara. "US Navy Proposing Major Show of Force to Warn China." *CNN Politics.* October 4, 2018. https://edition.cnn.com/2018/10/03/politics/us-navy-show-of-force-china/index.html.

Trump, Donald. *National Security Strategy of the United States of America.* 2017. https://www.whitehouse.gov/wp-content/uploads/2017/12/NSS-Final-12-18-2017-0905.pdf.

Trump, Donald, and Tony Schwartz. *Trump: The Art of the Deal.* New York: Ballantine Books, 2015.

Tucker, Robert C. "The Theory of Charismatic Leadership." *Daedalus* 97, no. 3 (1968): 731–756. http://www.jstor.org/stable/20023840.

Wike, Richard, et al. "U.S. Image Suffers as Publics Around World Question Trump's Leadership." *Pew Research Center.* June 26, 2017a. https://www.pewglobal.org/2017/06/26/u-s-image-suffers-as-publics-around-world-question-trumps-leadership/.

Wike, Richard, et al. "2. Worldwide, Few Confident in Trump or His Policies." *Pew Research Center.* June 26, 2017b. https://www.pewglobal.org/2017/06/26/worldwide-few-confident-in-trump-or-his-policies/.

Wittkopf, Eugene, Christopher Jones Jr., and Charles Kegley. *American Foreign Policy: Pattern and Process,* 7th edition. Boston: Cengage Learning, 2007.

Woodward, Bob. *Fear: Trump in the White House.* New York: Simon & Schuster, 2018.

Wright, Thomas. "Trump's 19th Century Foreign Policy." *Politico.* January 20, 2016. https://www.politico.com/magazine/story/2016/01/donald-trump-foreign-policy-213546.

Yong, Charissa. "US Announces US$300 Million to Fund Security Cooperation in Indo-Pacific Region." *The Straits Times.* August 4, 2018. https://www.straitstimes.com/politics/us-pledges-nearly-us300-million-security-funding-for-south-east-asia.

Yoon, Young-kwan. "How the Vacuum Left by America Bolsters China's 'Asia for Asians' Strategy." *Huffington Post.* Last date modified April 4, 2015. https://www.huffpost.com/entry/china-asia-for-asians_b_6595550.

Zizek, Slavoj. *Was Antigone a Man? Masculinity and Other Toxic Entities.* Birkbeck, University of London. Podcast Audio. April 29, 2019. http://zizekpodcast.com/2019/05/01/ziz233-was-antigone-a-man-masculinity-and-other-toxic-entities-29-04-2019/.

Zumbrun, Josh, and Siobhan Hughes. "To Counter China, U.S. Looks to Invest Billions More Overseas." *The Wall Street Journal.* August 31, 2018. https://www.wsj.com/articles/to-counter-china-u-s-looks-to-invest-billions-more-overseas-1535728206.

CHAPTER 3

The Great Distraction: The Near East and North Korea

Just when I thought I was out, they pull me back in.[1] —Michael Corleone, *The Godfather*

There is no instance of a country having benefitted from prolonged warfare.[2] —Sun Tzu, *The Art of War*

Americans should not go abroad to slay dragons they do not understand in the name of spreading democracy.[3] —John Quincy Adams, Secretary of State (1817–1825)

The cradle of civilizations is also the graveyard of Western empires. From Alexander of Macedonia in the ancient world to the Franco-British imperial condominium in the twentieth century, a slew of Western powers have stubbornly sought, but ultimately failed, to build a lasting order on the ashes of indigenous empires, from the mighty Acheamenids to the cosmopolitan Ottomans.[4] Only the Romans came close to establishing a centuries-old semblance of organized order in parts of the region, but just to find themselves at constant loggerheads with the Parthian and Sassanid rivals; overwhelmed by the religious fervor of Abrahamic

---

[1] The Godfather III (1990).

[2] Sun Tzu (2007).

[3] Brown and Winslow (2012).

[4] Fisk (2007).

© The Author(s) 2020
R. J. Heydarian, *The Indo-Pacific: Trump, China, and the New Struggle for Global Mastery*, https://doi.org/10.1007/978-981-13-9799-8_3

religions hailing from the region; and later, broken into halves as the Dark Ages descended amid the barbarian invasion from the north.[5] The United States is only the latest, and perhaps the last, Western power to have been ineluctably drawn into this age-old geopolitical maelstrom from which it desperately struggles to break free, yet so far in vain.

No postcolonial region has so disproportionately absorbed American geopolitical bandwidth than the Greater Middle East, stretching from the pristine deserts of Morocco to the rugged mountains of Afghanistan and lush forests of the Caspian Sea. In many ways, the region is the new Vietnam War,[6] which enervated American power abroad and divided it from within, except on a far larger scale and stretched across a longer time horizon with broader implications for civilizational ties between the West and the Islamic world.[7] In *The Clash of Civilizations*, a controversial work which was fundamentally anchored by a semantic-normative framework rather than an analytic-empirical insight, the late Samuel Huntington foresaw nothing short of a civilizational conflict between the West and the Islamic world as one of the defining features of the twenty-first century. As the American political scientist claimed, "Some Westerners...have argued that the West does not have problems with Islam but only with violent Islamist extremists. Fourteen hundred years of history demonstrate otherwise."[8] As eminent scholars such as Edward Said, however, have pointed out,[9] what Huntington failed to underscore, however, was the intra-civilizational conflict among competing centers of powers in the Middle East, the Shia Safavids and Sunni Ottomans[10] in early modern times and, more recently, between Shia-Persian Iran and Sunni-Arab nations, particularly Iraq (during Saddam) and Saudi Arabia.[11] Not to mention, the competition among different Sunni schools of jurisprudence, particularly the more liberal Hanafi branch, which was predominant during the golden age of Islam, as opposed to the more austere Hanbali branch,

---

[5] See Beard (2015), Dignas and Winther (2007), and Gibbon and Womersley (2000).
[6] History (2009).
[7] Huntington (1993).
[8] Abu-Rabi (2006).
[9] Said (2001).
[10] Hodgson (1977).
[11] Mabon (2015).

which gained the upper hand in the contemporary era.[12] And contrary to arguments on supposed "Islamic exceptionalism,"[13] which implies a fundamental civilizational-theological-political incompatibility with the Judeo-Christian world, the Islamic world did also have a semblance of separation of state and religion throughout centuries of Ottoman rule.[14] Moreover, the Islamic empires of the Medieval and early modern period didn't necessarily subscribe to a binary division between *Dar al-Islam* (Abode of Islam) and *Dar al-Harb* (Territory of War),[15] but instead a more nuanced distinction across a spectrum of relations with other civilizations, which included Dar al-Sulh (lit. Territory of treaty), pertaining to areas governed by peace treaties between Islamic empires and their (friendly) Christian and non-Muslim counterparts.[16]

Even more crucially, Huntington's work falsely represented Muslim societies as monolithic entities devoid of the ability for transformation and exercise of agency. In many ways, Said argues, the American political scientist relied on a caricature of what are actually highly complex, evolving Middle Eastern societies—an orientalist defect that has its roots in the works of historians such as Bernard Lewis.[17] In the words of Said, "certainly neither Huntington nor Lewis has much time to spare for the internal dynamics and plurality of every civilization, or for the fact that the major contest in most modern cultures concerns the definition or interpretation of each culture, or for the unattractive possibility that a great deal of demagogy and downright ignorance is involved in presuming to speak for a whole religion or civilization... the problem with unedifying labels like Islam and the West: They mislead and confuse the mind, which is trying to make sense of a disorderly reality that won't be pigeonholed or strapped down as easily as all that."[18] Said's works and insights are crucial, not only for their analytic nuance and rigor, but also for the fact that at least one American President, Barack Obama, may have attended and been deeply influence by his lectures in Columbia University.[19]

---

[12] Akyol (2011).

[13] Hamid (2017).

[14] Danforth (2014).

[15] See Kissinger's (erroneous) analysis in Kissinger (2015, 97–111).

[16] See The Oxford Dictionary of Islam (2019) and Hamid (2017).

[17] See Lewis (1990).

[18] Said (2001).

[19] Weiner (2008).

And this may partly explain, as will be discussed later in this chapter, Obama's unique approach toward America's imperial conundrum in the Middle East. In the same breath, Huntington's works have deeply influenced American elite's geopolitical paradigm in the Near East, particularly among neoconservatives and liberal hawks.[20] In a way, twenty-first century American foreign policy in the Greater Middle East is the operationalization of the debate between Huntington and Said.

Today's Middle East is fundamentally a realm of clash within civilizations, namely between a Persian-Shia realm versus the majority Arab-Sunni nations. The Arab uprisings—which have pitted Iran and its proxies, including the Alewite regime in Syria, against Sunni powers and protesters—has only exacerbated the sectarian, intra-civilizational conflict in the Islamic realm, which has now spread well beyond the region and all the way to Southeast Asia.[21] Thus, unlike in the Medieval and early modern times when the Islamic empires expanded all the way to the doors of Western Europe, the modern Middle East is instead more like a geopolitical abyss rather than the site of a new imperial rival to the West.

If there is anything that Donald Trump has been consistent about over the years is his recognition of the gnawing geopolitical predicament of imperial overstretch in the Middle East, which has been hemorrhaging American power over the past two decades. Not to mention, this is one of the few, if not only, issues on which he seems to be on the same page as his predecessor (and nemesis), Barack Obama, whose chief foreign policy objective was to Pivot to Asia (P2A) precisely out of the Middle East (see Chapter 6).[22] In the words of Kurt Campbell, one of the architects of the Asia-focused policy, the Obama administration's strategy was to reorient American foreign policy to "a rising Asia even in the midst of punishing and inescapable challenges in the Middle East," which he bluntly described as an "arc of instability" as opposed to the "arc of ascendance" in East Asia.[23]

Trump put it in even blunter terms, declaring: "Does the USA want to be the Policeman of the Middle East, getting nothing but spending precious lives and trillions of dollars protecting others who, in almost all cases, do not appreciate what we are doing? Do we want to be there

---

[20] Algeriani and Mohadi (2018).
[21] See Saleem (2016) and Formichi (2014).
[22] Campbell (2016).
[23] Ibid., 1.

forever? Time for others to finally fight..."[24] This is why Obama was among the few political leaders who openly opposed the 2003 Iraq War, while Trump was among few celebrities who, at least he claims, to have taken the same position ahead of the devastating conflict. Throughout his presidential campaign, Trump repeatedly berated his Republican rivals and the George W. Bush administration for its misadventures in the Middle East.[25]

To be fair, there is hardly anything fundamentally new with the policy preference of the two American presidents. If anything, the Richard Nixon administration was arguably the first contemporary American president to have sought disentanglement from the Near East in favor of greater engagement with rising powers in the Far East. The Nixon Doctrine was anchored by a policy of "strategic retrenchment," whereby Washington will (i) delegate responsibility to favored regional partners; (ii) reassess overseas strategic priorities; and (iii) streamline defense spending and diplomatic commitments.[26] By reaching out to Beijing, the Nixon administration hoped to build partnerships with emerging powers, which would truly reconfigure the global order. Meanwhile, Washington was more than happy to designate the Shah of Iran (Mohammad Reza Pahlavi) as a regional gendarmerie in the Persian Gulf, with Saudi Arabia, Israel, and Turkey jointly stabilizing the region against Soviet-backed revisionist Arab nations. Up until the 1979 Iranian Revolution, the Persians were part of the "alliance of the periphery" along with Turkey and Israel against Soviet-aligned Arab nations.[27]

Through retrenchment, the Nixon administration tried to address two primary concerns, namely (i) recovering from the devastating impact of the Vietnam War, and (ii) shaping a favorable future when America is no longer the dominant global power. But as Nixon embarked on his own pivot to East Asia, the Middle East morphed into a strategic black hole, beginning with the oil shocks of the 1970s, which went hand in hand with a new round of Arab–Israeli war, and culminated with the disintegration of the pro-Western Iranian monarchy.[28] In the words of Henry Kissinger, the chief architect of the Nixon Doctrine, "Nowhere

[24] Heavey (2018).
[25] Finnegan and Mehta (2016).
[26] Porter (2013).
[27] Sachs (2019).
[28] See Fisk (2007) and Yergin (2008).

is the challenge of international order more complex – in terms of both organizing regional order and ensuring compatibility of that order with peace and stability in the rest of the world" than in the Middle East. To him, the region has been embroiled in intractable conflicts, because it "seems destined to experiment with all of its historical experiences simultaneously – empire, holy war, foreign domination, a sectarian war of all against all – before it arrives (if it ever does) at a settled concept of international order."[29] In short, the Middle East is trapped in a crucible of intra-civilizational discord with cross-civilizational implications. Considering the centrality of the region, which produces the bulk of global energy output, to the global "fossil capitalism,"[30] external powers like the United States have been inevitably dragged into the region with no end in sight.

Thus, even Trump ended up choosing the Middle East, particularly Saudi Arabia, as his first overseas state visit, underscoring the gravitational pull of the world's cauldron of conflict. In fact, both Nixon (think of the Yum Kippur War and the 1973 Oil Crisis) and Obama (think of the Arab uprisings, the Iran nuclear negotiations and the Syrian Civil War) were eventually embroiled in and enervated by major crises across the region, which significantly undermined their ability to reorient American foreign policy. Washington's latest strategy under Trump, however, seems to combine two elements, namely (i) Nixon's delegation of new regional gendarmeries, namely Saudi Arabia and Israel, against a revisionist Iran; and (ii) drastic and swift reduction of American military footprint across the region's hotspots, particularly Syria and Afghanistan, amid the ostensible defeat of the so-called Islamic State (IS) as a rogue quasi-state actor. Far from stabilizing the region, however, Trump's version of strategic entrenchment is likely to cause even greater chaos and instability in the region. On the most fundamental level, the United States lacks a real strategy in the Greater Middle East, especially one that maintains "a balance between ends, ways, and means" based on clear identification of final objectives.[31]

---

[29] Kissinger (2015).

[30] For further analysis refer to Angus (2016) and Yergin (2008).

[31] Freedman (2015, xi).

Anatomy of Imperial Entanglement

Within a century, the region went from an afterthought to a new realm strategic of focus and, in more recent decades, an American imperial obsession. As London School of Economics' Fawaz Gerges explains, "Until the end of World War II the United States did not actively participate in Middle Eastern politics, It limited its engagement to educational and missionary activities and commercial investment in the region's oil sector. On the whole, American foreign policy had been isolationist from birth of the Republic."[32]

The advent of the Cold War, however, changed everything. Following Washington's 1953 participation in the coup against the democratically elected government in Iran, then under nationalist, anti-colonial Prime Minister Mohammad Mossadeq, America injected itself right into the heart of regional politics with devastating consequences for future of peace and democracy in the Middle East.[33] And in spite of countless American military interventions[34] (see Table 3.1)[35] as well as military bases (see Fig. 3.1) across the Middle East,[36] ostensibly for stabilization purposes, the region has instead turned into a seemingly irredeemable arc of conflict, namely a modern Game of Thrones on steroids.

The upshot is seemingly "endless wars,"[37] which have eroded both the imperial morale as well as moral ascendancy of America as a global leader, not to mention the significant strain on its powerbase. As an authoritative study by the RAND Corporation put it, "...stationing U.S. forces can be an effective tool in deterring state aggression, but it is not likely to have an effect in deterring intrastate conflict. There is also an important trade-off, in that U.S. troop presence may provoke more militarized activities."[38] To put things into perspective, let's assess the cost of containing Saddam's Iraq alone. As Samuel Huntington noted, the First Gulf War, which was meant to repel Saddam Hussein's invasion

[32] Gerges (2013, 27).
[33] See Kinzer (2008), Ansari (2007), Sick (2001), and Mishra (2012).
[34] See Myre (2014) and Zunes (2003).
[35] Jeffrey and Eisenstadt (2016, 20, 24–25).
[36] Zenko (2018).
[37] Chivers (2018).
[38] O'Mahony et al. (2018, 83).

Table 3.1 US military interventions in the Middle East

Major wars
- Gulf War, 1990–1991
- Afghanistan invasion, 2001
- Afghanistan counterinsurgency, 2001–present
- Iraq invasion, 2003
- Iraq counterinsurgency, 2003–2011

Other large-scale conflicts
- Operation Earnest Will (reflagging of Kuwaiti tankers to protect them from Iranian aggression), 1987–1988
- Containment of Iraq post-Gulf War:
  - Operation Provide Comfort, 1991–2003
  - Operation Northern Watch, 1991–2003
  - Operation Southern Watch, 1991–2003
  - Strike on Iraq in response to alleged Bush assassination plot, 1993
  - Operation Desert Fox, 1998
- GWOT, 2001–present
- Counter-IS campaign, 2014–present

Other operations and engagements
- Lebanon, 1958
- Attack on *USS Liberty*, 1967
- Jordan crisis, 1970
- Naval task force in support of Pakistan, 1971
- Iran hostage rescue mission, 1980
- U.S. intelligence support to Iraq in the Iran-Iraq war
- Beirut operation, 1983–1984
- U.S. airstrikes on Syrian air defense in Lebanon, 1983
- TWA hijacking alert, 1985
- *Achille Lauro* hijacking intercept, 1985
- Libya bombing, 1986
- Attack on *USS Stark*, 1987
- Somali peacekeeping operation, 1992–1993
- Khobar Towers bombing, 1996
- U.S. engagements with Al-Qaeda, 1998–2001
- Anti-piracy operations, Horn of Africa, 2006–present
- Operational support to Turkey against the Kurdistan Workers Party (PKK), 2007–present
- Libya Operation, 2011
- Syria overt and covert train-and-equip efforts, 2011–present
- Syria chemical weapons threat of military action, 2013
- Patriot missiles, F-16s and other forces deployed to Jordan, oriented toward Syria, 2013–present
- U.S. Patriot unit as part of NATO deployment to Turkey oriented toward Syria, 2013–2015
- U.S. air-to-air aircraft deployed to Turkey to counter Russian deployments to Syria, 2013–2015

Major noncombat operations
- U.S. responses to contain Soviet encroachment in Iranian Azerbaijan and Kurdistan and threats against Turkey, 1946–1950
- Military equipment airlift to Israel, 1973
- Yom Kippur War global alert, October 1973
- U.S. military support for the Afghan mujahedin, 1980–1989
- Coercive nuclear diplomacy with, and containment of Iran, 2003–present

Source Jeffrey and Eisenstadt (2016)

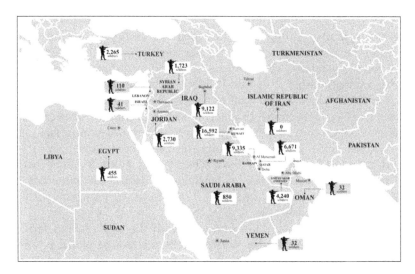

Fig. 3.1   US military bases across the Middle East (*Source* Zenko 2018)

of Kuwait, saw Washington deploying "75 percent of its active tactical aircraft, 42 percent of its modern battle tanks, 46 percent of its aircraft carriers, 37 percent of its army personnel, and 46 percent of its marine personnel."[39] This doesn't even include contributions by American allies, from Western Europe to Saudi Arabia and Japan, to the grand coalition efforts. The Iraqi forces were handily routed, forced to withdraw in utter humiliation and under constant bombardment,[40] but the strain on American resources was significant, putting into question whether Washington was in a position to make any meaningful response were there another simultaneous contingency in the region (i.e., conflict with Iran) or other geopolitical hotspots elsewhere in the world, particulalry in East Asia or in the post-Soviet space.

The Second Gulf War, this time to displace and supplant the Saddam regime, was even more exacting. At first, the Rumsfeld Doctrine, namely the deployment of a limited number of ground troops and high reliance on aerial bombardments, created an illusion of swift, cheap regime

[39] Huntington (2011, 90).
[40] Fisk (2007).

change in Mesopotamia. But as leading economists such as Joseph Stiglitz (Columbia University) and Linda Bilmes (Harvard University) have calculated, the true cost of the war, including healthcare expenditures for the veterans, was closer to $4.5 trillion dollars, about a third of the country's Gross Domestic Product. Together with the simultaneous war in Afghanistan, the total cost topped $7 trillion, just under half of the US Gross Domestic Product.[41] Not to mention, America's war against Jihadi groups, namely al-Qaeda and its derivatives, most famously the so-called IS; cost of containment of post-revolutionary Iran, which has spread its influence from Central Asia to the Mediterranean; America's annual multi-billion military aid to Israel; and hundreds of millions of dollars in annual geopolitical rent to strategic partners such as Pakistan, Jordan, and Egypt.

But why America's seeming obsession with the region? Four factors made the Middle East so disproportionately relevant to global powers, namely the discovery and development of fossil fuel reserves in the early twentieth century; the founding of the State of Israel by the middle of the century; and the emergence of indigenous revisionist powers, particularly post-revolutionary Iran and Saddam's Iraq, in the latter decades of the century; and the Global War on Terror after the September 11 attacks at the dawn of the new century. Without a question, the Middle East is geopolitically relevant. The region is the world's largest oil producer, accounting for a third of global production, 45% of crude oil exports, and host to almost half of global oil reserves.[42] Iran and Qatar have the world's second and third largest reserves of natural gas, respectively.[43] The region's geography, perched in the middle of the industrial hubs of Asia and Europe and historically the heartland of the ancient Silk Road, only accentuates its natural geopolitical importance. In many ways, the Middle East, particulalry Iran, is where Halford Mackinder's Eurasian "heartland" meets Nicholas John Spykman "rimland," thus the centrality of the region during the Cold War.[44] The special alliance between the United States and Israel, undergirded by a powerful pro-Israel lobby in Washington, further wedded the global superpower to

---

[41] Bilmes and Stiglitz (2008).

[42] British Petroleum (2018).

[43] Hydrocarbons Technology (2013).

[44] Kaplan (2013).

the region, especially as the Jewish-majority state fought for its survival against multiple waves of Arab invasions and, later, geopolitical rivalry with revolutionary Persians.[45] The third factor was the emergence of post-revolutionary Iran and Saddam's Iraq—two countries blessed with significant population, natural resources, and military-industrial base, in addition to close strategic ties with Russia and China—as revisionist powers seeking to establish a post-American order in the region. The elimination of the Saddam regime in Iraq ended up strengthening the hands of Iran, which turned much of eastern Iraq into its own sphere of influence, enjoying significant influence on the fellow Shiite ruling elite in Baghdad for years, if not decades, to come.[46] Iran's quest for mastery of nuclear technology only deepened America's sense of panic over the emergence of a new pillar of power in the region with full nuclear impunity. And lastly, al-Qaeda's brazen terrorist attacks on no less than the World Trade Center and Pentagon in the American heartland, which has provoked a two-decades-long global campaign against every Jihadi extremist group across the planet.

America's involvement in the Middle East was ultimately a kiss of death. The more it intervened in regional affairs, the more destabilizing its effect on the region. In the case of Iran's Shah, he became the country's last monarch amid a nationwide backlash against his strategic flirtations and ideological alignment with the West.[47] As the French philosopher Michel Foucault described the 1979 Iranian revolution, "[i]t is not a revolution...it is perhaps the first great insurrection against [Western-dominated] global systems, the form of revolt that is the most modern and the most insane."[48]

A BRAVE NEW MIDDLE EAST

One American president, however, tried to radically recast the coordinates of American imperial engagement with the region. Barack Obama, born to a (nominally) Muslim Kenyan father and an American mother,

---

[45] Mearsheimer and Walt (2008).

[46] Nasr (2016).

[47] Ansari (2019).

[48] Afary and Anderson (2005).

was the ultimate anti-Huntingtonian—fundamentally rejecting the "clash of civilizations" thesis in favor of an alternative vision, where America acts as a mediator between competing Muslim powers.[49] Obama was arguably Edward Said's most important student. In effect, he ultimately sought to deploy American power to contain the gushing wound of intra-civilizational discord in the Middle East by reaching out to both Sunnis and Shias.[50]

In his historic 2009 speech in Cairo, Obama declared: "I've come here to Cairo to seek a new beginning between the United States and Muslims around the world, one based on mutual interest and mutual respect, and one based upon the truth that America and Islam are not exclusive and need not be in competition. Instead, they overlap, and share common principles – principles of justice and progress; tolerance and the dignity of all human beings."[51] For Obama, the twenty-first century is one of globalization and, to use the words of the former Iranian reformist President Mohammad Khatami, a "dialogue among civilizations."[52] Obama's efforts to reach out to the Arab world were ultimately tested by the 2010–2011 Arab uprisings, which caught all major powers off-guard. After all, the revolts were the upshot of decades of structural contradictions in the political economy of Arab nations, where economic stagnation went hand in hand with political sclerosis and widespread corruption.[53] Washington sought to both preserve its interests in the region, while welcoming change. This balancing act ultimately proved an impossible, if not counterproductive, task. On one hand, the Obama administration rhetorically supported the popular revolts in Tunisia, Egypt, and Libya against ossified autocrats. But this meant Washington abandoning its regional autocratic allies such as Hosni Mubarak. To many of America's regional allies, Obama's America threw its friends under the bus by abandoning them during the revolutionary upheavals. Washington's subsequent support for the Muslim Brotherhood and its affiliates' ascendance via elections in post-revolutionary Arab world, however, alienated both liberal-democrats as well as reactionary regimes in the Middle East, particularly in the Persian Gulf. When the Egyptian

[49] Shahi (2017).
[50] Gardner (2017).
[51] Obama (2009).
[52] For instance, see Petito (2004).
[53] Heydarian (2014a).

military, long a key recipient of US military aid, toppled the Muslim Brotherhood-run government in 2013, the Obama administration found itself in an impossible spot. The situation got even more complicated when the protests spread to the Persian Gulf, particularly Bahrain, which hosts America's biggest naval base in the region, the US Navy Fifth Fleet. In response, the Obama administration largely stood by as a Saudi-led 'The Peninsula Shield Force' brutally crushed the largely Shia-driven protests for democratic reform. By standing idly by, Washington exposed its strategic hypocrisy and ended up alienating democratic forces across the world. On the other hand, Obama's support for armed intervention in Libya under the so-called Responsibility to Protect (R2P) principle, violated his own pacifist pronouncements, while precipitating a dangerous power vacuum across North Africa which is yet to be filled a decade henceforth. The episode also saw Obama's potential abuse of his war powers by effectively circumventing congressional scrutiny.[54] Obama's greatest failure vis-à-vis the Arab world, however, was his inability to convince a hostile Israeli government, led by Benjamin Netanyahu, to effectuate the two-state solution with the Palestinian Authority. The upshot of these strategic blunders, some almost ineluctable and largely immanent-structural to the geopolitics of the region, was a dramatic collapse of Obama's popularity across the Arab world. A year before he stepped down from office, a Pew Research Center survey found that only 15% of Palestinians and 14% of Jordanians and Pakistanis approved of Obama's foreign policy.[55]

The Great Détente

Obama proved more successful, however, in his efforts to reach out to Shia Iran. While realizing that a return to the pre-1979 relations with Iran was out of question, he deeply understood the significance of a détente with post-revolutionary Iran to anchor greater regional stability. After all, Iran was too powerful to ignore, the seat of multiple empires that once dominated the whole Middle East and beyond. More crucially, there were sufficient number of moderate-pragmatic forces among the country's elite and largely middle-class society to support a recalibration

---

[54] Savage (2017).
[55] Wike (2015).

in Iran–West relations.[56] Thus, the 2015 Joint Comprehensive Plan of Action (JCPA)[57] framework agreement, announced in Lausanne, Switzerland, after days of grueling 11th hour haggling between Tehran and the major world powers led by the United States, was the crown jewel of Obama's foreign policy in the Middle East. It was the closest one could get to a "win-win" deal. It paved[58] the way for an end to the anti-Iranian nuclear hysteria[59] and rollback of punitive Western sanctions, which collectively punished tens of millions of ordinary Iranian citizens.[60] It was also a deal that perfectly reflected the democratic will of the American and Iranian peoples. After all, polls consistently suggested that a solid majority of Americans favored a diplomatic compromise with Iran, despite their reservations about the effectiveness of a deal.[61] And a majority of the Iranian people, who twice voted for the moderate President Hassan Rouhani based on his promise to restore Iran's ties with the outside world primarily through effective nuclear negotiations, also welcomed an agreement that ends Iran's isolation without violating its basic rights to peaceful nuclear enrichment. While the war-weary American people could rejoice in preventing another conflict in the Middle East, the Iranian people wasted no chance in celebrating the promise of economic recovery and reintegration into the global community.[62] Upon the conclusion of the agreement, horns, chants, and cheers filled the air across Tehran and major cities in Iran, echoing the country's euphoric celebrations during the 2014 World Cup.[63] The grueling, suspense-laden, and years-long Iranian nuclear negotiations were a powerful testament to the wisdom of diplomacy—and a major boost to the diplomatic credentials of the Obama and Rouhani administrations, both of which largely staked their foreign policy legacies on disentangling decades of mistrust between Washington and Tehran. The two powers now suddenly became

---

[56] Ansari (2007).
[57] U.S. Department of State (2015a).
[58] Morello (2015).
[59] Porter (2014b).
[60] Heydarian (2012).
[61] Montanaro (2015).
[62] Calamur (2015).
[63] Rezaian (2014).

de facto allies in the war against Wahabi-Salafist extremism across the Middle East, quietly embracing a "neither foes, nor friends" relationship.[64]

By stubbornly pursuing a diplomatic compromise, despite vehement pushback from hardliners at home and abroad, the two sides played a key role in preventing a destructive war in a region that's already the world's most turbulent and traumatized. Obama's détente with Iran had an important historical precedence. The historic Nixon-Mao opening in the 1970s cemented the foundations of a decades-long symbiotic relationship between Washington and Beijing, allowing one of the world's most sophisticated civilizations to rejoin the community of nations—and transform the global economy along the way.[65] The Obama-Rouhani negotiations held a similar promise, allowing the Persian civilization to retake its pride of place on the global stage, unleashing the talents and potentials of the 75 million Iranians who have been besieged and isolated for years under escalating external pressure. The Iranian nuclear deal was by no means expected. The two sides excruciatingly discovered the optimal point of convergence, thanks to the stubborn willingness of negotiators to respect each other's "red lines." In fact, the US Secretary of State John Kerry spent more time with his Iranian counterpart than any single diplomat from any other country during the years-long negotiation process.[66] Iran made it clear that it will not under any circumstance agree to a complete dismantlement of its much-prized domestic enrichment capacity. Indeed, Iran maintained that it's entitled to domestic enrichment as a signatory to the Non-Proliferation Treaty, which, under Article IV(I), affirms the "inalienable right of all the Parties to the Treaty to develop research, production, and use of nuclear energy for peaceful purposes without discrimination," provided they're not otherwise involved in any nuclear-weapons-related activity.[67] As Iran's Foreign Minister Javad Zarif asserted, the country's nuclear program "has always been and always will remain exclusively peaceful."[68] Iran's other key demand was that concessions on its part should be reciprocated by the removal—as swiftly as possible—of all sanctions, particularly the unilateral punitive measures imposed by Washington and Brussels in late 2012.

[64] Cooper (2015).

[65] Kissinger (2012).

[66] Wright (2014).

[67] International Atomic Energy Agency (1970).

[68] Associated Press (2015).

The Obama administration, in turn, made it clear that it will settle for nothing less than a comprehensive, real-time, and verifiable inspection regime to ensure there is no diversion of fissile material for nuclear weapons production (which even US intelligence agencies admit Iran has never yet decided to attempt[69]). More precisely, Washington settled for at least a one-year "breakout time" cushion[70]: That's the time necessary for Iran to amass enough enriched uranium for building a single bomb were it to defy existing non-proliferation safeguards. These restrictions, and the accompanying inspections regime, are meant to allow Washington and its allies sufficient time to respond—whether through sanctions or military intervention—if any weapons-related diversion in Iran's nuclear activities is detected. As Obama bluntly put it, the aim is to "cut off every pathway that Iran could take to develop a nuclear weapon."[71] Any agreement, he added, would "not [be] based on trust," but instead "unprecedented verification." Among the most important concessions Iran agreed to was a reduction of its installed centrifuges by two-thirds; the halting of any uranium enrichment over 3.67% (which is only useful for power generation) for at least 15 years; the reduction of its current stockpile of about 10,000 kg of low-enriched uranium to 300 kg; and a promise not to build any new facilities for the purpose of enriching uranium for 15 years. Iran also agreed to repurpose and freeze uranium enrichment at its heavily fortified Fordow facility for at least 15 years, to remove the more advanced centrifuges from its Natanz facility, and to freeze enrichment at the heavy-water reactor in Arak. It also consented to subject itself to the history's most robust inspection regime under the auspices of the International Atomic Energy Agency, which will even have access to uranium mines and will exercise continuous surveillance at Iran's uranium mills for 25 years.[72]

The JCPA provided enough room for both sides to claim victory before their domestic constituencies. Iranian negotiators projected what their Supreme Leader Ali Khamanei called "heroic flexibility" before their domestic audience, including hardliners, because they've fundamentally preserved Iran's right to peaceful nuclear enrichment

[69] Porter (2014a).
[70] Wroughton (2015).
[71] Memoli and Parsons (2015).
[72] U.S. Department of State (2015b).

at home.[73] More importantly, the rollback in punitive sanctions—
the exact mechanics of which would be under negotiation for years to
come—allowed Iran's economy to recover, a centerpiece of Rouhani's
campaign in 2013.[74] The removal of Western sanctions, particularly targeted measures against Iran's oil and financial sectors, were expected
to pave the way for a huge and much-needed inflow of foreign investment, the recovery of Iran's oil industry, and a resurgence of its heavily battered currency.[75] A lot was at stake, namely the world's greatest
untapped market. Western multinationals also celebrated the deal. As
economists put it, Iran combines the consumer market and human capital potential of Turkey with the hydrocarbon riches of Saudi Arabia and
Russia and the mineral resources of Australia. Iran also has one of the
world's biggest auto-manufacturing industries, which could tremen-
dously benefit from cheaper and easier access to intermediate goods and
technology.[76] In short, Iran is the hottest emerging market in waiting.[77]
The nuclear agreement could also provide Iran much-needed strategic
space, allowing it to get out of the shadow of Eastern powers such as
China and Russia, which have exploited Iran's isolation in recent years.
After all, Iran's revolutionary slogan was "neither East, nor West, [but]
only the Islamic Republic" (*Na Sharghi, Na Gharbi, Faghad Jomhoriye
Eslami*). In light of the nuclear program-related sanctions against
Tehran, which intensified in 2012, China effectively forced the Middle
Eastern country to provide huge discounts on its hydrocarbon exports
and engage in barter deals—trading precious oil for surplus Chinese
consumer products, which heavily disrupted Iran's domestic manufacturing sector—while gaining privileged access to Iran's vast energy
and infrastructure sectors.[78] Meanwhile, Russia repeatedly reneged
on its earlier agreement to deliver advanced S-300 missile-defense systems to Iran, which Tehran has desperately sought for years.[79] Russia
only delivered it a year after the Iranian nuclear deal.[80] Many Iranians

---

[73] Bozorgmehr (2015).

[74] Habibi (2018).

[75] Rascouet and Kalantari (2015).

[76] Defterios (2015).

[77] Heydarian (2014b).

[78] Bozorgmehr (2011).

[79] Soldatkin (2015).

[80] Cappacio (2018).

heavily resented this exploitation by the Eastern powers of Russia and China. With Iran's Supreme Leader Ali Khamenei, who has the final say on its domestic and foreign affairs, repeatedly expressing his support for Iran's negotiators,[81] much of the Iranian establishment eventually rallied behind the Rouhani administration's effort to resolve the nuclear crisis.[82]

The Obama administration, in contrast, had to contend with a largely hostile, Republican-dominated Congress at home as well as skeptical allies in the Middle East, particularly Saudi Arabia and Israel, and their lobbies in the United States. This explains, for instance, Obama's spirited defense of the JCPA, which came after difficult phone calls with his Saudi and Israeli counterparts. Obama described the emerging final nuclear agreement, which barely escaped a congressional sabotage, as the best way to resolve the Iranian nuclear crisis, decrying his opponents for failing to provide a "reasonable alternative" and for politicizing a delicate issue, which demands nuanced diplomacy if war is to be avoided.[83] But more than the alleged threat of nuclear proliferation, the real issue at hand was really the balance of power in the Middle East.

First of all, both American and Israeli intelligence agencies indicate that despite mastering the fuel cycle, Iran hasn't even developed the necessary decision-making structure for weaponizing its program.[84] Leaked documents show that Israel's Mossad recently concluded that Iran is "not performing the activity necessary to produce weapons," despite Prime Minister Benjamin Netanyahu's assertions to the contrary. Objective observers, including top intelligence and military officials in the West and Israel, agree that Iran is a rational actor, driven by a largely predictable cost-benefit calculus. Developing a nuclear weapon would not only violate the Iranian clerical leadership's unequivocal *fatwa* against nuclear weapons, but it would also be irrational for Iran to nullify its conventional superiority over most of its neighbors by providing a perfect excuse to its neighbors to develop their own nuclear weapons.[85]

[81] Karami (2014).
[82] Erdbrink (2015).
[83] Tharoor (2015).
[84] Risen and Mazzetti (2012).
[85] U.C. Berkeley Events (2007).

In *A Single Roll of the Dice*, Iran analyst Trita Parsi persuasively argues that "balance of power" considerations have largely shaped Israel's strategic predisposition toward Iran, both before and after the 1979 Iranian Revolution.[86] The late Kenneth Waltz, among the most prominent foreign policy scholars, similarly argued that the hysteria over Iran's nuclear program is largely driven by concerns over preserving Israel's strategic superiority in the Middle East.[87] As he wrote in a controversial essay for *The Foreign Affairs*, "In no other region of the world does a lone, unchecked nuclear state exist. It is Israel's nuclear arsenal, not Iran's desire for one, that has contributed most to the current crisis."[88] So the Obama administration faced a two-pronged task. First, it had to prove the viability of the emerging agreement in ensuring that Iran's nuclear program is purely peaceful. And second, it had to assure its allies that it won't fundamentally alter the balance of power in the Middle East at their expense. This proved as a remarkably difficult task. Thus, the fate of the comprehensive nuclear agreement was founded on a full-scale mobilization on the part of the Obama administration—and supporters of diplomacy, inside and outside the government—to overcome domestic opposition and get the US Congress on board. But given the seismic implications of a comprehensive nuclear agreement that could potentially redraw the Middle East's geopolitical map, both Washington and Tehran faced vehement opposition following the agreement.[89]

The Third Coalition

Then everything changed, for the worse. The opposition to the deal culminated with Trump's decision in early 2018 to unilaterally renege on the agreement despite vehement resistance by allies in Western Europe, namely Germany and France and, to a lesser degree, the United Kingdom, as well as China and Russia. For Obama's successor, the Iranian nuclear deal was "the worst deal ever" signed by the American government, providing windfalls for Iran's regional ambitions at the expense of the United States and its allies.[90] A year after, Washington refused to even grant waivers of exemptions to allies and partners seeking reduced purchases of Iranian oil.

[86] Parsi (2013).
[87] Waltz (2012).
[88] Ibid.
[89] Bennis (2015).
[90] Beauchamp (2018).

The Trump administration threatened secondary sanctions against foreign companies seeking oil purchases from Iran.[91] The decision was warmly welcomed by Saudi Arabia, which promised to compensate for any potential shortfall in oil markets.[92]

To up the ante, the Trump administration designated Iran's Revolutionary Guard (*Sepah-e-Pasdaran-e-Iran*), roughly the Iranian equivalent of the People's Liberation Army, as a "terrorist organization." It also actively supported the Marxist-Islamist opposition group, the foreign-based People's Mojahedin Organization of Iran (Mojahedin-e Khalq), which Tehran designates as a terrorist organization. Meanwhile, European powers have struggled to operationalize the Instrument in Support of Trade Exchanges (INSTEX) mechanism, which is crucial to bypassing American sanctions against Iran and impact of Trump's withdrawal from the nuclear deal.[93] Senior American officials such as Secretary of State Mike Pompeo have gone so far as claiming that Trump was sent by God to protect Israel from Iran, adding a dangerous element of religious zealotry and ideological conflict to what is a fundamentally geopolitical contest for mastery in the Middle East.[94] Trump's all-out economic warfare on Iran, which will likely lead to the disintegration of the 2015 JCPOA nuclear deal, places the two countries on a potential war footing.[95] What's even clearer, however, is Washington's decision to fully align itself with Israel and Saudi Arabia against Iran and its regional proxies. Trump has effectively given Israel's hardline Netanyahu administration a *carte blanche* to push ahead with annexation of West Bank in violation of international law and the two-state solution[96]; continue the siege on Gaza that has gone hand in hand with often indiscriminate use of violence and potential war crimes against civilians in the area[97]; and formalize occupation of the Syrian-claimed portions of the Golan Heights.[98] The Trump administration's decision to move the American embassy to Jerusalem also

---

[91]Wadhams et al. (2019).

[92]Batchelor (2019).

[93]Davenport (2019).

[94]BBC (2019a).

[95]Bishara (2019).

[96]Wong and Edmonson (2019).

[97]Batchelor (2019).

[98]Romo (2019).

threatened the two-state solution, which calls for portions of the holy city to be part of a future Palestinian state.[99] Trump's unconditional support may further embolden Israel to take the fight to Iran and, at the very least, dangerously escalate the minimal border skirmishes between the two countries in recent years in the Syrian–Israeli border.[100]

More troublingly, however, is Washington's all-out support to the Saudi Kingdom, which is now under the de facto rule of Crown Prince Mohammad Bin Salman, a.k.a. "MBS." The Saudi ruler is known as a brash and aggressive leader who is pejoratively called "little Saddam" across the region.[101] His brazen and brutal military campaign in neighboring Yemen against Houthi rebels,[102] supposedly part of a broader conflict with Iran, has led to one of the greatest humanitarian disasters of the century.[103] As the largest weapons supplier to Saudi Arabia, the United States is automatically complicit in the Yemen conflict where there are widespread allegations of war crimes against the Saudi-led coalition forces. As a *Washington Post* editorial put it, "In reality, the Saudi bombing campaign would be unsustainable without that U.S. support, or the continuing sale of bombs and other materiel. That makes the Trump administration complicit in the continuing atrocities, such as the latest school and hospital bombings."[104]

Trump even went so far as vetoing a congressional resolution calling for an end to any kind of American involvement in the Yemen conflict, both operationally and in terms of arms sales. In another nod to the Saudis, Washington is also moving closer to designating the moderate political Islamic movement, the Muslim Brotherhood, as a terrorist organization, a move that will provoke anger among other key allies such as Turkey and Qatar. But Trump's most controversial, and morally reprehensible, act vis-à-vis Saudi Arabia was his unwillingness to censure the MBS regime for its alleged involvement in the gruesome murder of Washington Post columnist and Saudi activist Jamaal Kashoggi in late 2018 inside the Saudi

---

[99] See Arnold (2019) and Shapiro (2019).

[100] Hincks (2019).

[101] Burleigh (2018).

[102] For a more nuanced analysis of the war in Yemen and who the Houthis are see Abdul-Ahad (2015).

[103] *The Washington Post* (2019).

[104] Ibid.

consulate in Istanbul.[105] Both Turkish and American intelligence sources implicated the Saudi crown prince in Kashoggi's shocking murder, which forced many Western countries to downgrade their defense relations with the kingdom. While recognizing that MBS "could very well" have known about the murder, Trump argued that Saudi Arabia remains a "steadfast partner."[106] Trump also vetoed a congressional demand for a proper report into the brutal murder of the prominent Saudi activist,[107] a longtime resident in America who would end up as one of the Time's Person of the Year.[108] Not to mention, Trump's implicit approval of Saudi Arabia's siege on Qatar, a crucial partner that hosts America's largest military base in the region. Qatar's Al Udeid Air Base, which permanently hosts 11,000 American troops, has been a staging ground for B-52 airstrikes against IS targets in neighboring Iraq and Syria as well as F-16 fighters and E-8C Joint Stars reconnaissance planes used during the Afghanistan campaign following 9/11 attacks. It also serves a crucial bulwark against Iranian military footprint in the Persian Gulf.[109]

Nowadays, Doha is a completely different place. Across the once tranquil and complacent city, one sees ubiquitous expressions of nationalistic fervor and collective defiance, as the tiny petro-state proudly stands up to a Saudi-led siege that was unthinkable only few years ago. Instead of succumbing to pressure, Qatar has maintained its independence of action when it comes to dealing with Turkey, Iran, and the Muslim Brotherhood groups across the region. It was precisely this deep sense of strategic independence that prompted Saudi Arabia and the United Arab Emirates to shut off trade with and travel to as well as their airspace to their fellow Sheikhdom—all seemingly with the tacit approval of the American president.[110] The broader picture, however, is clear. In effect, Washington has provided both Israel and Saudi Arabia a carte blanche that could very well be used as a springboard for an all-out conflict with Iran, a perilous prospect which would ignite the whole region. And there are indications that the two American allies are seriously contemplating a joint military action against Iran (The Times 2010). Visiting Tehran in early 2018 and 2019, as the winter cold began to set in,

---

[105] Landler (2018).
[106] BBC News (2018).
[107] BBC News (2019, March).
[108] Haag and Grynbaum (2018).
[109] Lendon (2017).
[110] Landler (2017).

one could detect the impending sense of doom and destruction among a besieged people. Many see, across Iran, Trump's anti-Iran policy as an even more dangerous incarnation of the Bush administration's in the mid-2000s.

Break It, Disown It

To make matters worse, the Trump administration is negotiating a new order in the region amidst a planned (premature) withdrawal of American troops from Syria and Afghanistan. The perfunctory "December surprise" decision to withdraw 2000 American troops involved in the anti-IS operation in Syria, announced by the American president just as the world leaned into Christmas holidays, prompted the resignation of Trump's most trusted cabinet member, Secretary of Defense James Mattis. The decision for withdrawal came ahead of IS' decisive defeat at the hands of US-backed Syrian Democratic Forces (SDF) as a state-building enterprise in the battle of Baghouz, an eastern Syrian village on the bank of the Euphrates River.[111]

For Trump, the IS threat was no longer significant enough to justify American direct military intervention, whether through airstrikes, Special Forces deployment, and training and logistical support to anti-IS elements in Syria and Iraq. In his resignation letter, the former Pentagon chief was unsparing in his criticism of the administration, stating "My views on treating allies with respect and also being clear-eyed about both malign actors and strategic competitors are strongly held and informed by over four decades of immersion on these issues. We must do everything possible to advance an international order that is most conducive to our security, prosperity and values, and we are strengthened in this effort by the solidarity of our alliances."[112] For almost two years, Mattis and Trump constantly clashed over America's role in and commitment to the existing liberal international order.

Mattis' crucial post would remain empty for months to come, an unprecedented vacancy in contemporary American history, which went hand in hand with existing and upcoming vacancies in various senior positions in the State Department and the Pentagon.[113]

---

[111] Francis (2019).
[112] Ward and Kirby (2018).
[113] Seligman and Gramer (2019).

Ironically, Trump is arguably leading the most libertarian "small government" policy in the realm of American imperial foreign and defense policy in decades, just as he seeks to reassert global primacy and reshape the international order along his instincts. He is running a global empire with a skeletal bureaucracy. The American president also proved extremely adamant in ending the country's military presence in Afghanistan, even if this meant the potential collapse of the current government in Kabul and, subsequently, Taliban's swift, vengeful return. In fact, Trump, in a moment of consummate transnationalism amid heated discussions over America's Afghan strategy, even suggested (reportedly upon suggestion by Azerbaijan's dictator Ilham Aliyev earlier) that the "U.S. needed to get some of Afghanistan's valuable minerals in exchange for any support. I'm not making a deal on anything until we get minerals."[114] He showed limited appreciation for unintended consequences of inchoate American military withdrawal from the Middle East theater after decades of imperial onshore balancing in the area.

Trump's visceral and even impulsive policy in the Middle East has two important strategic implications. First, it means that Washington is negotiating from a position of weakness, rather than strength, leaving more room for discretion to its regional surrogates, namely the hardliners in charge of Saudi Arabia and Israel with potentially disastrous implications. A regional war involving Iran and the United States' allies will severely hamstring the Trump administration's ability to respond to contingencies in and compete with its archrival in East Asia, namely China. And secondly, Trump's policy provides space for IS resurgence, especially given the dependence of SDF and the government in Kabul on sustained American support.

While the US-backed Kurdish forces in Syria will have to contend with a hostile Turkey, the democratically elected government in Kabul will have to grapple with the Taliban forces. The ensuing power vacuum will provide a perfect space for new permutations of the IS franchise across the Middle East. Following the 9/11 attacks, President George W. Bush promised to "starve terrorists of funding, turn them one against another, drive them from place to place, until there is no refuge or no rest." But the al-Qaeda and its franchises are now at the peak of their

[114]Woodward (2018).

power in decades.[115] What Trump fails to appreciate is that when you break a region, you own its troubles for decades to come. Precipitous strategic retreat will only worsen the situation. In fact, it was precisely the relatively perfunctory withdrawal of American troops from Iraq in the late 2000s that paved the way for the emergence of IS.[116] Yet, the American president surprisingly proved more adept in handing another great strategic distraction at the far eastern end of the Eurasian landmass, though this was a very risky gamble that is yet to pay off.

THE NOT-SO-HERMIT KINGDOM

Weeks before the historic inter-Korean summit in Panmunjom in 2018, I visited North Korea (April 3–7) as part of a delegation of Asian scholars, led by former Indonesian diplomat Dino Djalal. During my stay, we met and exchanged views with senior officials, including Kim Yong Dae, vice-president of the Presidium of Supreme People's Assembly, and Ri Gil Song, vice minister for Foreign Affairs, and a coterie of other senior diplomats and bureaucrats in charge of trade, investments and external relations. Unwilling to rely on any single source to decipher North Korea, our delegation also met diplomats from foreign countries posted to North Korea, who also shared their points of view on developments in the country. Days before and after the trip, I also had the chance to talk to senior officials from China and South Korea, who oversaw the North Korean portfolio for years. The purpose of the trip was simple: To discover why the Hermit Kingdom, in a remarkable twist of events, had returned to the negotiating table. After careful examination of (known and knowable) facts, as well as deliberation with countless officials and experts within and outside North Korea, what became clear to me is that the regime is open to negotiation simultaneously out of a sense of strength as well as weakness.

The late April summit between the North Korean Supreme Leader Kim Jong-un and South Korean President Moon Jae-in has, quite understandably, triggered euphoric expectations of a permanent peace regime in the peninsula. The prominent South Korean academic and presidential adviser Chung-in Moon, who attended the summit, even claimed, "a comprehensive peace deal including real denuclearization by North

---

[115]Bulos (2018).
[116]For instance, see Stern and Berger (2016) and Weiss and Hassan (2016).

Korea is achievable in a couple of years, if not in the months ahead."[117] To be fair, the so-called Panmunjom Declaration, which emanated from the meeting between South Korean President Moon Jae-in and North Korean supreme leader Kim Jong-un, is unprecedented in its precision and ambition.[118] For the first time in history, North Korea not only agreed to place the nuclear issue at the heart of its summit with its southern neighbor, but it also agreed to openly discuss the prospect of full denuclearization on the peninsula.[119] In another major break from the past, North Korea's official mouthpiece, *Rodong Sinmun*, reported the supreme leader's commitment to denuclearization. This is a potentially huge development, considering the tendency for North Korea to say completely different things at home as opposed to abroad as well as the profound prestige the domestic elite and the broader masses attach to their possession of nuclear weapons. Crucially, the two sides arrived, in a written agreement, at a specific timetable for upcoming high-level civil and military meetings, the resumption of reunion events among separated families (August 15), and the visit of the South Korean president to Pyongyang (fall of 2018).

To express its goodwill, North Korea also promised to close down its nuclear test site in Punggye-ri, even opening it up for verification via inspection by foreign experts and observers, including those from America.[120] Moreover, the North Korean leader displayed an uncanny sense of pragmatism by not insisting on the severance or downgrade of the US-South Korea alliance as a precondition for denuclearization. Yet, none of these truly explain why North Korea has returned to the negotiating table. Why the change of heart? How did Kim Jong-un go from threatening America with nuclear war to proposing complete denuclearization within a span of months? Is he for real?

A New Opening

The strength stems from their virtual mastery of both the nuclear enrichment cycle as well as the weapons delivery system. Although they are yet

[117] Moon (2018b).

[118] ABC News (2018).

[119] Moon (2018b).

[120] Moon (2018a).

to perfect the "re-entry" technology,[121] which allows a nuclear power to precisely target faraway enemies with intercontinental ballistic missiles, North Korea is now a de facto member of the exclusive club of nuclear powers. As one of their senior officials told me, the country is now negotiating as a "full-fledged strategic state." In the regime's view, it can now deal with major players on a symmetrical basis. For sure, the reported collapse of the Mount Mantap at the Punggye-ri nuclear test site in the country's northwest, after the sixth nuclear blast in the area last year, limits the ability of the regime to improve and exhibit its nuclear prowess.[122] Nonetheless, the fact is that North Korea has already developed a nuclear deterrence, augmented by its ever-improving cache of ballistic missiles. Thus, it's quite reductionist, if not totally erroneous, to suggest that Kim has put forward the prospect of denuclearization,[123] simply because the regime can't test its nuclear weapons with similar ease as the past. Yet, what's often missed in the analyses of North Korea's motivations is the country's vision of building a "strong socialist state," one that isn't only militarily powerful, but also economically viable. In fact, as the North Korean supreme leader stated in his New Year's speech, he is willing to sacrifice nuclear weapons for economic development.[124] The sanctions have not been tough enough to erode the foundations of the regime, as in the case of Apartheid South Africa. Nor have they been severe enough to completely alter the regime's strategic calculus, as happened in Libya in mid-2000s.[125] Yet, they have been severe enough to encourage North Korea to return to the negotiating table, similar to the case of Iran after the imposition of robust sanctions against the Middle Eastern state in 2012. Unlike the Soviet Union, revisionist and ambitious powers today are more aware of the fact that regime stability and national power can't rely on military prowess alone. They are also cognizant of how international isolation allows rivals to leap ahead in terms of overall national development. For instance, Tehran is aware of the fact that sanctions have not only weakened its hand within the Organization of Petroleum Exporting Countries (OPEC), thanks to oil and financial embargoes, but have also allowed

[121] Kim (2017).
[122] Chen (2018).
[123] Brewer and Pak (2018).
[124] Revere (2013).
[125] Leverett (2004).

rivals such as Saudi Arabia, Israel, and Turkey to widen their technological edge over Iran. It was precisely within this context of the fear-
of-being-left-behind dynamics that pragmatists within Iran were able to
convince the top leadership to contemplate a nuclear compromise. The
North Korean elite (including the Swiss-educated supreme leader) are
acutely aware of the fact that the country is well behind its neighbors,[126]
especially its cousins across the 38th Parallel, in overall level of development. This undeniable fact must have been a great source of humiliation, envy, and insecurity for Pyongyang's leadership, notwithstanding
its propaganda bombast and militaristic posturing. Based on discussions
with informed foreign officials, North Korea's access to fuel, food, and
basic capital goods has been dramatically reduced in the past years. Major
trading partners have severely downgraded or completely cut off trade
and investment ties.[127] Even China has begun to tighten the noose, leaving Pyongyang at the mercy of its giant benefactor.[128] In 2017, North
Korea's Gross Domestic Product shrunk by 3.5%, according to the
Sejong-based Korea Institute for International Economic Policy. The
country's trade deficit almost quadrupled from $56 billion in 2016 to
$20 billion in 2018. Bilateral trade with China halved in 2018, from
almost $5 billion to only $2.4 billion.[129] As a result, Kim Jong-un has
found it increasingly impossible to reform and modernize the country.[130]

Having developed a deterrence capability to ensure regime survival,
however, the young North Korean leader is now interested in pushing ahead with his plans of modernizing and reforming a long-isolated
nation, which has been left behind by its neighbors, most especially the
enterprising cousins to the south of the 38th Parallel. The country is
like no other frontier market, thanks to its highly educated population,
extremely cheap labor, relatively decent basic infrastructure, proximity
to three major global economies (China, Japan, and South Korea), and
highly disciplined and internally coherent state apparatus. North Korea
possesses precisely the combination of human, bureaucratic and resource
capital, which allowed communist nations such as China and Vietnam to
join the ranks of the world's fastest-growing economies in recent decades.

---

[126] Pearson-Jones (2018).

[127] Mogato (2017).

[128] Hjelmgaard (2018).

[129] Lee (2019).

[130] Pan (2006).

New Horizons

During my visit to North Korea, we dropped by a modern, automated shoe-making factory, powered by an army of solar panels, state-of-the-art monitoring and accommodation facilities, and well-trained artisans and designers that flaunted indigenously crafted products. Then there were the urbane and articulate professors at Kim Il-sung University, the country's most prestigious educational institution, discussing their country's economic policies and hopes of reengagement with the outside world. What struck me the most during the visit was the capital city, Pyongyang, which is arguably the cleanest, most meticulously designed and emptiest urban center anywhere in the world. Atop the Juche Tower, the highest structure in the country, one could see the impeccably clean Taedong River, embellished by perfectly arranged rows of blossoming trees. On one side of the city, one sees buildings carefully painted across the color spectrum, morphing into a rainbow far into the horizon. At the heart of Pyongyang is the pyramid-shaped Ryugyong Hotel, which dominates the city's skyline, flashier and more surreal than even the glitziest skyscrapers one sees in the Persian Gulf Sheikhdoms. In the Ryomyong New Town, a new posh quarter in the city, there are columns of space ship looking skyscrapers, shopping centers, amusement parks, and a shiny, newly minted asphalted boulevard. Throughout our stay in the city, we dropped by several restaurants, where the menu was as varied as it was rich.

We also dropped by shopping centers, where products from across the world were available. The people in Pyongyang, meanwhile, seemed dressed beyond our stereotypes of Soviet-style uniformity, with many carrying fashionable bags and coats, with colorful sartorial taste. Surely, there was an element of theatrics and Pomkin Village drama. In recent years, however, the regime has introduced nascent elements of capitalism, including the establishment of quasi-private businesses, particularly restaurants and shopping centers. In rural areas, there is also experimentation with a North Korean version of household-responsibility system,[131] whereby farmers can keep some of their surplus production in designated collective farms. The upshot is the emergence of a parallel market economy, which has raised productivity even under most difficult conditions. What stands between the country's current predicament and an economic miracle is a final peace agreement. Such an agreement

[131] Lin (1988).

would ensure the regime's survival in exchange for a less confrontational foreign policy, which, at some point in the future, may include complete denuclearization. Yet, given the deep history of mutual-enmity among the protagonists as well as the world's concerns over North Korea's true intentions, achieving a permanent peace regime in the Korean Peninsula will be an uphill battle. There is no room for complacency.

Trump's Gamble

The American president's unprecedented decision to, first, pick a social media war with the North Korean leader, calling each other "rocket man" and "dotard," which quickly morphed into expressed openness to a historic bilateral summit, sent shockwaves across the world. Many questioned the wisdom of Trump's word war and, later, bromance with the North Korean strongman. Upon closer examination, however, Trump's North Korea strategy was likely both calculated and calibrated. It was partly based on the recognition of shifts in the strategic calculus of Pyongyang under the young Kim. But, more crucially, it was in response to North Korea's impending capability to strike major American cities with nuclear weapons. The burgeoning nuclear threat and ballistic missiles threat from North Korea (see Fig. 3.2)[132] prompted the Obama administration, in its twilight years in office, to consider potential preemptive strike against the Hermit Kingdom. In fact, Trump's predecessor authorized a Special Access Programs (SAP), the "most classified and compartmented operations conducted by the [US] military and intelligence" to this end. This was the most urgent geopolitical crisis that Trump inherited from Obama, likely a key topic of discussion during their meeting in the White House in November 2016.[133]

One person, however, has played a key role in shepherding the Korean peace efforts. The South Korean president—born to North Korean parents and a former Special Forces squad leader who directly witnessed the dangerous sleepwalk toward all-out war during border clashes in mid-1970s—has acted as a perfect matchmaker. Far from a naïve pacifist, as his critics imply, Moon spent much of his early political career observing the foreign policy of Nobel Peace Prize laureate and former President Kim Dae-jung, who oversaw the so-called Sunshine Policy that established years of thaw

---

[132]Bowden (2017).
[133]Woodward (2018).

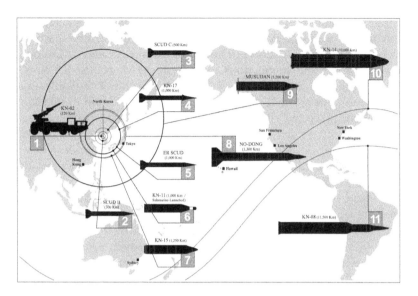

Fig. 3.2 North Korea's burgeoning ballistic missile capability (*Source* The Atlantic)

in inter-Korean relations. In fact, it was their meeting in 2009, where the former president implored his protégé to continue his foreign policy legacy, which convinced Moon to run for presidency: "That was the moment... He spoke those words as if they were his last will."[134] Initially, Moon and Trump were at loggerheads over the latter's threat to withdraw from the US-Korea Free Trade Agreement and blatant call for imperial tribute in exchange for American military presence in South Korea.[135] Eventually, however, Moon managed to convince Trump to consider direct diplomatic engagement with Pyongyang by dangling the possibility of a Nobel Peace Prize for the vainglorious American president.[136]

Both Trump and Moon realized that there were no good options in dealing with North Korea. Some were impeccably undesirable, while others were utterly unthinkable. Any form of military intervention—ranging from all-out invasion and aerial bombardment of nuclear and ballistic missiles installation to limited surgical strikes and

[134] Broder (2018).
[135] Shin and Smith (2019).
[136] Ibid.

political assassination—will likely lead to the immediate evisceration of Seoul and, in worst cases, great power conflict, with possible participation of China and even Russia in an expanded war theater.[137] Dialogue, combined with punitive sanctions and deterrence via robust US-Korean military alliance, seemed like the only option forward. The highly anticipated meeting between Kim and President Donald Trump in mid-2018 in Singapore produced the outlines of a grand bargain composed of a peace agreement, a nuclear disarmament regime, and an end of sanctions on and isolation of North Korea.[138] To strengthen the peace momentum, Trump offered confidence-building measures such as cancelation of certain US-Korean joint military exercises, which directly aimed at decapitation of North Korean regime. By the end of 2018, however, it became clear that neither the Trump administration, dominated by hawks such as Pompeo and National Security Adviser John Bolton, was interested in relaxing sanctions,[139] nor were the North Koreans showing any rush in dismantling their nuclear weapons anytime soon. If anything, Pyongyang sought to expand its bargaining chip by further entrenching their ballistic missile capability,[140] just as Washington sought the same by ramping up sanctions. The upshot was a two-level game, with one track dominated by cordial rhetoric, while the other driven by tit-for-tat escalation. North Korans, however, remained optimistic that Trump was a man they could make a deal with. As one North Korean official told the author during his 2018 visit to Pyongyang, with some American leaders there is a "need to make decisions quickly" in order to achieve their desired goal, while they could have more patiently "waited out" others. They clearly saw Trump belonging to the first category of American leaders. As the deadlock became clear, with Pompeo's several visits to North Korea failing to achieve any concrete outcome, Trump and Kim gave it a second shot, agreeing to hold another summit in Hanoi in March 2019. This time, however, both leaders faced great pressure to achieve a more concrete agreement. But to the surprise of many observers, Trump walked out halfway into the summit. No deal was better than a bad deal, he argued. North Korean reportedly sought

---

[137]Bowden (2017).

[138]Rosenfeld (2018).

[139]Partly based on discussions with a senior advisor to the Trump administration during one of the visits to Washington, DC in 2018.

[140]Choe (2018).

sanctions relief before any rollback in their nuclear weapons capability, while Trump insisted on the reverse order.[141]

Interestingly, Trump was also likely distracted by domestic politics, namely the congressional hearing that featured his longtime aid Michael Cohen providing potentially incriminating accusations against his former boss. As Trump tweeted hours after the collapse of the Hanoi Summit, "For the Democrats to interview in open hearings a convicted liar & fraudster [Cohen], at the same time as the very important Nuclear Summit with North Korea, is perhaps a new low in American politics and may have contributed to the 'walk [out].' Never done when a president is overseas. 'Shame'!"[142] This was an unsurprising refrain. The broader Muller investigation into Trump's alleged collusion with Russians served a major distraction and consumed the president's attention for months. As he told his former chief legal counsel, "John [Dowd], this thing is an enormous burden. It interferes particularly with foreign affairs. It's embarrassing to be in the middle of a deal and the guy, the premier or the prime minister on the other side says, 'Hey Donald, are you going to be around?' It's like a kick in the nuts."[143]

There are two ways to look at the Hanoi summit failure. On one hand, it exposed the utter lack of preparation and realistic expectations on the part of Trump. After all, resolving the Korean Peninsula crisis requires a meticulous, step-by-step peace regime, which, in turn, requires years of technical negotiations backed by political support at the highest levels on both sides, not to mention other interested parties such as South Korea, Japan, Russia and China. The North Koreans blamed the American side for the summit's collapse, arguing that Trump may have lost a once in a lifetime opportunity to the resolve the crisis peacefully. "It's hard to say there will be something better than what we offered. We may not have such an opportunity again...Our fundamental stance will never change and even if U.S. seeks further talks, our position won't change," North Korean Foreign Minister Ri Yong Ho said hours after the summit's premature end.[144] A visibly frustrated North Korea soon reshuffled its negotiating team, reportedly demoting chief negotiator Kim Hyok Chol,

---

[141] Liptak and Diamond (2019).
[142] *The Guardian* (2019).
[143] Woodward (2018).
[144] Mason and Shin (2019).

a former spy chief, and the supreme leader's sister Kim Yong Chol, who has accompanied her brother throughout crucial visits.[145] And this brings us to the other way of looking at the issue, namely that the North Koreans were the truly naïve party, thinking Trump was committed to go the extra mile to strike a deal after a grand summit or two. After all, it's possible that Trump is primarily interested in the optics of his North Korean diplomatic gamble, and the Public Relations capital it will generate ahead of his reelection bid in 2020, rather than ever being sincerely committed to end the conflict in the Korea Peninsula anytime soon, which haunted his predecessors since the end of World War II. What's clear, however, is that the way forward is slightly awkward: Trump will have to do what Obama did with respect to Iran, whereby a series of highly technical, snail-paced, and calculated negotiations produced a step-by-step, phased concessions that culminated in a historic non-proliferation deal—the very agreement which Trump dismissed as "the worst deal ever."

As the Trump administration grapples with the twin challenges of North Korea and the Middle East, a greater struggle for mastery is emerging on the horizon. Infrastructure development has quickly become the new pivot of geopolitics. Power and influence is no longer measured by the military prowess or economic size alone, but also the ability of international actors to provide the necessary capital and technology for overhauling decaying or underdeveloped public infrastructure around the world. Asia's leading economies have all pitched in, ranging from Japan's Connectivity Initiative and Partnership for Quality Infrastructure projects, to South Korea introducing the "New Northern" and "New Southern" Policies, and India's International North–South Transport Corridor. The biggest of all, however, is China's. On May 14, 2017, Beijing formally launched the One Road, One Belt (OBOR) project as a global initiative. At its very core, the event served as the chief register for China's new role in the international economic system and, more personally, Xi's emergence as a global leader. And the timing couldn't be any more perfect, given America's abrupt withdrawal from its historical role as the anchor of the global free trade regime. Through the BRI, which Xi has dubbed as "the project of the century," not only does China reiterate its commitment to globalization, but it will also be in the prime position to shape the post-American international economic order.

---

[145]Lee (2019).

REFERENCES

Abdul-Ahad, Ghaith. "Diary." *London Review of Books* 37, no. 10 (2015). https://www.lrb.co.uk/v37/n10/ghaith-abdul-ahad/diary.

Abu-Rabi, Ibrahim. *The Blackwell Companion to Contemporary Islamic Thought.* Hoboken: Wiley-Blackwell, 2006.

Afary, Janet, and Kevin Anderson. *Foucault and the Iranian Revolution: Gender and the Seductions of Islamism*, annotated edition. Chicago: University of Chicago Press, 2005.

Akyol, Mustafa. *Islam Without Extremes: A Muslim Case for Liberty.* New York: W.W. Norton & Company, 2011.

Algeriani, Adel Abdul-Aziz, and Mawloud Mohadi. "Huntington's Clash of Civilizations and Its Influence on the U.S. Foreign Policy (an Analytical Study)." *Journal of Global Business and Social Entrepreneurship* 4, no. 10 (2018): 1–9. http://gbse.com.my/v4no10JANUARY2018/Paper-147-i-.pdf.

Angus, Ian. *Facing the Anthropocene: Fossil Capitalism and the Crisis of the Earth System.* New York: Monthly Review Press, 2016.

Ansari, Ali. *Confronting Iran: The Failure of American Foreign Policy and the Next Great Crisis in the Middle East and the Next Great Crisis in the Middle East.* New York: Basic Books, 2007.

Ansari, Ali. "The Iranian Revolution: Why 1979's Uprising Still Shapes the Middle East." *BBC World Histories Magazine.* February 20, 2019. https://www.historyextra.com/period/20th-century/how-last-shah-lost-iran-mo-hammad-reza-pahlavi-iranian-revolution-middle-east/.

Arnold, Michael. "Two-State Solution." *Bloomberg.* April 11, 2019. https://www.bloomberg.com/quicktake/two-state-solution.

Batchelor, Tom. "Israel Security Forces May Be Guilty of War Crimes Over Killings of Palestinians in Gaza, UN Says." *Independent.* February 28, 2019. https://www.independent.co.uk/news/world/middle-east/israel-war-crimes-gaza-palestine-un-human-rights-report-a8800891.html.

Beard, Mary. *SPQR: A History of Ancient Rome*, 1st edition. New York: Liveright, 2015.

Beauchamp, Zack. "Trump's Withdrawal from the Iran Nuclear Deal, Explained." *Vox.* May 8, 2018. https://www.vox.com/world/2018/5/8/17328520/iran-nuclear-deal-trump-withdraw.

Bennis, Phyllis. "Iran Deal: A Game-Changer for the Middle East." *Foreign Policy in Focus.* April 2, 2015. https://fpif.org/iran-deal-a-game-changer-for-the-middle-east/.

Bilmes, Linda, and Joseph Stiglitz. *The Three Trillion Dollar War: The True Cost of the Iraq Conflict.* New York: W. W. Norton, 2008.

Bishara, Marwan. "Arrogance, Fanaticism and the Prospect of a US-Iranian War." *Aljazeera*. April 30, 2019. https://www.aljazeera.com/indepth/opinion/arrogance-fanaticism-prospect-iranian-war-190430085736682.html.

Bowden, Mark. "How to Deal with North Korea." *The Atlantic*. July/August 2017. https://www.theatlantic.com/magazine/archive/2017/07/the-worst-problem-on-earth/528717/.

Bozorgmehr, Najmeh. "Ayatollah Invokes 'Heroic Flexibility' to Justify Iran Deal." *Financial Times*. July 15, 2015. https://www.ft.com/content/33a7545c-249b-11e5-9c4e-a775d2b173ca.

Bozorgmehr, Najmeh. "China and Iran Plan Oil Barter." *Financial Times*. July 25, 2011. https://www.ft.com/content/2082e954-b604-11e0-8bed-00144feabdc0.

Brewer, Eric, and Jung H. Pak. "How to Tell When North Korea Starts to Denuclearize." *The Atlantic*. https://www.theatlantic.com/international/archive/2018/10/north-korea-nuclear-weapons-kim-jong-un-trump-pompeo/572635.

Broder, Jonathan. "South Korea's President Played Matchmaker for Trump and Kim, but Will It End War or Start Another?" *Newsweek*. July 5, 2018. https://www.newsweek.com/2018/07/13/south-korean-president-north-korea-kim-trump-moon-north-koreas-nuclear-1008030.html.

Brown, Harold, and Joyce Winslow. *Star Spangled Security: Applying Lessons Learned Over Six Decades Safeguarding America*. Washington, D.C.: Brookings Institution Press, p. 187, 2012.

Bulos, Nabih. "Seventeen Years After Sept. 11, Al Qaeda May Be Stronger Than Ever." *Los Angeles Times*. September 10, 2018. https://www.latimes.com/world/middleeast/la-fg-al-qaeda-survive-20180910-story.html.

Burleigh, Michael. "No Wonder They Call Him Little Saddam: MICHAEL BURLEIGH says Saudi Arabia's Mohammed Bin Salman Is an Unstable Despot Whose Bloodlust Threatens the Entire Middle East." *Daily Mail*. October 20, 2018. https://www.dailymail.co.uk/debate/article-6298711/No-wonder-call-Little-Saddam-MICHAEL-BURLEIGH-Saudi-Crown-Prince.html.

Calamur, Krishnadev. "Iran Talks: In Tehran, Blaring Horns, Chants, Cheers." *National Public Radio*. April 2, 2015. https://www.npr.org/sections/thetwo-way/2015/04/02/397099134/iran-talks-in-tehran-blaring-horns-chants-cheers.

Campbell, Kurt. *The Pivot: The Future of American Statecraft in Asia*. New York: Twelve, 2016.

Cappacio, Anthony. "Iran's Russian Anti-Aircraft Missile Now Operational, U.S. Says." *Bloomberg*. March 7, 2018. https://www.bloomberg.com/news/articles/2018-03-07/iran-s-russian-anti-aircraft-missile-now-operational-u-s-says.

Chen, Stephen. "North Korea's Nuclear Test Site Has Collapsed… and That May Be Why Kim Jong-Un Suspended Tests." *South China Morning Post.* April 25, 2018. https://www.scmp.com/news/china/diplomacy-defence/article/2143171/north-koreas-nuclear-test-site-has-collapsed-and-may-be-why-kim-jong-un.

"China Hosts Silk Road Forum to Revive Trade Route." *Aljazeera.* May 14, 2017. https://www.aljazeera.com/news/2017/05/china-hosts-silk-road-forum-revive-trade-route-170514035154982.html.

Chivers, C.J. "War Without End." *The New York Times.* August 8, 2018. https://www.nytimes.com/2018/08/08/magazine/war-afghanistan-iraq-soldiers.html.

Choe, Sang-Hun. "North Korea Is Expanding Missile Base with Eye Toward U.S., Experts Warn." *The New York Times.* December 6, 2018. https://www.nytimes.com/2018/12/06/world/asia/north-korea-missile-bases.html.

Cooper, Heleen. "U.S. Strategy in Iraq Increasingly Relies on Iran." *The New York Times.* March 5, 2015. https://www.nytimes.com/2015/03/06/world/middleeast/us-strategy-in-iraq-increasingly-relies-on-iran.html.

Danforth, Nick. "The Myth of the Caliphate." *Foreign Affairs.* November 19, 2014. https://www.foreignaffairs.com/articles/middle-east/2014-11-19/myth-caliphate.

"Dar al-Sulh." In John L. Esposito (ed.), *The Oxford Dictionary of Islam.* Oxford Islamic Studies Online. Accessed May 4, 2019. http://www.oxfordislamicstudies.com/article/opr/t125/e496.

Davenport, Kelsey. "EU Trade Tool Seeks to Save Iran Nuclear Deal." *Arms Control Association.* March 2019. https://www.armscontrol.org/act/2019-03/news/eu-trade-tool-seeks-save-iran-nuclear-deal.

Defterios, John. "Iran Deal Could Unlock Huge Economic Potential." *CNN Business.* April 1, 2015. https://money.cnn.com/2015/04/01/news/economy/iran-nuclear-deal-economic-potential/.

Dignas, Beate, and Engelbert Winther. *Rome and Persia in Late Antiquity: Neighbours and Rivals.* Cambridge: Cambridge University Press, 2007.

Erdbrink, Thomas. "Iran's Hard-Liners Show Restraint on Nuclear Talks with U.S." *The New York Times.* March 23, 2015. https://www.nytimes.com/2015/03/24/world/middleeast/irans-hard-liners-nuclear-talks.html.

Finnegan, Michael, and Seema Mehta. "Trump Says He Opposed Iraq War from the Start: He Did Not." *Los Angeles Times.* October 9, 2016. https://www.latimes.com/nation/politics/trailguide/la-na-second-presidential-debate-live-trump-says-he-opposed-iraq-war-from-the-1476065104-htmlstory.html.

Fisk, Robert. *The Great War for Civilisation: The Conquest of the Middle East.* New York: Vintage Books, 2007.

Formichi, Chiara. "Violence, Sectarianism, and the Politics of Religion: Articulations of Anti-Shi'a Discourses in Indonesia." *Indonesia* 98 (2014): 1–27. https://doi.org/10.5728/indonesia.98.0001.

Francis, Ellen. "Islamic State Faces Final Territorial Defeat in Eastern Syria Battle." *Reuters.* March 2, 2019. https://www.reuters.com/article/us-mideast-crisis-islamic-state/islamic-state-faces-final-territorial-defeat-in-eastern-syria-battle-idUSKCN1QJ04X.

Freedman, Lawrence. *Strategy: A History.* Oxford: Oxford University Press, 2015.

Gardner, David. "Barack Obama Failed to Fulfil Promise of His Middle East Policy." *Financial Times.* January 11, 2017. https://www.ft.com/content/eaa2622e-d74f-11e6-944b-e7eb37a6aa8e.

Gerges, Fawaz. *Obama and the Middle East: The End of America's Moment?* New York: St. Martin's Griffin, 2013.

Gibbon, Edward, and David Womersley. *The History of the Decline and Fall of the Roman Empire.* London: Penguin, 2000.

Haag, Matthew, and Michael Grynbaum. "Time Names Person of the Year for 2018: Jamal Khashoggi and Other Journalists." *The New York Times.* December 11, 2018. https://www.nytimes.com/2018/12/11/business/media/jamal-khashoggi-person-of-the-year-time.html.

Habibi, Nader. "The Iranian Economy Two Years After the Nuclear Agreement." *Crown Center for Middle East Studies.* 2018. https://www.brandeis.edu/crown/publications/meb/MEB115.pdf.

Hamid, Shadi. *Islamic Exceptionalism: How the Struggle Over Islam Is Reshaping the World.* New York: St. Martin's Griffin, 2017.

Heavey, Susan. "Trump Defends U.S. Withdrawal from Syria, Says Others Must Fight." *Reuters.* December 20, 2018. https://www.reuters.com/article/us-mideast-crisis-syria-trump/trump-defends-u-s-withdrawal-from-syria-says-others-must-fight-idUSKCN1OJ1KW.

Heydarian, Richard Javad. "Iran Sanctions: Collective Punishment." *The Huffington Post.* October 30, 2012. https://www.huffpost.com/entry/iran-sanctions-collective_b_2008211.

Heydarian, Richard Javad. *How Capitalism Failed the Arab World: The Economic Roots and Precarious Future of the Middle East Uprisings.* London: Zed Books, 2014a.

Heydarian, Richard Javad. "Post-sanctions Iran: The Next China?" *Aljazeera.* June 30, 2014b. https://www.aljazeera.com/indepth/opinion/2014/06/post-sanctions-iran-next-china-20146308302594267.html.

Hincks, Joseph. "Israel and Iran Are Waging a Secret War in Syria: Here's How It Finally Went Public." *Time.* January 25, 2019. http://time.com/5513411/israel-iran-secret-war-syria/.

Hjelmgaard, Kim. "China Clamps Down on North Korea Trade as Part of U.N. Sanctions." *USA Today.* January 5, 2018. https://www.usatoday.com/story/news/world/2018/01/05/china-tightens-north-korea-trade-limits-under-un-sanctions/1006632001/.

Hodgson, Marshall. *The Venture of Islam, Volume 3: The Gunpower Empires and Modern Times.* Chicago: University of Chicago Press, 1977.

Huntington, Samuel. "The Clash of Civilizations?" *Foreign Affairs.* June 1, 1993. https://www.foreignaffairs.com/articles/united-states/1993-06-01/clash-civilizations.

Huntington, Samuel. *The Clash of Civilizations and the Remaking of World Order.* New York: Simon & Schuster, 2011.

International Atomic Energy Agency. *Treaty on the Non-Proliferation of Nuclear Weapon (Information Circular).* April 22, 1970. https://www.iaea.org/sites/default/files/publications/documents/infcircs/1970/infcirc140.pdf.

"Iran Sanctions Raise Saudi Doubts." *Aljazeera.* February 16, 2010. https://www.aljazeera.com/news/middleeast/2010/02/201021641617847397.html.

Jeffrey, James, and Michael Eisenstadt. *U.S. Military Engagement in the Broader Middle East.* Washington: Washington Institute for Near East Policy, 2016.

Kaplan, Robert. *The Revenge of Geography: What the Map Tells Us About Coming Conflicts and the Battle Against Fate.* New York: Penguin Random House, 2013.

Karami, Arash. "Iran Negotiator Thanks Supreme Leader for Support." *Al-Monitor.* November 10, 2014. https://www.al-monitor.com/pulse/originals/2014/11/iran-negotiator-praises-khamenei-support.html.

Kim, Christine. "N.Korea Still Needs Time to Perfect Re-Entry Technology—S. Korea Vice Def Min." *Reuters.* August 14, 2017. https://www.reuters.com/article/northkorea-missiles-technology-idUSL4N1L017Q.

Kinzer, Stephen. *All the Shah's Men: An American Coup and the Roots of Middle East Terror*, 2nd edition. Hoboken: Wiley, 2008.

Kissinger, Henry. *On China.* London: Penguin Books, 2012.

Kissinger, Henry. *World Order.* London: Penguin Books, 2015.

Landler, Mark. "In Extraordinary Statement, Trump Stands with Saudis Despite Khashoggi Killing." *The New York Times.* November 20, 2018. https://www.nytimes.com/2018/11/20/world/middleeast/trump-saudi-khashoggi.html.

Landler, Mark. "Trump Takes Credit for Saudi Move Against Qatar, a U.S. Military Partner." *The New York Times.* June 6, 2017. https://www.nytimes.com/2017/06/06/world/middleeast/trump-qatar-saudi-arabia.html.

Lee, Youkyung. "Kim Jong Un's Cryptic Moves Puzzle North Korea Watchers." *Bloomberg.* March 2, 2019. https://www.bloomberg.com/news/articles/2019-05-02/kim-jong-un-s-game-of-thrones-puzzles-north-korea-watchers.

Lee, Kyung-Min. "Sanctions Push N. Korean Economy to Brink." *The Korea Times*. March 2019. https://www.koreatimes.co.kr/www/biz/2019/03/488_264778.html.

Lendon, Brad. "Qatar Hosts Largest US Military Base in Mideast." *CNN*. June 6, 2017. https://edition.cnn.com/2017/06/05/middleeast/qatar-us-largest-base-in-mideast/index.html.

Leverett, Flynt. "Why Libya Gave Up on the Bomb." *Brookings.edu*. January 23, 2004. https://www.brookings.edu/opinions/why-libya-gave-up-on-the-bomb/.

Lewis, Bernard. "The Roots of Muslim Rage." *The Atlantic*. September 1990. https://www.theatlantic.com/magazine/archive/1990/09/the-roots-of-muslim-rage/304643/.

Lin, Justin Yifu. "The Household Responsibility System in China's Agricultural Reform: A Theoretical and Empirical Study." *Economic Development and Cultural Change* 36, no. 3 (1988): S199–224. http://www.jstor.org/stable/1566543.

Liptak, Kevin, and Jeremy Diamond. "'Sometimes You Have to Walk': Trump Leaves Hanoi with No Deal." *CNN Politics*. February 28, 2019. https://edition.cnn.com/2019/02/27/politics/donald-trump-kim-jong-un-vietnam-summit/index.html.

Lutz, Meris. "Iran, Saudi Arabia: Islamic Solidarity Games in Tehran Canceled Over 'Persian Gulf' spat." *Los Angeles Times*. January 18, 2010. https://latimesblogs.latimes.com/babylonbeyond/2010/01/iran-tehran-loses-islamic-solidarity-games-over-persian-gulf-spat.html.

Mabon, Simon. *Saudi Arabia and Iran: Power and Rivalry in the Middle East*. London: I.B. Tauris, 2015.

Mason, Jeff, and Hyonhee Shin. "Summit Collapse Clouds Future of U.S.-North Korea Nuclear Diplomacy." *Reuters*. February 25, 2019. https://ru.reuters.com/article/worldNews/idUKKCN1QE0B8.

Mearsheimer, John, and Stephen Walt. *The Israel Lobby and U.S. Foreign Policy*. New York: Farrar, Straus and Giroux, 2008.

Memoli, Michael, and Christi Parsons. "Obama: Outline of Nuclear Deal with Iran Could Make 'Our World Safer'." *Los Angeles Times*. April 2, 2015. https://www.latimes.com/world/middleeast/la-fg-iran-talks-obama-20150402-story.html.

Mishra, Pankaj. "Why Weren't They Grateful?" *London Review of Books* 34, no. 12 (2012): 19–20. https://www.lrb.co.uk/v34/n12/pankaj-mishra/why-werent-they-grateful.

Mogato, Manuel. "Philippines Suspends Trade with North Korea to Comply with U.N. Resolution." *Reuters*. September 8, 2017. https://www.reuters.com/article/uk-philippines-northkorea/philippines-suspends-trade-with-north-korea-to-comply-with-u-n-resolution-idUKKCN1BJ113.

Montanaro, Domenico. "Americans Support Iran Talks, but Doubt They'll Prevent a Weapon." *National Public Radio.* April 2, 2015. https://www.npr.org/sections/itsallpolitics/2015/04/02/397106022/americans-support-iran-talks-but-doubt-theyll-prevent-a-weapon.

Moon, Chung-in. "A Real Path to Peace on the Korean Peninsula." *Foreign Affairs.* April 30, 2018a. https://www.foreignaffairs.com/articles/north-korea/2018-04-30/real-path-peace-korean-peninsula?cid=int-fls&pgtype=hpg/.

Moon, Chung-in. "The Progress and Promise of the Moon-Kim Summit." *Foreign Affairs.* April 30, 2018b. https://www.foreignaffairs.com/articles/north-korea/2018-04-30/real-path-peace-korean-peninsula.

Morello, Carol. "Iran Talks to Be Extended Another Day." *The Washington Post.* April 1, 2015. https://www.washingtonpost.com/world/negotiators-prepared-to-start-drafting-preliminary-agreement-on-iran-talks.

Myre, Greg. "America's Middle East Scorecard: Many Interventions, Few Successes." *National Public Radio.* August 25, 2014. https://www.npr.org/sections/parallels/2014/08/25/341892606/america-s-middle-east-scorecard-many-interventions-few-successes.

Nasr, Vali. *The Shia Revival.* New York: W. W. Norton, 2016.

Obama, Barack. "The President's Speech in Cairo: A New Beginning." 2009. Accessed April 4, 2019. https://obamawhitehouse.archives.gov/issues/foreign-policy/presidents-speech-cairo-a-new-beginning.

O'Mahony, Angela, Miranda Priebe, Bryan Frederick, Jennifer Kavanagh, Matthew Lane, Trevor Johnston, Thomas Szayna, Jakub Hlavka, Stephen Watts, and Matthew Povlock. *U.S. Presence and the Incidence of Conflict.* Santa Monica, CA: RAND Corporation, 2018.

Pan, Esther. "North Korea's Capitalist Experiment." *Council on Foreign Relations.* June 7, 2006. https://www.cfr.org/backgrounder/north-koreas-capitalist-experiment.

"Panmunjom Declaration for Peace, Prosperity and Unification of the Korean Peninsula." *ABC News.* April 27, 2018. https://www.abc.net.au/news/2018-04-27/panmunjom-declaration-for-peace2c-prosperity-and-unification-o/9705794.

Parsi, Trita. *A Single Roll of the Dice: Obama's Diplomacy with Iran.* New Haven: Yale University Press, 2013.

Pearson-Jones, Bridie. "School Friends of Kim Jong-un Describe How He Was a Good Basketball Player Despite Only Being 5′ 6″ and 'Good for a Laugh'." *Daily Mail.* January 15, 2018. https://www.dailymail.co.uk/news/article-5272341/Childhood-friends-Kim-Jong-school-days.html.

Petito, Fabio. "Khatami' Dialogue Among Civilizations as International Political Theory." *Journal of Humanities* 11, no. 3 (2004): 11–29. http://eijh.modares.ac.ir/article-27-9945-en.pdf.

"Pompeo Says God May Have Sent Trump to Save Israel from Iran." *BBC News.* March 22, 2019. https://www.bbc.com/news/world-us-canada-47670717.

Porter, Gareth. "In an Exclusive Interview, a Top Iranian Official Says That Khomeini Personally Stopped Him from Building Iran's WMD Program." *Foreign Policy.* October 16, 2014a. https://foreignpolicy. com/2014/10/16/when-the-ayatollah-said-no-to-nukes/.

Porter, Gareth. "Manufactured Crisis: The Untold Story of the Iran Nuclear Scare." *Foreign Affairs.* April 21, 2014b. https://www.foreignaffairs. com/reviews/capsule-review/2014-04-21/manufactured-crisis-untold-story-iran-nuclear-scare.

Porter, Patrick. "Sharing Power? Prospects for a U.S. Concert-Balance Strategy." *Strategic Studies Institute.* April 26, 2013. https://ssi.armywarcollege.edu/pubs/display.cfm?pubID=1149.

Rascouet, Angelina, and Hashem Kalantari. "Iran Can Add Million Barrels a Day of Oil if Sanctions Halt." *Bloomberg.* March 17, 2015. https://www.bloomberg.com/news/articles/2015-03-16/iran-can-add-million-barrels-a-day-of-oil-if-sanctions-are-ended.

"Reaction from Around the World to Nuclear Deal with Iran." *The Associated Press.* April 3, 2015. https://www.apnews.com/865c8f37d6b9443caa9a0e45cee92f9c.

"Regional Insight—Middle East." *British Petroleum.* 2018. https://www.bp.com/en/global/corporate/energy-economics/statistical-review-of-world-energy/country-and-regional-insights/middle-east.html.

Revere, Evans. "Kim Jong-un's New Year's Speech: A Kinder, Gentler North Korea?" *Brookings.edu.* January 3, 2013. https://www.brookings.edu/opinions/kim-jong-uns-new-years-speech-a-kinder-gentler-north-korea/.

Rezaian, Jason. "In Iran, Narrow World Cup Loss to Argentina Is Still Cause for Celebration." *The Washington Post.* June 21, 2014. https://www.washingtonpost.com/news/soccer-insider/wp/2014/06/21/in-iran-narrow-world-cup-loss-to-argentina-is-still-cause-for-celebration.

Risen, James, and Mark Mazzetti. "U.S. Agencies See No Move by Iran to Build a Bomb." *The New York Times.* February 24, 2012. https://www.nytimes.com/2012/02/25/world/middleeast/us-agencies-see-no-move-by-iran-to-build-a-bomb.html.

Romo, Vanessa. "Trump Formally Recognizes Israeli Sovereignty Over Golan Heights." *National Public Radio.* March 25, 2019. https://www.npr.org/2019/03/25/706588932/trump-formally-recognizes-israeli-sovereignty-over-golan-heights.

Rosenfeld, Everett. "Read the Full Text of the Trump-Kim Agreement Here." *CNBC.* June 12, 2018. https://www.cnbc.com/2018/06/12/full-text-of-the-trump-kim-summit-agreement.html.

Sachs, Natan. "Iran's Revolution, 40 Years On: Israel's Reverse Periphery Doctrine." *Brookings.edu.* January 24, 2019. https://www.brookings.edu/

blog/order-from-chaos/2019/01/24/irans-revolution-40-years-on-israels-reverse-periphery-doctrine/.

Said, Edward. "The Clash of Ignorance." *The Nation*. October 4, 2001. https://www.thenation.com/article/clash-ignorance/.

Saleem, Saleena. "Saudi Arabia's Shaken Pillars: Impact on Southeast Asian Muslims." *RSIS Commentaries No. 133.* June 1, 2016. https://dr.ntu.edu.sg/bitstream/handle/10220/40768/CO16133.pdf.

"Saudi Arabia Gives Israel Clear Skies to Attack Iranian Nuclear Sites." *The Times*. June 12, 2010. https://www.thetimes.co.uk/article/saudi-arabia-gives-israel-clear-skies-to-attack-iranian-nuclear-sites.

Savage, Charlie. *Power Wars: The Relentless Rise of Presidential Authority and Secrecy*. New York: Back Bay Books, 2017.

Seligman, Lara, and Robbie Gramer. "At Trump's Pentagon, Empty Offices Are the New Normal." *Foreign Policy*. March 12, 2019. https://foreignpolicy.com/2019/03/12/at-trumps-pentagon-empty-offices-are-the-new-normal-department-of-defense-mattis-resignation-vacancies-trump-administration-shanahan/.

Shahi, Deepshikha. "Revisiting the Clash of Civilizations Thesis After 9/11." *E-International Relations*. March 23, 2017. https://www.e-ir.info/2017/03/23/revisiting-the-clash-of-civilizations-thesis-after-911/.

Shapiro, Daniel. "Trump Kill the Two-State Solution." *Foreign Policy*. January 23, 2019. https://foreignpolicy.com/2019/01/23/dear-democrats-dont-let-trump-kill-the-two-state-solution/.

Shin Hyonhee, and Josh Smith. "South Korea Pushes Back at Trump Claims About More Money for Troop Agreement." *Reuters*. February 13, 2019. https://www.reuters.com/article/us-usa-southkorea-troops/south-korea-pushes-back-at-trump-claims-about-more-money-for-troop-agreement-idUSKCN1Q20AU.

Sick, Gary. *All Fall Down: America's Tragic Encounter with Iran*. Bloomington: iUniverse, 2001.

Soldatkin, Vladimir. "Russian Offers Iran Latest Anti-Aircraft Missiles: TASS." *Reuters*. February 23, 2015. https://www.reuters.com/article/us-iran-nuclear-russia-missiles/russian-offers-iran-latest-anti-aircraft-missiles-tass.

Stern, Jessica, and J.M. Berger. *ISIS: The State of Terror*. Bredebro: Ecco, 2016.

Sun Tzu. *The Art of War*, first thus edition. Las Vegas: Filiquarian, 2007.

Tharoor, Ishaan. "A Step-by-Step Guide to What the Iran Agreement Actually Means." *The Washington Post*. April 2, 2015. https://www.washingtonpost.com/news/worldviews/wp/2015/04/02/a-step-by-step-guide-to-what-the-iran-agreement-actually-means/?utm_term=.0834ebf94bf1.

The Godfather III. Directed by Francis Coppola. Beverly Hills: Paramount Pictures, 1990.

"The Trump Administration Is Complicit in Saudi Atrocities." *The Washington Post.* April 24, 2019. https://www.washingtonpost.com/opinions/global-opinions/the-trump-administration-is-complicit-in-saudi-atrocities/2019/04/24/c830a86e-651d-11e9-89854cf30147bdca_story.html?utm_term=855b99729230.

"The World's Biggest Natural Gas Reserves." *Hydrocarbons Technology.* November 11, 2013. https://www.hydrocarbons-technology.com/features/feature-the-worlds-biggest-natural-gas-reserves/.

"Trump Blames Cohen Testimony for Collapse of Summit with Kim Jong-un." *The Guardian.* March 4, 2019. https://www.theguardian.com/us-news/2019/mar/04/trump-blames-cohen-testimony-for-collapse-of-summit-with-kim-jong-un.

"Trump Defends Saudi Arabia Ties Despite Khashoggi Murder." *BBC News.* November 20, 2018. https://www.bbc.com/news/world-us-canada-46283355.

U.C. Berkeley Events. "Conversations with History—Trita Parsi." Youtube Video, 1:00:08. Posted December 3, 2007. https://youtu.be/SVGqDfX_pgA.

U.S. Department of State. *Joint Comprehensive Plan of Action (Full Text).* July 4, 2015a. https://www.state.gov/documents/organization/245317.pdf.

U.S. Department of State. *Parameters for a Joint Comprehensive Plan of Action Regarding the Islamic Republic of Iran's Nuclear Program.* April 2, 2015b. https://2009-2017.state.gov/r/pa/prs/ps/2015/04/240170.htm.

"Vietnam War." *History.com.* October 29, 2009. https://www.history.com/topics/vietnam-war/vietnam-war-history.

Wadhams, Nick, Glen Carey, and Margaret Taley. "Trump to Escalate Iran Feud by Ending Waivers; Oil Prices Climb." *Bloomberg.* April 22, 2019. https://www.bloomberg.com/news/articles/2019-04-22/u-s-said-to-eliminate-iran-oil-waivers-after-may-2-expiration.

Waltz, Kenneth. "Why Iran Should Get the Bomb." *Foreign Affairs.* June 15, 2012. https://www.foreignaffairs.com/articles/iran/2012-06-15/why-iran-should-get-bomb.

Ward, Alex, and Jen Kirby. "James Mattis, the Last "Adult" in the Trump Administration, Resigns as Defense Secretary." *Vox.* December 20, 2018. https://www.vox.com/2018/12/20/17168030/mattis-trump-defense-secretary-retires-tweet.

Weiner, Jon. "Obama and the Palestinian Professors." *The Nation.* April 10, 2008. https://www.thenation.com/article/obama-and-palestinian-professors/.

Weiss, Michael, and Hassan Hassan. *ISIS: Inside the Army of Terror.* New York: Regan Arts, 2016.

Wike, Richard. "7 Charts on How the World Views President Obama." *Pew Research Center.* 2015. https://www.pewresearch.org/fact-tank/2015/06/24/7-charts-on-how-the-world-views-president-obama/.

Woodward, Bob. *Fear: Trump in the White House*. New York: Simon & Schuster, 2018.

Wong, Edward, and Catie Edmonson. "Pompeo Refuses to Say What U.S. Would Do if Israel Annexes West Bank." *The New York Times*. April 9, 2019. https://www.nytimes.com/2019/04/09/us/politics/pompeo-israel-west-bank.html.

Wright, Robin. "The Adversary: Is Iran's Nuclear Negotiator, Javad Zarif, for Real?" *The New Yorker*. May 19, 2014. https://www.newyorker.com/magazine/2014/05/26/the-adversary-2.

Wroughton, Lesley. "U.S., Iran Positive After Nuclear Talks, Say Much Left to Do." *Reuters*. February 24, 2015. https://www.reuters.com/article/us-iran-nuclear/u-s-iran-positive-after-nuclear-talks-say-much-left-to-do.

Yergin, Daniel. *The Prize: The Epic Quest for Oil, Money & Power*. New York: Free Press, 2008.

Zenko, Micah. "US Military Policy in the Middle East: An Appraisal." *Chatham House: The Royal Institute of International Affairs*. October 18, 2018. https://www.chathamhouse.org/sites/default/files/publications/research/2018-10-18-us-military-policy-middle-east-zenko.pdf.

Zunes, Stephen. "A History Lesson: US Intervention in the Middle East." *Global Policy*. February 10, 2003. https://www.globalpolicy.org/component/content/article/167/35415.html.

CHAPTER 4

Xi Must Be Obeyed: The New Peking Order

[T]o prevent collusion and maintain security dependence among the vassals, to keep tributaries pliant and protected, and to keep the barbarians from coming together.[1] —Zbigniew Brzezinski on imperial geo-strategy, *The Grand Chessboard*

Yet, however slowly this great leviathan [China] evolved, it was never immobile. Like all civilizations, it accumulated experience, and made continual choices among its resources and possibilities.[2] —Fernand Braudel, *A History of Civilizations*

[W]e do not need to chase [after other countries] – we are the road.[3] —Xi Jinping, 2018 Speech in Hainan

The year 2013 will likely be remembered as the beginning of modern China's full-fledged bid for global primacy. It marked the rise of a new Chinese paramount leader, Xi Jinping, who, within a matter of months, managed to secure his grip on the three pillars of the Middle Kingdom's political system: presidency of the state, the office of the secretary-general of the Chinese Communist Party (CCP), and the head of the Central Military Commission (CMC). The swift—though far from

[1] Brzezinski (1998, 40).
[2] Braudel (1993, 171).
[3] Shim (2018).

© The Author(s) 2020
R. J. Heydarian, *The Indo-Pacific: Trump, China, and the New Struggle for Global Mastery*, https://doi.org/10.1007/978-981-13-9799-8_4

completely uncontested—consolidation of formal power ensured that, unlike in the case of Jiang Zemin and Hu Jintao in the mid-2000s, a single figure now sat undisputedly atop the pyramid of power in Beijing.[4] Over the next five years, Xi would unleash a dramatic anti-corruption crackdown, which virtually eliminated all potential rivals (e.g., Bo Xilai, Sun Zhengcai), sidelined or intimidated critics, placed practically all key-decision-making agencies under the control of a single man (much at the expense of Premier Li Keqiang), and paved the way for the creation of a unique and pervasive cult of personality unseen since the heady days of Cultural Revolution (1966–1976). Within four years in office, Xi oversaw the punishment of close to 1.4 million Party members, including "seventeen full and seventeen alternate Central Committee members, a pair of sitting Politburo members, an ex-member of the Politburo Standing Committee, and more than a hundred generals and admirals."[5] By 2018, Xi went one step further: eliminating term limits on the office of presidency, unequivocally placing himself in the position to become, should he choose to, a Mao-like "leader for life."

Thus, the year 2013 saw the beginning of the end of the two-decades-long collective leadership regime, which supplanted the tumultuous days of Chairman Mao Zedong's bloody reign, under the guidance of Deng Xiaoping and his reformist coterie. The upshot of Xi's political machinations is an ultramodern absolutist rule by a single man rather than, in the tradition of post-Stalinist and post-Maoist China, the oligarchy of collective-consociational party leadership. (In this sense, today's China is beginning to resemble archaic North Korea rather than post-war Vietnam, which has adopted a Deng-like system of party-led oligarchic rule.) Leaving nothing to imagination, Xi has personally overseen—through small working groups populated by loyalists, most notably Wang Qishan and the so-called Zhejiang clique—the management of the People's Liberation Army (PLA) and the domestic security apparatus in order to stave off any potential challenge to his power base. As one Chinese scholar put it, "No other Chinese Communist Party leader, not even Mao Zedong, has controlled the military to the same extent as Xi does today, [since] Mao had to share power with powerful revolutionary-era marshals." The centralizing bureaucratic reforms, coupled with Xi's

[4]Osnos (2015).
[5]Shirk (2018, 24).

refusal to formally designate a heir apparent in defiance of tradition, not only reflects Xi's political acumen, but arguably also his appetite for staying in power for the long haul.[6]

This earthshaking revolution within the Chinese political system has been accompanied by the emergence of China as the new global superpower and, potentially, the new anchor—if not, in Marxist lexicon, "vanguard"—of the international economic order. As the former United States House of Representatives Tip O'Neill once memorably said, "all politics is local." Thus, understanding China's overarching foreign policy initiative, the One Road, One Belt (OBOR) initiative, later renamed to Belt and Road Initiative (BRI), can't be divorced from the fundamental reconfiguration in Beijing's internal politics. Great leaders rarely leap into, to use the words of German Philosopher G.W.F. Hegel, "the slaughter-bench" of history without forwarding a grand vision of the future, both for their country and the wider world.[7] And Xi Jinping—as China's most powerful leader in decades, who presides over a newly minted global superpower—hasn't shied away from crafting and forwarding his own grand vision of, first, "national rejuvenation" at home and, secondly, placing China at the center of an emerging post-American global order through the revival and recreation of the ancient Silk Road.[8]

BIRTH OF A GLOBAL VISION

In 2013, Xi made two important speeches. In a high-profile conference in October that year, which was attended by the entire Standing Committee of the Politburo (SCP) and practically all key foreign policy players in the country, the Chinese president held the first-ever policy meeting about "peripheral nations" (China's immediate neighbors) since the founding of the modern Chinese state. Dubbed as the "Peripheral Diplomacy Work Conference," the event saw the Chinese paramount leader emphasizing the "extremely significant strategic value" Beijing supposedly attaches to its relations with neighboring countries. He highlighted the centrality of deepening economic cooperation and security partnership with nations in Middle Kingdom's historical backyard.

[6] See Shirk (2018) and Economy (2018).
[7] Hegel (1837).
[8] Xinhua (2017).

There was, of course, a sense of urgency that drove the formulation and implementation of the "peripheral diplomacy" strategy. A year earlier, as Xi prepared to take over the leadership of China from his (embattled and emaciated) predecessor, Hu Jintao, the CCP held its first Foreign Affairs Leading Group meeting in nearly a decade. The aim of the high-level meetings was to explore specific measures to stave off growing regional backlash against China's rising territorial and maritime assertiveness across the East and South China Seas. Countries such as Vietnam, the Philippines, and Japan were increasingly aligning with America, which was pushing forward with its own Pivot to Asia policy (P2A). The leadership in Beijing feared the possibility of an American-led encirclement and growing diplomatic isolation in the region unless China managed to restore relations with neighboring states. In particular, the Philippines, then under the Benigno Aquino III administration, made the unprecedented move of taking China to international court over the territorial disputes in the South China Sea. As one prominent Chinese scholar, Yan Xuetong, bluntly put it: "The policy now is to allow these smaller [neighboring] countries to benefit economically from their relationships with China. For China, we need good relationships more urgently than we need economic development. We let them benefit economically, and in return we get good political relationships. We should 'purchase' the relationships."[9] To facilitate the effectiveness of its strategy, Xi appointed a leading Asia expert, Wang Yi, as the new Chinese foreign minister in early 2013. Mr. Wang was a capable China hand and dexterous diplomat, who was at the center of the negotiation of the 2002 Declaration on the Conduct of Parties in the South China Sea (as deputy minister for Asia affairs at the Chinese [MOFA]), a former director of Taiwan Affairs Office, and proved an extremely capable ambassador in Tokyo at the height of Sino-Japanese tensions in mid-2000s.

During the Peripheral Diplomacy conference, Xi called on China to "strive to promote regional security cooperation" and "insist on mutual trust and benefit, equality and cooperation, propose the overall, common and cooperative security idea to push ahead security cooperation with peripheral countries." Highlighting the centrality of "maintaining stability in China's neighborhood" to his new foreign policy strategy, the

---

[9] Moriyasu (2015).

Chinese leader underscored his country's commitment to "encourage and participate in the process of regional economic integration, speed up the process of building up infrastructure and connectivity. We must build the Silk Road Economic Belt and 21st Century Maritime Silk Road, creating a new regional economic order."[10] Same month, during the ASEAN–China Summit, Premier Li Keqiang proposed the "2+7 cooperation framework," which envisioned a two-point political consensus on enhancing good neighborliness and mutual trust, likely through an augmented form of a Treaty of Amity and Cooperation (TAC) agreement between the two sides, as well as a seven-point economic cooperation package, focusing on trade, investment and infrastructure development.[11] Months earlier, Xi made another important speech, this time in Almaty, Kazakhstan, a key energy-rich nation in China's BRI vision, particularly under its "belt" strategy that cuts Eurasia, passes through Iran and Turkey, and extends all the way to Western Europe (see Fig. 4.1).

During his address at the Nazarbayev University (7 September 2013), Xi, in a typically Sino-centric manner, claimed that "the Silk Road linking east and west, Asia and Europe" goes as far back as "2,100 years ago during China's Han Dynasty," when China sent envoys, particularly Zhang Qian, to Eurasian nations such as Kazakhstan to expand trade and diplomatic relations.[12] He discussed how, "Shaanxi, my home province, is right at the starting point of the ancient Silk Road," claiming (falsely) that China was the genesis of the ancient Silk Road, even though historians contend that there was neither a single road, nor a single point of origin, and that, crucially, silk wasn't the primary trading item among nations back then. As Georgetown historian James Millward notes, "In fact, there never really was a single Silk Road (nor several roads) linking East to West that you could draw on a map; rather, trade fanned out in networks across the breadth of Eurasia — as it did elsewhere. And machinations of empires always played a larger role in promoting exchanges than did intrepid private traders."[13] In fact, as Peter Frankopan, the author of *The Silk Roads* explains, it was the Persian Achaemenid Empire, stretching from North Africa and Southeastern Europe all the way to

---

[10]China Council for International Cooperation on Environment and Development (2013).

[11]Parameswaran (2013).

[12]Xi (2013).

[13]Millward (2018).

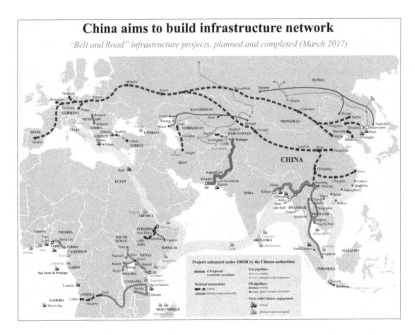

Fig. 4.1 China's Vision of a Global Infrastructure Network (*Source* Mercator Institute for China studies)

Central Asia and the Indian Subcontinent, which served as the foundation, and at times the central nervous system, of the ancient Silk Road.[14] The Achaemenid Empire, Amy Chua argues, was in fact the world's first true "hyperpower," an unrivaled transcontinental imperium. China only achieved a comparable status more than a millennia after during the highly cosmopolitan, though geographically less expansive, Tang Dynasty.[15]

Thus, the BRI's reference to the Silk Road is more a calculated appeal to nostalgia in order to present China's modern ambitions in more benign terms rather than the replication of a historically accurate Sino-centric proto-globalization in ancient times. To be fair, Xi himself,

---

[14]Frankopan (2017).

[15]Chua (2009).

speaking before his Central Asian audience, made it clear that reviving the ancient Silk Road was his grand foreign policy vision, with peripheral Eurasian neighbors acting as the linchpin of the overall strategy:

> To forge closer economic ties, deepen cooperation and expand development space in the Eurasian region, we should take an innovative approach and jointly build an "economic belt along the Silk Road"... we need to improve road connectivity. The [Shanghai Cooperation Organization] is working on an agreement on transportation facilitation. If signed and implemented at an early date, it will open up a major transportation route connecting the Pacific and the Baltic Sea. Building on that, we will actively discuss the best way to improve cross-border transportation infrastructure and work toward a transportation network connecting East Asia, West Asia and South Asia to facilitate economic development and travel in the region... we need to promote unimpeded trade. The proposed "economic belt along the Silk Road" is inhabited by close to 3 billion people and represents the biggest market in the world with unparalleled potential. The potential for trade and investment cooperation between the relevant countries is enormous. We should discuss a proper arrangement for trade and investment facilitation, remove trade barriers, reduce trade and investment cost, increase the speed and quality of regional economic flows and achieve win-win progress in the region... we need to enhance monetary circulation... it will significantly lower circulation cost, increase our ability to fend off financial risks and make our region more competitive economically in the world.[16]

EMPIRE BY OTHER MEANS

Zbigniew Brzezinski, a former U.S. National Security Advisor (1977–1981), identified three elements that define (China's) imperial geostrategy, namely "to prevent collusion and maintain security dependence among the vassals, to keep tributaries pliant and protected, and to keep the barbarians from coming together."

The BRI initiative, however, has both land-based ("belt") and maritime ("road") dimensions. Thus, one might ask, which dimension is more urgent or important to China? Moreover, why does Beijing insist on having two different transcontinental routes? Wouldn't this lead to

---

[16]See the full speech here http://www.fmprc.gov.cn/mfa_eng/wjdt_665385/zyjh_665391/t1078088.shtml.

overstretching China's (finite) resources, or represent a fanciful flight of ambition? More fundamentally, is BRI primarily an economic project or a geopolitical one? The best way to understand the strategic logic behind Xi's vision is to look at the evolving geography of Chinese power. As Robert Kaplan, building on his earlier works[17],[18] perspicaciously notes:

> China's infrastructure expansion across Central Asia is directly related to its maritime expansion in the South and East China seas. *After all, China is only able to act aggressively in its adjacent seas because it is now, for the time being, secure on land to a degree it has never been in its history* [author's own emphasis]. Threatened constantly by the peoples of the steppe in the west, southwest, and north, with the exception of the voyages of Admiral Zheng He during the Ming Dynasty in the early fifteenth century, China never actually did have a maritime tradition in the east. But globalization, with its exaggerated emphasis on sea lines of communication, has necessitated Chinese power projection into the blue-water extensions of its own continental landmass. Because that requires China to remain secure on land, it also means the permanent subjugation of the Muslim Uighurs, Tibetans, and Inner Mongolians. And thus we have the One Belt, One Road strategy.[19]

What's in play in here is what one can describe as "dialectics of empire": With the expansion of China's productive capacities, industrial, energy, and consumer needs, and overseas trade, inevitably came greater stake in secure and reliable global channels of communications, both on land and in seas. Prosperity also brought about an expansion in defensive capabilities, with the PLA closing its vast technological and tactical gap with rival powers. The result is the emergence of new interests, new insecurities, new ambitions, and, ultimately, the reevaluation, if not complete reconstitution, of a power's own identity. In geopolitics, there aren't permanent friends, nor permanent enemies; moreover, even interests aren't permanent, especially for rising powers such as modern China.

Over the past century, modern China has gone from a tenuously reconstituted post-Qing Empire in the early twentieth century to a land power surrounded by hostile continental neighbors (i.e., Russia) during the Cold War and, in recent decades, a global economic power with vast and expanding maritime interests. And as China's spheres of interest

---

[17]Kaplan (2010).
[18]Kaplan (2013).
[19]Kaplan (2018).

and arch of influence expands, so thus (the real and imaginary) necessity of creating buffer zones, defensive perimeters, and expanded areas of strategic posturing and military operation (Holmes and Yoshihara 2011). And with a booming economy comes an ineluctable march toward securing precious resources across the world.[20] As Robert Kaplan correctly observes: "Empires rarely come about by design; they grow organically. As states become stronger, they cultivate new needs and – this may seem counterintuitive – apprehensions that force them to expand in various forms."[21] The BRI's ambitious scale has drawn inevitable comparisons with America's key domestic and global projects at the peak of its industrial and geopolitical power. Some have compared the BRI to the Transcontinental Railroad project in the late nineteenth century (Hillman 2018), as America began to dominate the global industrial output, while others have compared it to the Marshall Plan in the mid-twentieth century, when America became the de facto global policeman, responsible for the bulk of military expenditures and economic output on earth. In the case of China, however, it is approaching likely both the peak of its economic and geopolitical power simultaneously. In contrast, there was a significant lag between America's emergence as an economic power, on one hand, and its geopolitical hegemony, on the other. And, even more astonishingly, China has managed to achieve its current status within a (i) single generation of unprecedented economic transformation and (ii) without the advantages of American geography, which left the North American power unscathed during the two world wars and, throughout its history, bereft of any significant indigenous rival in the entire Western Hemisphere. In contrast, China was (i) at the center of destruction wrought by the two world wars, primarily through the brutal and destructive Japanese Imperial occupation, and (ii) has been hemmed in by a coterie of hostile and capable rivals, ranging from Japan to India and Russia throughout the past century.[22]

In Xi's worldview, his country's rapid rise to riches and influence—coming on the heels of decades of domestic instability and economic insecurity—stands as an indubitable validation of China's potential, if not historical destiny, to once again become the center of the world. Thus, the BRI, at its very heart, is both a reflection of China's emergence as a global power as well as an instrument for the realization of a Sino-centric

[20] See for instance Economy and Levi (2014).

[21] Kaplan (2010).

[22] See for instance Kissinger (2012) and Allison (2017).

order in the future. The BRI, however, is far from just a vanity fair project (see Chapter 5). It's a comprehensive, deliberate, yet flexible strategy, which aims to achieve seven key objectives simultaneously:

1. Develop hinterlands and underdeveloped regions, particularly in minority-dominated regions in western regions;
2. Outsource internal infrastructure glut and productive overcapacity amid an economic slowdown, first at home but now also globally (Appelbaum 2016; Jacobs 2017; Sharma 2012);
3. Develop export markets' infrastructure for next stage of trade;
4. Expand domestic supply-chain beyond the Pearl River Delta, and internationalize Chinese industrial standards;
5. Save China's troubled State-Owned Enterprises (SOEs), which employ millions of workers;
6. Lock in rare commodities key to Chinese long-term development;
7. Gain foothold in key sectors of foreign countries for geopolitical gain, push back against Western influence.

The ultimate goal is to mitigate, if not eliminate, existing imbalances in the Chinese economy, while shaping the next chapter of the international economic order along Beijing's preferences, standards, and interests. Within a single generation, China precipitated a fundamental rebalancing within the international system, first economically (rising to become the second largest economy and largest trading nation), then militarily (as Asia's undisputed indigenous powerhouse with rapidly advancing asymmetrical as well as conventional military capabilities), and, finally, ideationally, as China doubles down on its soft power through exporting its cultural preferences, worldviews (i.e., *Tianxia*), industrial standards, and cutting-edge technological innovation (i.e., Alibaba). Before going into the details of the BRI (see Chapter 5), however, one must understand China's decades-old charm offensive strategy toward Asia. After all, the Peripheral Diplomacy initiative is a repackaged and updated version of an earlier regional policy. In China's ancient civilization, strategy is primarily a matter of remembering the past, rather than true innovation.

THE BEIJING CONSENSUS

Jiang Zemin's rise to power marked the first peaceful transfer of power in modern Chinese history. Though Deng would maintain informal levers of power for few more years, the early 1990s saw the gradual and steady establishment of a new form of authoritarian regime in Beijing. China transformed from, to use the classification of American political scientist Jack Goldstone, a "sultanistic" dictatorship into a "party-state" of collective leadership.[23] It was an endogenously driven change that was born out of the specter of Mao-era terror. As Deng warned, the horrors of the Maoist era weren't solely the fault of the former leader, Mao Zedong, but instead an inevitable outcome of an inherent systemic flaw: namely, how "[o]ver-concentration of power is liable to give rise to arbitrary rule by individuals at the expense of collective leadership."[24]

One should, of course, take into consideration the fact that the establishment of institutionalized collective leadership came after the Tiananmen protests (1989), which shook the foundations of the communist regime.[25] It also came on the heels of an economic takeoff that saw per capita income levels increasing by a factor of five across urban centers, the seat of massive nationwide protests in 1989, and increase by three times in rural areas after the introduction of economic reforms a decade earlier.[26] Under Jiang's stewardship, the Chinese political system was dramatically pluralized, as competing ideological currents coalesced under the umbrella of capitalist experimentation. Overtime, even the entrepreneurial class—the much-derided "bourgeoisie" in Marxist-Leninist universe—was gradually incorporated into the upper echelons of the CCP.[27] The diversification of the membership of the political establishment was clearly an attempt to co-opt new centers of power, namely the burgeoning middle class as well as business tycoons, but it also had the inevitable result of creating powerful interest groups, which favored greater openness, particularly in the economic realm.[28]

The seismic changes in the outlook and composition of the Chinese leadership went hand in hand with a dramatic overhaul of China's foreign policy. Both Jiang and his successor, Hu Jintao, would oversee the operationalization of Deng's famous dictum: "Hide our capacities and bide our time, *but also get some things done* [author's own emphasis]." Far from a pacifist, Deng encouraged more friendly external relations as well as greater economic

---

[23] Goldstone (2011).

[24] Shirk (2018).

[25] See Shirk (2008) and Li (2010).

[26] Kissinger (2011, 479).

[27] Andreas (2012).

[28] Kurtlantzick (2008).

engagement with the outside world as a *means* to empowering China after decades of self-imposed isolation, which brought about technological and scientific backwardness. It was a fundamentally opportunistic, calibrated call for (temporary) strategic self-restraint. Low-key foreign policy was not Deng's preferred strategic 'end' for a re-emerging China following centuries of humiliation at the hands of foreign powers and vicious internal divisions.

As John Mearsheimer explains, "The reason it ma[de] sense for China to bide its time is that if it avoids trouble and merely continues growing economically, it will eventually become so powerful that it can just get its way in Asia."[29] Together, Jiang and Hu, the two protégés of Deng, launched the third phase of PRC's foreign policy, better known as the "charm offensive."[30] Under Mao, China engaged in a protracted ideological warfare across its "near neighborhood," particularly in Southeast Asia, where indigenous communist movements relied on both material and political support of Beijing throughout the early phase of Cold War. Mao's China largely shunned the international order as an illegitimate construct of capitalist West, while openly supporting revolutionary movements across the "Third World." After the Sino-Soviet split in the 1960s, Maoist China launched a two-front global struggle against both the West (America) and the East (Soviet Union). This era of combative cohabitation vis-à-vis the great powers and their regional allies, including Japan and Western-oriented regimes in the Third World, peaked right before the Richard Nixon administration shepherded a historic détente between Beijing and Washington by skillfully tapping into Mao's strategic anxieties toward Moscow. Yet, it was not until the ascent of Deng to the pinnacle of power in late 1970s, shortly after Mao's death and the purge of radical-leftist elements within the regime, that the second phase of Chinese foreign policy gained its full expression. In 1978 and 1979, Deng embarked on high-profile diplomatic visits to key Southeast Asian countries, namely Singapore, Malaysia, and Thailand, as well as the United States, signaling the beginning of a new chapter in China's relations with the outside world. This phase was anchored by a singular impulse, namely the normalization of Beijing's ties with the West and its immediate neighbors, including Japan and the Association of Southeast Asian Nations (ASEAN). Similar to Mao, however, Deng remained aloof towards the liberal international order, viewing active Chinese participation in

[29] Mearsheimer (2014).
[30] Kurtlantzick (2008).

Western-led global organizations as strategic distractions, even traps or entanglements, which may frustrate efforts at modernizing his country. In other words, Deng sought engagement with the outside world, but only to the extent that it helps turbocharge economic development at home. Greater assertiveness on the international stage, he maintained, is a luxury that China could afford if and only if it managed to reach a certain level of development, which necessitated stronger global presence for protection of emerging Chinese interests overseas. This is precisely why Deng counseled his protégés to "keep a low profile and never take the lead"—making sure development at home remained at the apex of the communist regime's national priority for the time being. The meteoric rise of China, however, meant that Deng's successors would soon afford to undertake an increasingly proactive foreign policy.[31] As political scientists Taylor Fravel and Evan Medeiros explain, from the mid-1990s onwards Beijing entered the third phase of its foreign policy, which was characterized by "an attempt by China's [new] leaders to break out of their post-Tiananmen isolation, rebuild their image, protect and promote Chinese economic interests, and enhance their security," while "hedg[ing] against American influence around the world."[32]

China's Charm Offensive

As the dialectics of empire gained pace, so did China's interest in developing warm and cordial relations with the outside world. Rapid industrialization at home meant growing appetite for raw materials, agricultural produce, minerals, and energy resources from across the world, particularly in resource-rich developing regions of Africa, Asia, and Latin America. In sub-Saharan Africa, China became, within a span of a decade, a top trading and investment partner. The blossoming economic partnership was soon accompanied by the migration of millions of Chinese citizens, a mélange of workers and businessmen, who, in the words of former New York Times bureau chief Howard French turned Africa into "China's second continent."[33] In Latin America, China became an indispensable partner to the left-leaning, populist regime of

[31] Ibid., 16.
[32] Medeiros and Fravel (2003).
[33] French (2014).

Hugo Chavez, who launched an ambitious transnational 'Bolivarian' bloc of mostly anti-American nations. China became a key export partner, investor, and supplier of technology, both civilian and military, to the *Chavismo* regime, which leveraged Venezuela's oil riches to bankroll a region-wide geopolitical earthquake. China, however, also developed close relations with other Latin American powers, ranging from Brazil to Argentina and Chile, which served as precious sources of minerals and food produce for voracious Chinese industries and consumers.

Shifts in China's political economy undergirded a reformulation in China's foreign policy and, ultimately, self-perception. And this had profound geopolitical implications: By the end of Jiang's leadership, China began to fancy itself as a potential development model for the postcolonial world. In particular, China wasn't only attracted to autocratic regimes, which seemed as more reliable and straightforward partners for business, but also began to attract autocrats, who, in China, saw a seemingly perfect fusion of political control (under one party) and economic dynamism (managed capitalism). By the turn of the century, Beijing no longer viewed itself as an isolated, ideologically righteous force for the liberation of the Third World, nor as a fragile power undergoing uncertain domestic economic transformation. Instead, China began to see itself as a rising economic power with global interests. In fact, by the mid-2000s, Sinologist Joshua-Cooper Ramo observed: "China's rise is already reshaping the international order by introducing a new physics of development and power ... China is in the process of building the greatest asymmetric superpower the world has ever seen ... marking a path for other nations around the world who are trying to figure out not simply how to develop their countries but also how to fit into the international order in a way that allows them to be truly independent, to protect their way of life and political choices in a world with a single massively powerful center of gravity."[34]

In fact, Ramo coined the term "Beijing Consensus," pertaining to the country's supposedly nonideological, no-strings-attached, pragmatic approach to its global trade and investment engagement, as opposed to the World Bank and the IMF-driven "Washington Consensus" approach, which, based on principles of neoclassical economics, calls for structural, pro-market reforms. China's flexible, heterodox approach to development at home, on one hand, and expanding trade and investment

---

[34]Ramo (2004, 2–3).

abroad, on the other, rapidly transformed it into a model of development and preferred strategic partner to developing nations around the world, which opposed or lamented the orthodoxies of neoliberalism under the aegis of International Financial Institutions (IFIs). As the material conditions of China transformed, the country's leaders embraced new ideas about China and its place in the world. Under Jiang and Hu, as Asia's rising superpower economically matured, it advanced a series of new strategic concepts, including the slogans of "new security concept" and "peaceful development," which emphasized the centrality of diplomacy, multilateralism, and cooperation to a "win-win" relationship between Beijing and its external partners.

The Jiang administration (1989–2001) was primarily focused on strengthening the foundations of China's relations with America and the broader West, a critical export market and source of capital and technology, while the Hu administration (2002–2012) extended the horizons of China's proactive diplomatic engagement with much of the developing world. Improving relations with the West, however, meant, in instrumental terms, the need for stable and robust relations with Western-leaning powers in the region, including American treaty allies and strategic partners in East Asia. Jiang saw stable relations with great powers as key to creating the right conditions for China's rise, which was accelerated by the country's entry into the World Trade Organization (WTO) with the full backing of the Clinton administration. Hu built on Jiang's strategic achievements by deepening diplomatic engagement with the West, especially in light of the Global War on Terror (GWOT) in the first decade of the twentieth century, while doubling down on rapidly deepening trade and investment relations with the developing world.[35] As Fravel and Medeiros put it, under the Jiang-Hu period, China "expanded the number and depth of its bilateral relationships, joined various trade and security accords, deepened its participation in key multilateral organizations, and helped address global security issues."[36] And true to Deng's vision of collective leadership, even "[f]oreign policy decision-making [became] less personalized and more institutionalized, and Chinese diplomats [became] more sophisticated in their articulation of the country's goals."[37]

[35] Shirk (2008, 111).
[36] Medeiros and Fravel (2003).
[37] Ibid.

Thus, to (i) anchor China's economic breakout, (ii) ensure stability at home, and (iii) secure friendly relations with neighbors became the three primary and inseparable strategic imperatives of the ruling party. Between 1988 and 1994, China normalized/established diplomatic relations with as many as 18 nations, many emerging from the ruins of the Soviet empire and bordering the restive, Turkic-populated region of Xinjiang. China also upgraded strategic relations with the ASEAN, while ending its support for anti-regime communist movements across Southeast Asia. By 1991, China had established formal relations with all the members of the ASEAN. That year, Chinese Foreign Minister Qian Qichen made China's inaugural attendance at the ASEAN Foreign Ministers Meeting (AMM). Three years later, the energetic Chinese diplomat cofounded the ASEAN Regional Forum (ARF), the prime platform for strategic dialogue among all relevant powers, including Russia, China, the United States, Japan, and India, in the Asia-Pacific region. Between 1995 and 1997, China regularly held annual meetings with senior ASEAN officials and successfully advocated for the establishment of the "ASEAN+3" initiative, which brought the three historically hostile powers of Japan, (South) Korea and China together under the umbrella of the ASEAN-related platform. China also became the first major power to finalize a free trade agreement with the ASEAN. China's prestige among its neighbors, particularly in Southeast Asia, was further boosted during the 1997 Asian Financial Crisis, which wrecked havoc across emerging markets of the region as well as undermined confidence in America and the IFIs of World Bank and the International Monetary Fund (IMF). While America refused to rescue troubled Asian economies, which, under Washington's influence, opened up their financial sector to Western hot money, the IFIs failed to adopt effective measures during the crisis and, subsequently, imposed onerous structural adjustment programs across multiple Southeast Asian nations in its aftermath. In contrast, China not only refused to opportunistically revalue its currency and adjusting its interest rates, in order to attract equity investors fleeing collapsing East Asian markets, but also emerged as an enthusiastic supporter of a regional—rather than Western-dominated—multilateral institutions to avoid another financial catastrophe as well as aid post-crisis economies of the region.[38]

---

[38] See for instance Anderson (1998), Stiglitz (2003), and Goh (2014).

To the delight of its neighbors, Beijing supported the establishment of an Asian Monetary Fund as well as information-sharing and currency-swap arrangements to hedge against future financial crises. China also contributed to the IMF's aid package to postcrisis Thailand. Its highly constructive, if not "altruistic" role, during the crisis, won praise from across the world, including the Clinton administration, which invited China to attend the G8 finance ministers' meeting in 1998 as an honorary guest. The Asian Financial Crisis was a crucial boost to China's regional standing, because (i) it undermined confidence in Washington's pro-financial liberalization prescriptions and (ii) damaged Japan's reputation as the anchor of East Asian economy, the de facto regional economic hegemon then. Tokyo's decision to devalue its currency at the height of the crisis was seen as both irresponsible and even opportunistic. In the preceding decades, Japan, under the so-called "flying geese" phenomenon, became the core element of an elaborate, ever-expanding network of vertically integrated regional production chain. Through bilateral agreements and Japan-dominated Asian Development Bank (ADB), Japan also became the key source of infrastructure development across Asia. As Benedict Anderson explains: "Beginning in the Fifties, thanks to a series of war reparations agreements whereby Japan provided substantial funds to South-East Asian countries for the purchase of its manufactures, Tokyo's economic presence rapidly increased ... By the early Seventies, Japan had become the single most important external investor in the region, both as extractor of natural resources (timber, oil and so on) and in industrial and infrastructural development."[39]

By the turn of the century, however, Japan's reputation as the regional economic hegemon was in tatters, already struggling with a two-decades-long economic stagnation after the bubble burst of the 1980s. In contrast, China was now seen as the emerging, responsible regional leader. In 2003, barely five years after the Asian Financial Crisis, China and the ASEAN signed a strategic partnership agreement, cementing Beijing's new status as a trusted power in the Asian pecking order. Over the next decade, China–ASEAN trade expanded by more than sixfold, reaching US$400 billion in 2012, with two-way investments exceeding US$100 billion.[40]

[39]Anderson (1998).
[40]Parameswaran (2013).

Yet, China's diplomatic proactiveness, facilitated by a new generation of Western-trained and proficient diplomatic corps, extended to the more contentious Northeast Asian region. Cognizant of the absence of significant political integration among Japan, two Korea, and China, the leadership in Beijing encouraged greater participation in track 1.5 arrangements such as the Northeast Asia Cooperation Dialogue (NEACD). This was followed by China's central role in setting up the Six Party Talks, which brought all relevant powers together with North Korea in order to manage, if not resolve, the crisis in the Korea Peninsula. China also expanded its global profile by becoming a cofounder of the transcontinental Asia-Europe Meeting (ASEM), hosted the ninth Asia-Pacific Economic Cooperation summit in Shanghai (2001), and explored new avenues of cooperation with the European Union (EU) and the North Atlantic Treaty Organization (NATO). The hyperactive diplomatic push allowed China to simultaneously (i) enhance its profile in its immediate neighborhood, (ii) deepen ties with key regions, and (iii) drive a wedge between America and its allies, both in Europe and Asia, which welcomed China's charm offensive with gusto. By 2005, Malaysia hosted the inaugural East Asia Summit, which was seen as a Beijing-led effort to exclude America from the region, with Kuala Lumpur seeking to keep Washington out of regional groupings amid growing schism between the Bush administration and regional states amid the GWOT. In a strange twist of events, China was now seen by a growing number of nations as a credible alternative to and indispensable check on American hegemony.[41]

Toward the end of the Jiang administration, China began to present itself as a responsible global power. This new self-conception was expressed through supporting peacekeeping operations in various conflict zones, including in Congo and East Timor, and support for, among other international agreements, the UN Security Council Resolution 1441, which authorized weapons inspections and disarmament in Saddam's Iraq in 2002. China also ratified the Treaty on the Nonproliferation of Nuclear Weapons as well as the Chemical Weapons Convention. Earlier, despite its strategic nuclear inferiority to Russia and America, Beijing also signed up to Comprehensive Nuclear Test Ban Treaty (1996) and basic principles of the Missile Technology Control

---

[41] Shirk (2008, 120).

Regime. Beijing also became the convener of the Six-Party Talk to address the North Korean nuclear threat, and, over the years, China even censured and penalized its ally in Pyongyang.[42] During the early years of the Hu administration, China participated in US-organized joint naval exercise in the Sea of Japan aimed at preventing the spread of nuclear weapons.[43] Under the "new security" concept, forwarded by strategic minds within the increasingly influential and professionalized Chinese MOFA, China emphasized "mutual trust, mutual benefit, equality, and cooperation" as the basic operating principles of the country's foreign policy.[44]

Power to the Moderates The period saw the MOFA countering more hardline voices within the bureaucracy and the PLA, which advocated a more muscular and non-compromising position vis-à-vis China's territorial and strategic disputes overseas (Feigenbaum and Ma 2013). The Jiang administration largely sided with the reformist and pragmatic voices, including the MOFA, in order to gain the goodwill of neighbors, including newly emerging post-soviet states, and enhance China's standing in the international system. This was no easy feat, since China has had among the world's most contested borders. The country has six maritime neighbors and fourteen continental neighbors, not to mention a decades-long standoff with what it views as the "renegade province" of Taiwan. Yet, the Jiang administration, and to a lesser degree its successor, deftly dealt with this massive territorial conundrum.

As Taylor Fravel explains in his seminal work, *Strong Borders, Secure Nation,* the Jiang administration patiently and skillfully resolved seventeen border disputes, even if it meant yielding 1.3 million square miles of land along its continental brooders.[45] During Jiang's rule, Beijing settled border conflicts with post-Soviet nations of Kyrgyzstan, Tajikistan, and Kazakhstan as well as Russia, not to mention with Southeast Asian neighbors of Vietnam and Laos. In most cases, China abandoned as much as 50% of its original claim. In the case of Tajikistan, China settled for only 1000 out of 28,000 square kilometers of contested land areas in the Pamir Mountains (though the eventual deal was signed under suspicious

---

[42] See Medeiros and Fravel (2003), Shirk (2008), and Kurlantzick (2008).
[43] Shirk (2008, 122).
[44] Ibid., 128.
[45] Fravel (2008).

circumstances that will be discussed in next chapter).[46] As long-time Moscow-based corresponded Jonathan Steele explains: "Until the early 1990s Soviet Central Asia was hermetically sealed from China ... When Central Asia unexpectedly became independent, Beijing and the three republics that have borders with China built on these foundations and border treaties were concluded within a decade. Although Mao had argued that the nineteenth-century tsarist treaties, which set the borders, were 'unequal,' his successors accepted a deal that left 57 per cent of the territory China had claimed in Kazakh hands. In Tajikistan China took only 3 per cent of what it had asked for..." But China's charm offensive wasn't only limited to land borders of post-Soviet Central Asian countries and communist regimes in Southeast Asia.[47] In 2002, as the Jiang administration relinquished some levers of power (with the exception of the [CMC]) to the incoming leader, Hu Jintao, China signed up to Declaration on the Conduct of Parties in the South China Sea (DOC). The agreement, with Southeast Asian claimant states, namely Malaysia, Brunei, the Philippines and Vietnam, called upon all claimant states to resolve their disputes through peaceful dialogue instead of coercive and unilateral action. Over the succeeding years, China proposed maritime "joint development" agreements as well as confidence-building measures with other claimant states. Among the agreements were maritime delimitation in the Gulf of Tonkin (2002) with Vietnam and the 2005 Joint Maritime Seismic Undertaking with the Philippines and Vietnam. The period also saw China reaching out to other regional great powers, particularly Russia and China. The Shanghai Cooperation Organization (SCO), established in 2001, served as a crucial mechanism to manage Sino-Russian influence and strategic competition in post-Soviet Central Asia. In effect, Beijing established a condominium, if not a full-fledged co-dominion, with Moscow. It was China's proactive strategic engagement with Russia that paved the way for a new age of cooperation between the two former rivals, which almost went to war in the 1960s, not to mention centuries of Czarist conflict with Imperial China. Except, the Sino-Russia balance of power now increasingly favored the former junior partner, China.[48] The upshot of this carefully crafted diplomatic

---

[46] See Medeiros and Fravel (2003) and Steele (2013).

[47] Steele (2013).

[48] See Kotkin (2009) and Stokes (2017).

approach was a stable strategic partnership after centuries of rivalry. As Fu Ying, a veteran Chinese diplomat and Chair of the Foreign Affairs Committee of the National People's Congress, explains:

> The Chinese-Russian relationship is a stable strategic partnership and by no means a marriage of convenience: it is complex, sturdy, and deeply rooted. Changes in international relations since the end of the Cold War have only brought the two countries closer together...Beijing hopes that China and Russia can maintain their relationship in a way that will provide a safe environment for the two big neighbors to achieve their development goals and to support each other through mutually beneficial cooperation, offering a model for how major countries can manage their differences and cooperate in ways that strengthen the international system.[49]

Bridging differences with India, however, proved more daunting (see Chapter 7), thanks to the bitter memories of the 1962 border war, the historical rivalry within the global "Third World" movement, China's strategic alliance with Pakistan (India's archrival), as well as minimal economic engagement between the two Asian giants back then. As late as 2000, Sino-Indian bilateral trade was only US$3 billion, with no direct flights between Beijing and New Delhi until 2002.[50] By the end of the first decade of the twenty-first century, however, China became India's top trading partner, with two-way exchanges inching to the US$100 billion mark in 2015.[51] In addition to the SCO, China also established the Conference on Interaction and Confidence-Building Measures in Asia (CICA), which includes both Russia and China as its key members, while excluding Western powers as well as Japan. China's overall goal was to enhance its own "soft power." As American political scientist Joseph Nye argues, soft power is anchored by the recognition that "it is also important to set the agenda and attract others in world politics, and not only force them to change by threatening military force or economic sanctions."[52] By enmeshing regional powers in China-led networks of cooperation, Beijing hoped to not only protect its core interests, but also, even more ambitiously, orient its broader Eurasian neighborhood along its strategic preferences. As China enhanced its

---

[49] Ying (2015).
[50] Shirk (2008, 115–116).
[51] Krishnan (2011).
[52] Nye (2004, 5).

military muscle amid an economic boom, it sought greater influence internationally where persuasion, rather coercion, serves as the primary tool of foreign policy. In a keynote speech to the 17th National Congress of the Communist Party of China (CPC) in 2007, Chinese President Hu Jintao declared, "Culture has become a more and more important source of national cohesion and creativity and a factor of growing significance in the competition in overall national strength." The Chinese leader called on his country to "enhance culture as part of the soft power of [China] to better guarantee the people's basic cultural rights and interests."[53]

Yet, the Hu administration harbored no illusions vis-à-vis the limits of China's soft power and the exigencies of *realpolitik* in the international system. With greater economic resources came the early intimations of geopolitical assertiveness. Against this backdrop, the Hu administration also introduced "new historic missions" for its burgeoning military, including the protection of the country's ever-expanding trade linkages and supply lines, especially in the maritime space. Thus, the combination of expanding energy needs and trade linkages organically spurred a more assertive and capable Chinese maritime fleet operating across the Eurasian rimland (Kennedy 2010).[54] This marked the birth of China as a maritime power, as the Asian powerhouse broke out of its centuries-old continental geopolitical orientation amid (i) improved ties with land-based neighbors, (ii) rapidly growing naval capabilities, and (iii) the globalization of China's state-owned companies, and (iv) China's self reexamination as an increasingly global power. It was precisely against this backdrop of dialectically evolving Chinese role in the world, and its conception of itself and its interests, that Xi came to power and, shortly after, launched his twenty-first-century Silk Road initiative. The dragon was now awakened.

REFERENCES

Allison, Graham. *Destined for War: Can America and China Escape Thucydides's Trap*. Boston: Houghton Mifflin Harcourt, 2017.
Anderson, Benedict. "From Miracle to Crash." *London Review of Books* 20, no. 8 (1998): 3–7. https://www.lrb.co.uk/v20/n08/benedict-anderson/from-miracle-to-crash.

---

[53] Xinhua (2007).
[54] Kaplan (2013).

Andreas, Joel. "Sino-seismology." *New Left Review* 76 (2012). https://newlef-treview.org/issues/II76/articles/joel-andreas-sino-seismology.

Appelbaum, Binyamin. "A Little-Noticed Fact About Trade: It's No Longer Rising." *The New York Times*. October 30, 2016. https://www.nytimes.com/2016/10/31/upshot/a-little-noticed-fact-about-trade-its-no-longer-rising.html.

Braudel, Fernand. *A History of Civilizations*.New York: Penguin Books, 1993.

Brzezinski, Zbigniew. *The Grand Chessboard: American Primacy and Its Geostrategic Imperatives*. New York: Basic Books, 1998.

Cardenas, Kenneth. "Duterte's China Deals, Dissected." *Philippine Center for Investigative Journalism*. May 8, 2017. https://pcij.org/stories/dutertes-china-deals-dissected/.

China Council for International Cooperation on Environment and Development. *Important Speech of Xi Jinping at Peripheral Diplomacy Work Conference*. October 30, 2013. http://www.cciced.net/cciceden/NEWSCENTER/LatestEnvironmentalandDevelopmentNews/201310/t20131030_82626.html.

China Daily. "Hu Urges Enhancing 'soft power' of Chinese culture." China Daily, 2007. http://www.chinadaily.com.cn/china/2007-10/15/content_6226620.htm.

Chua, Amy. *Day of Empire: How Hyperpowers Rise to Global Dominance—And Why They Fall*. New York: Anchor, 2009.

Economy, Elizabeth. *The Third Revolution: Xi Jinping and the New Chinese State*. Oxford: Oxford University Press, 2018.

Economy, Elizabeth, and Michael Levi. *By All Means Necessary: How China's Resource Quest is Changing the World*, 1st edition. Oxford: Oxford University Press, 2014.

Feigenbaum, Evan, and Damien Ma. "The Rise of China's Reformers?" *Foreign Affairs*. April 17, 2013. https://www.foreignaffairs.com/articles/china/2013-04-17/rise-chinas-reformers.

Frankopan, Peter. *The Silk Roads: A New History of the World*. New York: Vintage Books, 2017.

Fravel, M. Taylor. *Strong Borders, Secure Nation: Cooperation and Conflict in China's Territorial Disputes*. Princeton University Press, 2008. http://www.jstor.org/stable/j.ctt7s2s6.

French, Howard. *China's Second Continent: How a Million Migrants Are Building a New Empire in Africa*. New York: Knopf, 2014.

"Full Text of President Xi's Speech at Opening of Belt and Road Forum." *Xinhua*. May 14, 2017. http://www.xinhuanet.com/english/2017-05/14/c_136282982.htm.

Goh, Evelyn. *The Struggle for Order: Hegemony, Hierarchy, and Transition in Post-Cold War East Asia*. Oxford: Oxford University Press, 2014.

Goldstone, Jack. "Understanding the Revolutions of 2011." *Foreign Affairs.* April 14, 2011. https://www.foreignaffairs.com/articles/middle-east/2011-04-14/understanding-revolutions-2011.

Hegel, Georg Wilhelm Friedrich. "Hegel's Philosophy of History." 1837. Retrieved May 8, 2019. https://www.marxists.org/reference/archive/hegel/works/hi/history3.htm.

Hillman, Jonathan. "Is China Making a Trillion-Dollar Mistake?" *The Washington Post.* April 9, 2018. https://www.washingtonpost.com/news/theworldpost/wp/2018/04/09/one-belt-one-road/.

Holmes, James, and Toshi Yoshihara. "Is China Planning String of Pearls." *The Diplomat.* February 21, 2011. https://thediplomat.com/2011/02/is-china-planning-string-of-pearls/.

Jacobs, Sarah. "12 Eerie Photos of Enormous Chinese Cities Completely Empty of People." *Business Insider.* October 4, 2017. https://www.businessinsider.com.au/these-chinese-cities-are-ghost-towns-2017-4?r=US&IR=T#/#when-caemmerer-found-out-about-these-empty-cities-he-was-immediately-fascinated-as-an-architectural-photographer-i-found-the-notion-of-a-contemporary-ghost-town-to-be-appealing-in-a-sort-of-unsettling-way-he-said-1.

Kaplan, Robert. "The Geography of Chinese Power." *Foreign Affairs.* May 1, 2010. https://www.foreignaffairs.com/articles/china/2010-05-01/geography-chinese-power.

Kaplan, Robert. *The Return of Marco Polo's World: War, Strategy, and American Interests in the Twenty-First Century.* New York: Random House, 2018.

Kaplan, Robert. *The Revenge of Geography: What the Map Tells Us About Coming Conflicts and the Battle Against Fate.* New York: Penguin Random House, 2013.

Kennedy, Andrew. "Rethinking Energy Security in China." *East Asia Forum.* June 6, 2010. https://www.eastasiaforum.org/2010/06/06/rethinking-energy-security-in-china/.

Kissinger, Henry. *On China.* New York: Penguin, 2011.

Kissinger, Henry. *On China.* London: Penguin Books, 2012.

Krishnan, Ananth. "India-China Trade Surpasses Target." *The Hindu.* January 27, 2011. https://www.thehindu.com/news/international/India-China-trade-surpasses-target/article15535404.ece.

Kotkin, Stephen. "The Unbalanced Triangle." *Foreign Affairs.* September/October 2009 Issue. https://www.foreignaffairs.com/reviews/review-essay/unbalanced-triangle.

Kurtlantzick, Joshua. *Charm Offensive: How China's Soft Power Is Transforming the World.* New Haven: Yale University Press, 2008.

Li, Nan. *Chinese Civil-Military Relations in the Post-Deng Era. Implications for Crisis Management and Naval Modernization.* Newport: U.S. Naval War College, 2010.

Mearsheimer, John. "Can China Rise Peacefully." *The National Interest*. October 25, 2014. https://nationalinterest.org/commentary/can-china-rise-peacefully-10204.

Medeiros, Evan, and Taylor Fravel. "China's New Diplomacy." *Foreign Affairs*. November 1, 2003. https://www.foreignaffairs.com/articles/asia/2003-11-01/chinas-new-diplomacy.

Millward, James. "Is China a Colonial Power." *The New York Times*. May 4, 2018. https://www.nytimes.com/2018/05/04/opinion/sunday/china-colonial-power-jinping.html.

Moriyasu, Ken. "China Needs to 'Purchase' Friendships, Scholar Says." *Nikkei Asian Review*. March 2, 2015. https://asia.nikkei.com/NAR/Articles/China-needs-to-purchase-friendships-scholar-says.

Nye, Joseph. *Soft Power: The Means to Success in World Politics*. New York: PublicAffairs, 2004.

Osnos, Evan. "Born Red." *The New Yorker*. March 30, 2015. https://www.newyorker.com/magazine/2015/04/06/born-red.

Parameswaran, Prashanth. "Beijing Unveils New Strategy for ASEAN–China Relations." *China Brief* 13, no. 21 (2013). https://jamestown.org/program/beijing-unveils-new-strategy-for-asean-china-relations/.

Ramo, Joshua. "Beijing Consensus." *The Foreign Policy Centre*. November 5, 2004. http://www.xuanju.org/uploadfile/200909/20090918021638239.pdf.

Sharma, Ruchir. "Breakout Nations: In Pursuit of the Next Economic Miracles." New York: W. W. Norton, 2012.

Shim, Elizabeth. "China Plans Underwater AI Base in South China Sea." *United Press International*. November 26, 2018. https://www.upi.com/China-plans-underwater-AI-base-in-South-China-Sea/1891543261199/.

Shirk, Susan. *China: Fragile Superpower*. Oxford: Oxford University Press, 2008.

Shirk, Susan. "China in Xi's 'New Era': The Return to Personalistic Rule." *Journal of Democracy* 29, no. 2 (2018). https://www.journalofdemocracy.org/articles/china-in-xis-new-era-the-return-to-personalistic-rule/.

Steele, Jonathan. "What Does China Want." *London Review of Books* 35, no. 20 (2013): 33–34. https://www.lrb.co.uk/v35/n20/jonathan-steele/what-does-china-want.

Stiglitz, Joseph. *Globalization and Its Discontents*. New York: Norton Paperback, 2003.

Stokes, Jacob. "Russia and China's Enduring Alliance." *Foreign Affairs*. February 22, 2017. https://www.foreignaffairs.com/articles/china/2017-02-22/russia-and-china-s-enduring-alliance.

Xi, Jinping. "Promote Friendship Between Our People and Work Together to Build a Bright Future." Speech, Nazarbayev University. September 7, 2013. *Ministry of Foreign Affairs of the People's Republic of China*. https://www.fmprc.gov.cn/mfa_eng/wjdt_665385/zyjh_665391/t1078088.html.

Ying, Fu. "How China Sees Russia." *Foreign Affairs*. December 14, 2015. https://www.foreignaffairs.com/articles/china/2015-12-14/how-china-sees-russia.

CHAPTER 5

The Belt and Road: China as the New Vanguard of Globalization

China is a sleeping giant. Let her sleep, for when she wakes she will move the world.[1] —Napoleon Bonaparte

The Euphrates, Tigris, and Oxus would be bitter
    As the salty sea, if they were not flowing.[2] —Jalal al-Din Rumi, 13th century Sufi poet along the Silk Road

[W]e should build the Belt and Road into a road connecting different civilizations. —Xi Jinping, the 2017 Belt and Road Forum for International Cooperation[3]

On May 14, 2017, Beijing launched the so-called "Belt and Road Initiative," previously known as the New Silk Road project and often also called as the BRI.[4] During the summit of global leaders, President Xi Jinping opened up the mega-event as the keynote speaker before leaders from as many as 28 nations, who were more than eager to tap into Chinese infrastructure development largesse. "We have no intention

---

[1] *Philippine Daily Inquirer* (2016).
[2] Gooch (2017, 53).
[3] Xinhua (2017, May).
[4] Aljazeera (2017).

© The Author(s) 2020
R. J. Heydarian, *The Indo-Pacific: Trump, China, and the New Struggle for Global Mastery*, https://doi.org/10.1007/978-981-13-9799-8_5

to form a small group detrimental to stability," the Chinese leader said during his keynote speech. "What we hope to create is a big family of harmonious co-existence."[5] At its very core, the event served as the chief register for China's new role in the international economic system and, more personally, Xi's emergence as a global leader. And the timing couldn't be any more perfect, given America's abrupt withdrawal from its historical role as the anchor of the global free trade regime.

Under President Donald Trump, Washington has adopted a neo-isolationist, unilateralist, anti-free trade "America First" foreign policy. Under Trump's watch, the historical anchor of the liberal international order abruptly reneged on the Paris Agreement on climate change, the Asia-Pacific-wide mega-free trade Transpacific Partnership Agreement (TPP) negotiations, and the Iranian nuclear deal—the three chief foreign policy initiatives of the Obama administration. The upshot was a global leadership vacuum. And China wasted no time in exploiting the historic opportunity. Earlier that year, as Trump began to assume office, Xi made the unprecedented decision of becoming the first Chinese head of state to attend the World Economic Forum at Davos, which annually brings together the world's economic and liberal policy-making elite. "Just blaming economic globalization for the world's problems is inconsistent with reality," declared Xi in his high-profile speech at Davos, indirectly attacking the protectionist, anti-trade rhetoric of the American president.[6] Though the purported leader of the world's largest and most powerful communist nation, he described globalization as a historically inevitability, a "big ocean that you cannot escape from," while criticizing protectionism as "locking oneself in a dark room."[7] In effect, the Chinese communist leader daringly presented himself as the new vanguard of globalization. Yet, this was more out of timely self-interest rather than vacuous rhetorical bombast. After all, China has arguably been the biggest beneficiary of globalization, which has allowed the communist nation to, within a single generation, lift 400 million citizens out of poverty, while transforming an agricultural backwater into the world's leading manufacturing power. In short, globalization has been the bedrock of China's economic miracle. Later that year, during the

[5] For full speech see Xinhua (2017).
[6] Stone (2018).
[7] For the full speech see CGTN (2017).

APEC summit in Da Nang (Vietnam), Xi described globalization as an "irreversible historical trend."[8] He advocated for an inclusive "multilateral trading regime and practice," which allows "developing members to benefit more from international trade and investment."

In stark contrast, Trump, during his first visit to Asia, emphasized bilateralism, and fair trade, while lambasting globalization as inimical to the interests of nations.[9] Through the BRI, which Xi has dubbed as "the project of the century," not only does China reiterate its commitment to globalization, but it will also place the Asian powerhouse in the position to shape the post-American international economic order. Over the coming decade, China is expected to invest up to $5 trillion[10] in transcontinental infrastructure projects, which will connect the country's industrial heartland to the world's largest consumer markets in Western Europe. The mega-project is slated to cover as many as 64 nations across four continents (Asia, Australia, Africa, and Europe), accounting for 62% of the world's population and about a third of the global Gross Domestic Product.[11]

Anatomy of a New Empire

The "belt" pertains to the "Silk Road Economic Belt," which runs through the post-soviet states of Central Asia, and West Asian powers of Iran and Turkey, then East-Central Europe all the way to the shores of Netherlands, while the "road" pertains to "Maritime Silk Road" (MSR), which starts from southern Chinese provinces of Fujian right through Southeast Asia, extending to South Asia and Western and North Africa then cutting through the Mediterranean to Europe. Since the launching of the BRI, Chinese companies have been, in accordance to the emerging architecture of the MSR, operating strategic port facilities from Piraeus in Greece to Darwin in Australia. Under the BRI, Chinese companies have been involved in the construction and operation of 42 ports across more than 30 nations. Chinese companies such as China

---

[8] *The Hindu* (2017).

[9] BBC News (2017).

[10] Depending on sources, the figure ranges from as low as $1.3 trillion to $8 trillion. Yet, the $5 seems as a more reasonable upper-limit, since the larger figures have yet to be reflected in China's own documents and pronouncements.

[11] Van der Leer and Yau (2016).

Merchants Group and China Ocean Shipping Company (COSCO) have been at the center of this "going global" strategy, which is transforming international maritime commerce.[12] The maps are flexible, a cornerstone of Chinese statecraft, and the number of participating nations could expand or contract over coming years. Similar to the ancient Silk Road, the BRI aims to connect East Asia to Europe via Central Asia and the Middle East. There are also several "economic corridors," with north-south orientation. The $46 billion China-Pakistan Economic Corridor, which crosses southward from the western Chinese promise of Xinjiang all the way through the Baluchistan Province and ending in the port of Gwadar in the Indian Ocean, is the most prominent and prized one. The Bangladesh, China, India, Myanmar (BCIM) Economic Corridor aims to bring about development to other western and southwestern provinces, connecting them to major maritime routes in the Indian Ocean.

It's more than just rhetoric. To prove its determination to realize the BRI vision, China has set up an initial $40 billion Silk Road Fund, with an additional $50 to be provided by the Beijing-based Asian Infrastructure Investment Bank (AIIB). In 2016, the AIIB approved $1.7 billion in loans to nine projects under the BRI. During the BRI summit in Beijing, Xi pledged another US$113 billion, with Chinese policy banks (e.g., China Development Bank, Bank of China, Export-Import Bank of China, The Industrial and Commercial Bank of China, etc.) expected to shoulder up to $1.3 trillion in investments over the coming years. Half-a-trillion dollars worth of projects and mergers and acquisitions (M&A) deals were announced in 2016 across seven infra-structure projects,[13] a third of them within China. Between 2013 to mid-2017, about 50 major Chinese state-owned enterprises were involved in about 1700 BRI-related projects.[14]

The China Development Bank (CDB) alone has been overseeing operations across 60 nations, where as many as 900 projects worth around $890 billion is at stake. The Industrial and Commercial Bank of China (ICBC) is evaluating up to 130 BRI-related projects worth about US$159 billion, while the Bank of China (BOC) pledged around $100

---

[12] Suokas (2018).
[13] Wong et al. (2017).
[14] Huang (2017).

billion between 2016 and 2018 alone.[15] The Xi administration has also established an elaborate, high-level bureaucratic structure to oversee the BRI vision. The Chinese president placed first-ranked Vice-Premier Zhang Gaoli, a member of Politburo Standing Committee (2012–2017), atop the BRI-focused bureaucracy, which includes heavyweights such as Vice-Premiere Wang Yang and chief foreign policy hand Yang Jiechi. The aim is to involve high-ranking officials from across the Chinese state apparatus in order to give a coordinated, comprehensive, and sustained momentum to the grand project. Xi has designated three agencies to coordinate the overall project, namely the Ministry of Foreign Affairs, Ministry of Commerce, and the National Development and Reform Commission. The BRI's first official blueprint was issued in March 2015, entitled "Vision and Actions on Jointly Building Silk Road Economic Belt and 21st Century Maritime Silk Road."[16]

The Economic Logic

The plethora of names attached to the transcontinental project reflects the inherently flexible, if not ambiguous, nature of the BRI project. Yet, as China analyst Peter Cai explains, "some of the key drivers behind BRI are largely motivated by China's pressing economic concerns."[17] China's economic troubles began shortly before Xi's ascent. Thanks to a US$586 billion stimulus program, China managed to overcome the Global Financial Crisis with a massive domestic infrastructure buildup. Over the succeeding years, China became the prime engine of global economic growth. Yet, the massive fiscal expansionary program, augmented by monetary easing (i.e., reduced interest rates), created systemic stress within an already-imbalanced economy. Add to these, growing public dissatisfaction with corruption, the decadent lifestyle among the "princeling" elite, and heightened inequality within and among Chinese provinces. It was precisely within this context that Xi pushed for a massive anti-corruption initiative to boost his legitimacy, while calling for structural reforms within the Chinese economy. Domestic reforms, once again, went hand in hand with global outreach, except, this time, even

---

[15] Cai (2017).
[16] Ibid.
[17] Ibid.

with greater zeal and ambition than in the past. In this sense, Xi represents the fourth phase in Chinese foreign policy in contrast to Mao's revolutionary struggle against the West and its regional allies (phase I), Deng Xiaoping's normalization of ties with neighbors and former adversaries (phase II), and Jiang's and Hu's charm offensive across the developing world (phase III).

In his early years in power, Xi also pushed forward with establishing multiple China-led multilateral initiatives, allocating $50 billion to the Beijing-based AIIB as well as $41 billion for the Shanghai-based New Development Bank (NDB) along Brazil, Russia, and China. Together, the AIIB and the NDB are tasked to provide alternative multilateral developmental organizations to the Western- and Japanese-dominated IFIs, namely the World Bank, the IMF, and the ADB. The Xi administration also allocated close to $10 billion in annual budget for "external propaganda," eclipsing the U.S. Department of State's $666 million budget for public diplomacy in 2014.[18] The beauty of the BRI project is that it allows Xi to strike multiple birds with a single stone. The objectives of the BRI fall under two key themes: (i) internal economic rebalancing and (ii) expansion of strategic presence across resource-rich and geographically important nations.

I. *Internal Economic Rebalancing.* The BRI is about accommodating China's domestic interest groups, namely the State-Owned Enterprises (SOEs) and national champions as well as policy banks; combating international economic contractions and geographic inequalities, and the need to sustain rapid economic growth as China confronts structural challenges that could lead to a "middle income trap."

A. *Facilitate China's long-term plans of developing landlocked hinterlands and underdeveloped regions.* As early as the Jiang administration, the Chinese regime launched the "western development strategy" (WDS) aimed at closing the developmental gap between underperforming hinterlands and high-performing coastal regions. Yet, despite massive injection of central government funds and a slew of preferential policies, the peripheral western regions contribution to Chinese GDP barely increased from 17.1% in 2000 to 18.7% a decade later (Cai 2017). Despite Beijing's preferential policies, large-scale fiscal injections, and state-directed investments, the western provinces' share of China's

---

[18]Shambaugh (2015).

total GDP increased only marginally from 17.1% in 2000 to 18.7% in 2010. In national economic rankings, the western, landlocked provinces and regions of Tibet, Xinjiang, Qinghai, and Gansu have consistently ranked well below the national average.[19] During the Xi administration, influential Chinese scholar Wang Jisi proposed the "March West" strategy, which was both a response to the US pivot to Asia as well as a revival of the earlier WDS strategy. In 2014, the BRI plan was officially integrated into China's national economic development strategy at the Central Economic Work Conference, with BRI serving as one of the three regional development plans.[20]

China's peripheral regions with large minority population cover up to two-thirds of the country's landmass and, crucially, host the bulk of the country's natural resources. This makes them hugely significant, even if more than nine out of ten Chinese citizens hail from the so-called "Han" majority. These regions are also important from a security point of view, since provinces such as Xinjiang and Tibet, which host Uighur Muslim minorities and Tibetan Buddhists, have also been a hotbed of political resistance to the communist regime (Hilton 2015). To the Chinese state, the root of the crisis is developmental deficit rather than sociocultural alienation. The communist regime hopes to purchase the hearts and minds of its restive minorities through an infrastructure offensive, offensive, while ignoring the ideational sources of the local populations' grievances against Beijing. The China-Pakistan Economic Corridor, in particular, is a flagship project that allows China to funnel large-scale infrastructure development funds to its troubled western province. The BCIM Economic Corridor aims to bring about development in other western and southwestern regions of China. It's hard to understate the gravity of China's politico-security dilemma in places such as Xinjiang, formerly known as East Turkistan. After decades of sociocultural alienation, which includes draconian restrictions on the expression of Islamic faith among the local population, the Uighur minority has embraced a more muscular form of resistance. Beginning in 2009, Xinjiang has been hit by a spate of terror attacks and violent clashes between the Uighur minority and Han settlers. In mid-2009, violent clashes between the two groups in the regional city of Urumqi led to as many as 184 casualties and injuries. China's repressive response has strengthened the hands of

[19] Cai (2017).
[20] Ibid.

more radical groups, including the East Turkestan Islamic Movement (ETIM), which have embraced a more violent form of resistance against the communist regime. In late-2013, the violence spread to Beijing, when several ethnic Uighurs, using an SUV, ploughed through visitors at Beijing's Tiananmen Square. The following year, in March, a group of knife-wielding individuals attacked civilians in Kunming, Yunan, followed by several terrorist attacks in Xinjiang in May that year. By July, a terrorist attack killed close to hundred individuals in the province, which was followed by the murder of an Imam close to the regime.[21] In recent years, there have also been cases of self-immolation and other forms of resistance adopted by Tibetan monks in protest against cultural oppression by the communist regime.[22] Through the BRI, in addition to virtual security lockdown in certain regions, the Xi administration hopes to bring stability to its restive western regions.

B. *Outsource internal productive glut and infrastructure overcapacity amid slowdown in global demand for its exports.* China simply has too much steel, cement, and infrastructure-related productive capacity that can't be absorbed domestically. And this all goes back to the unsustainable economic growth and stimulus programs it adopted in the past two decades. Back in the 1990s, China was already struggling with one of the highest rates of nonperforming loans in the world, which reached as high as 50%.[23] In the three years following the Global Financial Crisis, the Chinese banking system, controlled by the state, unleashed around US$4 trillion in new credit, expanded overall liquidity to US$10 trillion, around 20% larger than that of America. Much of the new credit was funneled into speculative sectors, including the real estate, which saw, in 2010 alone, more sales than the rest of the world combined. Others were invested in public infrastructure projects, which provided (temporary) economic reprieve though.[24] Inflation rates experienced a ten-fold increase in the 2009–2010 fiscal year, as real estate prices experienced bubble-like increase at the expense of middle-class families, whose earning barely kept up with inflation. Add to these, countless ghost cities, airports, roads, and railways across the country—infrastructure projects that ended up as elephant projects simply because their primary objective

[21] Rauhala (2014).
[22] Spegele (2012).
[23] Walker and Buck (2007).
[24] Sharma (2012, 24).

was creation of countercyclical growth in the immediate aftermath of the Great Recession.[25] To put things into perspective China's excess capacity, the steel industry's annual production surged from 512 million tons in 2008 to 803 million tons in 2015, with the extra 300 million tons outstripping the combined production of the entire European Union and the United States. Similar levels of excess capacity are seen in the cement industry.[26] In short, China desperately needs to address over-investment and overconstruction at home. In fact, the problem is so severe that China is considering not only exporting its excess production, but also the very production facilities themselves. In 2014, Chinese premier Li Keqiang, in a speech in Myanmar, the then ASEAN chairman, announced: "We have a lot of surplus equipment for making steel, cement and pleat glass for the Chinese market. This equipment is of good quality. We want companies to move this excess production capacity through direct foreign investment to ASEAN countries who need to build their infrastructure. These goods should be produced locally where they are needed."[27] China aims to export some of its heavy industry and low-end manufacturing production facilities to less industrialized neighboring countries. The Xi administration seeks to do this by tying together productive capacity and excess production under BRI-related projects, including construction of steel, railways, ports and highways across the Eurasian region, which hosts much of the world's emerging markets with heavy infrastructure needs.

C. *Assist and promote troubled State-Owned Enterprises (SOEs), which employ tens of millions of workers, through provision of lucrative projects overseas.* This is both a matter of strengthening national champions as well as preserving domestic order, the highest priority of the communist regime. The last time China oversaw a major overhaul of its SOEs, which led to the unemployment of as many as 60 million individuals, it sowed the seeds of political unrest throughout the 1980s, culminating in nationwide protests in 1989, most famously in the Tiananmen Square.[28] In recent years, China has had to layoff up to 1.8 million workers form the steel and coal industries due to excess capacity

[25] Jacobs (2017).
[26] Cai (2017).
[27] Ibid.
[28] Andreas (2012).

and production glut.[29] The transport equipment market across the BRI-covered regions was close to $263 billion in 2018 alone.[30] Almost 90% of BRI contracts have gone to Chinese SOEs.[31]

D. *By developing trading partners' basic infrastructure, China will also be able to reverse anemic growth in global trade by enhancing the absorption capacity of export markets in the emerging world.* This is crucial in light of the fact that the year 2016 saw, for the first time in recent memory, global trade stagnating.[32] Between 2007 and 2014, China's GDP growth halved, from a high of 14% to just above 7%. China hopes to achieve a global trade uptick through successfully deepening its hard infrastructure connection to BRI-covered nations as well as export its production capacity to less developed nations.[33]

II. *Enhancement of China's Global Influence.* Yet, the BRI is far from a purely economic enterprise. Its deep geopolitical underpinnings are reflected in the sheer breadth of its land-based as well as maritime blueprint. In fact, it's in the maritime portion of the BRI, where geopolitics is most alive and kicking. And this is crucial since the bulk of global trade is still carried through maritime trade, despite massive technological advancements that have promised to shrink trade and communication in time and space.[34]

While China's land-based linkages run through relatively friendly countries in Central (Russia and post-Soviet states), South (Pakistan and Afghanistan) and West (Iran and Turkey) Asia, the Eurasian rimland, stretching from the South China Sea and the Indian Ocean to the Persian Gulf and the Mediterranean, present a completely divergent geopolitical reality. The United States and its allies—along with key strategic partners such as India, Singapore, and the Gulf Cooperation Council—have dominated all these maritime routes since the end of Second World War. At least, this has been the perception of Chinese strategic planners, who have feared the prospect of US-led maritime encirclement and siege in an event of deeper Sino-American rivalry in the decades

[29] Cai (2017).
[30] Ibid.
[31] Hurley et al. (2018).
[32] Appelbaum (2016).
[33] Cai (2017).
[34] Kaplan (2013).

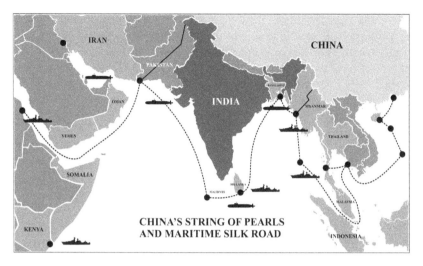

Fig. 5.1 China's "string of pearls" expanding Indo-Pacific footprint

ahead. Add to this, the more brutal reality of China's growing dependence on energy imports. From 2000 to 2008, the increase in the country's energy needs were so explosive that it now accounts for more than half of the world's total growth in energy demands. The period also saw China ending up consuming 10% of global oil, which is largely imported from the Persian Gulf region via the Indian Ocean, the Malacca Strait, and the South China Sea.[35] China's growing dependence on international imports of basic commodities has reinforced its sense of maritime vulnerability. Recognizing China's maritime vulnerability, and evermore confident with its land borders, the Hu administration placed the development of the PLA Navy's (PLAN) capabilities at the heart of its defense policy agenda. As Li explains: "Hu [Jintao] has been particularly concerned about China's newly emerging national interests in terms of energy security … [As early as November 2003] Hu, as the new CCP general secretary, advanced the concept of oil security, and stressed the need to develop a new energy-development strategy from a "strategic overall height" to achieve national energy security."[36] The PLAN's South Sea Fleet gained outsized attention, because "the South China Sea has

[35] Kennedy (2010).
[36] Li (2010).

potentially rich deposits of fossil fuels and natural gas and straddles major sea-lanes through the Strait of Malacca into the Indian Ocean."[37]

D. *Gain foothold across strategically located nations.* The BRI builds on the earlier efforts of the Hu administration. In order to protect China's emerging interests across maritime lanes of communications, the Hu administration steadily expanded the country's access to international ports across the Eurasian rimland. Unlike America, however, China didn't establish forward deployment bases across vast oceans, as the U.S. has done in places ranging from Hawaii and Guam to Japan and, during the Cold War, the Philippines' Subic and Clark bases. Instead, China went for a less costly and provocative alternative by instead developing as well as negotiating basing access across friendly nations across the Indian Ocean, stretching from the Seychelles, Chittagong (Bangladesh) in the east to Hambantota (Sri Lanka) and Gwadar (Pakistan) in the west (see Fig. 5.1). As Holmes and Yoshihara explain, "Beijing is negotiating agreements that grant Chinese vessels the right to call at ports like Gwadar, Hambantota, and Chittagong to rest, refuel, and perhaps refit, most likely for the purpose of laying the foundations for a hypothetical build-up of hard naval power while debating the wisdom of such an expensive, arduous, potentially hazardous course of action ... the port facilities under development in the Indian Ocean boast infrastructure that is 'clearly adequate' for military use should Beijing see the need."[38] By the second decade of the twenty-first century, China conducted massive rescue operations of its citizens in civil war-torn nations of North Africa, joined the international anti-piracy coalition in the Gulf Aden, and established its first full-fledged overseas naval base in Djibouti. What the BRI seeks to achieve is to strengthen Chinese foothold across the Indian Ocean by deepening Chinese stake and investment in ports, airports, and key infrastructure facilities in friendly Eurasian rimland nations, from Bangladesh and Sri Lanka to Pakistan and friendly Middle Eastern and West African nations.

E. *Lock in rare commodities key to Chinese long-term development.* The BRI also allows China to enhance its access to resource-rich nations in Central Asia, Middle East, Africa, and Southeast Asia. Enhanced infrastructure allows for more efficient and less costly transfer of precious minerals, food commodities, and hydrocarbon products from the

[37] Ibid.
[38] Holmes and Yoshihara (2011).

upstream in BRI-covered nations all the way to downstream Chinese consumer markets and industrial heartlands

F. *Globalize Chinese technological and industrial standards across emerging markets.* The BRI means Chinese national champions building massive infrastructure projects as well as partnering with foreign companies in production across the world. It will also help China diversify its heavily concentrated production base away from the Pearl River Delta (PRD), the manufacturing heartland of the world. The PRD, representing only 1% of the country's territory and 5% of its population, is responsible for 10% of the total GDP, quarter of total exports, and hosts a fifth of total FDI of China.[39] This means usage and diffusion of Chinese technology and engineering across the world, so that China's productive capacity, similar to Japan's, is extended beyond its immediate borders and the traditional industrial zones. Under the Internet Plus and Made in China 2025 strategies, which draw on Germany's "Industry 4.0" plan, the Asian powerhouse aims to become technologically self-sufficient as well as a global leader in cutting-edge industries. Based on the plan, China has identified 10 key sectors for national champions, namely biopharma and advanced medical products, new advanced information technology, aerospace and aeronautical equipment, automated machine tools and robotics, modern rail transport equipment, power equipment, maritime equipment and high-tech shipping, new energy vehicles and equipment, agricultural equipment and new materials. Quantitatively, China aims to raise domestic content of core components and materials from 40% by 2020 to 70% by 2025.[40] As Xi declared in a science event in May 2016, China will have to become "the world's major scientific and technological power," and it will require the state "to champion first-class institutes, research-oriented universities and innovation-oriented enterprises."[41] The initiative builds on the earlier "Go Out" or "Going Global" strategy of the Jiang administration, with the China Council for the Promotion of International Trade (CCPIT) playing a key role, which encouraged, beginning in 1999, for Chinese companies to increase their global presence, move up the value chain, and develop global brands. Pushing Chinese national champions up the value-chain is crucial to China becoming a consumer-based, service-oriented, high-tech and

---

[39] Vaitheeswaran (2017).
[40] Kennedy (2015).
[41] Reuters (2016).

innovation-driven economy. The seven objectives show how BRI is crucial to China's transformation into a comprehensive power by the middle of the century. It's Xi's road to the next stage of Chinese economic revolution and, accordingly, avoiding the much-dreaded 'middle income trap'.

GLOBALIZATION WITH CHINESE CHARACTERISTICS: BEIJING CONSENSUS 2.0

During the 19th Chinese Communist Party National Congress at the Great Hall of the People in central Beijing, Xi unveiled a two-stage national development plan. From 2020 to 2015, China will forge ahead with two 15-year development plans. The first one aims to turn China into a "moderately prosperous society" in 2035. By the middle of the century (2049), marking the 100th anniversary of the founding of the People's Republic of China (PRC), China aims to become a "great modern socialist country." At this point, the country should have achieved five objectives: (1) new heights are reached in every dimension of material, political, cultural, and ethical, social, and ecological advancement; (2) modernization of China's system and capacity for governance is achieved; (3) China has become a global leader in terms of composite national strength and international influence; (4) common prosperity for everyone is basically achieved; (5) the Chinese people enjoy happier, safer, and healthier lives. According to Xi, China has met two of three strategic goals, namely "ensuring that people's basic needs are met and that their lives are generally decent," ahead of time.[42] The final strategic goal of comprehensive modernization will be the chief focus in the three decades following the centenary of the founding of the CCP.[43] The BRI is key to China's achievement of a truly global superpower status, where the country not only wields instruments of power, but also rewrites the rules of international affairs according to its preferences and beliefs. Xi, who could remain in power for the foreseeable future, will not settle for anything less or else. The BRI means emerging countries across Asia, Africa, and Europe—and developing Oceana as well as Latin American nations may one day be included—increasingly relying on Chinese capital, engineering and, likely, even labor. Between 2000 and 2014, China

---

[42] Xinhua (2017, October).
[43] See full speech here *China Daily* (2017).

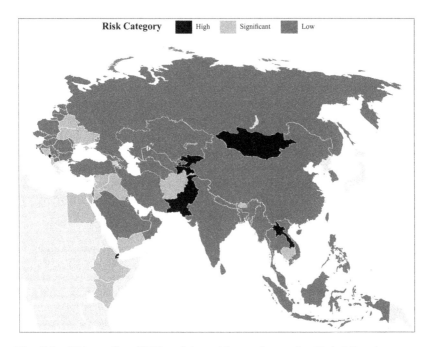

Fig. 5.2 Risk profile of BRI recipients (*Source* Center for Global Development 2018)

has invested up to $350 billion around the world, a staggering number that is expected to exponentially increase under the BRI strategy (see Fig. 5.2). Some put the final BRI tag price as high as $8 trillion.[44]

Crucially, the operationalization of the BRI means a growing proportion of the world relying on Chinese legal, regulatory and technological standards. This would make China a global cultural power, similar to where the West and Japan stand today. In fact, China is already establishing parallel international courts to oversee dispute-settlement cases vis-à-vis the BRI projects, especially in matters of debt-repayment and implementation standards.[45] The problem, however, is that,

[44]Hurley et al. (2018).
[45]Chandran (2018).

as Hurley et al. argue in an authoritative study on the BRI, "China's behavior as a creditor has not been subject to the disciplines and standards that other major sovereign and multilateral creditors have adopted collectively."[46] Now this is crucial in light of the fact that up to 33 BRI countries that are currently rated below investment grade or nonrated, while Bosnia, Belarus, and Herzegovina, Kenya and Ethiopia are at high-risk of developing unsustainable debt levels in the short-run, if they were to welcome significant BRI-related investments (see Fig. 5.2). Eight countries in particular: Tajikistan, Lao People's Democratic Republic (Laos), Kyrgyz Republic (Kyrgyzstan), Mongolia Maldives, Montenegro, and Pakistan are at high-risk of falling—or have already fallen into complete—debt trap.[47] To some critics, China is essentially engaging in "debt trap diplomacy," As Brahma Chellaney argues:

> China is using sovereign debt to bend other states to its will…states caught in debt bondage to the new imperial giant risk losing both natural assets and their very sovereignty…In exchange for financing and building the infrastructure that poorer countries need, China demands favorable access to their natural assets, from mineral resources to ports… Chinese financing can shackle its "partner" countries. Rather than offering grants or concessionary loans, China provides huge project-related loans at market-based rates, without transparency, much less environmental- or social-impact assessments.[48]

THE SHADOW OF DEBT TRAP

There is a fundamental element of transparency deficit built into China's BRI: The CDB and China Exim Bank tend not to disclose the terms of their loans, making it even difficult to trace BRI-related investments across the world, particularly in developing nations that lack institutional transparency or sufficient accountability regulations. China policy banks, the backbone of BRI's funding, tend to provide a variety of credit arrangements, ranging from fully commercial loans (Ethiopia-Djibouti railway, with upwards of 3% interest rates or more) to interest-free loans (mostly to key strategic partners such as Pakistan), with some carrying

---

[46] Hurley et al. (2018).

[47] Ibid.

[48] Chenalley (2017).

sovereign guarantees, meaning the receiving state has to cover, with tax-payers' money or/and national resources, any outstanding debt obligations. Even in cases where there is no formal sovereign guarantee, obscure and nontransparent deals with China carry such implication for incumbent governments in receiving nations. There are also concerns over foreign currency fluctuations, since Chinese loans tend to be made in Renminbi or dollars, to which the former is pegged. In fact, the Chinese regime itself fails to provide comprehensive, systematic, centralized and transparent cross-border reports of its projects. The terms of the agreements also lack transparency. In some cases, China has pushed for onerous debt-settlement measures including 80:20 debt-to-equity ratios, with financing ratios ranging from 75:25 to 80:20 (with Beijing in clear command position) (Hurley et al. 2018).

There have been several cases of debt relief, though on an ad hoc, case-by-case basis. China isn't a member of the Paris Club, the world's grouping of creditor nations, thus it doesn't abide by internationally acceptable standards of debt relief. Thus, China's debt structuring arrangements don't follow any multilateral framework on debt sustainability. In some cases, full or partial debt relief came along controversial compromises on the part of the receiving nation. In 2011, Tajikistan conceded 1158 square kilometers of disputed territory with China in exchange for debt relief. Most notoriously in the case of Sri Lanka, China demanded a 99-year lease for managing the Hambantota Port—echoing Britain's arrangement with Qing China over Hong Kong—as part of a debt-for-equity settlement in 2017. China demanded a whopping 6% interest rate on its $8 billion loan to Sri Lanka for the development of its main port. International credit rating agency Fitch recently warned that China's new Silk Road project is "driven primarily by China's efforts to extend its global influence," where "genuine infrastructure needs and commercial logic might be secondary to political motivations." In short, geopolitical considerations are embedded into the fabric of the BRI vision.[49]

Thus, the BRI could lead to the creation of elephant projects across the emerging markets, except on a far larger scale than the past. It's precisely the concerns over economic viability as well as China's aggressive, if not neo-colonialist-debt-settlement arrangements, have forced even Pakistan, a key strategic partner, as well as Myanmar and Nepal

---

[49] Reuters (2017).

to reject or reconsider major hydroelectricity projects under BRI worth close to $20 billion (Dasgupta and Pasricha 2017).[50] Chinese infrastructure projects across key Southeast Asian countries such as Thailand and Indonesia have also been hobbled by delays, concerns over quality, as well as onerous terms of agreement. In Laos, there is fear of long-term debt trap by China.[51] In Pakistan, a country that poetically describes its relations with China as "mightier than the Himalayas and deeper than the Arabian Sea," concerns over the BRI have taken a violent turn. In late 2018, gunmen targeted the Chinese consulate in Karachi. The assailants allegedly belong to Baluchi separatist movements, which vigorously oppose China's BRI projects in their Baluchistan region, especially in Gwadar, which have crowded out locals and largely benefited corrupt (Punjabi) government civilian and military elite.[52] The Balochistan Liberation Army (BLA), which claimed responsibility, described the attack as a resistance to "Chinese occupation" of their lands.[53] Seizing on the growing backlash against the BRI, the former US Secretary of State Rex Tillerson accused Beijing of "encourage[ing] dependency [by] using opaque contracts, predatory loan practices, and corrupt deals that mire nations in debt and undercut their sovereignty, denying them their long-term, self-sustaining growth...Chinese investment does have the potential to address Africa's infrastructure gap, but its approach has led to mounting debt and few, if any, jobs in most countries."[54] One country, in particular, became the poster boy for China's Beijing Consensus 2.0. Under President Rodrigo Duterte administration, the Philippines, a staunch US treaty ally, has tapped China as a major partner for national development (see Chapter 8). And this is taking place amid a historic infrastructure buildup dubbed as "Dutertenomics." Over the next decade, the government is set to embark on an ambitious $180 billion infrastructure spending bonanza, set to transform the Philippines' economy. Philippine Department of Finance (DOF) chief economist Karl Chua said in an interview with the author (February 12, 2018) that

[50] See Chenalley (2017) and Hurley et al. (2018).

[51] Cai (2017).

[52] See Chapter 5, https://www.amazon.com/s?k=Monsoon&i=stripbooks-intl-ship&ref=nb_sb_noss.

[53] https://www.theguardian.com/world/2018/nov/23/pakistan-blast-and-gunshots-heard-near-chinese-consulate.

[54] See full speech at Tillerson (2018).

the government is looking at 75 flagship projects, which include six airports, nine railways, three bus rapid transits, 32 roads and bridges, and four seaports that will help bring down the costs of production, improve rural incomes, encourage countryside investments, make the movement of goods and people more efficient, and create more jobs.[55] The government is also aiming to construct four energy facilities that will ensure stable power supply at lower prices; ten water resource projects as well as irrigation systems that will raise agricultural output; five flood control facilities that will help protect vulnerable communities as well as boost their resilience against the impact of climate change; and three redevelopment programs that will deliver sustainable solutions to best meet the needs of urban population.[56]

On one hand, infrastructure has been a major source of concern for foreign investors, who have been discouraged by the country's weak infrastructure and heavy utility costs. Those investments are crucial to create well-paying jobs for the millions of poor and unemployed Filipinos. According to an authoritative study by the Japan International Cooperation Agency (JICA), traffic congestion in Manila, caused by poor infrastructure, carried a daily price tag of P2.4 billion ($45 million) in 2012—a figure that is expected to almost triple by 2030.[57] According to the 2017 World Economic Forum's competitiveness report, the Philippines ranked 97th in the world in terms of infrastructure. In a separate report by the United Nations, the Philippines ranked 5th in Southeast Asia in terms of access to physical infrastructure.[58] Unlike his predecessors, Duterte is ditching the Public-Private-Partnership (PPP) modality in favor of larger reliance on government revenues as well as Official Development Assistance (ODA), particularly from Japan and China, as his main sources of infrastructure funding.[59] To support the new modality, Duterte has normalized relations with China, which has offered $7.3 billion in infrastructure investments, and assiduously courted Japan, which has been a leading investor in the Philippines for decades. Experts have expressed doubts over absorption capacity of

---

[55] Heydarian (2018a).
[56] Ibid.
[57] De Vera (2018).
[58] Dela Paz (2017).
[59] Heydarian (2018a).

government agencies to undertake projects competently and on time; risk of large-scale corruption and bidding anomalies affecting foreign, especially Chinese-led, projects; lack of construction workers and skilled labor; as well as growing pressure on Philippine peso and international reserves due to the need for importing intermediate goods and technology for infrastructure boom. And there is the issue of bad precedence. In the past, during the Gloria Macapagal Arroyo administration (2001–2010), China's big-ticket projects, namely the NBN-ZTE (embroiled in corruption cases) and Northrail projects (ruled unconstitutional by the Philippine Supreme Court for violation of bidding procedures), underscored the perils of Chinese investments across Southeast Asian. Critics claim that Duterte's increased reliance on China's higher-than-market-rate interest loans may drive the country into "debt bondage," similar to Sri Lanka, Venezuela, and Laos, and weaken the Philippines' delicate position in the South China Sea, where it faces continued threats to its territorial claims and maritime interests. To win Beijing's goodwill, the Filipino president, as the rotational chairman of the ASEAN in 2017, actively guarded China against any criticism over its massive reclamation activities in the South China Sea. He did the same when the Philippines took over the (rotational) position of Country Coordinator for ASEAN–China relations the following year. Meanwhile, to China's delight, Duterte has also sought to downgrade security cooperation with the US, the Philippines' sole treaty ally. Duterte has made it clear that he won't raise sensitive bilateral issues, namely territorial disputes, during his meeting with the Chinese president on the sidelines of the summit. "To date, I have nothing to say except [my profuse] thanks to China for helping us," the Filipino president said shortly before flying to Beijing after a stopover in Hong Kong in 2017.[60] "One thing is very certain actually: China, in all good faith, wants to help us." In a reflection of the tight nexus between geopolitical and economic considerations, Duterte secured a US$500 million loan for arms purchases from China during his visit to Beijing for the BRI Summit. While China has pledged as much as US$26 billion in aid and assistance to Manila since Duterte rose to power mid-2016, but only a fraction of which would be delivered in the following years.[61]

---

[60]Heydarian (2017).

[61]Koutsoukis and Yap (2018).

Chinese Chimera

Yet, a closer look at actual figures shows that China is yet to make any major investments in the Philippines, despite repeated announcements about a new "golden age" in bilateral relations. In fact, Chinese investment pledges have been at the heart of Duterte's pivot away from its traditional allies and increasingly warm relations with Beijing, despite years-long maritime disputes in the South China Sea. The bulk of investments in 2017 came from traditional trading partners such as the United States, Japan, and the Netherlands, as well as city-states of Singapore and Hong Kong. No major trace of Mainland Chinese investments in key sectors of Philippine economy yet, so far. In the first year of Duterte's administration, Japan and the United States led the way in investments. Japanese investment increased by 23.79%, from an already large base of $490 million in 2016 to $600 million in 2017. American investment was down by 69.62% (a 13-year low), from $530 million in 2016, but still stood at a high $160 million. South Korean investment, however, virtually collapsed, down by 92.61% from a high of $230 million in 2016 to only $16.6 million in 2017. In contrast, China's investment expanded by 15%, but from a very low base of only $27 million in 2016 to $31 million in 2017. That means Japan out-invested China by a whopping 23:1 ratio.[62]

Half way into Duterte's presidency in 2019, still no major Chinese infrastructure project was in motion. The other concern with BRI-related investments in the Philippines is the competence and economic viability of Chinese contractors, a number of which have been blacklisted by the World Bank for their anomalous track record. Not to mention, concerns over exorbitant interest rates (3–6%), willingness of China to observe bidding competitiveness procedures, follow standard practices in good governance and environmental sustainability, and, above all, provide jobs for the locals, rather than relying on fully integrated Chinese supply of capital, technology, and labor. As Filipino urban sociology expert Kenneth Cardenas writes in an authoritative study for the Philippine Center for Investigative Journalism (PCIJ)

> Among the Filipino parties to these deals are firms with no track record in major infrastructure projects, no recent operating profit, and alarmingly small asset bases. Of the 22 firms that returned from China with agreements, eight had a paid-up capitalization of less than PhP15 million. At

---

[62] Heydarian (2018b).

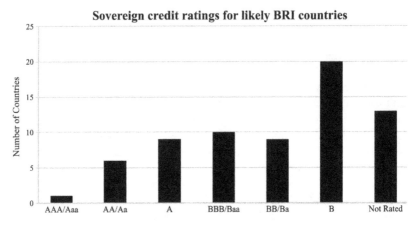

Fig. 5.3 BRI members' divergent sovereign credit rating (*Source* Center for Global Development [Hurley et al. 2018])

least three firms report their annual results under accounting rules for small and medium enterprises. Seven had not turned a profit over the past two years. *With a few exceptions, the reported value of their deals dwarf the firms' asset bases and turnovers by two or three orders of magnitude* [author's own emphasis]…Sometimes, though, a firm's track record is not in demonstrable success in running businesses, but in its ability to bring connections with the right offices, infrastructure outlays, and politically-guaranteed credit into fortuitous alignments… flagship infrastructure projects, with direct involvement of the Office of the President; the availability of guaranteed funding, whether in the form of soft-loan financing or a public-private partnership; a well-connected Filipino firm that just happens to be at the right place and the right time; and finally, projects that once delivered fall well short of the original promise [raise concerns].[63]

As Cardenas points out, "How did virtually unknown firms with no track record in bidding for—much less completing—major infrastructure projects, rise to billion-dollar prominence with the change of the administration?"[64] The Philippines' healthy growth rates and stable sovereign credit rating put into question whether there is any serious risk of "debt

[63]Cardenas (2017).
[64]Ibid.

trap." After all, the BRI beneficiaries fall across a broad spectrum when it comes to sovereign credit standing (see Fig. 5.3).

But, equally alarming, is the possibility of only a few Chinese investments reaching successful and sustainable completion due to lack of competence of involved contractors and massive corruption, which undermine the commendable intentions of the ambitious Dutertenomics project. Moreover, there are concerns that the Chinese investments, similar to those in Africa, Latin America, and Central Asia, will only reinforce undemocratic practices and undermine good governance standards, which, in effect, could strengthen autocratic tendencies in the Philippines. After all, transparency and accountability tend to be trumped by corruption and personalistic ties between China and the ruling elite in beneficiary nations. Then, there is the additional concern over whether China itself is solvent enough to undertake the BRI project along its lofty pronouncements. After all, the Xi administration is yet to address serious internal systemic weaknesses within the Chinese economy. The upshot of its post-Global Financial Crisis massive stimulus program was, inter alia, a dramatic increase in private debt, which reached 130% of the GDP. If one were to include the "shadow banking sector"—off-the-book transfers among depositors and corporations as well as informal lenders, which tend to charge dramatically higher interest rates—China's debt-to-GDP ratio could reach the 200% danger mark.[65] Chinese local government units accumulated up to US$1.8 trillion in debt by the time Xi took reign of the country. Externally, anemic growth in the West means limited opportunities for exporting domestic problems at home, protecting the export industries, and continuing the manipulative recycling of export dollars into consumer credit overseas. A credit crunch at home has been on the horizon, and may hit anytime in the near future.[66] On the other hand, one could simply look at China's AIIB, BRI, and other related initiatives as part of its "investment catch up" phase, which took off in mid-2000s, which may peak in not-so-distance future (see Fig. 5.4).

The Asian Development Bank's (ADB) estimates that Asia alone confronts an $8 trillion infrastructure spending gap over the next decade. Developing countries in Asia need $1.7 trillion annually to cover their infrastructure needs.[67] To be clear "debt trap" has a very specific

---

[65] Ibid., 26.

[66] Feigenbaum and Ma (2013).

[67] Asian Development Bank (2013).

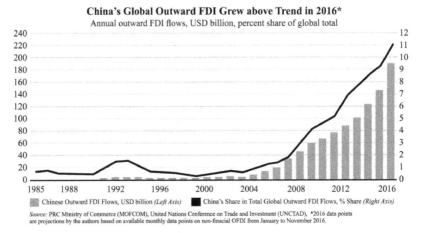

Fig. 5.4 China's global outward FDI (USD billion, percentage of global total) (*Source* The Financial Times)

definition. It essentially refers to a troubling fiscal situation, where the share of a nation's foreign debt relative to the size of its economy (the debt-to-GDP ratio) far exceeds sustainable levels. When a country's debt levels (to China) reach a critical threshold, they may be forced to give up strategic infrastructure as part of debt-for-equity arrangements. Looking at "debt trap" emerging when debt-to-GDP ratios breach the 50–60% threshold, Hurley et al. argue that the bigger concern with BRI is its modesty in addressing infrastructure needs of developing countries:

> Our analysis finds that BRI is unlikely to cause a systemic debt problem in the regions of the initiative's focus. While the aggregate numbers look large, when assessed in the context of the size of the economies that are likely to benefit from BRI investments, the amounts are consistent with current levels of infrastructure investment. Over a 20-year span, an $8 trillion investment program for BRI countries would amount to *less than 1.5 percent of GDP per annum, and about 2.5 percent excluding China* [author's own emphasis]. It is also likely that some of the China- sourced financing will merely substitute for other sources. *These levels are modest in comparison to the ADB's estimated infrastructure financing "needs" in Asia, which are projected to be 5.1 percent of the region's GDP.*[68]

---

[68] Hurley et al. (2018).

In short, the BRI may end up more as a chimera, falling several factors short of the infrastructure needs of targeted countries, rather than a strategic trap for many of its intended beneficiaries. In 2016, China's BRI-related investments dropped by 2% on a year-on-year basis. In fact, Xi himself acknowledged this tendency in recent years. In an important speech before senior officials in mid-2016, Xi underscored his sense of urgency by calling on officials to "get some model projects done and show some early signs of success and let these countries feel the positive benefits of our initiative."[69] Three years later, during the Second BRI in Beijing, the visibly sober, if not deflated, Chinese leader indirectly acknowledged growing concerns over the BRI's sustainability: "Everything should be done in a transparent way and we should have zero tolerance for corruption. We also need to ensure the commercial and fiscal sustainability of all projects so that they will achieve the intended goals as planned."[70]

In many ways, the BRI can better be compared to the American Transcontinental Railway bonanza in the nineteenth century, where, as Jonathan Hillman points out, the project became "an unquestionable national imperative," but the "actual construction…catered more to elite interests than collective wellbeing. Political favors trumped economic fundamentals thanks to shady financing, excessive subsidies and a heady dose of nationalism."[71] BRI investments may not be as large and consequential to the beneficiaries, yet they may have an extremely negative impact on the institutions of host nations, especially where transparency and accountability regimes are sorely lacking. For now, however, the BRI is both enhancing China's prestige and power, but also provoking a backlash both from recipient nations and, above all, the world's reigning superpower power, the United States. In fact, what we are witnessing is a brewing New Cold War, as China seeks to carve out a new Sino-centric Global Order in the emerging post-American world, where a growing number of nations "can say no" to Washington.

[69] Cai (2017).
[70] https://www.bbc.com/news/business-48061951.
[71] Hillman (2018).

REFERENCES

Allison, Graham. *Destined for War: Can America and China Escape Thucydides's Trap.* Boston: Houghton Mifflin Harcourt, 2017.

Andreas, Joel. "Sino-Seismology." *New Left Review* 76 (2012). https://newleftreview.org/issues/II76/articles/joel-andreas-sino-seismology.

"Apec Summit: Trump and Xi Offer Competing Visions for Trade." *BBC News.* November 10, 2017. https://www.bbc.com/news/world-asia-41937426.

Appelbaum, Binyamin. "A Little-Noticed Fact About Trade: It's No Longer Rising." *The New York Times.* October 30, 2016. https://www.nytimes.com/2016/10/31/upshot/a-little-noticed-fact-about-trade-its-no-longer-rising.html.

Cai, Peter. "Understanding China's Belt and Road Initiative." *Lowly Institute.* March 22, 2017. https://www.lowyinstitute.org/publications/understanding-belt-and-road-initiative.

Cardenas, Kenneth. "Duterte's China Deals, Dissected." *Philippine Center for Investigative Journalism.* May 8, 2017. https://pcij.org/stories/dutertes-china-deals-dissected/.

Chandran, Nyshka. "China's Plans for Creating New International Courts Are Raising Fears of Bias." *CNBC.* February 1, 2018. https://www.cnbc.com/2018/02/01/china-to-create-international-courts-for-belt-and-road-disputes.html.

Chenalley, Brahma. "China's Creditor Imperialism." *Project Syndicate.* December 20, 2017. https://www.project-syndicate.org/commentary/china-sri-lanka-hambantota-port-debt-by-brahma-chellaney-2017-12.

"China Hosts Silk Road Forum to Revive Trade Route." *Aljazeera.* May 14, 2017. https://www.aljazeera.com/news/2017/05/china-hosts-silk-road-forum-revive-trade-route-170514035154982.html.

"China's President Xi Pledges More Support for Technology Firms." *Reuters.* May 31, 2016. https://www.reuters.com/article/us-china-tech/chinas-president-xi-pledges-more-support-for-technology-firms-idUSKCN0YM089.

"CPC to Develop China into 'Great Modern Socialist Country' by Mid-21st Century." *Xinhua.* October 18, 2017. http://www.xinhuanet.com/english/2017-10/18/c_136688815.htm.

Dasgupta, Saibal, and Anjana Pasricha. "Pakistan, Nepal, Myanmar Back Away from Chinese Projects." *VOA.* December 4, 2017. https://www.voanews.com/a/three-countries-withdraw-from-chinese-projects/4148094.html.

De Vera, Ben. "Jica: Traffic Congestion now Costs P3.5 Billion a Day." *Inquirer.* February 22, 2018. https://newsinfo.inquirer.net/970553/jica-traffic-congestion-now-costs-p3-5-billion-a-day-metro-manila-traffic-jica-cost-of-traffic.

Dela Paz, Chrisee. "PH Inches Up in 2017 WEF Global Competitiveness Index." *Rappler.* September 27, 2017. https://www.rappler.com/business/183395-philippines-global-competitiveness-index-2017.

Feigenbaum, Evan, and Damien Ma. "The Rise of China's Reformers?" *Foreign Affairs*. April 17, 2013. https://www.foreignaffairs.com/articles/china/2013-04-17/rise-chinas-reformers.

"Fitch: China's One Belt, One Road Initiative Brings Risks." *Reuters*. January 26, 2017. https://www.reuters.com/article/idUSFit987609.

"Full Text of President Xi's Speech at Opening of Belt and Road Forum." *Xinhua*. May 14, 2017. http://www.xinhuanet.com/english/2017-05/14/c_136282982.htm.

"Full Text of Xi Jinping Keynote at the World Economic Forum." *CGTN*. January 17, 2017. https://america.cgtn.com/2017/01/17/full-text-of-xi-jinping-keynote-at-the-world-economic-forum.

"Full Text of Xi Jinping's Report at 19th CPC National Congress." *China Daily*. November 4, 2017. http://www.chinadaily.com.cn/china/19thcpcnationalcongress/2017-11/04/content_34115212.htm.

"Globalisation an 'Irreversible Historical Trend': Xi Jinping." *The Hindu*. November 10, 2017. https://www.thehindu.com/news/international/globalisation-an-irreversible-historical-trend-xijinping.

Goh, Evelyn. *The Struggle for Order: Hegemony, Hierarchy, and Transition in Post-Cold War East Asia*. Oxford: Oxford University Press, 2014.

Gooch, Brad. *Rumi's Secret: The Life of the Sufi Poet of Love*. New York: Harper Collins, 2017.

Heydarian, Richard Javad. "Duterte's Blossoming Liaison with China." *China-US Focus*. May 23, 2017. https://www.chinausfocus.com/foreign-policy/dutertes-blossoming-liaison-with-china.

Heydarian, Richard Javad. "Duterte's Ambitious 'Build, Build, Build' Project to Transform the Philippines Could Become His Legacy." *Forbes*. February 28, 2018a. https://www.forbes.com/sites/outofasia/2018/02/28/dutertes-ambitious-build-build-build-project-to-transform-the-philippines-could-become-his-legacy/#36460dd1a7f4.

Heydarian, Richard Javad. "Under Duterte, Philippines Enjoying an Investment Boom, but Don't Thank China." *Forbes*. March 25, 2018b. https://www.forbes.com/sites/richardheydarian/2018/03/25/under-duterte-philippines-enjoying-an-investment-boom-but-dont-thank-china/#7fe10659393e.

Hillman, Jonathan. "Is China making a trillion-dollar mistake?." *The Washington Post*. April 9, 2018. https://www.washingtonpost.com/news/theworldpost/wp/2018/04/09/one-belt-one-road/.

Hilton, Isabel. "Speak Bitterness." *London Review of Books* 37, no. 5 (2015): 22–23. https://www.lrb.co.uk/v37/n05/isabel-hilton/speak-bitterness.

Holmes, James, and Toshi Yoshihara. "Is China Planning String of Pearls." *The Diplomat*. February 21, 2011. https://thediplomat.com/2011/02/is-china-planning-string-of-pearls/.

"Hu Calls for Enhancing 'Soft Power' of Chinese Culture." *Xinhua*. October 15, 2007. http://www.china.org.cn/english/congress/228142.htm.

Huang, Zheping. "Your Guide to Understanding OBOR, China's New Silk Road Plan." *Quartz*. May 15, 2017. https://qz.com/983460/obor-an-extremely-simple-guide-to-understanding-chinas-one-belt-one-road-forum-for-its-new-silk-road/.

Hurley, John, Scott Morris, and Gailyn Portelance. "Examining the Debt Implications of the Belt and Road Initiative from a Policy Perspective." *Center for Global Development*. March 2018. https://www.cgdev.org/sites/default/files/examining-debt-implications-belt-and-road-initiative-policy-perspective.pdf.

Jacobs, Sarah. "12 Eerie Photos of Enormous Chinese Cities Completely Empty of People." *Business Insider*. October 4, 2017. https://www.businessinsider.com.au/these-chinese-cities-are-ghost-towns-2017-4?r=US&IR=T#/#when-caemmerer-found-out-about-these-empty-cities-he-was-immediately-fascinated-as-an-architectural-photographer-i-found-the-notion-of-a-contemporary-ghost-town-to-be-appealing-in-a-sort-of-unsettling-way-he-said-1.

Kaplan, Robert. *The Return of Marco Polo's World: War, Strategy, and American Interests in the Twenty-First Century*. New York: Random House, 2018.

Kaplan, Robert. *The Revenge of Geography: What the Map Tells Us About Coming Conflicts and the Battle Against Fate*. New York: Penguin Random House, 2013.

Kennedy, Andrew. "Rethinking Energy Security in China." *East Asia Forum*. June 6, 2010. https://www.eastasiaforum.org/2010/06/06/rethinking-energy-security-in-china/.

Kennedy, Scott. "Made in China 2025." *Center for Strategic and International Studies*. June 1, 2015. https://www.csis.org/analysis/made-china-2025.

Koutsoukis, Jason, and Cecilia Yap. "China Hasn't Delivered on Its $24-B Promise to PH." *Manila Bulletin*. July 26, 2018. https://business.mb.com.ph/2018/07/26/china-hasnt-delivered-on-its-24-b-promise-to-ph/.

Kurtlantzick, Joshua. *Charm Offensive: How China's Soft Power Is Transforming the World*. New Haven: Yale University Press, 2008.

Li, Nan. *Chinese Civil-Military Relations in the Post-Deng Era: Implications for Crisis Management and Naval Modernization*. Newport: U.S. Naval War College, 2010.

Moriyasu, Ken. "China Needs to 'Purchase' Friendships, Scholar Says." *Nikkei Asian Review*. March 2, 2015. https://asia.nikkei.com/NAR/Articles/China-needs-to-purchase-friendships-scholar-says.

Nye, Joseph. *Soft Power: The Means to Success in World Politics*. New York: PublicAffairs, 2004.

Osnos, Evan. "Born Red." *The New Yorker*. March 30, 2015. https://www.newyorker.com/magazine/2015/04/06/born-red.

Rauhala, Emily. "China Now Says Almost 100 Were Killed in Xinjiang Violence." *Time*. August 14, 2014. http://time.com/3078381/china-xinjiang-violence-shache-yarkand/.

Shambaugh, David. "China's Soft Power Push." *Foreign Affairs*. June 16, 2015. https://www.foreignaffairs.com/articles/china/2015-06-16/china-s-soft-power-push.

Sharma, Ruchir. *Breakout Nations: In Pursuit of the Next Economic Miracles*. New York: W. W. Norton, 2012.

Shirk, Susan. *China: Fragile Superpower*. Oxford: Oxford University Press, 2008.

Spegele, Brian. "Resistance on Tibet Is Conundrum for China, Dalai Lama." *The Wall Street Journal*. January 9, 2012. https://www.wsj.com/articles/SB10001424052970203513604577140753573184924.

Stone, Curtis. "China Stands Ready to Fight for Its Interests and the Future of Globalization." *People's Daily Online*. April 8, 2018. http://en.people.cn/n3/2018/0408/c90000-9446572.html.

Suokas, Janne. "China Invests in 42 Overseas Ports Under Belt and Road Project." *GB Times*. July 27, 2018. https://gbtimes.com/china-invests-in-42-overseas-ports-under-belt-and-road-project.

Tillerson, Rex. "U.S. Africa Relations: A New Framework." Speech, Fairfax, Virginia, March 6, 2018. *U.S. Department of State*. https://www.state.gov/secretary/20172018tillerson/remarks/2018/03/279065.

"Trump and Xi Visions Collide at Summit." *BBC News*. November 10, 2017. http://www.bbc.com/news/world-asia-41937426.

Vaitheeswaran, Vijay. "What China Can Learn from the Pearl River Delta." *The Economist*. April 8, 2017. https://www.economist.com/special-report/2017/04/08/what-china-can-learn-from-the-pearl-river-delta.

Van der Leer, Yeroen, and Joshua Yau. "China's New Silk Route the Long and Winding Road." *PWC*. February 2016. https://www.pwc.com/gx/en/growth-markets-center/assets/pdf/china-new-silk-route.pdf.

Walker, Richard, and Daniel Buck. "The Chinese Road." *New Left Review* 46 (July/August 2007). https://newleftreview.org/issues/II46/articles/richard-walker-daniel-buck-the-chinese-road.

"WHO Said That China Is a Sleeping Giant?" *Philippine Daily Inquirer*. October 23, 2016. https://www.pressreader.com/philippines/philippine-daily-inquirer.../281530815559032.

"Who Will Pay for Asia's $8 Trillion Infrastructure Gap?" *Asian Development Bank*. September 30, 2013. https://www.adb.org/news/infographics/who-will-pay-asias-8-trillion-infrastructure-gap.

Wong, Gabriel, Simon Booker, and Guillaume Barthe-Dejean. "China and Belt & Road Infrastructure: 2016 Review and Outlook." *PWC*. February 2017. https://www.pwchk.com/en/consulting/br-watch-infrastructure.pdf.

CHAPTER 6

The New Cold War: Sleep-Walking into Great Power Conflict

War is nothing but...more than the continuation of politics by other means. For political aims are the end and war is the means, and the means can never be conceived without the end. —Carl von Clausewitz[1]

China wants nothing less than to push the United States of America from the Western Pacific and attempt to prevent us from coming to the aid of our allies. —U.S. Vice-President Mike Pence, 2018 Speech at the Hudson Institute[2]

[P]repare for a comprehensive military struggle from a new starting point... Preparation for war and combat must be deepened to ensure an efficient response in times of emergency. —Chinese President Xi Jinping, January 2019 speech before the Central Military Commission (CMC)[3]

"China is getting more and more aggressive," Taiwan's President Tsai Ing-wen told to me during a meeting in the presidential palace in mid-2019 amid rising cross-strait tensions. "But we will not back down," she added with steely conviction.[4]

[1] Lindell (2009).
[2] Pence (2018).
[3] Lau (2019).
[4] Interview with the author, June 21, 2019, Taipei, Taiwan.

© The Author(s) 2020   149
R. J. Heydarian, *The Indo-Pacific: Trump, China, and the New Struggle for Global Mastery*, https://doi.org/10.1007/978-981-13-9799-8_6

Just as the northern hemisphere gently settled into the warming spring, earlier that year Chinese fighter jets brazenly violated, for the first time in recent years, Taiwan's airspace by crossing the "median line" delicately separating the two countries.[5] During their early April 2019 maneuver, the two Chinese J-11 planes, which crossed 43 nautical miles over a median line south of the Taiwan Strait, lingered for as long as 12 minutes within Taipei's airspace, the first incident of its kind since at least 1999.[6] In response, the outraged Taiwanese President Tsai Ing-wen, known for her pro-independence leanings, called for "forceful expulsion" of the Chinese warplanes. The incident took place months after Chinese President Xi Jinping declared that Taiwan's incorporation into Greater China is "inevitable" and that, dropping all pretense of pacifism, his country will "make no promise to give up the use of force and reserve the option of all necessary means."[7] Meanwhile, China also deployed an armada of paramilitary forces, up to 275 individual Chinese vessels over a span of three months, which laid siege on the Philippine-occupied Thitu Island in the South China Sea.[8] China's effort at dominating its adjacent waters at the expense freedom of navigation (FON) as well as the security of American allies such as Taiwan and the Philippines underscored a new and dangerous phase in the evolution of the Indo-Pacific order. Only six months earlier, a Chinese warship aggressively sailed within only 40 meters of the US destroyer, the USS Decatur, which was conducting routine Freedom of Navigation Operations (FONOPs) in the South China Sea.[9] From the Chinese point of view, the Americans were challenging its sovereignty in what it considers as its "blue national soil."[10] It was the closest the two superpowers got to a naval skirmish in modern times, and direct armed conflict since the end of the Korean War in 1953. The struggle for mastery in the Western Pacific is just warming up, with the year 2019 likely marking the inflection point in the brewing superpower rivalry.

Intent on checking Chinese strategic expansion, the Trump administration has stepped up its military deployment in the area and bolstered its commitments to regional allies. For the first time in years, it deployed

---

[5] Agence France-Presse (2019).

[6] Jennings (2019b).

[7] Haynes (2019).

[8] Aurelio (2019).

[9] Johnson (2018).

[10] Holmes (2013).

(March 25, 2019) among America's biggest and most advanced Coast Guard cutters, the USCGC *Bertholf*, through the 110-mile-wide Taiwan Straits.[11] In 2019 alone, Washington deployed guided-missile destroyer *USS McCampbell* and *USNS Walter S. Diehl* in January and, a month later, the *USS Stethem* destroyer and the ammunition and cargo vessel *USNS Cesar Chavez* through the same waterway for supposedly "routine" transits. To bolster the island nation's defensive capabilities, the Trump administration also authorized a $1.3 billion arms sale to Taiwan, which China treats as a renegade province. Increased defense assistance to Taipei is a direct challenge to Beijing's growing attempts at coercive reunification with Taiwan.[12] During his late February visit to Southeast Asia, the US Secretary of State Mike Pompeo also assured the Philippines that it would come to their rescue in an event of conflict in the South China Sea.[13] "As the South China Sea is part of the Pacific, any armed attack on any Philippine forces, aircraft, or public vessels in the South China Sea will trigger mutual defense obligations under Article 4 of our Mutual defense treaty," the American diplomat told his hosts in Manila. "We have your back," Pompeo reportedly told Filipino leaders.[14] It was the first time ever that a senior American official openly clarified the precise geographical scope of its 1951 Mutual Defense Treaty with the Philippines (see Chapter 8). Meanwhile, after an April visit by Philippine Defense Secretary Delfin Lorenzana to the United States, the two allies also discussed potential purchase of High Mobility Artillery Rocket System (HIMARS) system to deter Chinese militarization activities in disputed areas of the South China Sea.[15]

Aside from stepping up its commitment and defense sales to allies, the United States also directly took on China. In March, it dispatched, for the first time in history, two pairs of nuclear-capable bombers within a span of just over a week alone to challenge China's excessive claims in the South China Sea.[16] The aim of the operations is to ensure freedom of overflight in one of the world's most crucial waterways. This comes amid fears over a Chinese-imposed Air Defense Identification Zone (ADIZ) in the heavily contested area. With Beijing fully "weaponing" its

---

[11] Johnson (2019).
[12] Allen-Ebrahimian (2017).
[13] Ranada (2019).
[14] Ibid.
[15] Perper (2019).
[16] Doornbos (2019).

artificially-created islands in the South China Sea, including the deployment of HQ-9B surface-to-air-missiles (SAMs), YJ-12B anti-cruise ballistic missiles (ACBMs), and electronic jamming equipments,[17] many believe that it's just a matter of time before the Asian powerhouse establishes, or tries to establish, an exclusion zone in the area—and coercively drive out other smaller claimant states from the contested area.[18] The US Pacific Command has characteristically tried to downplay the aerial deployments as part of routine overflight operations: "U.S. aircraft regularly operate in the South China Sea in support of allies, partners, and a free and open Indo-Pacific," yet these operations have gone hand in hand with more frequent and aggressive FONOPs.[19] During Trump's first year in office, the US conducted four FONOPs in a span of only 5 months, the highest on record.[20] The Obama administration, in contrast, irregularly conducted similar operations, which demanded direct clearance from the White House, while the Trump administration largely delegated operational decisions to the Pentagon, including in the South China Sea.[21] As Dexter Filkins of *The New Yorker* observed, Trump has provided "total authorizations" to the Pentagon, which is "bringing a new calculus to global politics, in which the use of force plays a more prominent role, and that [senior Pentagon officials such as former defense secretary] Mattis may be the policy's principal driver."[22] The *New York Times* reported this trend as early as March 2017, when Trump began "shifting more authority over military operations to the Pentagon, according to White House officials, reversing what his aides and some generals say was a tendency by the Obama White House to micromanage issues better left to military commanders."[23] With freer reign, the more hawkish elements in Pentagon are now unshackled to push back against Chinese assertiveness with ever-growing verve and vigor. The US Navy now regularly deploys, often two at the same time, warships to the vicinity of Chinese-occupied islands in the South China Sea. In February, Admiral John Richardson,

[17] Heydarian (2018a).

[18] Jennings (2019a).

[19] Squitieri (2019).

[20] Panda (2017).

[21] Based on conversations with former senior Obama administration senior defense officials in Washington, DC, 2017–2018.

[22] On Trump's empowering of the Pentagon, also see Filkins (2017).

[23] Gordon (2017).

chief of US naval operations, also highlighted the Trump administration's pushback against China's "grey zone" or "short of conflict" operations in contested maritime spaces. It has openly accused China of deceptively using ostensibly civilian, though well-armed and coordinated, paramilitary and fishing vessels as camouflage for full-fledged military operations and territorial expansion in the area. The Pentagon has made it clear that it will now treat China's People's Armed Forces Maritime Militia (PAFMM) and other paramilitary Chinese forces as de facto military vessels. Thus, henceforth US warships will apply same rules of engagement to both the People Liberation Army Navy (PLAN) and the PAFMM and other supposedly "white hull" Chinese vessels engaged in expanding Beijing's strategic footprint in the South China Sea. The Trump administration made it clear that it will advance a new Indo-Pacific strategy to counter China's maritime assertiveness by the mid-2019.[24]

At the same time, the Trump administration has also stepped up its diplomatic offensive against China. During his high-profile speech at the 2019 Munich Conference (February 16), Vice-President Mike Pence warned allies and strategic partners from relying on Chinese technology in critical infrastructure lest they undermine their bilateral relations and depth of security cooperation.[25] "The United States has also been very clear with our security partners on the threat posed by Huawei and other Chinese telecom companies, as Chinese law requires them to provide Beijing's vast security apparatus with access to any data that touches their network or equipment,"[26] Pence warned, effectively compelling allies and partners to choose between China or America on matters pertaining to critical infrastructure policies. "We must protect our critical telecom infrastructure, and America is calling on all our security partners to be vigilant and to reject any enterprise that would compromise the integrity of our communications technology or our national security systems."[27] Weeks later in Iowa, US Secretary of State Mile Pompeo took aim at China's Belt and Road Initiative (BRI), describing it as a nefarious "debt [trap] diplomacy" strategy that is "almost certainly designed for foreclosure."[28] In a very undiplomatic lexicon, the

---

[24] See Heydarian (2018b) and Hayton (2014).

[25] Pence (2019).

[26] Ibid.

[27] Ibid.

[28] Pompeo (2019b).

American top diplomat described the initiative as a deceptive scheme, whereby China is "using the debt trap ... to put [recipient] countries in a place where it isn't a commercial transaction. It's a political transaction designed to bring harm and political influence in the country in which they're operating."[29] He called on the American private sector to join in the Trump administration's efforts against China: "We need to roll up our sleeves and compete by facilitating investments all across the world and encouraging partners to buy from us, and by punishing the bad [China] actors."[30] This was followed by an address (March 12, 2019) to leading energy executives in Houston, Texas, where the US chief diplomat lashed out at "China's illegal island building in international waterways," which, according to him, is not "simply a security matter," but also has major ramifications for the global economy and transport of energy resources.[31] "By blocking energy development in the South China Sea to coerce, it means China prevents ASEAN members from accessing more than 2½ trillion in recoverable energy resources," Pompeo said.[32] "To contrast, the United States government promotes energy security for those Southeast Asian nations. We want countries in the region to have access to their own energy."[33] In response, the Chinese foreign ministry has accused the United States of undue interference in regional affairs: "Nations outside the region [the U.S.] should refrain from stirring up trouble and disrupting the harmonious situation."[34] Amid growing US military footprint in China's adjacent waters, some Chinese hardliners have called for tougher response from Beijing during the 2019 Boao Forum in Hainan. Wu Shicun, who heads the prominent National Institute for South China Sea Studies in Hainan, called on Beijing to reinforce "deterrence facilities" in the disputed areas, because "we must deploy some defensive facilities that are able to overawe American warships entering [our] nearby [our] waters."[35] The Chinese academic emphasized that China will have to stand up to a US-led alliance if necessary: "The Americans feel that they alone are

[29] Pompeo (2019a).
[30] Ibid.
[31] Zhenhua (2019).
[32] Pompeo (2019a).
[33] Ibid.
[34] Panda (2019).
[35] Liu (2019).

not enough. They might also bring in allies such as Britain, Australia or Japan for exercises, or even create a regular joint action regime,"[36] Meanwhile in the US Senate, Republican Senators Marco Rubio and Tom Cotton along with Democratic Senator Ben Cardin reintroduced (May 2019) a bipartisan bill entitled *South China Sea and East China Sea Sanctions Act*, which calls for punitive sanctions against any Chinese individual or companies involved in China's "illegitimate activities" to "aggressively assert its expansive" claims in adjacent waters. For decades, Washington sought to maintain an "impossible trinity," whereby it claimed neutrality on the South China Sea disputes, while simultaneously developing closer strategic ties with China as well as upgrading partnership and alliances with rival claimant states such as the Philippines (treaty ally), Taiwan (de facto ally), and Vietnam (strategic partner). The bill, however, effectively abandons the United States' formal neutrality on the disputes by emphasizing the need to push back against Chinese activities in areas "contested by one or more ASEAN members or areas of the East China Sea administered by Japan or the Republic of Korea." If passed into law, the bill calls for sanctioning up to 25 Chinese companies, including the CCCC Dredging Group, a subsidiary of the state-owned China Communications Construction Company that has been instrumental in artificial island-building in contested areas of the sea.[37] Ultimately, it could even target the Chinese leadership, including President Xi Jinping, who has personally overseen the reclamation activities since 2013. Separately, two former senior Filipino officials, including former Philippine Ambassador to the US Albert Del Rosario, also sued (March 2019) the Chinese leader at the International Criminal Court for committing crimes against humanity vis-à-vis Filipino fishermen through, among others, inflicting damage to the ecological balance in the contested areas through massive reclamation activities.[38]

By all accounts, all gloves are off and neither United States nor China seem to be in a mood for comprise in the new Cold War that is gripping the twenty-first-century Asia. Unlike many of its predecessors, the Trump administration has taken the fight to China, challenging both its maritime expansionism as well as growing economic clout across the United

---

[36] Ibid.

[37] See Ghosh (2019) and the bill https://www.billtrack50.com/BillDetail/857770.

[38] Labog-Javellana (2019).

States' traditional spheres of influence. Washington's increasingly robust pushback against China, however, is part of a bigger shift in American policy and, more broadly, Sino-American relations. As months go by, the new phase of Sino-American rivalry more resembles a frozen conflict that could unexpectedly and suddenly melt into a hot war than a stable Cold War between two ideologically opposed superpowers. Individually, all points of tensions and areas of convergence, including disputes between China and US allies as well as FON and overflight in international waters, are more than manageable. But when put together, all these flashpoints and fault lines can congeal into a formidable black hole of total war. Both powers have found themselves in a situation where escalating structural tensions could turn even small frictions into explosive conflicts.[39] As Barbara Tuchman demonstrated in *The Guns of August*, great powers can easily sleepwalk into cataclysmic wars, since "in the midst of ... crisis nothing is as clear or as certain as it appears in hindsight."[40] The First World War, she warned, was after all the tragic upshot of personal miscalculations and shared misperceptions reaching a destructive apotheosis. What is most frightening is that no one intended it, and no one saw it coming—or believed it was even possible since it seemed just too apocalyptic even just for sheer contemplation. In her pioneering work, Tuchman highlighted the "disposition of everyone on all sides not to prepare for the harder alternative, [and] not to act upon what they suspected to be true," but instead embrace the convenient delusion that the opposing side will succumb short of armed conflict.[41] The precarious game of chicken in the Western Pacific, however, is just warming up.

TRAGEDY OF GREAT POWER RIVALRY

The Sino-American relationship has been far from monolithic, and Donald Trump's increasingly confrontational approach toward China marks a new low for arguably the world's most important bilateral relationship, or what Zbigniew Brzezinski termed as the "G2." As the former national security adviser explained in an influential column for *The Financial Times*: "The world will benefit, and so will our countries, if [bilateral cooperation] expands... the relationship between the US and

[39] Allison (2017).
[40] Tuchman (2009, 1199).
[41] Ibid., 114.

China has to be a comprehensive partnership...".[42] His call for a G2 informal alliance was partly embraced by the Obama administration, which described Sino-American relations as the most important bilateral relationship of the twenty-first century.[43]

To understand the root and trajectory of the Trump administration's China policy, and the dilemmas faced by the world's superpower, one must first look at the evolution—first symbiotic, but increasingly conflict-driven—of arguably the most indispensable bilateral relations in the modern century. Throughout modern history, ties between Beijing and Washington have oscillated between cooperation and rivalry, though they were never on a largely symmetrical field as they increasingly find themselves today. For the first time in a century, America is beginning to grapple with the prospect of a truly full-spectrum equal rival, a legitimate "strategic peer," in ways that the Soviet Union—or Imperial Japan and (Kaiser and Nazi) Germany for that matter—never was and ever managed to become. While the early twentieth century marked relatively cordial relations between the two powers, particularly during the Second World War, the first decades of the Cold War, in contrast, witnessed open conflict between Maoist China and the United States, specifically over the Korean Peninsula, Vietnam, and Taiwan. Yet, the two powers eventually moved toward détente during Mao's final years, with the Sino-Soviet split providing a strategic opening for the Nixon administration to explore a new relationship with Beijing. Thanks to the pragmatism of Deng Xiaoping and his handpicked successors, Jiang Zemin and Hu Jintao, China and the United States gradually moved toward economic interdependence. Bilateral relations in the post-Mao era increasingly resembled a strategic partnership rather than an ideological rivalry between a communist and a capitalist power. Robust economic relations and relatively cordial diplomatic exchanges, however, concealed deeper strategic tensions between the two powers.

Strategically, China's growing sense of security vis-à-vis its continental borders, deepening reliance on international trade and energy imports, and rapid military modernization underpinned its quest for maritime prowess, particularly in adjacent waters in the Western Pacific. Domestically, the post-Tiananmen demise of communist ideology gave way to the emergence of state-led popular nationalism, which rekindled China's historical

---

[42] Brzezinski (2009).
[43] Li (2016).

158 R. J. HEYDARIAN

grievances and augmented its appetite for territorial adventurism in near waters. The confluence of these primary factors largely explains China's assertive posturing in adjacent waters. China's maritime calculus, however, is also reflective of the shifting balance of power in the region. The intensification of East Asian maritime disputes was triggered by China's rising territorial assertiveness in the immediate aftermath of the 2008 Great Recession, which significantly undermined the economy of the Western world, including the United States. The Asian country was able to maintain robust growth rates at home while continuing its rapid military modernization, whereas the United States struggled with anemic growth and a shrinking military budget. Instead of conceding leadership to Beijing in East Asia, the United States, however, tried to reassert its Indo-Pacific hegemony by declaring the Pivot to Asia (P2A) policy, which seeks to communicate the country's determination to remain as an anchor of stability and prosperity in the region. The Trump administration has rhetorically and substantively distanced itself from its predecessor's P2A policy, yet it's doubling down on its military constrainment of its chief rival in Asia. As one senior Pentagon official admitted, "We are riding on the shoulderns of giants [the Obama administration]," when it comes to their strategic policy in East Asia.[44]

Xi is not only trying to reshape the global infrastructure landscape, but also the physics of China's territorial extent and spheres of influence. Of Kaiser's Germany, the imperial ambitions of which served as the fulcrum of the early twentieth century cataclysms, Barbara Tuchman wrote, "Believing themselves superior in soul, in strength, in energy, industry, and national virtue, Germans felt they deserved the dominion of Europe."[45] In many ways, China seems to be gripped by a similar sense of destiny, except in East Asia—the region it historically dominated under a *Tianxia* tributary system.[46] And far from accepting the ineluctable march toward a post-American order, the "Make America Great Again" Trump administration is more than eager to reassert Washington's hegemony in Asia. The product is a new period of complex, multi-dimensional and highly fluid strategic rivalry, which escapes all historical analogies, including the Cold War. The upshot is what Mearsheimer aptly described as the "tragedy of great power politics," where Washington can't afford to allow a regional power dominate

[44] Exchanges with the author, July 27, 2018, Washington DC.
[45] Li (2016), 137.
[46] Babones (2018).

East Asia without risking its own global leadership as well as century-old unchallenged primacy in the Western hemisphere, while Beijing is becoming too big to accept a secondary role in its own historical backyard, which it comfortably dominated for more than a millennium prior to the advent of Western imperialism.

The Forgotten Ally

For almost seven decades, the United States has undergirded the Asia-Pacific regional order. After its defeat and occupation of Japan (1945–1952), which required the full mobilization of America's vast resources, the United States had to contend with the Communist juggernauts of Soviet Union and China, who collectively proved to be a formidable adversary in the initial decades of the Cold War, most evidently during the proxy wars in Korea (1950–1953) and Vietnam (1955–1975). Enlisting postwar Japan as its new ally, and overseeing a vast hubs-and-spokes network of alliances in the region, the United States managed to not only survive the decades-long standoff with its ideological nemeses, but also eventually emerged as the indisputable victor. Toward the end of the twentieth century, the United States gleefully oversaw the disintegration of the Soviet empire, precipitated by Gorbachev's doomed efforts at reform, while cautiously integrating Communist China into the international liberal order. Beginning with President Nixon, especially his fateful (February 1972) visit to Mao's den, the United States began to explore a strategic partnership with Beijing's then seemingly implacable Red leadership. Pursuit of this partnership proved not only a question of exploring a Metternichean Holy Alliance with Beijing against the larger revisionist threat emanating from Moscow. There was a deep history of cooperation between China and the West to draw on, especially during World War II against the Axis powers. And Sino-American relations in particular were, after all, never straightforwardly hostile, often subjected to wild swings between confrontation and cooperation. During China's "Century of Humiliation," for instance, Washington was considerably less predatory than its European and Japanese counterparts, who brutally carved out little colonies on the prosperous peripheries of the Qing dynasty. As Niel Sheehan explains, Washington, from the late nineteenth century onwards, consciously sought to distinguish itself from other colonial powers: "Having overt colonies was not acceptable to the American political conscience.

Americans were convinced that their imperial system did not victimize foreign peoples. 'Enlightened self-interest' was the sole national egotism to which Americans would admit...Americans perceived their order as a new and benevolent form of international guidance."[47] Back then, Washington enjoyed a relatively more cordial relationship with China than other Western powers, and definitely Imperial Japan.

More than creating a favorable balance of power, based on Kissinger's conception of *Realpolitik*, the Nixon administration's efforts to come to terms with Communist China was also a way of rekindling the more constructive aspects of Sino-American relations in recent history. After all, China was, in the words of Oxford academic Rana Mitter, the West's "forgotten ally," a county that valiantly resisted Imperial Japan at a great cost. As many as 15 million lives were lost, with a staggering 100 million Chinese displaced during the Second World War—a mindboggling sacrifice that was only matched by the Soviet Union's own heroic resistance against Nazi Germany.[48] Exhausted and overstretched during their protracted confrontation with Imperial Japan, the Kuomintang (KMT)—a key element of the anti-fascist resistance during the Second World War—was too enervated to win the subsequent civil war against the Chinese Communist Party (CCP), who forced the KMT out of Mainland China into a seemingly eternal exile in Taiwan. Both the CCP and the KMT, who saw themselves as the true representative of the Chinese people, sought reunification on their own terms, so they constantly teetered on the verge of full-scale war.

Finding a *modus vivendi* with China was also an expedient way to avoid a large-scale conflict over Taiwan (Republic of China). Throughout the Second World War, the KMT forces stood shoulder-to-shoulder with the Allies. But as Sino-Soviet border clashes reached dangerous levels in the post-Stalin period, Chairman Mao, who voraciously sifted through Chinese classics on Warring States period and stratagems of Imperial China, welcomed a tactical alliance with "far barbarians" (Washington) against "near barbarians (Moscow)." In Mao's view, addressing the threat from the north was an existential question, which warranted a (temporary) postponement of the reunification issue. Nixon's disgraceful exit from power, over the "Watergate scandal," didn't torpedo the Sino-American rapprochement, however, as succeeding American administrations embraced the refreshing pragmatism of Mao's charismatic successor, Deng Xiaoping, who was

[47] Sheehan (1989, 131).
[48] *The Economist* (2015, August).

now intent on (i) pushing back against the Soviet-Vietnamese alliance and (ii) overhauling China's ossified economic system.[49]

Sino-American Symbiosis

Deng's January 1979 visit to the United States marked a watershed in Sino-American relations. Even the American media enthusiastically embraced China's new leader, who twice ended up on the cover of *Time* magazine. Deng was touted as a sober and good-humored leader, one who is committed to deepening Beijing's relations with the West and improving the lives of the Chinese people. What followed was, in the words of Sinologist Michael Pillsbury, "the greatest outpouring of American scientific and technical expertise in history,"[50] with the Carter and Reagan administrations overseeing new areas of cooperation with Deng's China. While the Carter administration granted China the much-vaunted most-favored-nation status as a trading partner, transforming America into a key consumer market for China's burgeoning exports, the Reagan administration, meanwhile, under various National Security Decision Directives (NSDD), sanctioned transfer of advanced military technology to the People's Liberation Army (PLA), cooperation in nuclear technology, and assistance in development of eight major research centers in China. The two sides cooperated to contain Hanoi's ambitions in Indochina, as well as Soviet designs in Afghanistan and Africa. Covert cooperation between the two powers involved intelligence-sharing, large-scale purchase of Chinese weaponry for anti-Soviet rebel groups, and huge transfer of American civil and military technology to China. In fact, Reagan's NSDD 140 called on America "to help China modernize, on the grounds that a strong, secure, and stable China can be an increasing force for peace, both in Asia and in the world."[51]

While Washington tried to build in China a reliable strategic partner, Deng was intent on closing China's military and civilian development gap with the West. Unimpressed with Communist catechism, Deng was more of a believer in Darwinian survival. He was deeply alarmed by how far China was left behind by its peers in Asia and the West, lamenting:

[49] For further analysis see Shirk (2008), Kissinger (2012), Osnos (2014), and Pillsbury (2015).

[50] Pillsbury (2015, 71).

[51] Ibid., 73.

"development is the only hard truth... [and] if we do not develop, then we will be bullied."[52] Instead of taking refuge in dogma, Deng confronted China's dilemmas with utmost courage and determination. As Henry Kissinger underscores, Deng "had the courage to base modernization on the initiative and resilience of the individual Chinese...The China of today – with the world's second largest economy and largest volume of foreign exchange reserves, and with multiple cities boasting skyscrapers taller than the Empire State Building – is testimonial to Deng's vision, tenacity, and common sense."[53] Under Deng's stewardship, China went through two key stages of reform. The first stage saw the abolition of communes, the revival of entrepreneurship in the rural areas, and the massive influx of capital from the Chinese diaspora, especially from Hong Kong, and across Special Economic Zones (SEZs) in Guangdong and Fujian.[54] Before Deng could shift gear to a second and more ambitious stage of reforms, however, China was hit by major protests, with demand for greater political freedom coming on the heels of economic insecurity, especially as ordinary citizens struggled with an inflationary spiral amid the retrenchment of "iron rice bowl" welfare programs and removal of price-controls.[55]

Social discontent eventually crystallized into massive protests in Tiananmen Square, and across major cities in China, presenting the greatest challenge to the CCP's grip on power in decades. Prodded by hardliners, Deng's subsequent decision to violently crackdown on the protesters not only undermined Beijing's ties with the West, which responded by imposing (arms exports) sanctions, but also divided the Chinese establishment and strengthened the position of the PLA. Cognizant of the CCP's declining legitimacy and the necessity for greater economic reforms if China were to continue developing, Deng decided to push ahead with economic reforms as well as a Patriotic Education campaign, which emphasized loyalty to the regime and fostered an aggrieved form of popular nationalism, which would later undergird China's territorial assertiveness in the East and South China Seas. As Zhao explains:

[52] Osnos (2014).

[53] Kissinger (2012, 321).

[54] For further analysis see Andreas (2008, 2010, 2012), and Walker and Buck (2007).

[55] See Shirk (2008), Kurlantzick (2009), Kissinger (2012), and Osnos (2015).

The patriotic education campaign was a state-led nationalist movement, which redefined the legitimacy of the post-Tiananmen leadership in a way that would permit the Communist Party's rule to continue on the basis of a non-Communist ideology. Patriotism was thus used to bolster CCP power in a country that was portrayed as besieged and embattled. The dependence on patriotism to build support for the government and the patriotic education campaign by the Communist propagandists were directly responsible for the nationalistic sentiment of the Chinese people in the mid-1990s.[56]

The need for robust economic reform was further augmented by the collapse of the Soviet Union (1991) and America's rise as a *hyperpower*, evident in the coalition forces' swift defeat of Saddam's massive Soviet-armed military in the First Gulf War (1991). Deng's 1992 "Southern tour" signaled his commitment to push ahead with the second stage of economic reforms, which included loosening certain financial sector restrictions, progressive streamlining of State-Owned Enterprises (SOEs), liberalization of the urban property sector, and courtship of foreign capital by offering a wide range of investment incentives (e.g., low labor costs, modern infrastructure, attractive tax rates, etc.) to companies from neighboring states such as Japan and Taiwan and, over the years, the West.[57]

Though the Clinton administration had signaled a tough line on China prior to winning the US Presidency, his administration ended up as a surprisingly congenial partner for China. While the Carter and Reagan administration were more low-key, if not fully covert, in their cooperative arrangements with Beijing, the Clinton administration, more openly embraced China as a potential strategic partner. Eager to integrate China's booming economy in the global markets, Clinton pushed for China's membership in the World Trade Organization (WTO), prompting a showdown with the Republican-dominated Congress.[58] In line with prevailing views of globalization at the time the Clinton administration believed that a more integrated China would transform it into a more peaceful and cooperative power. For China's part, deeper trade and investment relations with the West were also seen as desirable, both to

---

[56]Zhao (1998, 287).
[57]Heydarian (2015a, 28–33).
[58]Shirk (2008).

continue to advance economic growth and to rebuild ties undermined by the 1989 Tiananmen massacre. The 1990s also witnessed a highly successful diplomatic charm offensive by Jiang Zemin, Deng's handpicked successor, vis-à-vis China's neighbors.

The Good Old Days

Under Jiang's watch, China transformed into a prized partner of the Association of Southeast Asian Nations (ASEAN), resolved border disputes with almost all of its continental neighbors (with the notable exception of India), and shunned monetary opportunism during the 1997 Asian Financial Crisis. It was also a period that saw the gradual transformation of China into a resource-hungry industrializing power, which began investing across resource-rich countries in the Global South. Jiang's greatest success was arguably his ability to oversee the restoration of confidence in China's overseas relations, which contributed to the growing belief in the idea of a peacefully rising China.[59] Thanks to Jiang's astute diplomacy, his successor, Hu Jintao (also handpicked by Deng) took over an increasingly popular rising nation, which, in the mid-2000s, enjoyed a higher approval rating than America among Australians.[60] In fact, as leaked cables suggest, Washington was even impressed by China's charm offensive in the Philippines, a former American colony and postwar treaty ally. For instance, in a cable entitled "More on Hu Jintao's visit to the Philippines," the American embassy in Manila was largely sanguine vis-à-vis deepening Philippines–China relations, stating "President Hu's charm offensive in Manila does not appear significantly different from that in other ASEAN capitals. Better and broader bilateral ties advance regional interests, as other ASEAN members have also discovered."

The Mirage of Harmony

Stable and cordial ties facilitated China's integration into international markets as a "socialist market economy," a hybrid capitalist system that became the beneficiary of unprecedented amounts of foreign

---

[59] For further analysis see Medeiros and Fravel (2003), Kurlantzick (2008), Shirk (2008), Fravel (2012), and Heydarian (2015a, 39–45).

[60] Kurlantzick (2008, 4).

direct investment (FDIs) and technology transfer. As China's stakes in the existing international order increased, the Clintonite liberal argument went, the more incentive it had to cooperate with status quo powers. The vast asymmetry of power between America and China, however, was always the elephant in the room. While Washington saw itself as a benevolent power eager to integrate former foes into a liberal international order, as it did with postwar Japan and Germany, Beijing remained acutely aware of America's *hyperpower* status. In fact, though Deng Xiaoping advised caution by stating, "Hide our capacities and bide our time…" he also added a caveat: "*but also get some things done*" [author's own emphasis]. As John Mearsheimer explains, "The reason it ma[de] sense for China to bide its time is that if it avoids trouble and merely continues growing economically, it will eventually become so powerful that it can just get its way in Asia".[61] In fact, in August 1994, Deng Xiaoping was already calling for a more assertive Chinese foreign policy, which rested on two principles: "First, to oppose hegemonism and power politics and safeguard world peace; second, to build up a new international political and economic order."[62]

During the Clinton administration, on at least two occasions Washington and Beijing found themselves at loggerheads. The first occasion arose during the 1995/96 Taiwan Strait Crisis, when a beleaguered Jiang, pressured by hardliners at home to respond to pro-independence posturing in Taipei, stepped up military exercises and engaged in intimidation tactics against the Taiwanese leadership. The United States responded with force, deploying two aircraft carrier battle groups, USS *Nimitz* and USS *Independence,* to rein in Chinese intimidation. The second incident occurred three years later, when an American B-2 mistakenly bombed the Chinese Embassy in Belgrade, provoking mass uproar among Chinese populace, with Beijing demanding unequivocal apology from the American leadership.[63] Aware of its acute military inferiority, China displayed considerable self-restraint and shunned further escalation of the crisis. After all, Saddam's lightning defeat at the hands of American military behemoth exposed the vulnerability of Soviet

---

[61] Mearsheimer (2014).
[62] Brzezinski (1998).
[63] Shirk (2008).

technology, which formed the core of Chinese military platforms, and underscored the supremacy of air power and high-tech warfare.[64]

It didn't take long before another incident, the collision between a Chinese jetfighter and a US EP-3 surveillance plane close to Hainan in the South China Sea, stoked anti-American sentiments in China, reinforcing age-old mistrust toward and perception of Washington as an overbearing superpower.[65] Gladly, once again, the two powers were able to avoid an unwanted escalation, successfully managing the dispute and preventing it from sabotaging broader bilateral relations. Focused on the Global War on Terror (GWOT), the George W. Bush administration had little interest in taking on a rising power, which also shared similar concerns with radicalism, especially among the Uighur population in Xinjiang. Bereft of the military and ideological credentials of Mao and Deng, both Jiang and his successor Hu Jintao—bland but reliable apparatchiks—were always under pressure to prove their mettle, especially vis-à-vis a skeptical and increasingly influential PLA military brass. Facing an American *hyperpower*, they had sufficient reason to bide their time, while keeping the PLA on their side in exchange for considerable institutional autonomy and fiscal incentives. As China expanded its capabilities, and broadened its trade and investment relations across the globe, it steadily developed its ability to project power across multiple theaters and major Sea Lines of Communications (SLOCs) such as the South China Sea. As early as 2003, with China becoming increasingly dependent on hydrocarbon imports, Hu Jintao called for "oil security," bestowing, in an influential speech the following year, the PLA Navy with "new historic missions" such as the protection of China's energy security interests.[66] As China's stakes in global trade and commodity transport increased, its strategic orientation swung toward greater global assertiveness but not necessarily along America's preference. China had its own ideas about its interests, and the shape of the international order. Soon, America's *hyperpower* status would be shaken by a financial crisis, providing a perfect opportunity for China to flex its muscles, just as aggrieved nationalism began to grip the popular imagination in the run up to the 2008

---

[64]Kazianis (2014).
[65]Shirk (2008).
[66]Li (2010).

Beijing Olympics.[67] The two powers now quickly moved from cooperative co-dependence toward combative coexistence. Soon, China would be engulfed by a dangerous cocktail of triumphalism and jingoistic fire.

THE WAR OF POSITION

For decades, China was able to close its economic gap with the West, particularly the United States. But China's leaders most likely didn't expect to come to close the development gap at such an accelerated pace: In 1980, the US' Gross Domestic Product (GDP) was ten times larger than that of China, but by 2007 it was only four times larger. By 2012, America's GDP was only twice as large as China's. And by 2014, the country was poised to have the world's biggest economy in Purchasing power Parity (PPP).[68] China's rapid catch-up with the West perhaps created the impression—especially among hawks in Beijing—that China could now more independently pursue its ambitions in the region and beyond.[69]

The early twentieth-century Italian thinker Antonio Gramsci, who devoted his intellectual life to understanding the concept of hegemony, made a distinction between War of Position and War of Maneuver. While the War of Maneuver pertains to a direct confrontation of the status quo powers, or the 'hegemonic bloc', the War of Position is more about undermining the influence and sway of the existing leadership.[70] With respect to Sino-American relations, Pillsbury, for instance, shows that even hardliners (*Ying Pai*) in Beijing are aware of the huge (quantitative and qualitative) military gap between China and the West, so a direct confrontation is out of the question for, at the very least, the next two decades. In the meantime, however, China could engage in a War of Position against the United States.[71]

During the 2009 World Economic Forum in Davos, the Chinese premier, Wen Jiabao, joined Russian President Vladimir Putin, in lambasting (Anglo-American) capitalism. He lamented the West's "inappropriate macroeconomic policies," its "unsustainable model of

---

[67] Barmé (2009).

[68] See Colby and Lettow (2014), Pei (2014), and Allison (2015).

[69] See Pillsbury (2015) and Luttwak (2012).

[70] For the deeper analysis of the concepts of War of Position and War of Maneuver see Egan (2013).

[71] Pillsbury (2015).

development characterized by prolonged low savings and high consumption," its "blind pursuit of profit" and the widespread "failure of financial [regulatory] supervision" in the United States. In particular, China's neighboring countries, as well as the United States, began to notice an uptick in the country's naval assertiveness and hardening of its overall diplomatic language. In a 2010 diplomatic cable, entitled "Stomp around and carry a small stick: China's new 'global assertiveness'," the American embassy in Beijing noted a growing and shared worry among the international community vis-à-vis China's new posturing:

> The harsh (per usual) PRC [People's Republic of China] reaction to the recent U.S. announcement of arms sales to Taiwan and President Obama's intention to meet with the Dalai Lama has focused Chinese domestic attention on a phenomenon already observed (and criticized) abroad: China's muscle-flexing, triumphalism and assertiveness in its diplomacy. Foreign diplomats note that China is making no friends with its newly pugnacious attitude, but the popular assessment of China's stance, personified by the nationalistic, jingoistic and Chinese Communist Party-affiliated newspaper Global Times (Huanqiu Shibao), is *it's about time.*[72] [author's own emphasis]

In another cable, the US ambassador to Beijing, Clark T. Randt, shared growing worries about the possibility that China would use its economic leverage to squeeze American allies: "Perceived threats to China's security posed by Japan's participation in missile defense or by future high-tech US military technologies might cause tomorrow's Chinese leaders to change their assessment and to exert economic pressures on U.S. allies like Thailand or the Philippines to choose between Beijing and Washington."[73] What particularly caught the attention of neighbors and the United States was China's efforts to assert primacy along the First Island Chain, stretching from water off the northern coast of Japan all the way south to the westernmost portions of the South China Sea, embracing Vietnamese and Malaysian waters.

---

[72] Assaunge, Julian. The WikiLeaks Files: The World According to US Empire, eds. Verso: New York.

[73] Assaunge, Julian. The WikiLeaks Files: The World According to US Empire, eds. Verso: New York.

China's Backyard

In fact as early as mid-2000s, China was signalizing its intent to dominate the near waters, or, at the very least, keep America as far away as possible. After all, China harbored deep suspicion toward the United States and its strategic intentions. Surrounded by a wide network of American bases, with American navy constantly roaming the Western Pacific, China always grappled with the fear of an American-led containment strategy lurking on the horizon. Fundamentally, China's assertiveness was driven by triumphalism as much as paranoia over America's supposed malicious intentions. Influential Chinese opinion makers such as Ni Feng, the deputy director of the Chinese Academy of Social Sciences' Institute of American Studies, have gone so far as claiming that since America is "worried about a more powerful China" it will resort to "multiple means to delay its development and to remake China with U.S. values."[74] It is not clear whether such statements reflect a true sense of paranoia or/and are only provocative statements intended to justify China's renewed assertiveness. But one can't deny how anyone placed in the shoes of the current Chinese Communist leadership wouldn't exactly relish the fact that Beijing is surrounded by a sprawling network of American bases from the Korean Peninsula and Japan to Guam and Australia, not to mention the United States' extensive and expanding (rotational) basing access to and/or strategic partnerships with countries across the First and Second Island Chains, ranging from the Philippines and Singapore to Vietnam and Malaysia (Fig. 6.1).[75]

In short, for some in China since the United States is supposedly unwilling to accept a powerful Communist peer, it will never abandon containment and regime change vis-à-vis Beijing. According to this worldview, pure opportunism has underpinned America's cooperative and seemingly benevolent gestures toward China in recent decades. Suspicious vis-à-vis America's intentions, and caught in a structural

[74]Nathan and Scobell (2012).
[75]Kaplan (2014).

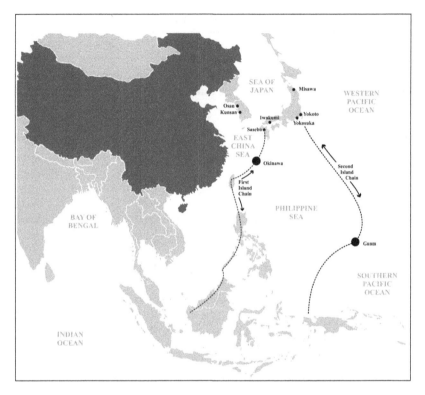

Fig. 6.1 First and Second Island Chains

competition for regional dominance, China has gradually carved out a zone of control in near waters. Henry Kissinger aptly describes the pernicious persistence of mutual mistrust between Washington and Beijing despite decades of détente:

> Some American strategic thinkers argue that Chinese policy pursues two long-term objectives: displacing the United States as the preeminent power in the western Pacific and consolidating Asia into an exclusionary bloc deferring to Chinese economic and foreign policy interests ... [For them] Beijing possesses the ability to pose unacceptable risks in a conflict with Washington and is developing increasingly sophisticated means to negate traditional U.S. advantages. Its invulnerable second-strike nuclear capability will eventually be paired with an expanding range of antiship ballistic

missiles and asymmetric capabilities in new domains such as cyberspace and space. China could secure a dominant naval position [in the region] … [eventually] lead[ing] to the creation of a Sinocentric Asian bloc dominating the western Pacific … On the Chinese side … They see the United States as a wounded superpower determined to thwart the rise of any challenger, of which China is the most credible. No matter how intensely China pursues cooperation, some Chinese argue, Washington's fixed objective will be to hem in a growing China by military deployment and treaty commitments, thus preventing it from playing its historic role as the Middle Kingdom.[76]

Mahan in Beijing

The timing of China's increased maritime assertiveness is an important indication of the calibrated nature of its (expansionist) maritime strategy, which is sensitive to the prevailing balance of power or alignment of forces (*Shi*) in the international system. A more careful look at China's actions suggests that its maritime assertiveness in adjacent waters preceded the Great Recession, but progressively expanded in scope and intensity in recent years. As early as 1974, when the United States signaled its disengagement from the Vietnamese civil war, and effectively abandoned its ally in Saigon, Chinese forces took on South Vietnam in the Paracel Islands in the northern portion of the South China Sea. By 1988, as the Soviet Union signaled its unwillingness to stand by its ally in Hanoi, China turned its attention to the Spratly Islands in the southern portion of the South China Sea, engaging in violent skirmishes against (unified) Vietnam forces for prized features such as the Johnson South Reef and Fiery Cross.[77]

In 1994, shortly after American bases in Subic and Clark were closed, China seized control of the Philippine-claimed Mischief Reef in the Spratly Islands, sparking a bilateral crisis the following year. In all instances, China was obviously exploiting the regional power vacuum as the reigning superpowers, Washington and Moscow, either effectively abandoned their allies and/or refused to deter Chinese maritime adventurism with military force. By astutely employing a salami-slicing strategy—usage of low-intensity skirmishes and intimidation

---

[76] Kissinger (2012).
[77] Garver (1992).

tactics to gradually gobble up one contested feature after the other—China was able to avoid triggering a broader conflict, and contain further escalation. In short, China kept its assertiveness below a threshold of full confrontation. To be fair, China was essentially replicating America's nineteenth-century strategy of dominating near waters (the Caribbean)—just as ancient Rome did vis-à-vis the Mediterranean—on its path to first regional then later international primacy. Reflecting on the foundations of Great Britain's dominance in the eighteenth century, specifically in his groundbreaking work *The Influence of Sea Power Upon History: 1660–1783*, the American naval strategist Alfred Thayer Mahan (1840–1914) played an influential role in advocating a strategic doctrine, which emphasized the centrality of developing a robust naval force that could exert control over vital international waterways, protect important trade linkages, and deny access to other powers across key SLOCs.[78] Such Mahanian strategy was seen as not only essential to preserving the more immediate interests of a rising power such as the United States, but also creating a perimeter of defense and broader 'zone of deference' that could serve as a linchpin for greater global ambitions. This is among the chief motivations behind China's rising territorial assertiveness in near waters.

The Blue Soil

Under the Monroe Doctrine, America first tried to dominate the Western Hemisphere and the Caribbean, before venturing into the Western Pacific toward the end of the Nineteenth Century. China's maritime assertiveness in adjacent waters resembled America's (and Rome's) similar efforts in their own backyards. For more than a millennium, specifically under the Han, Tang, and Ming dynasties, China was effectively the undisputed power in a Sino-centric East Asian order, but it was largely focused on threats from "barbarians" in the north than, say, oriented toward (European-style) maritime domination in the Western Pacific.[79]

With the disappearance of the Soviet threat, and resolution of the bulk of its continental border disputes, twenty-first-century China began to transform from a continental to a maritime power, now interested in dominating near waters and playing a key role in an era of the global maritime competition (Kaplan 2010). China's formal rapprochement

---

[78] Kaplan (2013).
[79] Chua (2009).

with Vietnam in the post-Cold War period didn't prevent it from imposing its will on its smaller communist neighbor. In early 2005, Chinese forces killed nine Vietnamese fishermen. By 2007 and 2008, China sought to sabotage Vietnam's efforts at developing hydrocarbon resources in the South China Sea by threatening Exxon Mobil and British Petroleum with sanctions if they continued their joint ventures with Hanoi in the contested area. In 2009, 210 Vietnamese fishermen were detained by Chinese forces, who seized their seventeen boats. The following year, China declared a unilateral fishing ban in the South China Sea.[80] For China, the battle was no longer over continental soil, but now extended to what it called its "blue soil."[81] China wasn't only motivated by the strategic imperative of creating a perimeter of defense in near seas. By now, unlike the United States in the Nineteenth Century, China was also swept over by a wave of popular nationalism—anchored by the Patriotic Education program—that espoused the belief that adjacent waters, particularly the South China Sea, are an extension of Chinese national territory.[82]

The intersection of strategic interests (i.e., establishment of perimeter of defense) and nationalistic (i.e., reclaiming China's historical territories) claims in near waters encouraged China to progressively seek to push the American juggernaut out of the Western Pacific. In early 2009, five vessels, belonging to varying Chinese law enforcement agencies, coordinated a joint effort at harassing the USS *Impeccable* about 75 nautical miles off the coast of Hainan. The American vessel was forced to make an emergency "all stop" to avoid a collision with the Chinese paramilitary forces. A few months later, two Chinese fishing vessels staged a similar operation against the USS *Victorious*. Even in the Yellow Sea, a site of overlapping claims between China and a relatively cordial neighbor in the Korean Peninsula, Beijing stepped up its assertiveness. As early 2001, a Chinese frigate threatened a US oceanographic survey ship (USNS *Bowditch*), which was conducting a routine survey in the area, to exit China's 200 nautical miles Exclusive Economic Zone (EEZ).[83]

---

[80] Pedrozo (2010).

[81] See Shirk (2008), Johnson (2014), and Hayton (2014).

[82] See Hayton (2014) and Holmes (2015).

[83] A coastal state is only allowed to do so within its territorial sea and, at most, in its (non-overlapping) contiguous zone, provided its safety and interests are clearly in danger as specified by international law (see Part II of UNCLOS).

In 2009, a similar operation was staged against another American surveillance vessel in the area. By July 2010, Beijing openly opposed joint exercises between America and South Korea in response to North Korea's alleged sinking of South Korean warship (*Cheonon*) few months earlier. That year, amid China's vehement protestations, America's super-carrier USS *George Washington* was forced to conduct joint exercises with South Korea in the Sea of Japan instead of the Yellow Sea as originally planned. In 2007, China—or to be more specific, the PLA—jolted American attention when it conducted an anti-satellite (ASAT) test in 2007, shooting down a weather satellite with a ballistic missile (without giving prior notice to Washington). This was an important warning to Washington, which heavily relies on satellite technology for coordinating its naval maneuvers.[84]

Meanwhile, China was also developing its underwater military capabilities, an area of particular concern to Washington. Beginning in the 1980s, Admiral Liu Huaqing, seen as China's own Mahan, played a critical role in advocating greater Chinese attack submarine presence in near waters. In the past four decades, China has divested from diesel submarines in favor of nuclear submarines, which can stay deep below the ocean's surface for an extended period, and are less easy to detect. The Chinese admiral called for China to achieve naval dominance in the First Island Chain by 2010 and in the Second Island Chain in the following decade. The Great Recession provided a major opening for China's military to actualize Liu's plans. By 2014, China launched "boomer"-type submarines, which are capable of launching nuclear missiles from the sea to much of East Asia, Alaska, Hawaii, and the continental United States.[85]

Shifting Gears

China's growing assertiveness in the near seas, however, was also influenced by the actions of other claimant states. The years 2010 and 2011 saw an even more assertive China, which rattled smaller neighbors—driving many of them into America's embrace.[86] In response to Vietnam and Malaysia's decision to submit their continental shelves claims to the UN Commission on the Limits of the Continental Shelf (CLCS), China

---

[84] See Gill and Kleiber (2007) and Kaplan (2013).

[85] Page (2014).

[86] Luttwack (2012).

officially unveiled its notorious "nine-dashed-line" claims,[87] covering much of the South China Sea. During the 2010 ASEAN Regional Forum (ARF), China's Foreign Minister Yang Jiechi became uncharacteristically combative, reportedly warning his counterparts in Southeast Asia: "China is a big country and other countries are small countries, and that's just a fact."[88] Recognizing growing worries over American commitment to rein in China's rising assertiveness, then Secretary of State Hillary Clinton effectively injected Washington into the heart of the disputes by offering assistance in negotiating a Code of Conduct (COC) in the South China Sea, while declaring that FON constitutes a "national interest" issue for her government just when Beijing signaled that it treated its claims in the area as a "core interest."[89,90] This was, in many ways, the beginning of the Obama administration's P2A policy, which was perceived in Beijing as a hostile and thinly veiled containment strategy, but fully welcomed by treaty allies such as Japan and the Philippines, which were deeply perturbed by China's maritime posturing. The following year saw an even more assertive China, which began harassing not only Vietnam, but also an American treaty ally, the Philippines. Between February and March 2011, there were at least five major incidents involving Chinese forces taking on South China Sea claimant states. There were also secondary factors, which affected China's posturing in the near seas, particularly in the South China Sea. The discovery of or speculations over huge hydrocarbon reserves in the area, the fragmented nature of China's maritime law enforcement structure ("five dragons in the high seas" phenomenon[91]), the growing influence of the PLA Navy's

---

[87] Actually, it isn't yet clear whether China is claiming the entire South China Sea, or just the land features in the area and their surrounding territorial waters. The Philippines' arbitration case against China was partly designed to force China to clarify this issue.

[88] Pomfret (2010).

[89] The term "core interest" is widely believed to mean that China is willing to risk military conflict and completely shuns any compromise.

[90] Buckley (2013).

[91] The 'Five Dragons' are China Marine Surveillance, General Administration of Customs (under the State Council), the Maritime Border Police (formerly under the Ministry of Public Security), the Fishing Regulation Administration (FRA, formerly under the Ministry of Agriculture), and the Maritime Safety Administration (under the Ministry of Transport) under the supervision of the State Ocean Administration (SOA). Until Xi's reforms in early 2013, which placed SOA as the lead agency to oversee China's maritime law enforcement bureaucracy, these agencies precariously jostled over jurisdiction in the South China Sea, injecting tremendous unpredictability into the picture.

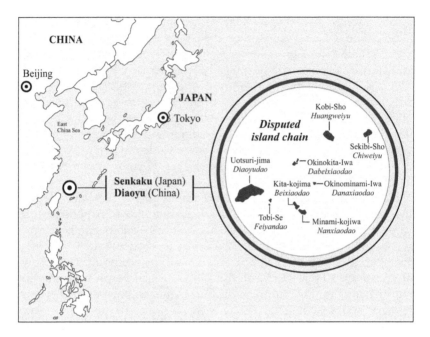

Fig. 6.2   Senkaku/Diaoyu Islands in the East China Sea

South Sea Fleet and paramilitary forces engaged in "people's war" at sea, and the growing interest of provincial government units (e.g., Hainan and Fujian) in exploiting fisheries resources[92] across the disputed waters collectively further compounded the South China Sea conundrum.[93]

The Revenge of History

Despite earlier efforts by the Democratic Party of Japan (DPJ) administration, under Prime Minister Yukio Hatoyama, for a reset in

---

[92] Confronting fisheries shortage due to overexploitation in their adjacent waters, local governments units such as Hainan encouraged its fishermen to venture deep into the South China Sea, as far as 670 miles to the south and deep into waters off the coast of Indonesia and the Philippines, providing fuel subsidies (US$320–US$480 per day) for larger vessels, renovation grants of up to US$322,500 for vessels fishing Companies, and advanced GPS gadgets for tens of thousands of fishermen.

[93] See Ruwitch (2014) and Erickson and Collins (2013).

Japan–China relations—as a crucial element of a broader post-American Asian community—the year 2010 marked the rekindling of age-old territorial disputes (see Fig. 6.2). The apprehension of a Chinese fisherman by Japan's Coast Guard forces close to the Senkaku (*Diaoyu* to the Chinese) islands in the East China Sea sparked a major diplomatic crisis, with Beijing demanding the unconditional release of the Chinese citizen. There was a lot of historical baggage involved: The disputed features were the spoils of the Sino-Japanese naval war (1894), which were reacquired by postwar Japan in 1972. Over the past four decades, Japan has exercised continuous and effective administrative control over the area, and has refused to even acknowledge its contested nature. But for the Chinese, as Asia scholar McCormack (2013) explains, a "single line may be drawn from Ryukyu (1879), Senkaku/Diaoyu (1895), Taiwan (1895), to Dongbei or 'Manchuria' (1931) …International law offered no system to which aggrieved colonial or semi-colonial countries could appeal and no such recourse was open to China…" For Beijing, the occupation of the Senkakus—beginning in the late nineteenth century—symbolized the demise of Sino-centric order and the rise of Imperial Japan—a living embodiment of China's historical humiliation in the nineteenth and early twentieth centuries. Though the late twentieth century saw varying efforts by both sides to shelve sovereignty disputes in the area in favor of stronger economic ties, Beijing began to betray signs of impatience as the first decade of the twenty-first century drew to a close.

Beyond avenging its historical humiliation, China's renewed assertiveness over the disputed features also reflected a fundamental shift in power between China and Japan (see Chapter 7).[94] Over the succeeding years, China stepped up "gray-zone" provocations[95]—deployment of paramilitary patrols close to the disputed features, harassment of Japanese jetfighters, imposition of ADIZ that compels other countries to seek Chinese permission before entering the airspace in the area,[96] unilateral drilling close to disputed waters, among others—against Japan. Over the years, China progressively stepped up its contestation of Japanese administrative control of the Senkakus by deploying an armada of paramilitary and military patrols to the area (see Fig. 6.3).

---

[94]See De Koning and Lipscy (2013), Walton (2014), Kang (2014), and Bitzinger (2015).

[95]Holmes and Yoshihara (2017).

[96]For more discussion on ADIZ see Welch (2013).

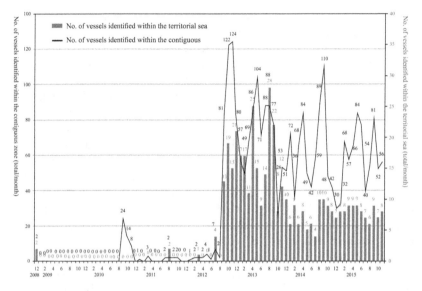

Fig. 6.3 Chinese paramilitary deployments into Senkau/Diaoyu Islands (*Source* Japanese Ministry of Foreign Affairs)

China was now openly expressing its intent on dominating the "Three Seas" (San Hai), namely the East and South China Seas as well as the Yellow Sea.

March to the East

China's growing maritime assertiveness perturbed American allies such as Japan and the Philippines, which welcomed greater American strategic footprint in the region. This coincided with—and provided a perfect backdrop for—the Obama administration decision to rebalance its strategic commitments from the Eurasian landmass to the Western Pacific. The P2A policy rested on three core principles: First, it marked the Obama administration's interest in decoupling American assets and strategic focus from the quagmire in Iraq, Afghanistan and the Greater Middle East, which severely enervated the global superpower and undermined its legitimacy (see Chapter 3); second, it signaled Washington's interest in tapping the vast consumer markets in the Asia-Pacific area, which emerged as the new pivot of global economy in the twenty-first century; and finally, it underlined America's growing suspicions vis-à-vis China's strategic designs in East Asia and the Western Pacific.[97] Though Secretary of State Clinton informally kicked off the P2A during the 2010 ARF summit, Obama officially launched the new policy before the Australian parliament in late 2011, where he underlined Washington's commitment to remain as the anchor of regional order and prosperity:

> Our new focus on this region reflects a fundamental truth – the United States has been, and always will be, a Pacific nation ... Here, we see the future. As the world's fastest-growing region – and home to more than half the global economy – the Asia Pacific is critical to achieving my highest priority, and that's creating jobs and opportunity for the American people ... As President, I have, therefore, made a deliberate and strategic decision – as a Pacific nation, the United States will play a larger and long-term role in shaping this region and its future, by upholding core principles and in close partnership with our allies and friends ... We will keep our commitments ... we will constantly strengthen our capabilities to meet the needs of the 21st century. Our enduring interests in the region demand our enduring presence in the region.[98]

In an influential article for the *Foreign Policy* magazine, entitled "America's Pacific century," Clinton provided a more in-depth articulation of the P2A policy:

> The Asia-Pacific has become a key driver of global politics ... At a time when the region is building a more mature security and economic architecture to promote stability and prosperity, U.S. commitment there is essential. It will help build that architecture and pay dividends for continued American leadership well into this century, just as our post-World War II commitment to building a comprehensive and lasting transatlantic network of institutions and relationships has paid off many times over – and continues to do so ... Harnessing Asia's growth and dynamism is central to American economic and strategic interests and a key priority for President Obama ... The region is eager for our leadership and our business – perhaps more so than at any time in modern history.[99]

[97] Kaplan (2014).
[98] Obama (2011).
[99] Clinton (2011).

America's refocus on the Asia-Pacific region didn't only look reasonable, but was also urgently needed, especially among American allies and partners along the First Island chain. On trade policy, the Obama administration pushed for the Trans-Pacific Partnership (TPP) agreement, which sought to bind together twelve of the most promising economies across the Pacific theater under a "high-standard" trade liberalization regime. To put things into perspective, the Asia-Pacific region is a top destination for American products, outstripping transatlantic trade by 50%, while two-way flow of direct investments between Washington and its Asian partners have doubled in the last decade, with South Korea, Singapore, India, and China featuring among America's top ten most rapidly growing sources of FDI.[100] In the words of former senior American diplomat Kurt Campbell, one of the architects of the Obama strategy, "The Pivot is premised on the idea that the Asia-Pacific region not only increasingly defines global power and commerce, but also welcomes US leadership and rewards US engagements with positive returns on political, economic, and military investments."[101] It's a region that, according to former Australian Ambassador to the United States Kim Beazley, "is the sunny uplands for America, and no region appreciates [it] more."[102] As an ambassador from a major Middle Eastern (revisionist) nation told the author, "In our region, the U.S. is [seen as] the bogeyman and source of all destruction. Here [in Asia], it's a beloved sheriff."

One could argue that Singapore's legendary founder, former Prime Minister Lee Kuan Yew, may have been among the important voices that encouraged Washington to push ahead with the TPP agreement in order to counter China's lurch toward economic hegemony in Southeast Asia. In a 2007 cable,[103] the Singaporean leader reportedly "urged the United States to pursue more Free Trade Agreements to give the region options besides China," lest Beijing leverage its economic prowess to squeeze out strategic concessions from its smaller and increasingly dependent neighbors.[104] In military terms, Washington promised to commit 60% of

---

[100] Campbell and Ratner (2014).

[101] Campbell (2016).

[102] Ibid., 2.

[103] Wikileaks (2007).

[104] Conversation with the author October 2014, Manila. The conversation was in a Middle Eastern language, hence the quote is a rough translation by the author.

its massive naval assets to the region, with the planned relocation of expeditionary forces and/or expanded (rotational) basing access to partners and allied countries such as Australia, the Philippines, and Singapore. By 2012, it had already deployed 60% of its aircraft carriers to the Pacific theater. Yet, America's refocus on the region failed to prevent further provocative posturing from China.[105] On one hand, China's massive economic resources gave it sufficient confidence and room for maneuver, allowing Beijing to leverage trade and investment incentives to win friends, counter American influence, and divide the region. On the other hand, China's hardliners saw the P2A as a perfect excuse to justify a more muscular policy in the region, with the leadership in Beijing—amid a rise in popular nationalism—coming under pressure to prove it wouldn't be intimidated by Washington's growing strategic footprint. The P2A also encouraged treaty allies such as Japan and the Philippines to up the ante, testing America's commitment to keep China's territorial ambitions in check. The result was a "provocation dialectic," whereby Beijing, Tokyo, and Manila pushed the envelope in order to clarify how far America was committed to preserving the status quo. Aside from challenging American naval dominance in adjacent waters, China also more directly sought to shape the regional economic order.

The Soft Power Coup

In early 2014, China dealt a huge blow to the United States' leadership in the region when it managed to enlist leading European economies as well as American allies in Asia as founding members of the Asian Infrastructure Investment Bank (AIIB), which would be headquartered in Beijing. Former Treasury Secretary Larry Summers (2015) went so far as claiming that the AIIB episode possibly marked "the moment the United States lost its role as the underwriter of the global economic system."[106] Meanwhile, the United States came under growing criticism for struggling to forge a coherent strategy on the TPP free trade agreement, as the Obama administration scrambled for legislative support to expedite the trade negotiations involving key Asian partners such as Japan, Vietnam, Malaysia, and Singapore. As the Obama administration and

---

[105] See Ross (2012) and Kaplan (2014).
[106] Summers (2015).

the Congress, particularly Democrats, squabbled over granting Obama fast track authority, Singapore's then Foreign Minister K. Shanmugam warned, "American credibility will be seriously impacted if this [the TPP] doesn't go through," underscoring the repercussions of continued political squabbles over the TPP in Washington.[107] To drive home his point, Singapore's top diplomat stressed the importance of trade to regional leadership in Asia: "In a sense the history of East Asia and the Asia-Pacific is being re-written through trade deals…Can you as a Pacific power, a world power, afford to not fully engage in this region?"[108] Further emphasizing the strategic significance of the TPP, the then US Defense Secretary Ashton Carter astonishingly claimed "passing TPP is as important to me as another aircraft carrier."[109]

The strategic lesson of the continuous back-and-forth hegemonic struggles between the United States and China is clear: Leadership in Asia is as much about serving as an anchor of stability—as Washington has sought to do for the past seven decades—as it is about undergirding the regional economic order by providing trade and investment incentives, as China has been efficiently doing for the past decade or so. If the United States wants to remain as the undisputed regional leader, which is essentially the logic behind the P2A, it will have to not only deter further Chinese provocations in adjacent waters, particularly in the South China Sea, but also enhance its economic footprint in Asia in ways that are consistent with the developmental imperatives of the regional states. Back in 2007, Lee Kuan Yew described China's strategy in East Asia as pretty straightforward and outright domineering: "China tells the region, 'Come grow with me.' At the same time, China's leaders want to convey the impression that China's rise is inevitable and that countries will need to decide if they want to be China's friend or foe when it 'arrives.' China is also willing *to calibrate its engagement to get what it wants or express its displeasure*" [author's own emphasis]. For instance, China effectively placed an investment freeze on the Philippines, until the Rodrigo Duterte presidency (see Chapter 8), which dared to take China to international court over the South China Sea disputes, while dangling large-scale investments to other Southeast Asian countries, which have

---

[107] Agence France-Press (2015).

[108] Wikileaks (2007).

[109] Cooper (2015).

not openly stood up to it.[110] Between 2001 and 2011, China pledged more than $600 billion in foreign aid and government-sponsored investment activity (FAGIA) to developing countries around the world, with ASEAN countries such as Indonesia ($38 billion), Malaysia ($14 billion), and Thailand ($13 billion) featuring among the biggest beneficiaries.[111] China also doubled down on its commercial diplomacy by propping up alternative international financial institutions, from the BRICs New Development Bank to the AIIB and the "One Road, One Belt" new Silk Road initiative. While in the past China's FAGIA was more focused on resource-rich Latin America and Africa, the Xi administration is instead more interested in courting the goodwill of its more immediate neighbors. In short, China can theoretically avoid a full diplomatic backlash so long as it dominates the economic landscape—the core interest of states and peoples across Asia. So long as China maintains its position as a key trading partner and source of large-scale investments, particularly in strategic sectors such as utilities and infrastructure, Beijing will maintain significant (but not irreversible) influence over its neighbors.

This is why it is important, as Singapore's late leader advised, to provide alternative options for the region. The negotiations over the TPP, however, were repeatedly hobbled by delays and disagreements at home as well as among trading partners. At home, Obama was, quite ironically, saved by 11th-hour Republican votes, which granted him the trade promotion authority (TPA) to expedite the negotiations. Many Democrats fiercely opposed the TPP on the grounds that it hurts the domestic workforce. A key challenge, however, was the concern among many negotiating partners, particularly developing countries in Asia, over provisions that seemed to overwhelmingly favor (American) corporate interests at the expense of domestic industrial policy and the general welfare of consumers.[112] The Obama administration reportedly made necessary concessions in order to win the support of other negotiating countries to seal a deal before its term in office is finished, but securing the support of the US Congress for the final approval of the TPP agreement proved another major hurdle.[113] Eventually, the Obama administration failed to get the

---

[110] Heydarian (2015c).
[111] Wolf et al. (2013).
[112] Finnegan (2015).
[113] *The Economist* (2015, October).

TPP pass the Congress in time, leaving it to Trump to decide its fate, or at least America's participation in it. Economic inducements are a crucial component of what American Political Scientist Joseph Nye termed as "soft power," namely the ability to shape the preferences of other nations through noncoercive means, including attraction, persuasion, and co-optation. According to Nye, soft power is based on the premise that "it is also important to set the agenda and attract others in world politics, and not only force them to change by threatening military force or economic sanctions."[114] The attractiveness of one's culture, the traction of its values and political system, and the pace, shape, and conduct of its foreign policy are other important elements of soft power. Paradoxically, modern China seemingly became a more eager student of Nye's advice.[115]

Throughout its repeated cycles of rise and decline, soft power was at the heart of Imperial China's enduring tributary system in East Asia, which reached its zenith under the Tang dynasty (AD 618–907). In *Day of Empire*, Amy Chua shows how it was primarily China's civilizational prestige cosmopolitan outlook, and gigantic economic resources that undergirded its status as the preeminent power in the region until the advent of European colonialism.[116] Modern China, specifically toward the latter years of Deng Xiaoping's rule and thereafter, also leveraged commercial diplomacy to enhance Beijing's influence across the region. As far as China is concerned, commercial diplomacy took two interrelated forms. First, rapid capitalist expansion encouraged China to actively employ the diplomatic apparatus of the state to expand China's trade and investment relations globally, particularly with respect to the industrialized world as well as resource-rich countries in Africa and Latin America. Second, over time, a prosperous China began to actively leverage its newfound wealth— thanks to a successful neo-mercantilist strategy based on currency manipulation and an aggressively export-oriented industrial base—for facilitating specific strategic goals overseas. While the first stage of its commercial diplomacy was more reflective of the policies of Deng Xiaoping and Jiang Zemin, the second stage of commercial diplomacy was more apparent during the late–Hu Jintao and Xi Jinping administrations. Dissatisfied by the outcome of Structural Adjustment Programs (SAPs) and

---

[114]Nye (2004, 5).

[115]Ibid., 11.

[116]Chua (2009).

policy prescriptions of the World Bank and the IMF, under the so-called "Washington Consensus," many developing countries welcomed the emergence of China as an alternative global creditor (see Chapter 4).[117]

Economic Statecraft

Initially, China's commercial diplomacy seemed largely benign and beneficial to the developing world and the global economy. The Beijing Consensus was based on a simple bargain (see Chapter 4). For the industrialized world, China provided an attractive investment destination, thanks to its shiny infrastructure and surplus labor. As the world's factory, China subsidized the precipitous decline of manufacturing costs for a whole host of products, which empowered global consumers who could now afford an ever-growing volume and range of products. For the resource-rich developing world, China became a primary customer and foreign investor, transforming the fortunes of countries such as Brazil and much of sub-Saharan Africa. Throughout the early 2000s, China's seemingly insatiable demand for raw materials and minerals pushed up global commodity prices to new heights, creating a bubble-like commodity boom. Over the years, however, there was a growing backlash against China's "going global" strategy. In Africa and Latin America, complaints centered on China's preference for employing its own citizens for overseas projects handled by SOEs, the dangerous working conditions under Chinese employers, entrenchment of autocratic and inefficient institutions that survived on China's no-strings-attached largesse and the environmental costs of China's mining activities More fundamentally, China was criticized for reorienting the economies of other developing countries toward unsustainable extractive industries at the expense of domestic manufacturing and agriculture. From sub-Saharan Africa to Southeast Asia and Latin America, a number of countries, particularly commodity-exporting nations, began to experience de-industrialization and rising economic inequality as resource-extraction became the primary source of income for the ruling elite. China's scramble for Africa provided a modern infrastructure, which primarily catered to the efficient transfer of mineral resources from mines to ports.[118]

---

[117] Kurlantzick (2008).
[118] See Kurlantzick (2008), Sharma (2012), and French (2014).

Meanwhile, the industrialized world bemoaned the outsourcing of domestic jobs to China's SEZs, a factor behind the depressed wages of and stubborn unemployment among the American middle class, while Western multinational companies raised concerns over increasingly restrictive and arbitrary investment rules and regulations under the CCP. It didn't take long before China employed its commercial diplomacy to challenge the existing order. With the 2008 Great Recession undermining Western economies, China began to speak its mind more forcefully. Countering the American-backed TPP free trade agreement, which excludes China but includes Vietnam, Xi also called for a pan-regional Free Trade Area of the Asia-Pacific (FTAAP), which will essentially be a consolidation of existing free trade deals between China and other regional economies.[119] At the 2014 Conference on Interaction and Confidence Building Measures in Asia (CICA), a gathering of Eurasian continental nations that includes Russia and Iran, Chinese president Xi Jinping called for "a new regional security cooperation architecture" where Asian problems will "be solved by Asians themselves," a thinly veiled jab at extra-regional powers like the United States, which has stood as the anchor of the Asian order for the past seven decades.[120] Eager to close the military gap, China is turbocharging its military modernization program with double-digit defense-budget growth.[121] China's rising territorial assertiveness in adjacent waters is perhaps indicative of its plans, as envisioned by Admiral Liu Huaqing (founder of China's modern navy), to dominate the First Island Chain in the medium term, paving the way for dominating East Asia by pushing the United States out of the Second Island Chain in the Western Pacific by the middle of the twenty-first century.[122] In response, a growing number of Asian countries, from treaty allies such as Japan and the Philippines (until Duterte's ascendance) to fence-sitters such as Singapore and former rivals such as Vietnam, have welcomed a greater American military footprint in the region, giving rise to an informal "maritime coalition of the willing."[123]

---

[119] Heydarian (2015a).

[120] Tiezzi (2014).

[121] Bitzinger (2015).

[122] Page (2014).

[123] See Kaplan (2014) and Heydarian (2015b).

Cognizant of the regional pushback, the Xi administration launched the so-called "peripheral diplomacy" (*zhoubian waijiao*) strategy, which calls on China to "strive to promote regional security cooperation" and "insist on mutual trust and benefit, equality and cooperation, propose the overall, common and cooperative security idea to push ahead security cooperation with peripheral countries."[124] For skeptics, the peripheral diplomacy strategy is essentially aimed at leveraging China's massive economic resources to buy off the goodwill of neighbors and, if needed, fully divide-and-conquer the region. In the last two years, China has pledged more than $100 billion to various regional economic initiatives, from the AIIB to the "One Belt, One Road" Strategy, with another $1.25 trillion allocated for a global investment splurge by 2025 (see Chapter 4). To further boost its soft power, China spends as much as $10 billion annually on external propaganda, which is powered by a plethora of state-dominated global media outlets under the supervision of the State Council Information Office (SCIO). By 2015, China was estimated to have roughly $4 trillion in currency reserves, a gigantic cache to fund a soft power splurge. Meanwhile, the Obama administration struggled to effectuate its Asia policy.[125]

THE PIVOT AND ITS DISCONTENTS

The P2A wasn't only about increased American focus on and strategic footprint in East Asia. It was also about introducing a more effective burden-sharing arrangement, whereby key regional allies such as Japan would begin to play a more consequential role in preserving the regional balance of power. In an era of sequestration and anemic growth—compounded by continued geopolitical tremors in other regions of the world such as Eastern Europe and the Middle East, which also demand American strategic commitment—the United States has had no choice but to jointly guard the international order along with its trusted allies. Under the Shinzo Abe administration, Japan has increasingly become

---

[124]See a summary of the speech at China Council for International Cooperation and Environment and Development (2013).

[125]Shambaugh (2015).

a proactive contributor to preserving the US-led order in the region. Intent on challenging China's economic hegemony, the Abe administration has stepped up its investments across Asia, pledging as much as $20 billion in loans and aid to the ASEAN, up to $35 billion to India, and up to $110 billion for Asian infrastructure development (see Chapter 7). For many Southeast Asian countries, a Sino-Japanese rivalry in the economic realm is a much-welcomed development, since it means more trade and investment opportunities.[126] But the P2A has had a mixed record with respect to managing maritime tensions in the area. Though it signaled growing American strategic footprint in the region, it didn't clarify how far Washington is willing to go to protect the territorial integrity and maritime interests of its allies. It took until his 2014 state visit to Tokyo for Obama to explicitly state that the US–Japan Mutual Defense Treaty covers the Senkaku Islands.[127] But such assurances seemed reluctant at best, a grudging recognition of Japan's administrative control over the disputed features. Given the tremendous level of economic interdependence between China and the United States, with the Obama administration officials describing Sino-American relations as the most important bilateral relationship of the century, there were always bound to be doubts as to the depth of American commitment to its allies. If anything, the Obama administration—similar to the Clinton administration—was, and continues to be seen, as extremely reticent in confronting China. As Harvard Professor Stephen Walt observed:

> Both Obama and Clinton were committed to maintaining U.S. 'global leadership.' Both favored spreading democracy where possible, but turned a blind eye toward various dictatorships when circumstances seemed to require it. Both sought to engage a rising China, while hedging against a future rivalry. (Obama did more of the latter, of course, because there is now more to hedge against). But most importantly, both Clinton and Obama were highly risk-averse regarding the use of American military power.[128]

---

[126] Heydarian (2015a).

[127] Article I of the US–Japan MDT declares that 'Japan grants, and the United States of America accepts, the right ... to dispose United States land, air and sea forces in and about Japan. Such forces may be utilized to contribute to the maintenance of international peace and security in the Far East and to the security of Japan against armed attack from without.'

[128] Walt (2014).

The P2A also reinforced Chinese suspicions vis-a-vis American attitudes toward its rise. As Wu Xinbo (a prominent Chinese scholar from Fudan University) argues, "Beijing also suspects that Washington's intended role of balancer serves only to check a rising China, undermining its legitimate national interests in the region."[129] The result was a self-fulfilling prophecy of intensified Sino-American rivalry. As prominent Sinologist Robert Ross explains:

> The decision to pursue the pivot was based on the premise that a newly emboldened China was challenging U.S. interests and undermining regional stability simply because it could – that is, because its growing military power made aggressive diplomacy easier and more attractive than in the past ... The new U.S. policy unnecessarily compounds Beijing's insecurities and will only feed China's aggressiveness, undermine regional stability, and decrease the possibility of cooperation between Beijing and Washington ... By threatening China and challenging its sovereignty claims over symbolic territories, Washington has encouraged Chinese leaders to believe that only by adopting belligerent policies will a rising China be able to guarantee its security. Herein lies the great irony of the pivot: a strategy that was meant to check a rising China has sparked its combativeness and damaged its faith in cooperation.[130]

Another problem with the P2A was that it was stronger in rhetoric than in substance. To begin with, as early as 1997, the US was already devoting a large portion of its military assets to the region. Both Clinton and George W. Bush administration deployed major naval and air assets to Japan and Guam, strengthened defense cooperation with treaty allies like the Philippines, and enhance American access to port facilities of friendly nations such as Singapore. Back in 2005, Washington already announced that it would deploy 60% of its submarines to the Asia-Pacific theater, with the Bush administration assigning an additional aircraft carrier to the area.[131] In 2007, the US Navy expressed its willingness to have a sustained forward presence across the region, which, in the words of Robert Kaplan, represented "a momentous shift in overall US maritime strategy."[132]

---

[129] Wu and Green (2014, 201).
[130] Ross (2012).
[131] Ibid.
[132] Kaplan (2010).

In military terms, the P2A's added-value therefore is questionable, since America never really left the region to begin with and was already increasing its commitment under the Clinton and Bush administrations. In short, the P2A unnecessarily raised expectations by repackaging existing trends in American strategic orientation towards Asia amid much fanfare.

There was also the issue of mixed signals. The departure of Secretary Clinton in 2013 added additional uncertainty about American commitment to its allies, especially when her incoming replacement, John Kerry, expressed reservations vis-à-vis growing American military footprint in the region, stating during his confirmation hearing: "I'm not convinced that increased military ramp-up is critical yet. I'm not convinced of that."[133] Such statements weren't very reassuring to treaty allies such as the Philippines, which tragically lost the Scarborough Shoal to China after a precarious standoff in mid-2012. During the crisis, Washington refused to commit militarily, instead encouraging the Philippines to diplomatically manage the dispute, as an armada of Chinese paramilitary vessels surrounded a Filipino frigate (Gregorio Del Pilar), which apprehended Chinese fishermen straddling a contested feature that lay well within the Philippines' 200 nautical miles EEZ. For some observers, the Philippines' decision to use a naval frigate (gray hull) rather a coast guard vessel (a white hull) to apprehend Chinese fishermen reflected a precarious level of adventurism on the part of Manila, which was most probably expecting American military assistance in an event of military confrontation with Beijing—to no avail. For Australian strategist Hugh White, the whole point of the P2A was precisely to show that Washington is willing to "use all elements of American power to resist China's challenge to regional status quo based on US leadership in Asia."[134]

Obviously this wasn't the case during the Scarborough Shoal standoff, underscoring the Obama administration's failure to pass White's test of regional leadership. Amid a budget dispute with Congress, President Obama had to even cancel his much-awaited Asia trip in 2013, where he was expected to attend the APEC summit and make state visits to Malaysia and the Philippines. Obama's no-show was a huge disappointment, with varying leaders, especially Singapore's, openly questioning America's ability to get its house in order and remain as an anchor

---

[133]Economy (2013).
[134]White (2014).

of stability in Asia. Few months earlier, however, Obama held a high-level and intimate summit with Xi, who called for a "new type of great power relationship," with both leaders barely mentioning the territorial disputes in Asia during their formal pronouncements. The following year saw the American president visiting the Philippines, but refusing to clarify whether the Mutual Defence Treaty between the two countries would apply in an event of conflict over disputed features in the South China Sea,[135] especially since the Philippines will have to supposedly prove administrative control over all features it claims.[136] To cement greater American commitment to its territorial interests, Manila desperately negotiated an Enhanced Defense Cooperation Agreement (EDCA) with Washington, providing America with greater rotational access to Philippine bases in Subic and Clark. But the EDCA failed to explicitly commit America to Philippine interests in the South China Sea under the Obama administration, just as Manila took the unprecedented decision of taking China to international court at The Hague over the South China Sea disputes.[137] As former US Assistant Secretary of State for East Asian and Pacific Affairs Kurt Campbell (2009–2013) and Ely Ratner of the Center for a New American Security, bluntly put it as early as 2014: "Almost three years later, the Obama administration still confronts the persistent challenge of explaining the concept and delivering on its promise…"[138] And this is the context within which one should understand Trump's perilous confrontation with China, and how other middle powers are rising to the occasion lest the Indo-Pacific's peace and prosperity is irredeemably damaged by a new great power conflict.

[135] Article IV of the Philippine–U.S. MDT states: 'Each Party recognizes that an armed attack in the Pacific Area on either of the Parties would be dangerous to its own peace and safety and declares that it would act to meet the common dangers in accordance with its constitutional processes [author's own emphasis] …'. Article V states: 'an armed attack on either of the Parties is deemed to include an armed attack on the metropolitan territory of either of the Parties, or on the island territories under its jurisdiction in the Pacific or on its armed forces, public vessels or aircraft in the Pacific'.

[136] See for instance analysis of former US Navy rear admiral Michael McDevitt (2013) on the limits of American commitment to Philippine-claimed features in the South China Sea, particularly the Scarborough Shoal.

[137] See Vitug (2018).

[138] Campbell and Ratner (2014).

REFERENCES

Agence France-Presse. "Taiwan Blasts China for 'Reckless and Provocative' Fighter Jet Incursion." *South China Morning Post.* April 1, 2019. https://www.scmp.com/news/china/military/article/3004049/taiwan-blasts-china-reckless-and-provocative-fighter-jet.

Agence France-Presse. "US Credibility at Stake Over Asia Trade Pact: Singapore." *Rappler.com.* June 17, 2015. https://www.rappler.com/world/global-affairs/96592-us-credibility-at-stake-asia-trade-pact-singapore.

Allen-Ebrahimian, Bethany. "Trump Comes Through for Taiwan with $1.3 Billion Arms Sale." *Foreign Policy.* June 29, 2017. https://foreignpolicy.com/2017/06/29/trump-comes-through-for-taiwan-with-1-3-billion-arms-sale/.

Allison, Graham. *Destined for War: Can America and China Escape Thucydides's Trap.* Boston: Houghton Mifflin Harcourt, 2017.

Allison, Graham. "The Thucydides Trap: Are the U.S. and China Headed for War?" *The Atlantic.* September 24, 2015. https://www.theatlantic.com/international/archive/2015/09/united-states-china-war-thucydides-trap/406756/.

Andreas, Joel. "Changing Colours in China." *New Left Review* 54 (2008). https://newleftreview.org/issues/II54/articles/joel-andreas-changing-colours-in-china.

Andreas, Joel. "A Shanghai Model?" *New Left Review* 65 (2010). https://newleftreview.org/issues/II65/articles/joel-andreas-a-shanghai-model.

Andreas, Joel. "Sino-Seismology." *New Left Review* 76 (2012). https://newleftreview.org/issues/II76/articles/joel-andreas-sino-seismology.

"Asia's Second World War Ghosts." *The Economist.* August 10, 2015. https://www.economist.com/news/essays/en/asia-second-world-war-ghosts.

Aurelio, Julie. "PH Protests Presence of Chinese Boats Near Pag-asa." *Inquirer.* April 2, 2019. https://globalnation.inquirer.net/174045/ph-protests-presence-of-chinese-boats-near-pag-asa.

Babones, Salvatore. "Zhongguo and Tianxia: The Central State and the Chinese World." *Oup.* February 25, 2018. https://blog.oup.com/2018/02/zhongguo-tianxia-chinese-international-relations-terms/.

Barmé, Geremie R. "China's Flat Earth: History and 8 August 2008." *The China Quarterly* 197 (2009): 64–86. https://doi.org/10.1017/s0305741009000046.

Bitzinger, Richard. "China's Double-Digit Defense Growth." *Foreign Affairs.* March 19, 2015. https://www.foreignaffairs.com/articles/china/2015-03-19/chinas-double-digit-defense-growth.

Brzezinski, Zbigniew. *The Grand Chessboard: American Primacy and Its Geostrategic Imperatives.* New York: Basic Books, 1998.

Brzezinski, Zbigniew. "The Group of Two That Can Change the World." *The Financial Times.* January 14, 2009. https://www.ft.com/content/d99369b8-e178-11dd-afa0-0000779fd2ac.

Buckley, Chris. "China Leader Affirms Policy on Islands." *The New York Times.* January 29, 2013. https://www.nytimes.com/2013/01/30/world/asia/incoming-chinese-leader-will-not-to-bargain-on-disputed-territory.html.

Campbell, Kurt. *The Pivot: The Future of American Statecraft in Asia.* New York: Twelve, 2016.

Campbell, Kurt, and Ely Ratner. "Far Eastern Promises: Why Washington Should Focus on Asia." *Foreign Affairs.* April 18, 2014. https://www.foreignaffairs.com/articles/east-asia/2014-04-18/far-eastern-promises.

Chang, Gordon. "The Chinese and Japanese Economies Are Delinking: Prelude to Conflict?" *Forbes.* February 16, 2014. https://www.forbes.com/sites/gordonchang/2014/02/16/the-chinese-and-japanese-economies-are-delinking-prelude-to-conflict/#25cb3b2b3291.

Chua, Amy. *Day of Empire: How Hyperpowers Rise to Global Dominance—And Why They Fall.* New York: Anchor, 2009.

Clinton, Hillary. "America's Pacific Century." *Foreign Policy.* October 11, 2011. https://foreignpolicy.com/2011/10/11/americas-pacific-century/.

Colby, Elbridge, and Paul Lettow. "Have We Hit Peak America." *Foreign Policy.* July 3, 2014. https://foreignpolicy.com/2014/07/03/have-we-hit-peak-america/.

Cooper, Helene. "U.S. Defense Secretary Supports Trade Deal with Asia." *New York Times.* April 7, 2015. https://www.nytimes.com/2015/04/07/us/politics/defense-secretary-supports-trade-deal-with-asia.html.

De Koning, Philippe, and Phillip Lipscy. "The Land of the Sinking Sun." *Foreign Policy.* July 30, 2013. https://foreignpolicy.com/2013/07/30/the-land-of-the-sinking-sun/.

Doornbos, Caitlin. "US Sends B-52 Bombers Over South China Sea for Second Time in a Week." *Stars and Stripes.* March 15, 2019. https://www.stripes.com/news/pacific/us-sends-b-52-bombers-over-south-china-sea-for-second-time-in-a-week-1.572750.

Economy, Elizabeth. "Secretary of State John Kerry on China." *Council on Foreign Relations.* February 27, 2013. https://www.cfr.org/blog/secretary-state-john-kerry-china.

Egan, Daniel. "Rethinking War of Maneuver/War of Position: Gramsci and the Military Metaphor." *Critical Sociology* 40 no. 4 (2013). https://doi.org/10.1177/0896920513480222.

Erickson, Andrew, and Gabe Collins. "Limited Liftoff Looming: Y-20 Transport Prepares for 1st Test Flight." *The Diplomat.* January 8, 2013. https://thediplomat.com/2013/01/limited-liftoff-looming-y-20-transport-prepares-for-1st-test-flight/.

Filkins, Dexter. "James Mattis, a Warrior in Washington." *The New Yorker.* May 22, 2017. https://www.newyorker.com/magazine/2017/05/29/james-mattis-a-warrior-in-washington.

Finnegan, William. "Why Does Obama Want This Trade Deal So Badly." *The New Yorker.* June 11, 2015. https://www.newyorker.com/news/daily-comment/why-does-obama-want-the-trans-pacific-partnership-so-badly.

Fravel, M. Taylor. "All Quiet in the South China Sea." *Foreign Affairs.* March 22, 2012. https://www.foreignaffairs.com/articles/china/2012-03-22/all-quiet-south-china-sea.

French, Howard. *China's Second Continent: How a Million Migrants Are Building a New Empire in Africa.* New York: Knopf, 2014.

Garver, John W. "China's Push Through the South China Sea: The Interaction of Bureaucratic and National Interests." *The China Quarterly* 132 (1992): 999–1028. https://www.jstor.org/stable/654191.

Ghosh, Nirmal. "Renewed US Bid to Stop Beijing's South China Sea Plans." *The Straits Times.* May 25, 2019. https://www.straitstimes.com/world/united-states/renewed-us-bid-to-stop-beijings-south-china-sea-plans.

Gill, Bates, and Martin Kleiber. "China's Space Odyssey: What the Antisatellite Test Reveals About Decision-Making in Beijing." *Foreign Affairs.* May 1, 2007. https://www.foreignaffairs.com/articles/china/2007-05-01/chinas-space-odyssey-what-antisatellite-test-reveals-about-decision-making.

Gordon, Michael. "Trump Shifting Authority Over Military Operations Back to Pentagon." *The New York Times.* March 19, 2017. https://www.nytimes.com/2017/03/19/us/trump-shifting-authority-over-military-operations-back-to-pentagon.html.

Haynes, Suyin. "Xi Jinping Says Taiwan's Unification with China Is 'Inevitable'." *Time.* January 2, 2019. http://time.com/5491569/xi-jinping-taiwan-china-unification-inevitable/.

Hayton, Bill. *The South China Sea: The Struggle for Power in Asia.* New Haven: Yale University Press, 2014.

Heydarian, Richard Javad. *Asia's New Battlefield: US, China, and the Struggle for Western Pacific.* London: Zed, 2015a.

Heydarian, Richard Javad. "South China Sea: Forging a Maritime Coalition of the Willing." *Asia Maritime Transparency Initiative.* May 7, 2015b. https://amti.csis.org/south-china-sea-forging-a-maritime-coalition- of-the-willing/.

Heydarian, Richard Javad. "The Diplomatic Implications of Philippines-China Arbitration." *Asia Maritime Transparency Initiative.* January 21, 2015c. https://amti.csis.org/the-diplomatic-implications-of-philippines-china-arbitration/.

Heydarian, Richard Javad. "Crossing the Rubicon: Duterte, China and Resource-Sharing in the South China Sea." *Maritime Issues.* October 23, 2018a. http://www.maritimeissues.com/politics/crossing-the-rubicon-duterte-china-and-resourcesharing-in-the-south-china-sea.html.

Heydarian, Richard Javad. "Genealogy of Conflict: The Roots, Evolution, and Trajectory of the South China Sea Disputes." In Sumit Ganguly, Andrew Scobell, and Joseph Chinyong Liow (eds.), *The Routledge Handbook of Asian Security Studies*. Abingdon: Routledge, 2018b.

Holmes, James. "The Commons: Beijing's 'Blue National Soil'." *The Diplomat*. January 3, 2013. https://thediplomat.com/2013/01/a-threat-to-the-commons-blue-national-soil/.

Holmes, James. "When China Rules the Sea." *Foreign Policy*. September 23, 2015. https://foreignpolicy.com/2015/09/23/when-china-rules-the-sea-navy-xi-jinping-visit/.

Holmes, James, and Toshi Yoshihara. "Five Shades of Chinese Gray-Zone Strategy." *The National Interest*. May 2, 2017. https://nationalinterest.org/feature/five-shades-chinese-gray-zone-strategy-20450.

"Important Speech of Xi Jinping at Peripheral Diplomacy Work Conference." *China Council for International Cooperation and Environment and Development*. October 30, 2013. http://www.cciced.net/cciceden/NEWSCENTER/LatestEnvironmentalandDevelopmentNews/201310/t20131030_82626.html.

Jennings, Ralph. "Beijing Done, for Now, Acquiring Land in South China Sea." *Voa*. March 15, 2019a. https://www.voanews.com/a/beijing-done-for-now-acquiring-land-in-south-china-sea/4830326.html.

Jennings, Ralph. "China's Jets That Crossed into Taiwan Airspace: Not a First; Maybe Not the Last." *Voa*. April 3, 2019b. https://www.voanews.com/a/china-taiwan-airspace/4859810.html.

Johnson, Jesse. "Pentagon Sends Ships Through Taiwan Strait for Third Time in Three Months." *Japan Times*. March 25, 2019. https://www.japantimes.co.jp/news/2019/03/25/asia-pacific/pentagon-sends-ships-taiwan-strait-third-time-three-months.

Johnson, Jesse. "Photos Confirm U.S.-Chinese Warships' Near-Miss as Experts Say South China Sea Encounter Likely to Affect Allied Operations in Region." *Japan Times*. October 3, 2018. https://www.japantimes.co.jp/news/2018/10/03/asia-pacific/u-s-says-photos-near-collision-chinese-war-ship-south-china-sea-legitimate.

Johnson, Keith. "Lord of the Sea." *Foreign Policy*. May 16, 2014. https://foreignpolicy.com/2014/05/16/lord-of-the-sea/.

Kang, David. "A Looming Arms Race in East Asia?" *The National Interest*. May 14, 2014. https://nationalinterest.org/feature/looming-arms-race-east-asia-10461.

Kaplan, Robert. *Asia's Cauldron: The South China Sea and the End of a Stable Pacific*. New York: Random House Trade Paperbacks, 2014.

Kaplan, Robert. "The Geography of Chinese Power." *Foreign Affairs*. May 1, 2010. https://www.foreignaffairs.com/articles/china/2010-05-01/geography-chinese-power.

Kaplan, Robert. *The Revenge of History: What the Map Tells Us About Coming Conflict and the Battle Against Fate.* New York: Random House, 2013.

Kazianis, Harry. "The 'House of Cards' Lesson for the U.S. Military." *Defense One.* February 20, 2014. https://www.defenseone.com/threats/2014/02/house-cards-lesson-us-military/79091/.

Kissinger, Henry. *On China.* London: Penguin Books, 2012.

Kurlantzick, Joshua. *Charm Offensive: How China's Soft Power Is Transforming the World.* New Haven: Yale University Press, 2008.

Kurlantzick, Joshua. "Taking the Bosses Hostage." *London Review of Books* 31 no. 6 (2009): 9–13. https://www.lrb.co.uk/v31/n06/joshua-kurlantzick/taking-the-bosses-hostage.

Labog-Javellana, Juliet. "Ex-DFA Chief Del Rosario, Morales Sue China's Xi at ICC." *Inquirer.net.* March 21, 2019. https://globalnation.inquirer.net/173757/ex-philippine-officials-fishermen-file-crimes-against-humanity-case-vs-chinese-president-at-icc#ixzz5pEO1loZF.

Lau, Mimi. "Chinese President Xi Jinping Gives Army Its First Order of 2019: Be Ready for Battle." *South China Morning Post.* January 5, 2019. https://www.scmp.com/news/china/politics/article/2180772/chinese-president-xi-jinping-gives-army-its-first-order-2019.

"Lee Kuan Yew on Burma's 'Stupid' Generals and the 'Gambler' Chen Sui-Bian." *WikiLeaks.* October 19, 2007. https://wikileaks.org/plusd/cables/07SINGAPORE1932_a.html.

Li, Cheng. "Assessing U.S.–China Relations Under the Obama Administration." *Brookings Institution.* August 30, 2016. https://www.brookings.edu/opinions/assessing-u-s-china-relations-under-the-obama-administration/.

Li, Nan. *Chinese Civil-Military Relations in the Post-Deng Era: Implications for Crisis Management and Naval Modernization.* Newport: U.S. Naval War College, 2010.

Lindell, Jordan. "Clausewitz: War, Peace and Politics." *E-International Relations Students.* Last date modified November 26, 2009. http://www.e-ir.info/2009/11/26/clausewitz-war-peace-and-politics/.

Liu, Zhen. "'Time for Tougher Deterrence from China' as US Steps Up Patrols in South China Sea." *South China Morning Post.* March 29, 2019. https://www.scmp.com/news/china/diplomacy/article/3003895/time-tougher-deterrence-china-us-steps-patrols-south-china-sea.

Luttwack, Edward. *The Rise of China vs. the Logic of Strategy.* New York: Belknap Press, 2012.

McCormack, G. "Much ado over Small Islands: The Sino-Japanese Confrontation over Senkaku/Diaoyu." *Asia-Pacific Journal* 11, no. 21 (2013). japanfocus.org/-Gavan-McCormack/3947.

McDevitt, Michael. "Will China Refashion the Asian Maritime Order?" *Journal of International Security Affairs* (2013, December). www.cna.org/sites/default/files/McDevitt.pdf.

Mearsheimer, John. "Can China Rise Peacefully." *National Interest.* October 25, 2014. https://nationalinterest.org/commentary/can-china-rise-peacefully-10204.

Medeiros, Evan, and Taylor Fravel. "China's New Diplomacy." *Foreign Affairs.* November 1, 2003. https://www.foreignaffairs.com/articles/asia/2003-11-01/chinas-new-diplomacy.

Nathan, Andrew J., and Andrew Scobell. "How China Sees America: The Sum of Beijing's Fears." *Foreign Affairs* 91, no. 5 (2012): 32–47. http://www.jstor.org/stable/41720859.

Nye, Joseph. *Soft Power: The Means To Success In World Politics.* New York: Public Affairs, 2004.

Obama, Barack. "Remarks by President Obama to the Australian Parliament." Speech, Canberra, Australia. November 17, 2011. *White House Office of the Press Secretary.* https://obamawhitehouse.archives.gov/the-press-office/2011/11/17/remarks-president-obama-australian-parliament.

Osnos, Evan. *Age of Ambition: Chasing Fortune, Truth, and Faith in the New China.* New York: Ferrar, Straus, and Giroux, 2014.

Osnos, Evan. "Born Red." *The New Yorker.* March 30, 2015. https://www.newyorker.com/magazine/2015/04/06/born-red.

Page, Jeremy. "China's Submarines Add Nuclear-Strike Capability, Altering Strategic Balance." *Wall Street Journal.* October 24, 2014. https://www.wsj.com/articles/chinas-submarine-fleet-adds-nuclear-strike-capability-altering-strategic-balance-undersea-1414164738.

Panda, Ankit. "South China Sea: Fourth US FONOP in Five Months Suggests a New Operational Rhythm." *The Diplomat.* October 12, 2017. https://thediplomat.com/2017/10/south-china-sea-fourth-us-fonop-in-five-months-suggests-a-new-operational-rhythm/.

Panda, Ankit. "US Secretary of State Criticizes China's South China Sea Practices." *The Diplomat.* March 14, 2019. https://thediplomat.com/2019/03/us-secretary-of-state-criticizes-chinas-south-china-sea-practices/.

Pedrozo, Raul. "Beijing's Coastal Real Estate." *Foreign Affairs.* November 15, 2010. https://www.foreignaffairs.com/articles/east-asia/2010-11-15/beijing-s-coastal-real-estate.

Pei, Minxin. "How China and America See Each Other." *Foreign Affairs.* March/April 2014. https://www.foreignaffairs.com/reviews/review-essay/how-china-and-america-see-each-other.

Pence, Mike. "Remarks by Vice President Pence at the 2019 Munich Security Conference." Speech, Munich, Germany. February 16, 2019. *White House.* https://www.whitehouse.gov/briefings-statements/remarks-vice-president-pence-2019-munich-security-conference-munich-germany/.

Pence, Mike. "The Administration's Policy Towards China." Speech, Washington, DC. October 4, 2018. *Hudson Institute.* https://www.hudson.org/events/1610-vice-president-mike-pence-s-remarks-on-the-administrations-policy-towards-china102018.

Perper, Rosie. "The US and Philippines Are Reportedly Discussing Deploying a Rocket System in the South China Sea to Fend Off China." *Business Insider.* April 3, 2019. https://www.businessinsider.com/us-and-philippines-rocket-system-in-south-china-sea-2019-4.

Pillsbury, Michael. *Hundred-Year Marathon.* New York: Henry Holt, 2015.

Pomfret, John. "U.S. Takes a Tougher Tone with China." *Washington Post.* July 30, 2010. http://www.washingtonpost.com/wp-dyn/content/article/2010/07/29/AR2010072906416.html.

Pompeo, Michael. "Keynote Address at CERAWeek." Speech, Houston, Texas. March 12, 2019a. *U.S. Department of State.* https://www.state.gov/secretary/remarks/2019/03/290303.htm.

Pompeo, Michael. "Remarks to the Iowa Farm Bureau." Speech, Des Moines, Iowa. March 4, 2019b. *U.S. Department of State.* https://www.state.gov/secretary/remarks/2019/03/289888.htm.

Ranada, Pia. "South China Sea Covered by PH-U.S. Mutual Defense Treaty—Pompeo." *Rappler.* March 1, 2019. https://www.rappler.com/nation/224668-pompeo-says-south-china-sea-covered-philippines-us-mutual-defense-treaty.

Ross, Robert. "The Problem with the Pivot." *Foreign Affairs.* November 1, 2012. https://www.foreignaffairs.com/articles/asia/2012-11-01/problem-pivot.

Ruwitch, John. "Satellites and Seafood: China Keeps Fishing Fleet Connected in Disputed Waters." *Reuters.* July 28, 2014. https://www.reuters.com/article/us-southchinasea-china-fishing-insight.

Shambaugh, David. "China's Soft Power Push." *Foreign Affairs.* June 16, 2015. https://www.foreignaffairs.com/articles/china/2015-06-16/china-s-soft-power-push.

Sharma, Ruchir. *Breakout Nations: In Pursuit of the Next Economic Miracles.* New York: W. W. Norton, 2012.

Sheehan, Neil. *A Bright Shining Lie: John Paul Vann and America in Vietnam.* New York: Vintage, 1989.

Shirk, Susan. *China: Fragile Superpower.* Oxford: Oxford University Press, 2008.

Squitieri, Tom. "On Sea and in Air This Week, US Reminds China the South China Sea Is International and Open." *Talk Media News.* March 15, 2019. http://www.talkmedianews.com/world-news/2019/03/15/on-sea-and-in-air-this-week-us-reminds-china-the-south-china-sea-is-international-and-open/.

Summers, Lawrence. "A Global Wake-Up Call for the U.S.?" *The Washington Post*. April 5, 2015. https://www.washingtonpost.com/opinions/a-global-wake-up-call-for-the-us/2015/04/05/6f847ca4-da34-11e4-b3f2-607bd612aeac_story.

Tiezzi, Shannon. "At CICA, Xi Calls for New Regional Security Architecture." *The Diplomat*. May 22, 2014. https://thediplomat.com/2014/05/at-cica-xi-calls-for-new-regional-security-architecture/.

"The Trans-Pacific Partnership: Weighing Anchor." *The Economist*. October 10, 2015. https://www.economist.com/finance-and-economics/2015/10/10/weighing-anchor.

Tuchman, Barbara. *The Guns of August: The Outbreak of World War I*, reprint edition. New York: Random House, 2009.

Vitug, Marites. *Rock Solid: How the Philippines Won Its Maritime Case against China*. Manila: Ateneo De Manila Press, 2018.

Walker, Richard, and Daniel Buck. "The Chinese Road." *New Left Review* 46. July/August 2007. https://newleftreview.org/issues/II46/articles/richard-walker-daniel-buck-the-chinese-road.

Walt, Stephen. "Is Barack Obama More of a Realist Than I Am?" *Foreign Policy*. August 19, 2014. https://foreignpolicy.com/2014/08/19/is-barack-obama-more-of-a-realist-than-i-am/.

Walton, Timothy. "Are We Underestimating China's Military?" *The National Interest*. May 19, 2014. https://nationalinterest.org/feature/are-we-underestimating-chinas-military-10479.

Welch, David. "What's an ADIZ?" *Foreign Affairs*. December 9, 2013. https://www.foreignaffairs.com/articles/east-asia/2013-12-09/whats-adiz.

White, Hugh. "Why Obama Should Abandon the Pivot." *East Asia Forum*. May 4, 2014. http://www.eastasiaforum.org/2014/05/04/why-obama-should-abandon-the-pivot/.

Wolf, Charles, Jr., Xiao Wang, and Eric Warner. "China's Foreign Aid and Government-Sponsored Investment Activities: Scale, Content, Destinations, and Implications." *RAND Corporation*. 2013. https://www.rand.org/pubs/research_reports/RR118.html. Also available in print form.

Wu, Xinbo, and Michael Green. "Regional Security Roles and Challenges." In Nina Hachigian (ed.), *Debating China: The U.S.–China Relationship in Ten Conversations*. Oxford: Oxford University Press, 2014.

Zhao, Suisheng. "A State-Led Nationalism: The Patriotic Education Campaign in Post-Tiananmen China." *Communist and Post-Communist Studies* 31 no. 3 (1998): 287–302. https://doi.org/10.1016/S0967-067X(98)00009-9.

Zhenhua, Lu. "Beijing Hits Back at Secretary of State Michael Pompeo's 'Irresponsible' South China Sea Energy Claims." *South China Morning Post*. March 13, 2019. https://www.scmp.com/news/china/diplomacy/article/3001491/mike-pompeo-accuses-beijing-creating-debt-traps-and-energy.

CHAPTER 7

The Post-American World: Middle Powers and the Coalition of Deterrence

Who controls the Rimland rules Eurasia; Who rules Eurasia controls the destinies of the world.[1] —Nicholas Spykman, *The Geography of the Peace* (1944)

If one day China should change her color and turn into a superpower, if she too should play the tyrant in the world, and everywhere subject others to her bullying, aggression and exploitation, the people of the world should identify her as social-imperialism, expose it, oppose it and work together with the Chinese people to overthrow it. —Chinese Paramount Leader Deng Xiaoping's speech at the United Nations' General Assembly, April 10, 1974[2]

We have to take responsibility for our own security and prosperity while recognizing we are stronger when sharing the burden of collective leadership with trusted partners and friends. The gathering clouds of uncertainty and instability are signals for all of us to play more active roles in protecting and shaping the future of this region. —Australian Prime Minister Malcolm Turnbull, keynote speech Shangri La Dialogue 2017[3]

In *World Order*, Henry Kissinger points out how an existing order—a set of commonly accepted rules that govern interstate relations—loses its

[1] Gray (2015).
[2] Montelibano (2014).
[3] Dobell (2017).

© The Author(s) 2020
R. J. Heydarian, *The Indo-Pacific: Trump, China, and the New Struggle for Global Mastery*, https://doi.org/10.1007/978-981-13-9799-8_7

coherence when it is challenged by "either a re-definition of [its] legitimacy or a significant shift in the [international] balance of power."[4] One could argue that China represents a challenge to the existing order on both fronts: China is challenging the legitimacy of American leadership by pushing for alternative rules and arrangements—the so-called Beijing Consensus,[5] with the BRI as its key component—vis-à-vis regional economic integration, while also shifting the balance of power in the region through rapid military buildup. As Paul Kennedy observed in *The Rise and Fall of the Great Powers*, "there is a noticeable 'lag time' between the trajectory of a state's relative economic strength and the trajectory of its military/territorial influence."[6] For China, the lag time has rapidly shrunk in the past decade, especially since Xi's ascent to power. And Beijing's expanding ambitions and rising assertiveness is a function of both strategic triumphalism as well as an acute security dilemma. On one hand, China has experienced one of the most impressive strides for any rising power (see Figs. 7.1 and 7.2). Within a single generation, China has transformed from a rising regional economic powerhouse into a global engine of growth. In 1990, China's nominal GDP was only 6% of that of the United States. By 2016, it was already larger by 60% in purchasing power parity terms. This seismic shift has been most pronounced in the Indo-Pacific, particularly in East Asia, where China's share of regional GDP grew from only 8% in 1990 to 51% in 2014. In the same period, it's share of regional trade expanded from only 8% to a sizeable 39%.[7] The BRI is expected to only consolidate this trend. For some experts, Beijing's economic dominance means, "there is [and would be] little appetite for a containment strategy against China."[8]

---

[4] Kissinger (2014, 365).

[5] The Beijing Consensus, a term coined by Joshua Cooper-Ramo and further developed by Sinologists such as Stefan Halper, pertains to China's no-strings-attached, flexible approach to international trade and investment relations. Unlike the West and international financial institutions such as the IMF and World Bank, which have aggressively espoused structural adjustment programs and pro-market governance reforms in accordance to the neo-liberal principles of what John Williamson calls the "Washington Consensus," China doesn't demand drastic economic (or political) reforms when it engages in trade and investment with other countries. And this, for some experts, explains China's special attractiveness as an economic partner to many countries. See for instance Ramo (2004).

[6] Kennedy (1989, xxiii).

[7] Kang (2018).

[8] Kang (2017).

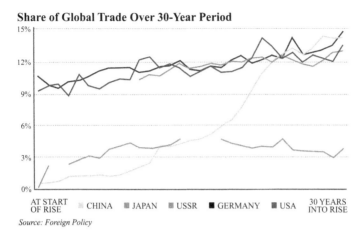

Fig. 7.1 Rising powers' share of global trade in their peak years (%)

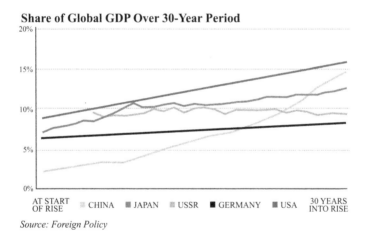

Fig. 7.2 Rising powers' share of global GDP during their peak decades (%)

Or, at the very least, that's what Beijing hopes for, namely locking in regional neighbors into a state of deferential dependence through a thick web of asymmetrical economic interdependence with, of course, China at the apex. As Sinologist Howard French observes, China is interested in restoring a kind of tributary system, where neighbors "will have no choice but to hitch their fortunes to it and bow to Beijing's authority." This is a crucial prerequisite for the "ultimate goal," however, which is "becoming a true global power" of the century.[9] In fact, this is perfectly consistent with China's millennia old imperial tradition. For instance, Liu Ching (199 BCE), a Han Dynasty imperial advisor and among the most respected Chinese strategists of all time, recommended "induced economic dependence," through export of high-grade silk woolen clothes, as a tool for subduing independent-minded and militarily capable, though less economically endowed, neighbors such as the Xiongnu. The process of economic inducement was followed by "indoctrination," namely socializing smaller neighbors to internalize Chinese worldview and Confucian values. As grand strategist Edward Luttwak put it, once the process of subjugation reaches a critical threshold, China would "withdraw all tokens of equality and [almost immediately] impose subordination."[10] This is relevant, especially given modern China's heavy reliance on ancient strategic traditions for modern application.[11] Chinese scholar Feng Zhang euphemistically terms this ancient statecraft that anchors tributary dynamics between Beijing (center) and its neighbors (periphery) as "relationalism," namely "the dynamic process of connections and transactions among actors in structured social relationships," with obviously China in the commanding position of hegemony.[12] And China is confident that its moment has arrived. In the blunt words of a prominent Chinese scholar, "We are entering into a new era where the United States will no longer be able to 'call the shots' alone, as its power in an increasingly multipolar world begins to wane."[13]

The other major driving force behind China's strategic assertiveness is, paradoxically, insecurity, which, quite paradoxically, intensified just as it closed its power gap with the West. As one leading Chinese scholar explained, the Obama administration's "strategic pivot to the Asia-Pacific region, especially during [sic] the financial crisis of 2008 and political riots in Northern Africa, makes China even more suspicious of U.S. strategic intentions."[14] Surrounded by tens of thousands of America troops—stationed from Guam to South Korea, Japan and the Philippines all the way to Diego Garcia and the Persian Gulf—China feels surrounded by a ring of

[9] French (2017, 11).
[10] Luttwak (2012, 28).
[11] See Kissinger (2012).
[12] Zhang (2015).
[13] Hachigian (2014).
[14] Ibid., 161–175.

hostility, which threatens both its territorial integrity as well as channels of communications, especially for its trade-dependent and energy-importing economy. From China's quasi-fatalistic point of view, the United States will never accept it as a peer, thus the almost inevitability of superpower conflict. And add to this, its profound sense of entitlement to hegemony in East Asia (Nathan and Scobell 2012).

Now, China is taking the fight to its rivals. As the Romans put it, if you want peace (on your own terms), (one must) prepare for war (*Si vis pacem, para bellum*). Buoyed by its burgeoning military capabilities, China has staked claim to adjacent waters, most especially the South China Sea, as the extension of its territory at the expense of military freedom of navigation for other powers and even, potentially, civilian freedom of navigation down the road. Over a span of 18 months, beginning in December 2013, China reclaimed 1170 hectares (2900 acres) across the disputed Spratly islands, giving birth to a sprawling network of advanced military and civilian facilities in the area, laying the foundations of an Air Defense Identification Zone (ADIZ) in the area. The Fiery Cross, widely seen as a potential command-and-control center for China's military operations in the area, was enlarged by 11 times its original size, now hosting a 3 kilometers-long airstrip, which is capable of accommodating the most advanced aircrafts. The same model has been replicated on the Mischief and Subi Reefs as well as in the Paracel and Woody Islands. Unlike other claimant states, which also have military presence in the area, the scale and sophistication of China's facilities in the area provide it with the ability to project power *from* its outposts, threatening the supply lines and freedom of overflight of rival claimant states as well as external powers that have enjoyed unimpeded access to the high seas in the area (see Fig. 7.3).

And China is backing up its expanding footprint with an increasingly capable military behemoth. If China continues its current defense spending trajectory, it will likely eclipse America's before the middle of this century. Of course, America is expected to keep a qualitative edge over China for the foreseeable future, but China's impressive strides in the development of stealth fighter programs (i.e., J-20 and J-31) and other advanced weaponries, including satellite-killer ballistic missiles, should serve as a cautionary tale against complacency. Not to mention, China's rapid development of anti-access/area-denial (A2/AD) capabilities, including "carrier killer" anti-ship ballistic missiles (ASBMS) such as the DF-21D and DF-26 platforms, which could dramatically raise the costs

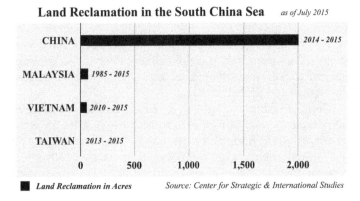

Fig. 7.3   China's reclamation and militarization in South China Sea

of an American military intervention in an event of conflict along the First Island Chain.[15] In fact, China today has the largest naval fleet in the world,[16] which has been bolstered by the addition of new aircraft carriers (including indigenously-made ones) and new generation of Type-052C guided-missile destroyers that far outsize many of their counterparts.[17] The combination of Beijing's rapidly growing conventional military muscle and cutting-edge asymmetrical anti-access/area-denial capability is giving China, still primarily a regional military power, growing confidence to challenge America's century-old naval dominance in the area. As one authoritative study by the RAND corporation explains: "Both sides would suffer large military losses in a severe conflict… [b]y 2025, U.S. losses could range from significant to heavy…" and that "China's A2AD will make it increasingly difficult for the United States to gain military-operational dominance and victory, even in a long war."[18] A 2018 bipartisan study, led by the National Defense Strategy Commission composed of 12 leading experts and former national security officials, warned that "America's ability to defend its allies, its partners and its own vital interests is increasingly in doubt," and that the country "might [even] struggle to win, or perhaps lose, a war against China or

[15] Erickson (2015).
[16] Lague and Lim (2019).
[17] *The Economic Times* (2019).
[18] Gompert et al. (2016).

Russia."[19] Recognizing China's rapid advancements in its conventional and asymmetric military capabilities, leading experts such as James Holmes have described China as the United States' "near-peer" in the emerging balance of military power in the Pacific theatre, where "60 percent of the U.S. Navy [stands] against [the almost entirety of] a peer navy, army, and air force — on [China's] home turf."[20] China's acquisition of its first full-fledged foreign military base in Djibouti could be only the beginning of a larger trend toward establishing a burgeoning global empire.

Yet, China is a fragile superpower and far from invincible, especially as its economy betrays signs of vulnerability. Its current economic troubles—from the massive stock market crash in mid-2015 to China's slowing growth and whimpering manufacturing exports—represent only the tip of the iceberg. There are even larger bubbles building up in the real estate and (over-leveraged) state-owned banks. The more fundamental concerns are structural and institutional, ranging from China's impending demographic winter to the rigidity of its regulatory framework and growing fiscal woes (Babones 2015b), especially among profligate local and regional governments.[21] A weaker Chinese economy down the road means a break on Beijing's soft power binge and, one could argue, a more sober foreign policy, both in outlook and capacity, which is geared at facilitating economic recovery at home rather than adventurism abroad. China's economic jitters could also impact the current calculations of neighboring countries, which not long ago saw China as an inevitable and boisterous economic hegemon that will have to be accommodated. As China struggles with economic slowdown and confronts structural shifts in its demographics and economic structure, it will also have to revisit its defense spending bonanza, as requirements on social spending consume a greater chunk of the state budget. It goes without saying that it's also conceivable that an economically besieged Beijing would instead (foolishly) choose to overcompensate for troubles at home by adopting an aggressive foreign policy with destructive consequences for China and the world. We are likely already seeing the intimations of such self-defeating rally round the flag impulse.

But aside from its gradually sputtering economy, China's image in the region has also taken a hit. Under the Obama administration, America's

---

[19] Gavis (2018).

[20] Holmes (2015).

[21] See Sharma (2012) and Babones (2015a).

approval ratings in Asia recovered from the Bush era lows, whereas China's approval ratings have dramatically slumped in recent years. According to a *Pew Research Center* survey in 2014, majorities in 8 out of 11 major countries in Asia were concerned over a prospect of war between China and its neighbors over territorial disputes, with majority of citizens in countries like the Philippines (58%), Vietnam (74%), and Japan (68%) viewing China as a national security threat.[22] A 2014 poll by the BBC showed that, since 2005 China's approval ratings and influence have declined year-on-year by 14 percentage points, with almost half of the respondents expressing negative views of China.[23] Even more crucially, in spite of lingering anxieties over Trump's temperament and leadership, most countries still prefer the United States rather China to remain as the world's preminent power, including in the Indo-Pacific (see Fig. 7.4).[24] The implication is clear: A future charismatic and multilateralist American president will be in a far better position to rally international support, especially if China's image continues to deteriorate.

Betting on China's economic collapse is likely misguided, given the country's time-tested dynamism and proven ability to overcome one crisis after the other over the past two decades. Yet, structural slowdown seems almost inevitable, as China becomes an older society and a more mature economy with new needs and challenges. An economically vulnerable and more unpopular China reflects the costs and limits of Beijing's bid for regional hegemony (see Chapter 8). Though China is just too big and powerful to be contained, there is an optimal "goldilocks approach" to dealing with China: namely, what political scientist Gerald Segal termed as "constrainment," a strategy that "is intended to tell [China] that the outside world has interests that will be defended by means of incentives for good behavior, deterrence of bad behavior, and punishment when deterrence fails."[25] But this strategy, as Segal correctly points out, can work if America and its allies "act in a concerted fashion both to punish and to reward China."[26] It's a strategy that combines both engagement and deterrence. And the aim is not only to balance against China's worst instincts, but, following

---

[22]Pew Research Center (2014).

[23]Shambaugh (2015).

[24]Wike et al. (2018).

[25]Segal (1996).

[26]Ibid.

Fig. 7.4 Survey on preference of countries on the world's preeminent power

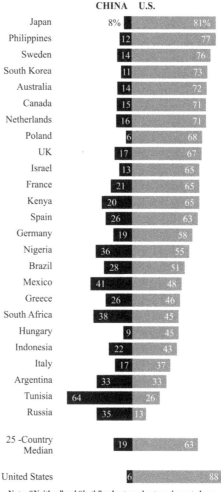

Most prefer U.S. as world leader

Having ___ as the world's leading power
be better for the world

Note: *"Neither" and "both" volunteered categories not shown.*

Source: *2018 Global Attitudes Survey. Q33.*

Nicholas Spykman's advise, also "the improvement of the relative power position" of the United States and its allies, since "there is no real security in being just as strong as a potential enemy; there is security only in being a little stronger."[27] In short, the aim is to preserve a favorable balance of power at the expense of China's imperial ambitions.

Without a question, Asia is at a crossroads. As Graham Allison aptly warns, the United States and China are facing a potential Thucydides trap, wherein the established power's "fear, insecurity, and determination to defend the status quo" rises in response to "the rising power's [China] growing entitlement, sense of its importance, and demand for greater say and sway."[28] Trump's lurch to all-out trade war with China, and America's expanding military footprint in the East and South China Seas, is the clearest manifestation of precisely this dangerous great power dynamic. For Graham Allison, in "high-stakes relationships" such as that between two superpowers, namely the United States and China, "predictability and stability—not friendship—matter most."[29]

The Dawn of Fragmegration

During Obama's visit to China in late 2009, the two countries issued an important joint statement, which largely escaped the attention of both media and experts. While large sections of it were relatively uncontroversial, one in particular stood out. Likely due to China's insistence, a section of the statement read: "The two sides agreed that respecting each other's *core interests* [author's own emphasis] is extremely important to ensure steady progress in U.S.-China relations." This seemingly trivial rhetorical insertion proved a huge strategic blunder. Over the succeeding years, Beijing expanded its list of "core interests" and, accordingly, instituted new policies to back it up. As Princeton academic and former Obama administration official Thomas Christensen writes, "Realizing that invoking 'core interests' was a mistake, senior U.S. officials stopped using it after the summit—but Chinese elites have often invoked the term in complaints that Washington has gone back on its word."[30]

---

[27] Anderson (2013).
[28] Allison (2015).
[29] Allison (2017, 236).
[30] See Christensen's article (2015b) and book (2015a).

China sensed that its time in the sun had arrived. After all, by the second decade of the twenty-first century, it became clear that the Indo-Pacific, particularly East Asia, no longer had a single undisputed leader. In 2013, during his high-profile meeting with Obama, a patently emboldened Xi bluntly declared: "The vast Pacific Ocean has enough space for two large countries like the United States and China."[31] Beijing was now effectively demanding the Obama administration to recognize its sphere of influence in adjacent waters and the de facto Finlandization of its near neighborhood.

The way forward, however, is not a Sino-American co-dominion in the Asia-Pacific theatre, but instead a truly multilateral and rule-based order that is undergirded by balance of power, legitimacy, and institutionalized engagement among relevant actors. So far, the United States and its allies are still struggling to mobilize enough assets to rein in Chinese territorial ambitions, while China's economic resources aren't also enough to buy the full acquiescence of key actors across the region. The result is neither a post-American order, nor a Sino-centric one. It's a legitimate strategic deadlock over the future of the regional security architecture. The Asia-Pacific order is entering a phase of intensified Sino-American rivalry and continued economic interdependence that can be called *Pax Chimerica*—a tenuous regional order characterized by Chinese predominance in the economic realm, while the United States is increasingly seen as an anchor of maritime security in the region, especially for a whole host of countries that are perturbed by China's territorial assertiveness.[32] Crucially, however, a number of middle powers in the Indo-Pacific have sought to establish a post-American order that is neither Chinese-led nor defined by the whims of the White House alone, especially amid the perilous polarization in American politics and rise of Trumpian isolationism untethered to the global liberal order. Instead, what they seek to establish is a multipolar order, which reflects their shared interests as well as the greatest common denominator among nations across the Pacific and Indian oceans. The upshot is the formation of a "coalition of deterrence," as Japan, India, Australia, and a number of European powers with possession of Indo-Pacific territories collectively

---

[31] BBC (2013).

[32] The term was actually coined by Niall Ferguson and Moritz Schularick, who analyzed the economic co-dependence between the two superpowers.

hold the line through initially ad-hoc but increasingly institutionalized cooperative mechanisms. The growing sentiment among these nations is that they should either hang together or risk getting hung apart.

As China emerges as the predominant indigenous power in Asia, it has become a pivotal force to a simultaneous process of integration and fragmentation in the region, or what American political scientist James N. Rosenau calls "fragmegration."[33] In economic terms, China has emerged as a center of gravity, forming the core of major proposed regional trading initiatives such as FTAAP and Regional Comprehensive Economic Partnership (RCEP), which, unlike American-led trading agreements such as the TPP, don't demand comprehensive and high-standard trade liberalization among member states. While China offers and supports "silver standard" trading regimes, America's "gold standard" versions have yet to gain traction. Countries such as the Philippines, for instance, may need to amend their constitution in order to qualify for TPP (and its successor's) negotiations. Other key East Asian countries such South Korea, Indonesia and Thailand were left out of the TPP (and its successor's) negotiations. With the exception of the Philippines (at least according to official numbers[34]), practically all Asia-Pacific countries count China as their top trading partner. When it comes to regional security, however, China has become a polarizing force, gradually threatening freedom of navigation in one of the world's most important SLOCs, the South China Sea, not to mention its dangerous jostling with Japan in the East China Sea; provocative maneuvers against India along contested Himalayan territories; and relatively obscure but intensified disputes with South Korea in the Yellow Sea. In fact, the anti-China backlash was gaining pace towards the end of the Obama administration.[35]

China's destabilizing behavior has actually become the central theme of Asia's premier security conference, the Shangri-La Dialogue (SLD), an annual conference in Singapore organized by the International Institute for Strategic Studies (IISS). Beginning with the 2015 edition of the SLD, for instance, a growing number of nations, including those with historically warm relations with Beijing such as Singapore, have openly expressed their disquiet over China's relentless alteration of the maritime

---

[33] Rosenau (2000).

[34] Philippine trading data tends to omit smuggled imports from China, which, if included in the data, could push up Beijing as the top trading partner of Manila.

[35] Luttwak (2012).

status quo. For long, the tiny and prosperous city-state of Singapore has punched well above its weight, serving as a critical mediator among Pacific powers, particularly Beijing and Washington. The late Lee Kuan Yew, among the twentieth century's greatest and longest-serving leaders, was a master of international diplomacy, carefully maintaining an optimal strategy of balancing toward the two great powers. Singapore's founding father constantly sought to assuage fears over the return of post-Mao China into the international fold, while advising his counterparts in Beijing to consider the strategic anxieties of its neighbors, maintain cordial ties with Washington, and embrace globalization with a pragmatic outlook. As a result, Singapore has arguably become a linchpin of and a prime platform for dialogue over the existing security architecture in Asia. For the tiny Southeast Asian nation, the future of Asia is anchored by a healthy competition and broadly symbiotic relationship between the United States and China. Since the late 2000s, however, Singapore has become increasingly alarmed by China's overbearing attitude and more aggressive pursuit of sweeping territorial claims in neighboring countries. As one of the world's most trade-dependent economies, which heavily relies on reprocessing imported basic commodities and producing high-value-added exports, Singapore has a direct stake in maintaining stability in SLOCs, particularly the Strait of Malacca and the South China Sea. Singapore has no illusions about the intentions of great powers, so it has also developed one of the most modern and well-equipped armed forces in the world. Fears of a power vacuum—and full-blown Chinese hegemony in Asia—has prompted Singaporean leaders to grant the US Navy greater rotational access. Lee Kuan Yew's son (Hsien Loong), the current prime minister and a former Brigadier-General, has become increasingly vocal about the necessity of a rule-based resolution of the South China Sea disputes. As a firm believer in balance of power, he has also emphasized the importance of America's commitment to the region, since Washington's naval muscle is the best possible deterrence against full-blown Chinese maritime adventurism. Singaporean Prime Minister Lee Hsien Loong's keynote speech at the 2015 SLD, for instance, was indicative of how even non-claimant states in Southeast Asia are now deeply alarmed by the developments on the ground, and are eager to see, if not directly facilitate, a mechanism to manage the disputes and prevent them from spiraling out of control. He was steadfast in emphasizing how the disputes "should be managed and contained," and warned "if the present dynamic continues, it must [sic] lead to more tensions and bad outcomes."[36] Interestingly, the Singaporean leader, whose country would soon take over as the ASEAN-China country coordinator, pushed the diplomatic envelope, declaring "China and ASEAN should conclude a Code of Conduct on the South China Sea as soon as possible" in order to arrest a "vicious cycle" in the region.[37] The Singaporean prime minister explicitly called for "all parties adhere to international law, including the UN Convention on Law of the Sea (UNCLOS)," boldly declaring, much to China's chagrin, "that is the best outcome"—an indirect statement of support for the Philippines ongoing arbitration case against China.[38]

A year earlier, when the Singaporean leader made a similar statement in the United States, China reportedly filed a diplomatic demarche, pressuring Singapore to retract its position. But it seems that Singapore is holding its ground. In another indirect jab against China, he also reiterated how "if the outcome [of disputes] is determined on the basis of might is right, that will set a very bad precedent," going on to note that the regional order "cannot be maintained by just by superior force."[39] It is not a farfetched proposition to assume that Singapore's point of view is shared by the majority of countries in the Asia-Pacific region and beyond. With the exception of Beijing, hardly anyone tried to justify or downplay China's destabilizing actions in international waters. Singapore's carefully and deliberately expressed strategic sentiments and sensibilities serve as a bellwether of the regional temperament toward China. That year also saw the much-anticipated speech by the then US Defense Secretary Ashton Carter, which came on the heels of a weeks-long American effort to push back against Chinese belligerence in the South China Sea. The American defense secretary emphasized that the United States "will fly, sail, and operate wherever international law allows, as U.S. forces do all over the world."[40] It was a justification of Washington's ongoing efforts to directly challenge China's construction activities. By mid-2015, the United States began to deploy surveillance aircrafts and warships close to the 12 nautical miles radius of China's artificially built islands in the South China Sea, prompting strong warning

[36] Heydarian (2015).
[37] The International Institute for Strategic Studies (2015).
[38] Lee (2015).
[39] Ibid.
[40] Sciutto (2015).

from China about potential escalation and military counter-action.[41] But Washington was determined to stick to its guns, and demonstrate its willingness to stand up to China and enforce "freedom of navigation" operations and oppose "restrictions on international air or maritime transit."[42] Carter was also careful to emphasize how Washington's efforts are in step with regional norms and the interests of allies and partners, who seek to maintain stability in international waters. The United States unveiled a $425 million defense initiative to enhance the naval and coast guard capabilities of Southeast Asian countries. It was a critical (and subtly packaged) initiative to enhance the ability of regional allies and strategic partners to push back against China and deter further adventurism. This was in step with earlier suggestions and efforts by the Pentagon to augment the capabilities of regional states, including the proposed establishment of an International Maritime Operations Center (IMOC) in Indonesia, which could provide necessary support for multilateral patrol operations in the Western Pacific and the Indian Ocean. Meanwhile, Australia signaled its determination to maintain patrols in the South China Sea, a clear sign of support for the American position, while Japan, under the revised United States–Japan bilateral defense guidelines, contemplated joint aerial patrols in the South China Sea.[43]

Shortly after President Xi Jinping's visit to the White House in late September 2015, Washington began to more decisively employ its military capabilities to rein in Chinese adventurism by pushing ahead with deploying destroyers and B-52 bombers close to or within the 12 nautical miles territorial sea of Chinese-occupied features in the South China Sea.[44] With China brazenly admitting that it could impose an ADIZ in the South China Sea, Washington and its regional partners began scrambling to protect freedom of (civilian and military) navigation in international waters.[45] Although, few expected the Obama administration

---

[41] The question is whether the United States will go so far as to enter into the 12 nautical miles of Chinese-claimed features in the Spratly chain of islands, since many of these features are low-tide elevations, which can't be appropriated and can't generate their own territorial waters. Carter didn't say anything that bars that option so clearly this is an operational and political decision under consideration.

[42] Torode (2015).

[43] Ibid.

[44] Spetalnick and Francisco (2015).

[45] Wong (2015).

to implement anything as robust as the Clinton administration's 1996 decision to deploy two aircraft carriers to the Western Pacific to keep China's territorial ambitions in check. The key challenge for the Obama administration, however, was deploying sufficient military muscle in order to deter China from imposing an ADIZ in the area and choking off the supply-lines of other claimant states, particularly treaty allies such as the Philippines, without triggering any clashes with China. In fact, China's 2015 "white paper" on defense strategy openly emphasized "offshore defense" and "open sea defense," reflecting Beijing's growing strategic and territorial ambitions in high seas. With reports suggesting China placed motorized artillery pieces and other advanced defensive systems on the islands, coupled with Chinese warnings against US surveillance operations in the area, it became clear that Beijing was bracing for more jostling with Washington.[46] To be fair, as early as 2013, Xi left little doubt as to how far his country is willing to go to pursue its territorial claims in adjacent waters: "No foreign country should ever nurse hopes that we will bargain over our core national interests …Nor should they nurse hopes that we will swallow the bitter fruit of harm to our country's sovereignty, security and development interests."[47] No wonder then, it became increasingly clear to everyone that the fate of Asia could very well be defined by the trajectory of the Sino-American jostling in the South China Sea. What Xi failed to realize, however, was that his confrontational approach would unleash a bipartisan backlash in America. Even the likes of former Treasury Secretary and Goldman Sachs executive Henry Paulson, a key player during China's liberalization in the 1990s and a longtime believer in "constructive cooperation" with the Asian powerhouse,[48] would shift gear and embrace growing skepticism toward engagement with China.[49] By the late 2010s, a new consensus would emerge in Washington, where going tough on China became the default strategic option. Even the American business sector, fed up with investment restrictions, bureaucratic harassment, and technological and intellectual property theft in China, has supported a tougher economic policy toward the Asian powerhouse. And despite rising import

---

[46] Sciutto (2015).
[47] Buckley (2013).
[48] Paulson (2016).
[49] Anderlini (2018).

costs, many American manufacturers across the Rust Belt and Deep South support the increasingly tough policy against China, believing that this is a necessary price for correcting a predatory and exploitative relationship with the Asian powerhouse.[50]

In a much-discussed essay for Foreign Affairs, Kurt M. Campbell and Ely Ratner, two former U.S. officials, effectively declared the death of the Age of Engagement with China: "Neither carrots nor sticks have swayed China as predicted. Diplomatic and commercial engagement has not brought political and economic openness. Neither US military power nor regional balancing has stopped Beijing from seeking to displace core components of the US-led system. And the liberal international order has failed to lure or bind China as powerfully as expected. China has instead pursued its own course, belying a range of American expectations in the process."[51] Despite his much-taunted personal rapport with Xi, Trump embraced this new strategic zeitgeist with gusto.

WAR BY OTHER MEANS

The aim of war, the Prussian military genius Carl Von Clausewitz wrote, is to "compel [an] opponent to fulfill our will."[52] True to his campaign promise, US President Donald Trump has unleashed what appears to be an all-out trade war against China.[53] In late 2018, the United States slapped new tariffs on $200 billion in Chinese imports, with the threat of additional duties reaching 25% the following year. This came on top of an earlier round of tariffs on $50 billion of Chinese products. China responded in kind, raising its own retaliatory tariffs (between 5 and 10%) on a total of $110 billion of American products.[54] As a result, the world's two largest economies ended up imposing new restrictions on close to $400 billion of bilateral trade, sending shockwaves across the global economy.

Despite repeated promises of a grand trade bargain, and multiple rounds of negotiations, both sides failed to finalize well into 2019.

---

[50] See Tejada (2018), Kitroeff (2019), and Tooze (2019).
[51] Campbell and Ratner (2018).
[52] Lindell (2009).
[53] Curran et al. (2018).
[54] Ibid.

218 R. J. HEYDARIAN

In May of that year, the Trump administration imposed an additional round of tariffs on $200 billion worth of Chinese products amid a breakdown in trade negotiations. In response, China warned of "necessary countermeasures," while a prominent Chinese academic, Jin Canrong, went so far as suggesting China should sell off its huge cache of American treasury bills; ban exports of rare earth minerals; and impose retaliatory measures against American businesses operating in the Mainland.[55] In an almost direct assault on China's industrial policy, the Trump administration also (temporarily) placed Huawei, the global telecommunications giant and among Xi's national champions, on a blacklist over national security considerations. Shortly after, Google as well Intel Corp., Qualcomm Inc., and Broadcom Inc. suspended their services to Huawei, sending shockwaves across the global telecommunications industry.[56] The Chinese company was already a hot topic in US–China relations following the arrest of Meng Wanzhou, Huawei's chief financial officer, in Canada in December 1. This was reportedly at the behest of American officials seeking to investigate the prominent Chinese executive for potential criminal charges. In response, China went so far as arresting two Canadian citizens, including a former diplomat, on trumped-up charges.[57] Almost exactly a year earlier, ZTE, the other Chinese telecommunications giant, found itself in same place, when the Trump administration imposed sanctions on the company for, among others things, its illegal transactions with Iran. In the words of one ZTE employee back then, the US sanctions represented "the biggest [existential] challenge" in his decade of work in the company.[58] Three months later, Washington gave a lifeline to the company after a $1.4 billion settlement deal. Huawei is hoping for a similar outcome, but it's likely that the emerging technological schism will be a permanent feature of bilateral relations with huge ramifications for global technological supply chain for decades to come. Despite their huge technological strides, Chinese national champions are still highly dependent on collaboration with and inputs from more established Western counterparts, not to mention Western markets. Thus, any sanctions on their suppliers and partners can severely

[55] Canrong (2019).
[56] King et al. (2019).
[57] Bilefsky (2019).
[58] Jiang (2018).

undermine their viability.[59] The biggest issue, however, is Washington's concern over Beijing's potential sabotage of technological supply chain of up to 30 major American and western companies, including that of Apple and Amazon, with alleged installation of, among others, micro-chips for espionage and other nefarious purposes.[60]

What we are entering, according to Center for American Security's Patrick Cronin, is "an intensifying competition punctuated by deals and crises," with Trump's strategy "designed to make [things] unpredictable" in order "preserve a psychological and perceptional edge" over China, while China, faced with a challenge to its core interests, will "likely [move] to ratchet up the risk [accordingly]."[61] The conflict is now officially structural, seemingly beyond the agential maneuvering of their respective leaders. As *The Atlantic*'s Uri Friedman correctly observes, "In truth, however, Trump's endgame with China may not actually be establishing a fairer trading relationship... they [Trump administration hawks] are aiming to do nothing less than 'decouple' the U.S. and Chinese economies so that American technologies and industries are less susceptible to Chinese theft and coercion."[62] For some hawks in Washington, DC, China has become too powerful to be engaged, thus better to constrain its ambitions and influence before it's too late. John Mearsheimer effectively predicted this "offensive realism" mindset in *The Tragedy of Great Power Politics*, where he argues: "A potential hegemon [China] does not have to do much to generate fear among other states [especially status hegemon] in the system. Its formidable capabilities alone are likely to scare neighboring powers...because a state's intentions are difficult to discern, and because they can change quickly, rival great powers will be inclined to assume the worst about the potential hegemon's intentions, further reinforcing the threatened states' incentive to contain it and maybe even weaken it if the opportunity presents itself."[63] The contemporary Sino-American relationship fully embodies this dynamic. Almost four decades since the formal restoration of bilateral diplomatic relations, Washington has once again identified

---

[59] Banjo and Yuan (2019).
[60] Robertson and Riley (2018).
[61] Interview with author, November 28, 2019.
[62] Friedman (2018).
[63] Mearsheimer (2014, 345).

Beijing as a strategic competitor. Except, this time, China is the most formidable challenger to American hegemony in history. The Trump administration's National Security Strategy (NSS) openly describes China as a "revisionist" power, which seeks to "challenge American power, influence, and interests" around the world, particularly in the Indo-Pacific, in an attempt "to erode American security and prosperity."[64] In its National Defense Strategy (NDS), Pentagon accused China of "leveraging military modernization, influence operations, and predatory economics to coerce continues its neighboring countries to reorder the Indo-Pacific region to their advantage" and "continue to pursue a military modernization program that seeks Indo-Pacific regional hegemony in the future" through the "displacement of the United States to achieve global preeminence in the future."[65] In both strategic documents, the Trump administration not only described our current era as one of great powers rivalry, but also embraces it with gusto. For some in the Trump administration, China is nothing short of an existential threat, given its unique combination of economic dynamism, burgeoning military might, and demographic weight—strengths the Soviet Union could only dream of at the height of the Cold War.[66] Within this paradigm, it has sought to challenge China not only in the high seas of the Western Pacific, but also in the realm of trade and investments.

Within his first year in office, Trump assessed the prospect of activating various legislation, namely Section 232 of the Trade Expansion Act of 1962 as well as Section 301 of the Trade Act of 1974, to aggressively reconfigure America's external trade relations. In its second year, the Trump administration's trade policy became increasingly dominated by the protectionist "iron triangle," composed of White House chief trade adviser Peter Navarro, US Trade Representative Robert Lighthizer, a former Reagan official who oversaw tough trading negotiations with Japan in the 1980s, and Commerce Secretary Wilbur Ross, who collectively view America's trade deficit as a national security concern.[67] Through ramped up tariffs, and punishment of China's alleged intellectual property theft, the Trump administration hopes to restore America's

[64] Trump (2017).
[65] Ibid., 2.
[66] Woodward (2018).
[67] Ibid.

manufacturing power. For Trump, this was not only about challenging China's rising economic influence, but also a genuine concern for his base, especially in the American rustbelt. As he reportedly told one of his former chief economic advisers during a heated discussion over tariffs, "I went to parts of Pennsylvania that used to be big steel towns and now they're desolate towns and no one had a job and no one has work there."[68]

Though trade diversion,[69] due to the ongoing Sino-American trade wars, has benefited some Asian nations, much of the region, so far, has greeted the Sino-American trade war with trepidation. There is increasing worry about the unintended consequences[70] not only for regional trade linkages,[71] where China plays a pivotal role, but also the decades-long cold peace in Asia, which is looking increasingly fragile. Despite repeated discussions of a trade war "truce," there is little sign of an irreversible breakthrough on the horizon. In fact, historically beggar-thy-neighbor policies, namely the spiral of retaliatory tariffs, most especially during the Great Depression, created new constituencies, which benefited from and advocated for maintenance, if not further escalation, of expanded protectionist measures. Through ramped-up tariffs and punishment of China's alleged intellectual property theft, the Trump administration hopes to restore America's manufacturing power. To be fair, within his first year in office, Trump assessed the prospect of activating various legislations, namely Section 232 of the Trade Expansion Act of 1962 as well as Section 301 of the Trade Act of 1974, to aggressively reconfigure America's external trade relations. So his subsequent protectionist policies should haven't come as a surprise, despite the short-term employment of prominent liberals such as former Goldman Sachs executive Gary Cohn and former EXXON Mobil CEO Rex Tillerson.

So far, Washington seems to have gained the upper hand. For a starter, the United States can double the scope of its tariffs, given the sheer volume of its Chinese imports. Trump has threatened to extend punitive tariffs to an additional $267 billion of Chinese imports.[72]

---

[68] Ibid.
[69] Pavlova (2018).
[70] FT Confidential Research (2018).
[71] OCBC Bank (2018).
[72] Curran et al. (2018).

This gives Washington a lot of leverage. By contrast, China may soon run out of American products to target and is beginning to show signs of serious vulnerability: Chinese stock markets have been hit hard, among the worst performing[73] in Asia, while the yuan lost 8% of its value[74] against the dollar between April and August of 2018. Though China is the world's biggest exporter, it suffered, for the first time in 20 years,[75] a current-account deficit in the first half of 2018. Trump's tax cuts have, meanwhile, powered American financial markets, with GDP growth and unemployment rates reaching their best levels in recent years.

It was precisely in recognition of this asymmetry that the Xi adminis-tration initially adopted a conciliatory approach,[76] offering to buy more American natural gas, agricultural produce, aircraft, and even go so far as to make adjustments to its Made in China 2025 strategic program, which aims to make China a technological leader in the coming decade. As a leading Chinese trade expert He Weiwen told *The New York Times*, "The red line is China's right to develop, not the concrete industrial policies and measures regarding Made in China 2025."[77] For now, Southeast Asian countries such as Vietnam and Cambodia have been benefiting from the relocation of light industries from China amid the ongoing trade war.[78] There will be winners in any war, but down the road, there are four key concerns for the region.[79]

First of all, other Asian economies are worried about being next in Trump's crossfire. After all, an emboldened Washington has already targeted India,[80] while major Southeast Asian countries like Indonesia, Thailand, the Philippines, and Vietnam are also wor-ried[81] about Trump's response to their trade surpluses with America. Second, increased tariffs on Beijing will have ripple effects,[82] given

[73] Zhang (2018).
[74] *The Economist* (2018, August).
[75] Varma (2018).
[76] Bradsher (2018).
[77] Ibid.
[78] Wu (2018).
[79] Asean Business Staff (2018).
[80] Achom (2018).
[81] Chin (2018).
[82] Krugman (2018).

the integrated nature[83] of the East Asian production network, with China at the center. Many "Made in China" products have significant value-added input from other regional economies, including Taiwan, South Korea, and Japan, thus tariffs will target all the regional co-producers. Shifting production from China to other regional states also carries its own costs, since it would entail shifting entire supply chains, which could be both expensive and risky.[84] This could mean an increased burden on consumers as production costs increase.

Third, an escalated trade war could severely hurt China's economy, with adverse effects for a region which is increasingly dependent[85] on Chinese markets, capital, tourists, and cheap technology imports. In a scenario of an all-out global trade war, the world could suffer from[86] up to a 70% contraction in international trade, which, in turn, could cause a global depression, with a 2–3% contraction[87] in the global Gross Domestic Product (GDP). Lastly, and most worryingly, the trade war is going hand in hand with a dramatic deterioration in Sino-American diplomatic and strategic ties. What initially looked like a Trump-style "Art of the Deal" bargaining strategy for measured adjustment of the American trade deficit has now turned into a full-blown Cold War,[88] with China viewing the trade war as part of a containment strategy,[89] if not a larger existential struggle.[90] A furious China has gone so far warning to indefinitely suspend[91] trade negotiations[92] as well as the upcoming bilateral strategic dialogue, while Trump has gone as far as to accuse the Asian powerhouse of interfering in domestic American politics[93] to undermine his trade policy. Meanwhile, geopolitical tensions

---

[83] Nakayama et al. (2018).

[84] Stevenson (2018).

[85] Biswas (2016).

[86] Krugman (2018).

[87] Ibid.

[88] Chang (2018).

[89] Jiangtao and Churchill (2018).

[90] Chang (2018).

[91] Walcott (2018).

[92] Tankersley and Rappeport (2018).

[93] Allen (2018).

in the South China Sea have intensified[94] just as defense and strategic diplomatic channels have atrophied. If left unchecked, the ongoing escalation could effectively end seven decades of relative peace and unprecedented prosperity in Asia. Yet, there is more to the Indo-Pacific saga than just the Sino-American rivalry.

As early as 2013, Rory Medcalf and Raja Mohan, the two leading experts on "middle power diplomacy," highlighted the considerable heft[95] of Indo-Pacific middle powers of India, Japan, Indonesia, and Australia, which have a combined GDP, population and defense spending that is on par with—and, over coming years, could even exceed—China's, especially as India and Indonesia continue their economic boom and defense buildup. With European powers of France and Britain, which have Indo-Pacific territories and interests, joining the naval scramble[96] against China, middle powers are even in a better position to augment ongoing efforts to keep Beijing's ambitions in check, arguably even irrespective of the vicissitudes of American power projection in Asia. Thus, quite paradoxically, Trump's unpredictability, and the seeming unreliability of America in extension, has proven as a catalyst for more middle power strategic proactiveness. Sure, many of them were already expected to increase their strategic commitments in the future, but one can't deny that Trump's unilateralism has forced a much-needed and timely strategic rethink among allies and partners in the Indo-Pacific. Trump's "Hedgehog"-like leadership is still drenched in "big dangers," but, at least for now, it has reset the Asian geopolitical landscape in many unexpectedly encouraging ways that were previously unthinkable. That's the ultimate paradox of Trump's presidency.

COALITION OF DETERRENCE

Nature abhors a vacuum and this is presently true in Asia, where regional states are fretting over the lack of reassuring leadership on the part of both the United States and China. Earlier in the decade, Ian Bremmer worried about a "G-Zero" world, where "America is increasingly unwilling, and incapable, of assuming" responsibilities for the preservation

---

[94] Martinez (2018).
[95] Medcalf and Mohan (2014).
[96] Heydarian (2018c).

of global order, while "rising powers aren't yet ready to take up the slack..."[97] But things are beginning to change. Caught between a reckless America,[98] led by an apparently unhinged populist, and a revanchist China, seemingly bent on recreating a neo-tributary system,[99] the middle powers have stepped into the fray. A new concert of middle powers,[100] including Japan, Australia, India, Singapore, Indonesia, and, more recently, even some European powers with Indo-Pacific territories, have stepped up their efforts to create a post-American order in Asia that isn't dominated by China. In fact, the Pentagon has encouraged and warmly welcomed this development, calling on Australia, Indonesia, South Korea, and other middle powers to pitch in, preserving freedom of navigation and overflight in vital sea lines of communications such as the South China Sea.[101] Even smaller powers such as the Philippines, Malaysia, and Vietnam have been playing an increasingly influential role[102] in shaping the regional post-American order. While the Philippines, under Rodrigo Duterte, has pursued rapprochement[103] with China at the expense of historically warm ties with US, Malaysia, under the leadership of Mahathir Mohamad, has taken up the cudgels[104] to warn the world about the dangers of wholehearted embrace of China. As for Vietnam, it has quietly welcomed closer security cooperation with Washington, New Delhi, Moscow and Tokyo in order to reduce its economic dependence on and security threats from China (see Chapter 8).

While almost everyone welcomes Chinese largesse, few are oblivious to the risks that come with a more powerful and militarily assertive Beijing. In fact, the era of optimism over a Chinese-led Asia was ultimately short-lived. It took off during[105] the height of the Asian financial crisis, when Beijing refused to opportunistically revalue its currency at the expense of beleaguered neighbors, while supporting Asia-driven

---

[97] Bremmer (2013, 4).
[98] Ikenberry (2017).
[99] Su-Yan and Lo (2015).
[100] Daalder and Linday (2018).
[101] McGrath (2019).
[102] Heydarian (2018b).
[103] Heydarian (2018d).
[104] Heydarian (2018e).
[105] Goh (2013).

multilateral efforts to address the roots and consequences of the financial contagion. In contrast, the Clinton administration and Japan came under fire for not providing sufficient assistance during the crisis. In fact, Washington, the World Bank, and the International Monetary Fund were largely blamed[106] for causing the crisis, thanks to their aggressive push for liberalization of underdeveloped financial markets in developing East Asia.

By the mid-2000s, China's "charm-offensive" strategy[107] essentially peaked, as Beijing relished blossoming ties with practically all of its neighbors, including American treaty allies such as the Philippines. From Seoul to Singapore, China was seen as a broadly self-restrained behemoth fast becoming a leading trade and investment partner and, over time, a constructive counterweight to a unilateralist America under the Bush administration. Paradoxically, the "Sino-mania" bubble began to burst shortly after Wall Street went bust, precipitating the 2008–2009 Great Recession, which undermined the foundations of American power and unleashed a dangerous phase of triumphalism[108] in Beijing. From 2009 onwards, China was more offensive than charming, aggressively pushing its excessive territorial claims in adjacent waters, while indulging in predatory investment practices,[109] which eventually brought small, poorer states such as Sri Lanka to the brink of strategic servitude.[110] In recent years, independent-minded states such as Malaysia[111] and regional powers such as Australia[112] have begun to sour over Chinese investments, contemplating a fundamental reexamination of their previously warm relations with Beijing. Meanwhile, the Philippines successfully took China[113] to international court for violating key provisions of the United Nations Convention on the Law of the Sea (UNCLOS) through massive reclamation and aggressive militarization of disputed land features in the South China Sea.

---

[106] Stiglitz (2003).
[107] Kurtlantzick (2008).
[108] Pillsburry (2016).
[109] Fernholz (2018).
[110] Chellaney (2017).
[111] Erickson (2018).
[112] Ballard (2018).
[113] Santos (2016).

Despite its best efforts, the Obama administration's "Pivot to Asia" strategy was widely seen as more rhetorical than substantive. The rhetoric raised expectations[114] of a highly engaged America, but the country was largely impotent in constraining Chinese maritime assertiveness and the creation of an expanding zone of Sino-centric economic dependency in developing Asia. The Trump administration, which has become the new champion of trade protectionism and nativist anti-immigration policies, has only crystalized existing concerns over American decline. Abruptly dispensing with Barack Obama's signature global economic policy—the Trans-Pacific Partnership Agreement—the Trump administration has yet to put forward any major economic initiative for Asia, while China forges ahead with its BRI[115] across the entire Eurasian landmass. While America remains militarily supreme, the Trump administration has also yet to introduce an optimally effective maritime strategy against China. Yet, as the Center for Strategic and International Studies' Greg Poling explains, despite Washington's expanded naval deployments to the Indo-Pacific waters and intensified security cooperation with allies in the region, "The Trump administration has so far not shown much initiative or creativity in tackling the South China Sea disputes...[thus] for now China continues to extend its control over the South China Sea with each passing day."[116]

Ongoing Freedom of Navigation Operations (FONOPs) have, so far, proved insufficient to constrain Beijing's maritime appetite, but provocative enough to give its target nation the pretext to further militarize[117] the disputes. It's not clear whether doing more of the same[118] will be enough. In short, the Trump administration is pushing back, and still has considerable resources at its disposal. But it's not enough, nor is it comprehensive, since Trump is yet to put an alternative to the TPP forward. But while a brewing Sino-American cold war is a cause for worry, it's also encouraging other regional players to step up to preserve the best elements of the liberal international order. This is happening on both economic and geopolitical fronts. Through negotiating a TPP-11

[114] Ford (2017).

[115] Kuo and Kommenda (2018).

[116] Interview with the author, March 24, 2019.

[117] Asia Maritime Transparency Initiative (2018).

[118] Glaser and Poling (2018).

(minus America),[119] the Indo-Pacific middle powers have moved closer to creating a truly post-American economic initiative, which is not dominated by China and preserves the "gold standard" of trade liberalization. The TPP-11 nations hope to bring about a consequential economic bloc, which focuses on protection of intellectual property rights, opening up of excessively protected and inefficient sectors in places such as Japan, and expansion of intra-regional trade through the removal of non-tariff barriers, enhanced economies of scale, and productivity enhancement brought about by easier flow of technology and capital. In defense of the global liberal economic order Japan, which also led the TPP-11 negotiations, finalized the world's largest bilateral free trade agreement with the European Union in 2019, covering a third of global GDP and more than 600 million consumers. Both sides agreed to reduce duties on close to 99% of products they trade with each other.[120]

The middle powers have also sought to push back against China's BRI due to concerns[121] over debt sustainability, good governance, environmental standards, and predatory practices, including debt-for-equity arrangements. Indonesia and other Southeast Asian countries are also playing a more proactive role[122] in shaping the RCEP in a truly inclusive way, i.e., so that it does not exclude China but, crucially, is also not dominated by it. They are also working to streamline tariff rates and customs procedures across a region with many overlapping bilateral free trade agreements, and to address the developmental concerns of poorer Indo-Pacific nations. Through the RCEP, middle powers hope to augment global free trade regimes, halt China's predatory trade practices[123] and push back against the Trump administration's trade war.[124] The middle powers have also invested vast sums into their own expansive infrastructure projects. Japan has formulated the multi-billion-dollar Connectivity Initiative,[125] which emphasizes sustainable infrastructure across Asia; India has forged ahead with the International North–South Transport

---

[119] Jennings (2018).

[120] Chu (2018).

[121] Heydarian (2018a).

[122] Hermansyah (2018).

[123] *The Economist* (2018, September).

[124] Primack (2018).

[125] Sunaga (2016).

Corridor (INSTC)[126] railway and port projects to strengthen regional integration; South Korea has introduced the "New Southern Policy,"[127] to focus on infrastructure development in key Southeast Asian countries; and Australia signed an investment agreement[128] with the Association of Southeast Asian Nations (ASEAN) to "develop a pipeline of high-quality infrastructure projects, to attract private and public investment."

Geopolitically, the middle powers have also been lending weight to America's pressure campaign against Chinese maritime assertiveness. At the heart of their concern is prevention of any single power, particularly China, from having sole control over sea lines of communications in the Indo-Pacific. At the forefront of these parallel efforts is Japan, the country that is arguably the most perturbed by China's rise. China's revanchist claims in adjacent waters cover the East China Sea, where Japan occupies the contested Senkaku islands, and the South China Sea, where the bulk of Japan's energy imports pass. In recent years, the Shinzo Abe administration has steadily increased defense spending and systematically chipped away[129] at pacifist legal restrictions in order to make Japan a major military force. Two years into Trump's presidency, Japan has engaged in many firsts. It deployed,[130] for the first time ever, its gigantic Kaga helicopter carrier, which was accompanied by two guided-missile destroyers on high-profile port calls across the Indo-Pacific. Aboard the Japanese warship, the country's underappreciated military prowess suddenly dawns upon you. This was particularly the case during my visit to one of their destroyers, which docked in Subic Bay in the Philippines in 2018. Along the way, Japan's Marine Self-Defense Forces (JMSDF) armada conducted joint drills with the US Navy's[131] Ronald Reagan aircraft carrier strike group and the UK Royal Navy's[132] HMS Albion, reflecting growing interoperability and concerted pushback among like-minded nations against China. Japan also, for the first time since the end of the Second World War, deployed an armored vehicle to participate

[126] Spector (2002).
[127] Parameswaran (2018).
[128] Westbrook (2018a).
[129] Liff (2018).
[130] Kubo (2018).
[131] Shim (2018).
[132] Ng (2018).

in joint US–Philippine military exercises. During his recent meeting with his Vietnamese counterpart, Nguyen Xuan Phuc, Abe reiterated his commitment to assist[133] ongoing efforts to preserve FONOPs and strengthen the maritime security capacity[134] of Southeast Asian states. Japan is even expected to help Hanoi[135] develop energy resources in areas contested by China. The year 2018 saw the British, French[136] and Australian[137] naval forces also conducting FONOPs close to Chinese-occupied land features in the South China Sea. India and the U.K. have also announced plans[138] for naval cooperation through carrier battle group operations, ahead of the UK's deployment of its latest aircraft carrier, the HMS Queen Elizabeth, to the Indo-Pacific. The following year, the United States, Japan, India, and the Philippines conducted their first ever quadrilateral naval exercises in the South China Sea, creating new "Quad" permutations that signal growing coordination among like-minded countries in the region.[139] No longer relying on America alone, the middle powers of the Indo-Pacific are taking matters into their own hands in order to uphold free trade and freedom of navigation in the world's most dynamic region. The Indo-Pacific isn't a simply a new theatre of superpower rivalry, but instead a highly fluid strategic chessboard that provides significant agency for middle powers to shape the future of the global order.

THE FULCRUM STATE

As mentioned in the first chapter, Japan played a pivotal role in the conceptualization, and later, promotion of the Indo-Pacific concept. In recent years, with almost vengeful dynamism, Prime Minister Abe has overseen many firsts for himself and his country. Under Abe, Japan has adopted its largest defense spending on record,[140] and seeking its first

---

[133] *The Japan Times* (2018).

[134] Parameswaran (2017).

[135] Keck (2018).

[136] Navaltoday (2018).

[137] *The Straits Times* (2018, August).

[138] Gurung (2018).

[139] Mangosing (2019).

[140] Reuters (2018).

aircraft carrier[141] and deployed first armored vehicle for overseas military exercises since the end of World War II.[142] He also became Japan's youngest leader, at the age of 52, during his first stint in power in 2006, and the first one to be born after World War II. Underscoring his pro-active diplomatic streak, he was well ahead of all his peers in reaching out to larger-than-life populist figures, who have upended two of the oldest democracies in the Indo-Pacific region. Abe was the first for-eign leader[143] to meet the US President Donald Trump shortly after his election victory as well as the first foreign leader to visit the Philippines under President Rodrigo Duterte.[144] In an adept display of personal touch, he enthusiastically joined Trump for golf in Mar-o-Lago, while sharing breakfast in Duterte's home in the provincial town of Davao. Based on discussions with senior Japanese officials, I was also told that Abe actively pushed for Trump and Duterte to restore frayed bilateral relations during the Obama administration.[145]

And perhaps, there is no leader as globally traveled as Abe. Between 2012–2014, less than two years since his return to power, Abe man-aged to visit as many as forty-two nations, shuttling across Asia, Africa, and Latin America, where he pledged large-scale Japanese investments, trade deals, and, most importantly, development assistance. Almost sin-glehandedly, he made Japan a truly global player for the first time in dec-ades. After being selected, for the third straight time, as the president of the ruling Liberal Democratic party (LDP) in September 2018, garnering 553 votes out of a total of 807 by party stalwarts, Abe is well on track to becoming the longest-serving Japanese leader in postwar history. This is a testament to his personal charisma and remarkable political savvy, a dramatic turnabout in political fortunes after a graceless exit from power in 2007. But this is also a reflection of the shifting mood in Japanese soci-ety that has gone hand in hand with a reconfiguration of power among the political elite, as the country grapples with the meteoric rise of China, the consummate marginalization of domestic opposition groups, and pro-found structural economic challenges amid a deepening demographic

[141] Ibid.
[142] Agence France-Presse (2018b).
[143] BBC (2016).
[144] Rappler (2017).
[145] Conversations with senior Japanese officials between 2017 and 2018.

winter. Ahead of his fateful reelection, Abe declared that he was determined to "build a new country together," promising to "take the lead in handing over a proud and hopeful Japan to younger generations."[146] In short, he sees himself as nothing short of a transformational leader, a world-historical figure that will resurrect Japan's lost self-confidence and dynamism after the "lost decades"[147] of the late twentieth century, where stubborn economic stagnation followed a major slump in the 1990s.[148]

The Other Thucydides Trap

It's not only pride—the hope to bring Japan back to its days of glory—that is driving Abe's agenda. It's also fear, particularly of China. Allison's Thucydides trap, namely the potentially explosive structural frictions between a rapidly rising power and an insecure status quo power, has been palpably at play in Asia. While the US GDP and military spending continues to pull ahead of China's, a dramatic role reversal has already taken place in East Asia with most frightening shock to one nation: Japan. Back in 1990, Japan's GDP, despite having a population about half of the United States' and ten times smaller than China's, represented 15% of the global economic output. By 2008, it fell to 10%, and is projected to shrink to as little as 6% within a decade from now. Between 1990 and 2030, China's share of global GDP is expected to balloon from only 2% to as much as 25%. The year 2008 represented a major shock to the Western world, with the Wall Street as the epicenter of the Global Recession. In the case of Japan, however, it saw China ending its long-held status as the world's second largest economy, effectively retiring Japanese economic hegemony in Asia (see Figs. 7.5 and 7.6).[149]

Economic rebalancing has come along with rapid shifts in the balance of military power. At the beginning of the twenty-first century, Japan's defense budget was 60% larger than China's. Just over a decade later in 2012, it was barely a third of China's. But it's more than just a matter of quantitative shift, given China's growing investments in cutting-edge military technology, which is rapidly chipping away at Japan's qualitative edge

---

[146] McCurry (2018).

[147] Horiaka (2006).

[148] Rickards (2016).

[149] Anderson (1998).

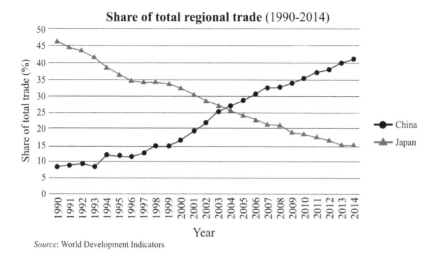

Fig. 7.5 China's and Japan's share of East Asian trade (1990–2014)

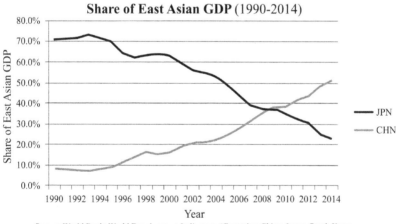

Fig. 7.6 China's and Japan's share of East Asian GDP (1990–2014)

over China.[150] To Tokyo's horror, the dramatic reversal in Sino-Japanese balance of power has been accompanied by China's most overt challenge to Japan's hold over the Senkaku/Diaoyu islands yet. In many ways, China's rising maritime assertiveness in the East China Sea is an attempt at reversing Japan's humiliating defeat of China in the 1884–1885 naval wars, which unleashed a decades-long imperial expansion by Tokyo well inside Beijing's sphere of influence and, later, heartland: namely, the acquisition of Taiwan in 1895, annexing of the Korean Peninsula in 1910, and later the invasion of Mainland China, beginning with the occupation of Manchuria (1931) and culminating in the 1937 Sino-Japanese war.[151]

Japan's occupation of the Senkaku/Diaoyu islands, which were reacquired in 1972 after temporary control by the occupying US forces, served as a painful reminder of China's humiliating defeats at the hands of a former vassal state. The age-old Zhou Enlai (and later Deng Xiaoping's) formula of "shelving" sovereignty disputes in favor of economic cooperation gave way to revanchist attempts by Beijing to wrest control of what it believes rightfully and historically belongs to it. Not long after a series of negotiations over joint exploration deals in the East China Sea in late 2000s, the territorial disputes reached a boiling point, which threatened to tear asunder bilateral relations.[152] This was particularly the case following the arrest of a Chinese fishing boast captain in 2010 by Japanese coast guard forces in the overlapping areas of claim,[153] which saw Beijing retaliating through imposition of restriction on rare earth exports to Japan,[154] as well as violent anti-Japanese protests in China two years later, following Tokyo's decision to nationalize ownership of the disputed land features in order to preempt a similar move by the then outgoing hardline governor of Tokyo Shintaro Ishihara.[155] As early as the mid-2000s, Abe saw China's rising maritime assertiveness as a direct threat to Japan's interest as well as the broader regional order. He correctly read the tectonic shifts in the regional, and more broadly global, balance of power with a great sense of urgency. His solution: the formation of a quadrilateral alliance, or better known as the Quad.

---

[150] See De Koning and Lipsey (2013) and Walton (2014).

[151] Holmes (2012).

[152] Watts (2008).

[153] Branigan and McCurry (2010).

[154] Bradsher (2010).

[155] Johnson and Shanker (2012).

In December 2006, barely three months into his premiership, Abe met his then Indian counterpart, Manmohan Singh in Japan. In their joint statement, the two leaders characterized India and Japan as "natural partners" and "largest and most developed democracies of Asia," which have "a mutual stake in each other's progress and prosperity."[156] They underscored "the usefulness of having dialogue among India, Japan and other like-minded countries in the Asia-Pacific region on themes of mutual interest."[157] Two months later, Abe reiterated the four countries' shared democratic values during the visit of then Australia Prime Minister John Howard. By April, Abe was in Washington to press a similar argument, hoping to convince the Bush administration to go beyond the trilateral alliance arrangements with Japan and Australia alone, and bring India into the fold.[158] Perhaps even more than Australia's then reticence to join any informal coalition of constrainment against China, which was solidified by Sinophile Kevin Rudd's rise to power, as well as India's ambivalence, given its sensitivity to maintaining normalized ties with Beijing, it was Abe's resignation in late 2007 that killed the Quad 1.0.[159] In its new iteration, however, the Quad seems more sustainable. In fact, it's largely welcomed by Southeast Asian nations (see Fig. 7.7).[160]

The Trump administration's call for a "Free and Open" Indo-Pacific is, in many ways, a reiteration, if not repacked version, of Abe's earlier thoughts on the emerging global order, with Asia at its very center.[161] One could even argue that the Free and Open Indo-Pacific (FOIP) is the other name for the Abe doctrine, paving the way for the creation of a Quad 2.0, with a greater sense of purpose, internal coherence, and urgency, as China begins to redraw the maritime heartland of Asia. As Stanford University academic Donald Emerson explains, while the FOIP can be understood in different ways, the emphasis on "free and open" is likely deliberate, namely designed "to keep the four Quad countries in and China out."[162] It was also designed to pave the way for the entry

---

[156] Ministry of External Affairs of India (2006).
[157] Ibid.
[158] David (2007).
[159] Madan (2017).
[160] Huong (2018).
[161] Pence (2018).
[162] Interview with author, March 1, 2019.

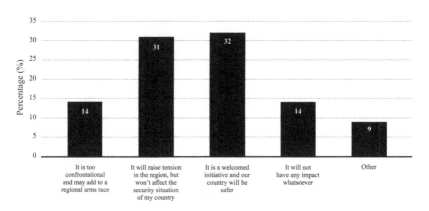

Fig. 7.7   Southeast Asian Nations' views on the Quad

of another Asian powerhouse. After all, Japan's Indo-Pacific concept was largely predicated on the rise and buy-in of another emerging superpower, which has long been confined to the sidelines due to a domestic developmental predicament, high trade protectionism (that sabotaged the World Trade Organization's Doha Round), and vicissitudes of a boisterous yet often dysfunctional democracy.

THE ELEPHANT IN THE ROOM

India is the ultimate pivot state of the twenty-first century. While maintaining stable relations with Russia (major arms supplier), China (top trading partner), and Iran (key energy supplier), the South Asian powerhouse has also stepped up its strategic engagement with Japan and major Western powers. With its sheer demographic weight and growing geopolitical ambitions, India will ineluctably play a central role in shaping the balance of power in the Indo-Pacific theatre. Under the leadership of Prime Minister Narendra Modi, the country has more confidently embraced its newfound global status. But given the depth of poverty and economic challenges at home, development remains a top priority for the Indian political elite. Not to mention, India is hemmed in by multiple territorial disputes on both its eastern and western borders (see Fig. 7.8). In February of 2019, India almost came to blows with Pakistan after the former deployed several fighter jets into Pakistani territory to bomb alleged hideouts and training ground of terrorists groups. Pakistani missile defense systems then shot down Indian planes, capturing one of

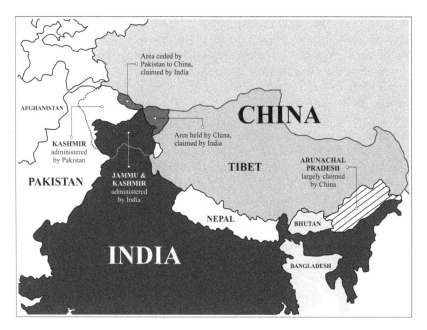

Fig. 7.8   India's territorial disputes

their pilots. The heightened tensions between the two nuclear powers came on the heels of a suicide bombing attack against Indian security forces in the contested Indian Administered Kashmir (IAK) by Jaish-e-Mohammad, an extremist group suspected of being supported by Pakistani intelligence services. India vowed to do everything necessary to diplomatically isolate Pakistan, even going so far as threatening to divert the flow of rivers downstream to Pakistan, while the chest-thumping Indian leader, facing a difficult reelection bid at home, indulged in round-the-flag rhetoric amid heightened climate of jingoism on both sides.[163] The months-long tension only underscored the fragility of cold peace between the two nuclear powers as well as India's insecure borders.

And many experts remain skeptical about India's role in the emerging Indo-Pacific security architecture, particularly in terms of dealing with the rise of China. As Australian National University academic William Tow explains, "India's level of enthusiasm for anything more than a

[163] BBC News (2019).

soft coalition of democracies deliberating on broad Indo-Pacific security issues will continue to be tempered by its residual instincts favoring a non-alignment posture. That country's postwar history points to an aversion to affiliating with formal security command structures with other states and not that much has changed in contemporary times to change this pattern of behavior. It also has no great desire to alienate China unnecessarily and believes that it can deal with China more effectively on a bilateral rather than a minilateral basis."[164]

No wonder why India, so far, seems more interested in having a seat at the table of global powers, while remaining reluctant to fully flex its muscle and, accordingly, commit resources to overly ambitious initiatives abroad. But just as climate, geopolitical orientations can also shift, at first imperceptibly, overtime. In coming the years, New Delhi will likely find itself at loggerheads with Beijing, which is becoming a "two-oceans" naval powerhouse, both in the Pacific and Indian seascapes, and is already a top source of development assistance in India's near neighborhood. The two Asian powers will have to focus on areas of common interest and greater economic cooperation lest they sleepwalk into a new Cold War after decades of "cold peace." In *The Post-American World*, Fareed Zakaria envisioned the country as one of the giants of the twenty-first century. Crucially, he saw India no longer as a "non-aligned" power, which jealously guards its strategic space by refusing to align with one superpower against, but instead as "the ally" of the United States in the coming decades.[165] Others view India as an independent pillar of a concert of powers, along with China and the United States, which will collectively shape and manage the emerging Indo-Pacific order.[166] So far, it seems India is striving to become both a pivot state courted by all superpowers as well as independent pole in its own right, particularly in the Indian Ocean and, over the coming decades, in the Western Pacific.

Economic rebalancing is one major factor. After decades of mediocre growth rates, the past two decades have seen India emerging as a dynamic emerging market, growing at an average rate of above 7% annually.[167] In a highly symbolic moment, India's Gross Domestic Product

[164] Interview with author, October 30, 2018.
[165] Zakaria (2008).
[166] Kaplan (2013).
[167] Trading Economics (2018).

is expected to surpass that of its former colonial master, the United Kingdom, 2019.[168] By the middle of this century, India will likely occupy its premodern age status as the world's second largest economy, only behind China.[169] A buoyant economy has allowed India to rapidly modernize its armed forces. In the past decade, India has been the world's largest arms importer, boasting an annual defense budget of $52.5 billion, the fifth largest in the world.[170] A growing share of its military expenditures is now devoted to developing the country's naval capabilities, with India expected to deploy two aircraft carriers in the near future. As early as 2020, India is expected to have the world's third largest defense budget. Meanwhile, India not only has rejected China's BRI, but has also sought to push back against rising Chinese influence in its near neighborhood by providing an alternative source of development as well as security assistance to nearby countries such as Bhutan,[171] Maldives, and Sri Lanka.[172] In fact, almost 64% of India's Ministry of External Affairs is spent on international aid initiatives, which include, among others, the International Technical and Economic Cooperation (ITEC) program. As Hudson Institute's Aparna Pande notes, "South Asia is not the only region where India seeks to expand its influence."[173] In what has been described as "the most significant exposition of its 'Act East' policy," India invited Southeast Asian heads of state as its chief guests during its 69th Republic Day parade in January 2018.[174]

Courting the Far East

The Commemorative Summit, with the theme "Shared Values, Common Destiny," marked the emergence of India as a major force in the broader Indo-Pacific theatre. Aside from the economic underpinnings of the "Act East" policy, China's rising assertiveness, and perceived threats to India's interests, has simply reinforced New Delhi's hopes of deepening

[168] McRae (2018).

[169] Access full report here https://www.pwc.com/gx/en/issues/economy/the-world-in-2050.html.

[170] PTI (2018).

[171] Mohan (2018).

[172] Satish (2018).

[173] Pande (2017, 164).

[174] Parashar (2018).

its cooperation with key regional actors, including the ASEAN. As for smaller Southeast Asian countries, they have gradually come to embrace India as a major trading partner and a potential stabilizing force in the region. China was very much the backdrop against which the summit was defined. The impressive pageantry of the whole event, which saw the attendance of 11 heads of state and government, underlined blossoming ties between India and the ASEAN. Both sides celebrated twenty-five years of Dialogue Partnership, fifteen years of Summit Level interaction, and five years of Strategic Partnership. As expected, trade and maritime security issues dominated the agenda. India's business-oriented and nationalist Prime Minister Narendra Modi deftly leveraged the event to project himself as a global statesman. During the summit, the Indian leader sought to deepen economic ties with Southeast Asian countries, while rallying them in defense of the existing regional order.

The economic stakes are significant and rapidly growing. In the mid-2010s, India's trade with the ASEAN expanded by 10%, rising from $65.1 billion to $71.6 billion.[175] As encouraging as these numbers are, they pale in comparison to China's $452.31 billion in trade with ASEAN countries in the same period. The Modi administration is intent on expanding trade and investment relations with booming Southeast Asia, which is moving toward greater economic integration with the hopes of creating a Common Market within a decade. India is also interested in engaging and influencing the direction of negotiations of ASEAN-led initiatives, namely the RCEP trading agreement. The Indian leader also sought to tap into underdeveloped bilateral relations across Southeast Asia. In particular, he held cordial exchanges with Filipino leader Rodrigo Duterte, who called for deeper economic ties between the two countries. The Philippines and India discussed $1.25 billion worth of bilateral investment pledges, largely in the area of energy, transportation, pharmaceutical industries, and information technology, which are expected to create as many as 10,000 jobs.[176] Yet, maritime security issues were also a key theme during the summit, with particular focus on China's rising naval and territorial assertiveness in the Pacific and Indian oceans.[177] During his speech before ASEAN heads of

---

[175] Gupta (2018).

[176] Romero (2018).

[177] Bhattacherjee (2018).

state, Modi identified "humanitarian and disaster relief efforts, security cooperation and freedom of navigation" as key areas for maritime cooperation. During the "Retreat" segment of the summit, the leaders held off-the-record discussions, which addressed maritime security issues. Aside from trade, maritime security issues were highly prominent in the joint India-ASEAN statement, dubbed as the "Delhi Declaration."[178] For instance, both sides reaffirmed their commitment to, "maintaining and promoting peace, stability, maritime safety and security, freedom of navigation and overflight in the region, and other lawful uses of the seas." They emphasized the necessity for protecting "unimpeded lawful maritime commerce," while "promot[ing] peaceful resolutions of disputes" in accordance with international law. India and the ASEAN, in a clear reference to China's disputes with Southeast Asian claimant states, called for "full and effective implementation of the Declaration on the Conduct of the Parties in the South China Sea (DOC)" as well as "early conclusion of the Code of Conduct in the South China Sea (COC)." The summit, therefore, underlined India's burgeoning interest in the South China Sea, where the bulk of India's trade and energy passes through, not to mention major energy investment deals, particularly with Vietnam. Perturbed by China's expanding footprint in the India Ocean, and rising tensions in disputed India–China borders in the Himalayas, the Modi administration is taking the fight to China via stronger cooperation with ASEAN countries. Yet, as Indian experts such as Abhijit Singh have warned, it's important that both sides will effectively manage their expectations lest they set themselves up for strategic disappointment.[179]

Bilateral relations are, in many ways, still in their developmental stages, especially when compared to the ASEAN's more robust relations with China, Japan, and the United States. Both sides are yet to discuss joint naval exercises, nor are there indications of a major boost to bilateral investments deals. What is clear, however, is that India is gradually emerging as a key strategic partner for the ASEAN, which is keen on reducing its increasing dependency on an overbearing China. Shared concerns over the rise of China are fast becoming the glue, which is bringing both sides closer together.

[178] FE Online (2018).
[179] Singh (2018).

Modifying the Nehruvian Doctrine

More fundamentally, under Modi's stewardship India has effectively cast away its tradition of strategic "non-alignment," a cornerstone of the opposition Congress Party and former Prime Minister Jawaharlal Nehru, in favor of a "web of allies." As a result, the South Asian powerhouse has more overtly tilted toward like-minded countries such as Japan, Australia, France, the United States, and the UK, which aim to constrain China's rise as Asia's preeminent military power. As Dhruva Jaishankar, a leading Indian foreign policy expert, told the author, "For all intents and purposes, non-alignment is not just over, but it is not particularly useful or applicable in today's context. Even the Congress Party, in opposition, speaks of non-alignment only as a valuable contribution of the past, rather than the basis for policy of the future."[180]

Much of this has to do with the fact that India's growing naval power and ambitions is colliding with that of China, as both Asian powers expand into each other's traditional spheres of influence. Despite booming economic ties between the two countries, with bilateral trade breaching $80 billion mark in 2017, there is still deep-seated mutual-suspicion. China has resolved most of its land-based border disputes with its continental neighbors, except with India in the Himalayas. More crucially, the oceans are becoming a new theatre of strategic rivalry. Two decades ago, Zhao Nanqi, a high-level Chinese military official, made it clear that "We can no longer accept the Indian Ocean as an ocean only of the Indians."[181] Zhang Ming, a prominent Chinese strategist, has gone so far as arguing that "India is perhaps China's most realistic strategic adversary," given New Delhi's increasing strategic presence in Southeast Asia and the Pacific under its "Act East" policy.[182]

In turn, India mirrors China's strategic anxiety. As Brahma Chellaney, one of India's most prominent strategic thinkers, told the author, "the main driver" behind India's naval buildup and deepening ties with Japan and the West is the perception that China is "encroach[ing] on India's maritime backyard" as part of a broader "strategic encirclement," with

---

[180]Interview with author dated October 22, 2019.
[181]Kaplan (2011).
[182]Scott (2008).

Pakistan and Sri Lanka acting as China's key allies against India.[183] It's precisely this security dilemma, which is gradually poisoning the once blossoming relations between Asia's two giants. During the Second World War, it were the Indian troops, operating under the aegis of the British Empire, that played a crucial role in rolling back Imperial Japan's march toward East Asia hegemony.[184] The question now is: Will India play a similar role against a revanchist China in the twenty-first century? Absent a reversal in current trend lines, growing Sino-Indian geopolitical frictions may ultimately define the Indo-Pacific order in coming decades.

THE INDO-PACIFIC CONTINENT-NATION

Not long ago, Malaysia's outspoken Prime Minister Mahathir Mohamad memorably dismissed Australia as a "deputy sheriff to America," which supposedly had little space in and common ground among the community of Asian nations.[185] Only a decade earlier, the continent-nation was seen by many of its Asian neighbors as an outpost of the Anglo-Saxon world, a consummate Western nation awkwardly perched at the intersection of Southeast Asia, and the Pacific and India Oceans. Today, however, Australia is seen as a critical stakeholder in the emerging security architecture across the Indo-Pacific. Three elemental forces have driven Australia's proactive engagement with Asia, namely fear, greed, and hope. It dreads the prospect of strategic isolation amid the rise of culturally distinct Asian nations as well as the emergence of China as a truly global power, now extending its influence into Australia's doorsteps in the southern Pacific.

Then there is the element of greed, namely tapping into the vast markets of Asia, which are hungry for Australia's raw materials, high-end agricultural products, and services. In more recent years, however, there is also growing hope and confidence that the country can play a crucial role in shaping and preserving an inclusive, free, and open order in the Indo-Pacific region through engagement and cooperation with all relevant powers, including China. Despite its relatively small population of only 25 millions souls, Australia does matter. It has managed to punch well

---

[183] Interview with author dated October 6, 2019.
[184] See Mohan (2019) and Harris (2014).
[185] Fickling (2004).

above its weight in international affairs. And along the way it has gradually staunched wounds in its historically troubled relations with Malaysia and Indonesia. Throughout the 1990s, Malaysia's Mahathir constantly expressed his dismay with Australia's ill-treatment of illegal migrants and long history of institutionalized racism, including the White Australia Policy that only ended in the late twentieth century. He lashed out at Canberra for supposedly "talk[ing] down to Asia—it tells the Asians how to behave themselves, even when the Australians themselves are not very well behaved."[186] In turn, Prime Minister Paul Keating of Australia once described the strong-willed Malaysian leader as "recalcitrant."[187] As for Indonesia, bilateral relations with Australia reached a nadir in 1999 when Canberra sent troops into East Timor for post-independence stabilization. This was seen by many Indonesians as evidence of Australia's efforts to undermine the country's territorial integrity. And along with fellow Muslim-majority Malaysia, Indonesia vehemently opposed Australia's support for the Iraq War. Australian foreign policy, however, took a decidedly Asia-oriented tilt under Prime Minister Kevin Rudd, the country's first Mandarin-speaking leader. What followed is a renaissance in Australia's economic and strategic relations with not only China, but also the broader Asian neighborhood to the north.

The 2012 "Australia in the Asian Century" White Paper under Julia Gillard administration represented a landmark document, which underscored the country's commitment to "a new phase of deeper and broader engagement" with its Asian neighbors.[188] Describing Asia as the new center of global geo-economic gravity, the paper ambitiously called for "whole-of-Australia effort," where "businesses, unions, communities and governments" are "partners in a transformation as profound as any that have defined Australia throughout our history." Far from just toeing Washington's line, Canberra has increasingly adopted a sophisticated, independent-minded foreign policy, reorienting its strategic identity as an Indo-Pacific nation. Though Australia has advocated for international law, including the Philippines' landmark arbitration award at The Hague, as a basis to resolve regional maritime disputes, it has refused overt joint

---

[186] Shenon (1993).

[187] Ibid.

[188] Australian Government (2013).

FONOPs with the United States against China in the South China Sea.[189] Advocating an inclusive regional vision that doesn't cast Beijing as a threat and an outsider has been a key pillar of Canberra's policy. Moreover, Australia believes that any stable regional security architecture recognizes the role of middle powers, particularly India and the ASEAN. To this end, Australia has established itself as a key dialogue partner of ASEAN by hosting the inaugural Australia-ASEAN summit in Sydney, while upgrading strategic cooperation with India. As Stephen Smith, among the chief architects of Australia's Indo-Pacific strategy, told the author, the future of the region shouldn't be defined by Sino-American competition, which "must be balanced and managed so that [it] does not see the potential for misjudgment or miscalculation."[190] In its 2017 Foreign Policy White Paper, Australia underscored its commitment to "strong and constructive ties with China," welcoming the Asian power's "greater capacity to share responsibility for supporting regional and global security."[191] It underscores the country's hope to "strengthen our Comprehensive Strategic Partnership for the benefit of both nations."[192] Amid rising Sino-American tensions, however, Australia has found itself, perhaps more than any other country in the region, at a strategic crossroads.

Nonetheless, following more than a decade of constructive engagement, Canberra has begun to take an increasingly tougher stance against China's influence operations in Australian politics as well as strategic penetration in the South Pacific Islands. In recent years, Canberra has imposed new restrictions on foreign electoral financing, with particular focus on the flow of money by Beijing or its intermediaries to influence domestic legislation, politics, thought leaders, veteran diplomats, and rising political figures in Australia. As one Australian analyst put it, what's surprising is "how Canberra is pushing back in the face of threats from Beijing and pressure from local business leaders worried about economic retaliation."[193] Canberra has also blocked Huawei and ZTE from gaining foothold in the country's 5G-network telecommunications sector over national security considerations, playing a leading global role, along

---

[189] Ku (2018).

[190] Interview with author dated October 31, 2018.

[191] Australian Government (2017).

[192] Ibid.

[193] Garnaut (2018).

with Washington, in curbing China's next-generation technological footprint in global critical infrastructure.[194] While there are concerns over China's growing influence in neighboring New Zealand,[195] long perceived as the weakest link in the Anglo-Saxon Five Eyes alliance,[196] a perception that has only exacerbated with the country's formal accession to the BRI in mid-2019,[197] Australia has pushed back against Chinese influence in its traditional sphere of influence, namely the South Pacific. In 2018, Australia effectively blocked Huawei from gaining a foothold in the area by providing an alternative package of investments that provide underwater Internet cables as well as a cyber security center for the Solomon Islands.[198] The same year also saw Australia effectively lobbying neighboring Fiji to block Chinese plans of developing a regional military hub, particularly the Fiji Military Forces' Black Rock Camp in Nadi.[199] Australia also agreed to co-develop a vital naval base in the Manus Island in Papua New Guinea, the historical site of Allied forces' resistance to Imperial Japan's expansion during World War II.[200] Perturbed by China's growing influence in the area,[201] Australia has also sought to tap into Pacific Islands' growing concerns over debt trap under China[202] by maintaining its position as the biggest source of development aid in the region (see Fig. 7.9).[203]

More broadly, Australia has adopted a largely skeptical position on China's global economic initiatives, joining the Chinese-led AIIB at the 11th hour,[204] while snubbing the BRI at the federal level.[205] Down the road, the Indo-Pacific continent-nation faces a difficult choice between tilting to its treaty ally (Washington) or assuaging its top trading partner

---

[194] Agence France-Presse (2018a).

[195] See Brady (2018).

[196] Roy (2018).

[197] ABC News (2019).

[198] Westbrook (2018b).

[199] Mudaliar (2018).

[200] Barrett (2018).

[201] See Dornan and Brant (2014).

[202] Dziedzic (2018a).

[203] Dziedzic (2018b).

[204] Rimmer (2015).

[205] Watkin (2019).

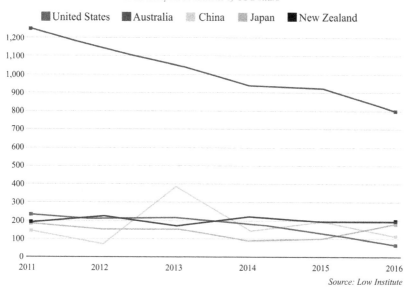

Top Donors to the Pacific Region
Total aid spent in millions of US Dollars

Fig. 7.9   Top donors in the South Pacific Islands

(Beijing). So far, however, it seems that Canberra has chosen a third way, namely transforming itself into the ultimate "strategic mediator" in the Indo-Pacific, which is not afraid to draw the line when superpowers threaten its interests, whether it's resisting the Trump administration's protectionist policies or China's interference in Australian politics and its neo-imperial ambitions in the South Pacific.[206] It's a smart and constructive position, which makes Australia crucial to avoiding a Sino-American Cold War in Asia. Yet, the middle powers are not the only players in the town, as populous and increasingly prosperous Southeast Asian states begin to harness their struggle for autonomy amid the Sino-American order, collectively shaping the future of the Indo-Pacific. And then, there is the ghost of the Soviet Union, and its successor's attempt to reassert strategic presence in the world's new pivot of history.

[206] *The Straits Times* (2018, March).

REFERENCES

Achom, Debanish. "'Tariff King' India Wants Trade Deal with US to Keep Me 'Happy': Trump." *NDTV.* October 2, 2018. https://www.ndtv.com/india-news/donald-trump-says-india-wants-to-start-trade-talks-with-us-immediately-news-agency-afp-1925242.

Agence France-Presse. "Australia Blocks Huawei, ZTE from 5G Network." *ABS-CBN News.* August 23, 2018a. https://news.abs-cbn.com/business/08/23/18/australia-blocks-huawei-zte-from-5g-network.

Agence France-Presse. "Japan Military Joins Historic PH-US War Games." *ABS-CBN News.* October 6, 2018b. https://news.abs-cbn.com/news/10/06/18/japan-military-joins-historic-ph-us-war-games.

Allen, Jonathan. "At U.N., Trump Accuses China of Interfering in Midterm Elections." *NBC News.* September 26, 2018. https://www.nbcnews.com/politics/politics-news/u-n-trump-accuses-china-interfering-midterm-elections-n913281.

Allison, Graham. "The Thucydides Trap: Are the U.S. and China Headed for War?" *The Atlantic.* September 24, 2015. https://www.theatlantic.com/international/archive/2015/09/united-states-china-war-thucydides-trap/406756/.

Allison, Graham. *Destined for War: Can America and China Escape Thucydides's Trap.* Boston: Houghton Mifflin Harcourt, 2017.

"An Accounting of China's Deployments to the Spratlys Islands." *Asia Maritime and Transparency Initiative.* May 9, 2018. https://amti.csis.org/accounting-chinas-deployments-spratly-islands/.

Anderlini, Jamil. "American Executives Are Becoming China Sceptics." *Financial Times.* November 14, 2018. https://www.ft.com/content/389a92c2-e738-11e8-8a85-04b8afea6ea3.

Anderson, Benedict. "From Miracle to Crash." *London Review of Books* 20, no. 8 (1998): 3–7. https://www.lrb.co.uk/v20/n08/benedict-anderson/from-miracle-to-crash.

Anderson, Perry. "Imperium." *New Left Review.* September–October 2013 Issue. https://newleftreview.org/issues/II83/articles/perry-anderson-imperium.

Asia Maritime Transparency Initiative. "An Accounting of China's Deployments to the Spratly Islands." *Center for Strategic and International Studies.* May 9, 2018. https://amti.csis.org/accounting-chinas-deployments-spratly-islands/.

ASEAN Business Staff. "US-China Trade War Could Be Good for South-East Asia, DBS Economist Argues." *The Business Times.* October 1, 2018. https://www.businesstimes.com.sg/asean-business/us-china-trade-war-could-be-good-for-south-east-asia-dbs-economist-argues.

"Australia Asserts Right to South China Sea Passage." *The Straits Times.* August 21, 2018. https://www.straitstimes.com/asia/australianz/australia-asserts-right-to-south-china-sea-passage.

Australian Government. "Australia in the Asian Century." 2013. www.defence.gov.au/whitepaper/2013/docs/australia_in_the_asian_century_white_paper.pdf.

Australian Government. "Opportunity, Security and Strength: 2017 Foreign Policy White Paper." 2017. https://dfat.gov.au/news/news/Pages/opportunity-security-strength-the-2017-foreign-policy-white-paper.aspx.

"Australia Warns of Trade War, Pushes for Trump Tariffs Exemption." *The Straits Times.* March 4, 2018. https://www.straitstimes.com/asia/australianz/australia-warns-of-trade-war-pushes-for-trump-tariffs-exemption.

Babones, Salvatore. "China Hits the Wall." *Foreign Affairs.* August 16, 2015a. https://www.foreignaffairs.com/articles/china/2015-08-16/china-hits-wall.

Babones, Salvatore. "Why China's Massive Military Buildup Is Doomed." *National Interest.* August 5, 2015b. https://nationalinterest.org/feature/why-chinas-massive-military-buildup-doomed-13494.

Ballard, Barclay. "Australia Looks to Curb Chinese Influence by Tightening Foreign Investment Rules." *World Finance.* February 1, 2018. https://www.worldfinance.com/markets/australia-looks-to-curb-chinese-influence-by-tightening-foreign-investment-rules.

Banjo, Shelly, and Gao Yuan. "After Huawei, Trump's Blacklist May Lead to a Global Tech Schism." *Bloomberg Businessweek.* May 22, 2019. https://www.bloomberg.com/news/articles/2019-05-22/after-huawei-trump-s-blacklist-may-lead-to-a-global-tech-schism.

Barrett, Jonathan. "U.S. Joins Australian Plan to Develop New Pacific Naval Base." *Reuters.* November 17, 2018. https://www.reuters.com/article/us-apec-summit-port/u-s-joins-australian-plan-to-develop-new-pacific-naval-base-idUSKCN1NM06X.

Bhattacherjee, Kallol. "India-ASEAN Ties to Focus on Freedom of Navigation." *The Hindu.* January 26, 2018. https://www.thehindu.com/todays-paper/india-asean-ties-to-focus-on-freedom-of-navigation/article22526632.ece.

Bilefsky, Dan. "Huawei Executive Gets New Bail Term: Staying in a $16 Million Home." *New York Times.* May 8, 2019. https://www.nytimes.com/2019/05/08/world/canada/huawei-meng-wanzhou-extradition.html.

Biswas, Rajiv. *Asian Megatrends.* London: Palgrave Macmillan, 2016.

Bradsher, Keith. "Amid Tension, China Blocks Vital Exports to Japan." *The New York Times.* September 22, 2010. https://www.nytimes.com/2010/09/23/business/global/23rare.html.

Bradsher, Keith. "Trump's Tariffs Are Changing Trade with China. Here Are 2 Emerging Endgames." *The New York Times.* August 8, 2018. https://www.nytimes.com/2018/08/08/business/trump-trade-china.html.

Brady, Anne-Marie. "China in Xi's 'New Era': New Zealand and the CCP's 'Magic Weapons'." *Journal of Democracy* 29, no. 2 (2018): 68–75. https://www.journalofdemocracy.org/articles/china-in-xis-new-era-new-zealand-and-the-ccps-magic-weapons/.

Branigan, Tania, and Justin McCurry. "Japan Releases Chinese Fishing Boat Captain." *The Guardian.* September 24, 2010. https://www.theguardian.com/world/2010/sep/24/japan-free-chinese-boat-captain.

Bremmer, Ian. *Every Nation for Itself: What Happens When No One Leads the World.* London: Portfolio, 2013.

Buckley, Chris. "China Leader Affirms Policy on Islands." *The New York Times.* January 29, 2013. https://www.nytimes.com/2013/01/30/world/asia/incoming-chinese-leader-will-not-to-bargain-on-disputed-territory.html.

Campbell, Kurt, and Ely Ratner. "The China Reckoning." *Foreign Affairs.* February 13, 2018. https://www.foreignaffairs.com/articles/china/2018-02-13/china-reckoning.

Canrong, Jin. "China Has Three Trump Cards to Win Trade War with US." *Global Times.* May 15, 2019. http://www.globaltimes.cn/content/1150061.shtml.

Chang, Gordon. "The Chinese See Trump's 'Trade War' as Existential Fight—And They're Right." *Daily Beast.* August 23, 2018. https://www.thedailybeast.com/the-chinese-see-trumps-trade-war-as-existential-fightand-theyre-right.

"Chapter 4: How Asians View Each Other." *Pew Research Center.* July 14, 2014. https://www.pewglobal.org/2014/07/14/chapter-4-how-asians-view-each-other/.

Chellaney, Brahma. "Sri Lanka: The Latest Victim of China's Debt-Trap Diplomacy." *Srilankanbrief.org.* December 26, 2017. http://srilankabrief.org/2017/12/sri-lanka-the-latest-victim-of-chinas-debt-trap-diplomacy/.

Chin, Stephen. "Trade War: Will ASEAN Be Next?" *The ASEAN Post.* July 16, 2018. https://theaseanpost.com/article/trade-war-will-asean-be-next-1.

"China Deploys New Missile Destroyer, Frigate in Its Anti-piracy Fleet." *The Economic Times.* April 4, 2019. https://economictimes.indiatimes.com/news/defence/china-deploys-new-missile-destroyer-frigate-in-its-anti-piracy-fleet/articleshow/68724333.cms.

"Chinese Leader Xi Jinping Joins Obama for Summit." *BBC News.* June 8, 2013. https://www.bbc.com/news/world-asia-china-22798572.

Christensen, Thomas. *The China Challenge: Shaping the Choices of a Rising Power.* New York: W. W. Norton, 2015a.

Christensen, Thomas. "Obama and Asia." *Foreign Affairs.* September/October 2015b. https://www.foreignaffairs.com/articles/asia/obama-and-asia.

Chu, Ben. "European Union seals major free trade deal with Japan." *The Independent.* December 12, 2018. https://www.independent.co.uk/

news/business/news/japan-european-union-free-trade-parliament-brexit-tariffs-a8679856.html.

Curran, Enda, Andrew Mayeda, and Jenny Leonard. "China Strikes $60 Billion of U.S. Goods in Growing Trade War." *Bloomberg*. September 18, 2018. https://www.bloomberg.com/news/articles/2018-09-17/trump-ratchets-up-tariff-pressure-on-china-with-200-billion-hit.

Daalder, Ivo, and John Lindsay. "The Committee to Save the World Order." *Foreign Affairs*. September 30, 2018. https://www.foreignaffairs.com/articles/2018-09-30/committee-save-world-order.

David, Camp. "President Bush and Prime Minister Abe of Japan Participate in a Joint Press Availability." *The White House*. April 26, 2007. https://georgew-bush-whitehouse.archives.gov/visit/japan/abe/index.html.

De Koning, Philippe, and Phillip Lipscy. "The Land of the Sinking Sun." *Foreign Policy*. July 30, 2013. https://foreignpolicy.com/2013/07/30/the-land-of-the-sinking-sun/.

Dobell, Graeme. "Malcolm Turnbull on Asia's Times and Trump's Hunger Games." *Australian Strategist Policy Institute*. July 3, 2017. https://www.aspistrategist.org.au/malcolm-turnbull-asias-times-trumps-hunger-games/.

Dornan, Matthew, and Philippa Brant. "Chinese Assistance in the Pacific: Agency, Effectiveness and the Role of Pacific Island Governments." *Asia & The Pacific Policy Studies*. June 11, 2014. https://doi.org/10.1002/app5.35.

Dziedzic, Stephen. "Tonga Called on Pacific Islands to Band Together Against China—Then Had a Sudden Change of Heart." *ABC News*. August 20, 2018a. https://www.abc.net.au/news/2018-08-20/tonga-prime-minister-changes-mind-on-china-loan-issue/10138068.

Dziedzic, Stephen. "Which Country Gives the Most Aid to Pacific Island Nations? The Answer Might Surprise You." *ABC News*. August 9, 2018b. https://www.abc.net.au/news/2018-08-09/aid-to-pacific-island-nations/10082702.

Erickson, Amanda. "Malaysia Cancels Two Big Chinese Projects, Fearing They Will Bankrupt the Country." *The Washington Post*. August 21, 2018. https://www.washingtonpost.com/world/asia_pacific/malaysia-cancels-two-massive-chinese-projects-fearing-they-will-bankrupt-the-country.

Erickson, Andrew. "Showtime: China Reveals Two 'Carrier-Killer' Missiles." *The National Interest*. September 3, 2015. https://nationalinterest.org/feature/showtime-china-reveals-two-carrier-killer-missiles-13769.

"EU-Japan Trade: Five Things About the World's Biggest Deal." *BBC News*. February 1, 2019. https://www.bbc.com/news/business-47086737.

Fernholz, Tim. "Eight Countries in Danger of Falling into China's 'Debt Trap'." *Quartz*. March 8, 2018. https://qz.com/1223768/china-debt-trap-these-eight-countries-are-in-danger-of-debt-overloads-from-chinas-belt-and-road-plans/.

Fickling, David. "Australia Seen as 'America's Deputy Sheriff'." *The Guardian.* September 10, 2004. https://www.theguardian.com/world/2004/sep/10/ indonesia.australia.

FE Online. "Full Text of Delhi Declaration of ASEAN-India Commemorative Summit to Mark 25th Anniversary of ASEAN-India Relations." *Financial Express.* January 26, 2018. https://www.financialexpress.com/india-news/full-text-of-delhi-declaration-of-asean-india-commemorative-summit-to-mark-25th-anniversary-of-asean-india-relations/1030898/.

Ford, John. "The Pivot to Asia Was Obama's Biggest Mistake." *The Japan Times.* January 23, 2017. https://www.japantimes.co.jp/opinion/2017/01/23/ commentary/world-commentary/pivot-asia-obamas-biggest-mistake/#. XGLTufZuLug.

"France, UK Announce South China Sea Freedom of Navigation Operations." *Navaltoday.com.* June 6, 2018. https://navaltoday.com/2018/06/06/ france-uk-announce-south-china-sea-freedom-of-navigation-operations/.

French, Howard. *Everything Under the Heavens: How the Past Helps Shape China's Push for Global Power.* New York: Knopf, 2017.

Friedman, Uri. "Donald Trump's Real Endgame with China." *The Atlantic.* October 4, 2018. https://www.theatlantic.com/international/archive/2018/ 10/trump-china-trade/572122/.

FT Confidential Research. "Vietnam Is Most Vulnerable in Southeast Asia to Trade War." *Nikkei Asian Review.* August 13, 2018. https:// asia.nikkei.com/Editor-s-Picks/FT-Confidential-Research/Vietnam-is-most-vulnerable-in-Southeast-Asia-to-trade-war.

Garnaut, John. "How China Interferes in Australia." *Foreign Affairs.* March 9, 2018. https://www.foreignaffairs.com/articles/china/2018-03-09/how-china-interferes-australia.

Gavis, Olivia. "U.S. Military Might 'Struggle to Win, or Perhaps Lose' War with China or Russia, Report Says." *CBS News.* November 14, 2018. https:// www.cbsnews.com/news/u-s-military-might-struggle-to-win-or-perhaps-lose-war-with-china-or-russia-report-says/.

Glaser, Bonnie, and Gregory Poling. "Vanishing Borders in the South China Sea." *Foreign Affairs.* June 5, 2018. https://www.foreignaffairs.com/ articles/china/2018-06-05/vanishing-borders-south-china-sea.

Goh, Evelyn. *The Struggle for Order.* Oxford: Oxford University Press, 2013.

Gompert, David C., Astrid Stuth Cevallos, and Cristina L. Garafola. *War with China: Thinking Through the Unthinkable.* Santa Monica, CA: RAND Corporation, 2016. https://www.rand.org/pubs/research_reports/RR1140. html. Also available in print form.

Gray, Colin. "Nicholas John Spykman, the Balance of Power, and International Order." *Journal of Strategic Studies.* 873–897 (2015). https://www.tandfonline.com/doi/abs/10.1080/01402390.2015.1018412.

Gupta, Surojit. "Indo-Asean Trade Rises 10% to $72bn in FY17 but Is Long Way Off Potential." *Times of India.* January 26, 2018. https://timesofindia. indiatimes.com/business/india-business/indo-asean-trade-rises-10-to-72bn-in-fy17-but-is-long-way-off-potential/articleshow/62657555.cms/.

Gurung, Shaurya Karanbir. "India, UK to Increase Joint Navy Training." *Economic Times.* October 4, 2018. https://m.economictimes.com/news/defence/india-uk-to-increase-joint-navytraining/amp.

Hachigian, Nina. *Debating China: The U.S.-China Relationship in Ten Conversations.* Oxford: Oxford University Press, 2014.

Harris, Gardiner. "A Largely Indian Victory in World War II, Mostly Forgotten in India." *The New York Times.* June 22, 2014. https://www.nytimes.com/2014/06/22/world/asia/a-largely-indian-victory-in-world-war-ii-mostly-forgotten-in-india.html.

Hermansyah, Anton. "Indonesia Targets to Conclude RCEP Negotiations This Year." *The Jakarta Post.* April 24, 2018. https://www.thejakartapost.com/news/2018/04/24/indonesia-targets-to-conclude-rcep-negotiations-this-year.html.

Heydarian, Richard Javad. "Chinese Chimera: The Real Concern with the BRI." *Lowly Institute.* July 24, 2018a. https://www.lowyinstitute.org/the-interpreter/chinese-chimera-real-concern-bri.

Heydarian, Richard Javad. "China's Premature Bid for Hegemony in Southeast Asia." *Brookings.edu.* November 28, 2018b. https://www.brookings.edu/blog/order-from-chaos/2018/11/28/chinas-premature-bid-for-hegemony-in-southeast-asia/.

Heydarian, Richard Javad. "Europe Lends America Muscle in South China Sea." *Asia Times.* June 6, 2018c. https://www.asiatimes.com/article/europe-lends-america-muscle-in-south-china-sea/.

Heydarian, Richard Javad. "Fire and Fury: Duterte's Revolutionary Foreign Policy." *The Diplomat.* September 1, 2018d. https://thediplomat.com/2018/08/fire-and-fury-dutertes-revolutionary-foreign-policy/.

Heydarian, Richard Javad. "Malaysia's Bold Play Against China." *The Washington Post.* November 14, 2018e. https://www.washingtonpost.com/news/theworldpost/wp/2018/11/14/Malaysia.

Heydarian, Richard Javad. "The Dangerous Battle for the South China Sea." *The National Interest.* June 3, 2015. https://nationalinterest.org/feature/the-dangerous-battle-the-south-china-sea-13029?page=2.

Holmes, James. "The Sino-Japanese Naval War of 2012." *Foreign Policy.* August 20, 2012. https://foreignpolicy.com/2012/08/20/the-sino-japanese-naval-war-of-2012/.

Holmes, James. "When China Rules the Sea." *Foreign Policy.* September 23, 2015. https://foreignpolicy.com/2015/09/23/when-china-rules-the-sea-navy-xi-jinping-visit/.

Horiaka, Charles Yuji. "The Causes of Japan's 'Lost Decade': The Role of Household Consumption." *Japan and the World Economy, Elsevier* 18, no. 4. (2006): 378–400. https://doi.org/10.3386/w12142.

Huong, Le Thu. "Southeast Asian Perceptions of the Quadrilateral Security Dialogue." *Australian Strategic Policy Institute.* October 2018. https://s3-ap-southeast-2.amazonaws.com/ad-aspi/2018-10/SR%20130%20Quadrilateral%20security%20dialogue.pdf.

Ikenberry, John. "The Plot Against American Foreign Policy." *Foreign Affairs.* April 17, 2017. https://www.foreignaffairs.com/articles/united-states/2017-04-17/plot-against-american-foreign-policy.

"India GDP Annual Growth Rate." *Trading Economics.* 2018. Last date accessed April 10, 2019. https://tradingeconomics.com/india/gdp-growth-annual.

"Is China Losing the Trade War Against America." *The Economist.* August 11, 2018. https://www.economist.com/finance-and-economics/2018/08/11/is-china-losing-the-trade-war-against-america.

"Japan and Vietnam Agree to Cooperate on Security in South China Sea." *The Japan Times.* October 9, 2018. https://www.japantimes.co.jp/news/2018/10/09/national/politics-diplomacy/japan-vietnam-agree-cooperation-secure-peace-south-china-sea.

"Japan PM Is First Foreign Leader to Meet Trump." *BBC News.* November 17, 2016. https://www.bbc.com/news/world-asia-37946613.

Jennings, Ralph. "How an Australia-Canada-Japan Led TPP-11 Trade Deal Compares to China's Alternative." *Forbes.* March 13, 2018. https://www.forbes.com/sites/ralphjennings/2018/03/13/how-japan-australia-and-nine-friends-will-resist-china-in-world-trade/#407568007dd6.

Jiang, Sijia. "China's ZTE Says Main Business Operations Cease due to U.S. Ban." *Reuters.* May 9, 2018. https://www.reuters.com/article/us-zte-ban/chinas-zte-corp-says-main-business-operations-have-ceased-due-to-u-s-ban-idUSKBN1IA1XF.

Jiangtao, Shi, and Owen Churchill. "More Than Tariffs: China Sees Trade War as a New US Containment Tactic." *South China Morning Post.* August 21, 2018. https://www.scmp.com/news/china/diplomacy-defence/article/2160375/more-tariffs-china-sees-trade-war-new-us-containment.

Johnson, Ian, and Thom Shanker. "Beijing Mixes Messages Over Anti-Japan Protests." *The New York Times.* September 16, 2012. https://www.nytimes.com/2012/09/17/world/asia/anti-japanese-protests-over-disputed-islands-continue-in-china.html.

Kang, David. *American Grand Strategy and East Asian Security in the Twenty-First Century.* Cambridge: Cambridge University Press, 2017.

Kang, David. "Trump's First Year in Asia: Accelerating a Long-Term Trend." *Journal of American-East Asian Relations* 25, no. 2 (2018). https://doi.org/10.1163/18765610-02502002.

Kaplan, Robert. *Monsoon: The Indian Ocean and the Future of American Power.* New York: Random House Trade Paperbacks, 2011.

Kaplan, Robert. *The Revenge of Geography: What the Map Tells Us About Coming Conflicts and the Battle Against Fate.* New York: Penguin Random House, 2013.

Keck, Zachary. "Japan Will Soon Help Vietnam Extract Gas from the South China Sea: How Will China Respond?" *The National Interest.* August 11, 2018. https://nationalinterest.org/blog/buzz/japan-will-soon-help-vietnam-extract-gas-south-china-sea-how-will-china-respond-28477.

Kennedy, Paul. *The Rise and Fall of the Great Powers.* Penguin: New York, p. xxiii, 1989.

King, Ian, Mark Bergen, and Ben Brody. "Top U.S. Tech Companies Begin to Cut Off Vital Huawei Supplies." *Bloomberg.* May 20, 2019. https://www.bloomberg.com/news/articles/2019-05-19/google-to-end-some-huawei-business-ties-after-trump-crackdown.

Kissinger, Henry. *On China.* London: Penguin Books, 2012.

Kissinger, Henry. *World Order.* London: Penguin Books, 2014.

Kitroeff, Natalie. "The President Takes on China, Alone." *The New York Times.* Podcast Audio. May 15, 2019. https://www.nytimes.com/2019/05/15/podcasts/the-daily/trump-china-trade-war.html.

Krugman, Paul. "Supply Chains and Trade War (Very Wonkish)." *The New York Times.* August 10, 2018. https://www.nytimes.com/2018/08/10/opinion/supply-chains-and-trade-war-very-wonkish.html.

Ku, Julian. "The British Are Coming to the South China Sea, and It's About Time." *Lawfare.* February 28, 2018. https://www.lawfareblog.com/british-are-coming-south-china-sea-and-its-about-time.

Kubo, Nobuhiro. "Exclusive: Japanese Helicopter Carrier to Tour South China Sea, Indian Ocean for Two Months." *Reuters.* July 4, 2018. https://www.reuters.com/article/us-japan-defence-southchinasea-exclusive/exclusive-japanese-helicopter-carrier-to-tour-south-china-sea-indian-ocean-for-two-months.

Kuo, Lily, and Niko Kommenda. "What Is China's Belt and Road Initiative." *The Guardian.* July 30, 2018. https://www.theguardian.com/cities/ng-interactive/2018/jul/30/what-china-belt-road-initiative-silk-road-explainer.

Kurtlantzick, Joshua. *Charm Offensive.* New Haven: Yale University Press, 2008.

Lague, David, and Benjamin Kang Lim. "China's Vast Fleet Is Tipping the Balance in the Pacific." *Reuters.* April 30, 2019. https://www.reuters.com/investigates/special-report/china-army-navy/.

Lee, Hsien Loong. "Transcript of Keynote Speech by Prime Minister Lee Hsien Loong at the Shangri-La Dialogue on 29 May 2015." Speech, Singapore. May 29, 2015. *Prime Minister's Office Singapore.* https://www.pmo.gov.sg/Newsroom/transcript-keynote-speech-prime-minister-lee-hsien-loong-shangri-la-dialogue-29-may-2015.

Liff, Adam. "Japan's Security Policy in the 'Abe Era': Radical Transformation or Evolutionary Shift?" *Texas National Security Review* 1, no. 3 (2018). https://tnsr.org/2018/05/japans-security-policy-in-the-abe-era-radical-transformation-or-evolutionary-shift/.

Lindell, Jordan. "Clausewitz: War, Peace and Politics." *E-International Relations Students.* Last date modified November 26, 2009. http://www.e-ir.info/2009/11/26/clausewitz-war-peace-and-politics/.

Luttwack, Edward. *The Rise of China vs. the Logic of Strategy.* New York: Belknap Press, 2012.

Madan, Tanvi. "The Rise, Fall and Rebirth of the 'Quad'." *War on the Rocks.* November 16, 2017. https://warontherocks.com/2017/11/rise-fall-rebirth-quad/.

Mangosing, Frances. "In a First, Philippines, US, Japan and India Navies Sail in South China Sea." *Inquirer.* May 9, 2019. https://globalnation.inquirer.net/175198/in-a-first-philippines-us-japan-and-india-navies-sail-in-south-china-sea.

Martinez, Luis. "Chinese Warship Came Within 45 Yards of USS Decatur in South China Sea: US." *ABC News.* October 2, 2018. https://abcnews.go.com/Politics/chinese-warship-45-yards-uss-decatur-south-china.

McCurry, Justin. "Shinzo Abe Set to be Japan's Longest-Serving PM After Winning Party Vote." *The Guardian.* September 20, 2018. https://www.theguardian.com/world/2018/sep/20/shinzo-abe-set-to-be-japans-longest-serving-pm-after-winning-party-vote.

McGrath, Ciaran. "South China Sea: US Navy Admiral Calls on Ally Australia to Act Amid Beijing Dispute." *Express.* May 17, 2019. https://www.express.co.uk/news/world/1128188/south-china-sea-us-navy-beijing-military-latest-news-australia-indonesia.

McRae, Hamsh. "This Year, India Will Surpass the UK to Be the Fifth Largest Economy—But We Shouldn't Worry Too Much." *Independent.* March 10, 2018. https://www.independent.co.uk/voices/uk-economy-india-china-g7-g20-industrial-revolution-western-technology-a8248341.html.

Medcalf, Rory, and C. Raja Mohan. "Responding to Indo-Pacific Rivalry: Australia, India and Middle Power Coalitions." *Lowly Institute.* August 8, 2014. https://www.lowyinstitute.org/publications/responding-indo-pacific-rivalry-australia-india-and-middle-power-coalitions.

Mearsheimer, John. *The Tragedy of Great Power Politics.* New York: W. W. Norton, 2014.

Ministry of External Affairs of India. *Joint Statement Towards India-Japan Strategic and Global Partnership.* December 15, 2006. https://mea.gov.in/bilateral-documents.htm?dtl/6368/Joint+Statement+Towards+IndiaJapan+Strategic+and+Global+Partnership.

Mohan, Geeta. "PM Modi Sanctions Rs 4,500 Crore Aid to Bhutan." *India Today.* December 29, 2018. https://www.indiatoday.in/india/story/pm-modi-sanctions-rs-4-500-crore-aid-to-bhutan-1419316-2018-12-29.

Mohan, C. Raja. "Raja Mandala: Integrating the Island." *Carnegie India.* January 2, 2019. https://carnegieindia.org/2019/01/02/raja-mandala-integrating-island-pub-78047.

Montelibano, Jose Ma. "China Defies Deng Xiaoping Warning." *Inquirer.* April 4, 2014. https://opinion.inquirer.net/73236/china-defies-deng-xiaoping-warning.

Mudaliar, Christopher. "Australia Outbids China to Fund Fiji Military Base." *The Interpreter: Lowly Institute.* October 4, 2018. https://www.lowyinstitute.org/the-interpreter/australia-outbids-china-fund-fiji-military-base.

Nakayama, Shuji, Setsuo Otsuka, and Issaku Harada. "US-China Tariff Showdown Uproots Global Supply Chains." *Nikkei Asian Review.* August 24, 2018. https://asia.nikkei.com/Economy/Trade-War/US-China-tariff-showdown-uproots-global-supply-chains.

Nathan, Andrew J., and Andrew Scobell. "How China Sees America: The Sum of Beijing's Fears." *Foreign Affairs* 91, no. 5 (2012): 32–47. http://www.jstor.org/stable/41720859.

"New Zealand Says It Will Find a 'Win-Win' Situation in China's Belt and Road Strategy." *ABC News.* May 7, 2019. https://www.abc.net.au/news/2019-05-07/nz-says-it-will-find-a-win-win-in-belt-and-road-strategy/11085564.

Ng, Teddy. "Japanese, British Warships Carry Out Joint Exercise in Indian Ocean in Latest Show of Strength to China." *South China Morning Post.* September 27, 2018. https://www.scmp.com/news/china/military/article/2165968/japanese-british-warships-carry-out-joint-exercise-indian-ocean.

Pande, Aparna. 2017. *From Chanakya to Modi: Evolution of India's Foreign Policy.* Harpercollins: New Delhi.

Parameswaran, Prashanth. "A New Boost for South Korea's New Southern Policy?" *The Diplomat.* July 27, 2018. https://thediplomat.com/2018/07/a-new-boost-for-south-koreas-new-southern-policy/.

Parameswaran, Prashanth. "ASEAN-Japan Coast Guard Cooperation in the Spotlight with Philippines Exercise." *The Diplomat.* November 25, 2017. https://thediplomat.com/2017/11/asean-japan-coast-guard-cooperation-in-the-spotlight-with-philippines-exercise/.

Parashar, Sachin. "India to Invite Heads of 10 Asean Nations for Republic Day Celebrations." *Times of India.* January 25, 2018. https://timesofindia.indiatimes.com/india/india-to-invite-heads-of-10-asean-nations-for-republic-day-celebtations/articleshow/59497883.cms.

Paulson, Henry. *Dealing with China: An Insider Unmasks the New Economic Superpower.* New York: Twelve, 2016.

Pavlova, Uliana. "'Made in Cambodia' May Become New Fashion Label with Tariffs Hitting China." *Bloomberg.* August 20, 2018. https://www.bloomberg.com/news/articles/2018-08-19/trade-war-surprise-gives-cambodia-added-appeal-for-u-s-firms.

Pence, Mike. "Mike Pence: The United States Seeks Collaboration, Not Control, in the Indo-Pacific." *The Washington Post.* November 9, 2018. https://www.washingtonpost.com/opinions/mike-pence-the-united-states-seeks-collaboration-not-control-in-the-indo-pacific/2018/11/09/.

Pillsbury, Michael. *Hundred-Year Marathon.* New York: St. Martin's Press, 2016.

Primack, Dan. "The Next Phase of the China Trade War." *Axios.com.* October 14, 2018. https://www.axios.com/the-next-phase-of-the-china-trade-war.

PTI. "India's Defence Budget Breaks into World's Top 5: UK Report." *The Economic Times.* February 15, 2018. https://economictimes.indiatimes.com/news/defence/indias-defence-budget-breaks-into-worlds-top-5-uk-report/articleshow/62929343.cms.

Ramo, Joshua. "Beijing Consensus." *The Foreign Policy Centre.* November 5, 2004. http://www.xuanju.org/uploadfile/200909/20090918021638239.pdf.

Reuters. "Japan's Defense Ministry Eyes Record Defense Budget Amid North Korean and Chinese Threats." *The Japan Times.* August 31, 2018. https://www.japantimes.co.jp/news/2018/08/31/national/politics-diplomacy/japan-eyes-record-defense-budget-amid-north-korean-chinese-threats/#.XLWzVvZuIpR.

Rickards, Jim. "Japan's in the Middle of Its 3rd 'Lost Decade' and a Recovery Is Nowhere in Sight." *Business Insider.* March 23, 2016. https://www.businessinsider.com/japans-3rd-lost-decade-recovery-nowhere-in-sight-2016-3.

Rimmer, Susan Harris. "Why Australia Took so Long to Join the AIIB." *The Interpreter: Lowly Institute.* March 30, 2015. https://www.lowyinstitute.org/the-interpreter/why-australia-took-so-long-join-aiib.

Robertson, Jordan, and Michael Riley. "The Big Hack: How China Used a Tiny Chip to Infiltrate U.S. Companies." *Bloomberg Businessweek.* October 4, 2018. https://www.bloomberg.com/news/features/2018-10-04/the-big-hack-how-china-used-a-tiny-chip-to-infiltrate-america-s-top-companies.

Romero, Alexis. "Philippines Secures $1.25-B Investments from India." *Philstar.* January 26, 2018. https://www.philstar.com/headlines/2018/01/26/1781449/philippines-secures-125-b-investments-india.

Rosenau, James. "The Governance of Fragmentation: Neither a World Republic Nor a Global Intestate System." *The George Washington University.* August 1, 2000. http://aura.u-pec.fr/regimen/_fich/_pdf/pub_002.pdf.

Roy, Eleanor Ainge. "New Zealand's Five Eyes Membership Called into Question Over 'China Links'." *The Guardian.* May 28, 2018. https://www.theguardian.com/world/2018/may/28/new-zealands-five-eyes-membership-called-into-question-over-china-links.

Santos, Matikas. "Philippines Wins Arbitration Case vs. China Over South China Sea." *Inquirer.net.* July 12, 2016. https://globalnation.inquirer. net/140358/philippines-arbitration-decision-maritime-dispute-south-china-sea-arbitral-tribunal-unclos-itlos.

Satish, D.P. "India Wins Maldives and Sri Lanka Back, Corners China." *Multidimension.* December 28, 2018. https://multidimension.co/magazine/india-wins-maldives-and-sri-lanka-back-corners-china/.

Sciutto, Jim. "U.S. Surveillance Detects Chinese Artillery on Disputed Islands." *CNN Politics.* May 29, 2015. https://edition.cnn.com/2015/05/28/politics/china-ashton-carter-south-china-sea-islands/.

Scott, David. "The Great Power 'Great Game' Between India and China: 'The Logic of Geography'." *Geopolitics* 13, no. 1 (2008): 1–26. https://www.tandfonline.com/doi/full/10.1080/14650040701783243.

Segal, Gerald. "East Asia and the 'Constrainment' of China." *International Security* 20, no. 4 (1996): 107–135. https://doi.org/10.2307/2539044.

Shambaugh, David. "China's Soft Power Push." *Foreign Affairs.* June 16, 2015. https://www.foreignaffairs.com/articles/china/2015-06-16/china-s-soft-power-push.

"Shangri-La Dialogue 2015: Strengthening Regional Order in the Asia-Pacific." Youtube Video, 1:22:51. *The International Institute for Strategic Studies.* May 30, 2015. https://youtu.be/P9KZUrukal4.

Sharma, Ruchir. *Breakout Nations: In Pursuit of the Next Economic Miracles.* New York: W. W. Norton, 2012.

Shenon, Philip. "Malaysia Premier Demands Apology." *The New York Times.* December 9, 1993. https://www.nytimes.com/1993/12/09/world/malaysia-premier-demands-apology.html.

Shim, Elizabeth. "Japanese Navy Trains with USS Ronald Reagan in East China Sea Drills." *UPI.com.* October 10, 2018. https://www.upi.com/Japanese-navy-trains-with-USS-Ronald-Reagan-in-East-China-Sea-drills/6851539175629/.

Singh, Abhijit. "India's 'Act-East' Must Satisfy ASEAN Expectations." *Observer Research Foundation.* January 24, 2018. https://www.orfonline.org/expert-speak/indias-act-east-must-satisfy-asean-expectations/.

Spector, Regine. "The North-South Transport Corridor." *Brookings.edu.* July 3, 2002. https://www.brookings.edu/articles/the-north-south-transport-corridor/.

Spetalnick, Matt, and Rosemarie Francisco. "Obama Puts South China Sea Dispute on Agenda as Summitry Begins." *Reuters.* November 17, 2015. https://www.reuters.com/article/us-apec-summit/obama-puts-south-china-sea-dispute-on-agenda-as-summitry-begins-idUSKCN-0T60RM20151117.

Stevenson, Alexandra. "Trump's Tariffs May Hurt, but Quitting China Is Hard to Do." *The New York Times.* September 24, 2018. https://www.nytimes.com/2018/09/24/business/china-tariffs-manufacturing-cambodia.html.

Stiglitz, Joseph. *Globalization and Its Discontents.* New York: W. W. Norton, 2003.

Sunaga, Kazuo. "Japan's Assistance to ASEAN Connectivity in Line with MPAC2025." *Embassy of Japan.* October 2016. https://www.asean.emb-japan.go.jp/documents/20161102.pdf.

Su-Yan, Pan, and Joe Tin-Yau Lo. "Re-conceptualizing China's Rise as a Global Power: A Neo-Tributary Perspective." *The Pacific Review* 30 (2015): 1–25. https://doi.org/10.1080/09512748.2015.1075578.

Tankersley, Jim, and Alan Rappeport. "China Cancels Plans for Trade Talks in Washington." *The New York Times.* September 22, 2018. https://www.nytimes.com/2018/09/22/business/china-cancels-plans-for-trade-talks-in-washington.html.

Tejada, Carlos. "Beg, Borrow or Steal: How Trump Says China Takes Technology." *The New York Times.* March 22, 2018. https://www.nytimes.com/2018/03/22/business/china-trump-trade-intellectual-property.html.

"The Perils of China's 'Debt-Trap Diplomacy'." *The Economist.* September 6, 2018. https://www.economist.com/asia/2018/09/06/the-perils-of-chinas-debt-trap-diplomacy.

Tooze, Adam. "Adam Tooze on US vs China." *Talking Politics.* Podcast Audio. May 11, 2019. https://www.talkingpoliticspodcast.com/blog/2019/163-adam-tooze-on-us-vs-china.

"Trade Tariffs & Its Impact on ASEAN." *OCBC Bank.* Last date accessed February 3, 2018. https://www.ocbc.com/assets/pdf/special%20reports/trade%20tensions%20and%20its%20impact%20on%20asean%20(jul18).pdf.

Torode, Greg. "China's Island Airstrips to Heighten South China Sea Underwater Rivalry." *Reuters.* September 17, 2015. https://www.reuters.com/article/us-southchinasea-china-submarines/chinas-island-airstrips-to-heighten-south-china-sea-underwater-rivalry-idUSKCN0RH0DA20150917.

Trump, Donald. *National Security Strategy of the United States of America.* 2017. https://www.whitehouse.gov/wp-content/uploads/2017/12/NSS-Final-12-18-2017-0905.pdf.

Varma, K.J.M. "China Records First Current Account Deficit in 20 Years in H1 2018." *Livemint.* August 7, 2018. https://www.livemint.com/Politics/nooie4BvcPsU6uwWVzGKQK/China-records-first-current-account-deficit-in-20-years-in-H.html.

Walcott, John. "China Cancels Security Talks with United States." *Channel News Asia.* October 1, 2018. https://www.channelnewsasia.com/news/world/china-cancels-security-talks-with-united-states-10774976.

Walton, Timothy. "Are We Underestimating China's Military?" *The National Interest.* May 19, 2014. https://nationalinterest.org/feature/are-we-underestimating-chinas-military-10479.

Watkin, Tim. "Australia, BRI Backlash Should Be a Warning on Loans." *The Interpreter: Lowly Institute.* February 12, 2019. https://www.lowyinstitute. org/the-interpreter/australia-bri-backlash-should-warning-loans.

Watts, Jonathan. "China and Japan Agree on Joint Gas Exploration of East China Sea." *The Guardian.* June 18, 2008. https://www.theguardian.com/ world/2008/jun/18/china.japan.

Westbrook, Tom. "Australia, ASEAN Agree to Start Regional Infrastructure Cooperation." *Reuters.* March 19, 2018a. https://www.reuters.com/article/ us-asean-australia-infrastructure/australia-asean-agree-to-start-regional-infrastructure-cooperation-idUSKBN1GV09V.

Westbrook, Tom. "Australia Keeps China Out of Internet Cabling for Pacific Neighbor." *Reuters.* June 13, 2018b. https://www.reuters.com/article/ us-australia-solomonislands-internet/australia-keeps-china-out-of-internet-cabling-for-pacific-neighbor-idUSKBN1J90JY.

"What Will Duterte, Abe Have for Breakfast in Davao?" *Rappler.com.* January 12, 2017. https://www.rappler.com/newsbreak/inside-track/158173-.

Wike, Richard, Bruce Stokes, Jacob Pushter, Laura Silver, Janell Fetterolf, and Kat Delvin. "4. Most Prefer That U.S., Not China, Be the World's Leading Power" in "Trump's International Ratings Remain Low, Especially Among Key Allies." *Pew Research Center.* October 1, 2018. https://www.pewglobal.org/2018/10/01/ most-prefer-that-u-s-not-china-be-the-worlds-leading-power/.

Wong, Edward. "China Says It Could Set Up Air Defense Zone in South China Sea." *The New York Times.* May 31, 2015. https://www.nytimes. com/2015/06/01/world/asia/china-says-it-could-set-up-air-defense-zone-in-south-china-sea.html.

Woodward, Bob. *Fear: Trump in the White House.* New York: Simon & Schuster, 2018.

Wu, Debby. "Trump's Tariffs Push Electronics from China to Southeast Asia." *Bloomberg.* August 1, 2018. https://www.bloomberg.com/news/arti-cles/2018-08-01/trump-s-tariffs-push-electronics-from-china-to-southeast-asia.

Zakaria, Fareed. *The Post-American World.* New York: W. W. Norton, 2008.

Zhang, Feng. *Chinese Hegemony: Grand Strategy and International Institutions in East Asian History.* Redwood: Stanford University Press, 2015.

Zhang, Shidong. "China Stocks World's Worst Performers in First Half of 2018, Volatility Surges in Hong Kong to Two-Year High." *South China Morning Post.* June 29, 2018. https://www.scmp.com/business/china-business/ article/2153074/shanghai-index-rebounds-first-time-after-entering-bear.

CHAPTER 8

China's Inchoate Hegemony: Small Powers' Struggle for Autonomy

In a world where the big fish eat small fish and the small fish eat shrimps, Singapore must become a poisonous shrimp. —Prime Minister Lee Kuan Yew[1]

In this venue, your honors, I announce my separation from the United States...America has lost now. I have realigned myself in your ideological flow, and maybe I will also go to Russia...there are three of us against the world, China, [the] Philippines and Russia. It is the only way. —President Rodrigo Duterte, State Visit to Beijing in October 2016[2]

You don't want a situation where there's a new version of colonialism happening because poor countries are unable to compete with rich countries in terms of just open, free trade. It must also be fair trade. —Prime Minister Mahathir Mohamad 2018 speech at Beijing[3]

Chinese President Xi Jinping's much-ballyhooed visit to Manila in late 2018 came at a critical juncture in the evolving Indo-Pacific order. It took place on the heels of that year's Asian summitries, namely the Association of Southeast Asian Nations (ASEAN) and the Asia Pacific Economic Cooperation (APEC) high-level meetings, which bore witness

---

[1] Koh (1990).
[2] Ide (2016).
[3] Bloomberg News (2018).

© The Author(s) 2020
R. J. Heydarian, *The Indo-Pacific: Trump, China, and the New Struggle for Global Mastery*, https://doi.org/10.1007/978-981-13-9799-8_8

to an undeclared Cold War between the United States and China.[4] Singapore's Prime Minister Lee Hsien Loong eloquently articulated the stark implications of rising Sino-American tensions for smaller regional states, which have been stubbornly, and even heroically, resisting the prospect of being forced "to take sides."[5]

As a regional swing state and an American treaty ally, the Philippines emerged as a critical node in the ongoing Sino-American competition for regional primacy. And this had a lot to do with geography and history. At the heart of the Indo-Pacific lay Southeast Asia, the most diverse region on earth and home to a dynamic mélange of post-colonial nations that have consciously and jealously guarded their hard-earned sovereignty and strategic autonomy in what has historically been a vicious theater of great power competition.[6] And perched at the very core of that pivotal region are the 7641 islands that constitute the Philippines, a vibrant archipelagic nation straddling the South China Sea, the Western Pacific, the interlocking seascapes that compose the maritime heartland of East Asia. A nation blessed in geography, the Philippines, described as the "pearl of the Orient" by the Spanish imperium, was the fulcrum of the Galleon trade, the greatest manifestation of maritime globalization in early modernity.[7] Manila served as a crucial entrepot, linking the New World to the complacent, and soon disintegrating, empires of the Orient, namely China, which would soon come to terms with the advent of full-fledged European imperialism. After three centuries of Spanish rule, the Philippines, at the turn of the twentieth century, turned into America's first and only colony in Asia.[8] The colonization of the Philippines' marked America's transformation into a global empire, stretching from the Atlantic all the way to East Asia.[9] For the next hundred years, the two countries became inseparable. Under the new colonial master's relatively benign rule, the Philippines rapidly became Asia's first liberal democracy and second most developed nation (only behind Imperial Japan).[10]

---

[4] Heydarian (2018g).
[5] Wong (2018).
[6] Weatherbee (2010).
[7] Philippine History.org (2019).
[8] Anderson (1997).
[9] Ferguson (2005).
[10] Karnow (1990).

By the middle of the twentieth century, the Southeast Asian country proudly possessed Southeast Asia's best-equipped armed forces, leading universities and modern public infrastructure.[11] Back then, it comfortably occupied the rarified position the city-state of Singapore enjoys today, albeit writ large. Though never forgetting its own valiant anti-colonial struggle against the United States, the Philippines stood shoulder-to-shoulder with its last imperial overlord through the First and Second World Wars as well as the hottest conflicts of the Cold War, namely the Korean and Vietnam Wars.[12] Until the twilight years of the twentieth century, the Philippines hosted America's biggest overseas military complex in Subic and Clark. In fact, even the end of Cold War, with the decisive collapse of the Soviet Union in 1991, failed to sever Manila's umbilical cord to Washington.

Even the collapse of the Soviet Union, which precipitated the withdrawal of American bases from the Philippines and elsewhere, failed to sever the umbilical cord between the two nations. Despite the exit of American bases in 1992, the 1951 Mutual Defense Treaty (MDT) served as a foundation for a series of post-Cold War defense agreements, including the Philippine–US mutual Visiting Forces Agreement (VFA) and the Enhanced Defense Cooperation Agreement (EDCA), which collectively undergirded the Philippine–US alliance and ensured its continued relevance well into the twenty-first century. Though largely underappreciated, the Philippine–US alliance—the oldest in Asia—served as a linchpin of the regional liberal order for more than a century. It's an alliance that enjoys remarkable popularity in the Philippines, with surveys showing that the Philippines is among the most pro-American nations on earth, even under the unorthodox and unpopular leadership of Donald Trump (see Fig. 8.1).[13]

At one time, Filipinos rated America's role in the world more favorably than Americans themselves.[14] Everything changed, however, with the election of a former provincial mayor to Philippine presidency. Under President Rodrigo Duterte, the Southeast Asian country turned into a potential crowning jewel for Xi's "peripheral diplomacy," which aims to

[11] Fallows (1987).

[12] Heydarian (2017b).

[13] Santos (2014).

[14] Rappler.com (2019).

Fig. 8.1 Asian countries views on Trump's leadership

People in the Philippines and Vietnam have confidence in Trump, while those in South Korea and Japan do not

Confidence in ___ to do the right thing regarding world affairs

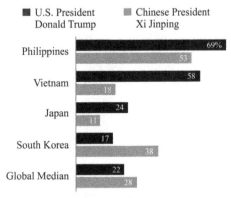

Note: Global medians based on 37 countries.

Source: Spring 2017 Global Attitudes Survey.

charm estranged neighbors through massive economic inducements.[15] The Chinese leader was desperate for a diplomatic breakthrough in the Philippines. In many ways, Xi was paying the cost of his misplaced strategic triumphalism, prematurely celebrating China's search for a place in the sun. Beginning in late 2018, Xi came under heavy criticism at home and abroad[16] for ditching Deng's "hide and bide[17]" dictum in favor of unrestrained assertiveness on the international stage.[18] No less than Long Yongtu, China's former chief trade negotiator who oversaw the country's accession to the World Trade Organization, has openly criticized the Xi administration for refusing to "think deeply enough" in dealing with international partners, particularly Washington.[19]

[15] China Council for International Cooperation on Environment and Development (2013).

[16] Kuo (2018).

[17] Heydarian (2014).

[18] Harshaw (2018).

[19] Tang (2018).

As a prominent China expert observed, there are "indication[s] that the disharmony within China's party elite is increasing."[20] China's rising influence has also provoked backlash across the region, with a growing number of countries, including Maldives,[21] Malaysia, Pakistan,[22] and Australia,[23] revisiting their strategic and economic relations with Beijing. China's much-vaunted Belt and Road Initiative (BRI) is now increasingly seen through the lens of Sri Lanka's debt trap.[24] Add to this China's ham-fisted "tantrum diplomacy,"[25] with Chinese diplomats dictating statements out of multilateral meetings to host nations, which has alienated a lot of smaller nations. This was poignantly on display during the 2018 APEC summit, when Chinese diplomats reportedly forced their way into Papua New Guinea's Foreign Minister's office to demand changes to the proposed joint communiqué. The upshot was a testy showdown between Washington and Beijing that prevented the APEC,[26] for the first time in its two-decades-long history, from issuing a joint communiqué.[27] Even worse, China has now provoked a reinvigorated US "Pivot" to Asia under the Trump administration, which has stepped up its efforts, together with like-minded regional powers, to constrain Chinese influence across the Indo-Pacific. In cooperation with Japan and Australia, Washington has launched the Indo-Pacific Transparency Initiative[28] to track, expose, and counter China's "debt trap" diplomacy and threats to freedom of navigation and overflight in the region.[29] Together with Canberra, Washington has decided to augment defense and strategic ties with South Pacific countries in order to check China's growing footprint in the region.[30] And together with India, Japan, and Australia, the Trump administration is countering China's growing strategic footprint across the Indian Ocean. In many ways, this is the real

---

[20] Kuo (2018).
[21] Reuters (2018).
[22] Sukumaran (2018).
[23] Garnaut (2018).
[24] Fernholz (2018).
[25] Rogin (2018).
[26] Vaswani (2018).
[27] Lendon and Murray (2018).
[28] Office of the Spokesperson (2018).
[29] *The Economist* (2018).
[30] Murphy (2018).

Pivot to Asia many were expecting earlier under the Obama administration. It was precisely against the backdrop of this regional backlash that Xi's visit to Manila took place.[31] And he had reasons for hope, since no Chinese leader has come this close to extracting the Southeast Asian country from America's orbit of influence. After all, under Duterte's watch, Manila has not only downplayed its bitter territorial disputes with Beijing but has also downgraded security relations with Washington.

The Filipino president, who views China as a critical ally, has rejected American requests to preposition weapons and equipment in critical military bases close to the disputed South China Sea, while blocking US warships from using Philippine ports en route for Freedom of Navigation Operations (FONOPs) in the area.[32] As a result, he has hamstrung Washington's ability to optimally deter Chinese maritime assertiveness in adjacent waters. Moreover, Duterte has granted China unprecedented military access to ports and airbases in his hometown of Davao, raising concerns over expanding Chinese military footprint in the Philippines.[33] No wonder then, China has described Duterte as its "most respected and most important friend,"[34] with Xi relishing how "[o]ur relations have now seen a rainbow after the rain," in an op-ed published by state news agency Xinhua ahead of his visit to Manila.[35] During his visit to Manila, the two leaders triumphantly upgraded their bilateral relations into a strategic partnership, which "sends a strong message to the world that our two countries are partners in seeking common development."[36] And yet, the two sides failed to achieve any major breakthrough on outstanding issues. Despite all the prior talk of a resource-sharing agreement in the South China Sea, they ended up only signing an exploratory memorandum of understanding (MOU) on potential joint exploration deals in the contested areas.[37] This was likely due to a deadlock in negotiations amid mounting domestic opposition,[38] including within the Philippine

[31] Sharma (2018).
[32] Poling and Cronin (2018).
[33] Viray (2018d).
[34] Esmaquel II (2018d).
[35] Xinhua (2018).
[36] Placido (2018).
[37] CNN Philippines (2018).
[38] Heydarian (2018a).

bureaucracy, against any capitulation to China.[39] The Philippine defense establishment, which has remained skeptical of China[40] and prefers maintaining robust security cooperation with traditional allies such as the United States, reportedly also shut down a Chinese proposal for a maritime and air liaison mechanism in overlapping areas of claim.[41] If anything, the Philippines and the United States decided to have 20 more joint exercises (from 261 to 281) in 2019, with greater focus on maritime security cooperation. This highlights the resilience and robustness of Philippine–US alliance despite Duterte's diplomatic pivot to China.[42] Above all, the Philippines was also frustrated with lack of movement on China's backlog of infrastructure investments, despite a prominent Filipino minister openly calling on the Chinese leader to "speed up" the processing of projects.[43] Many are beginning to ask what has happened to China's pledge of $24 billion of investments during Duterte's 2016 visit to China.[44] Three years into Duterte's presidency, out of the 29 deals signed during Xi's visit, mostly MOUs, frameworks, and letters, hardly a single one indicated a swift movement on any of China's packaged promise of big-ticket projects in the pipeline.[45] So far, among the ten proposed infrastructure projects, only one, the Chico River Pump Irrigation Project, has cleared the preliminary stages of implementation.[46] As a result, Duterte is coming under growing pressure to re-examine his strategic accommodation of China in favor of a tougher stance in the South China Sea.[47] Absent a breakthrough on major areas of concern, the momentum in Sino-Philippine rapprochement could soon peter out (see next section).

The underwhelming outcome of Xi's visit to the Philippines, the supposed crowning jewel of his peripheral diplomacy strategy, only highlights the fragility of China's bid for regional hegemony. China's greatest weakness, China expert David Shambaugh correctly explains, "is its

---

[39] Esmaquel II (2018c).
[40] Heydarian (2018d).
[41] Based on confidential data from author's sources.
[42] Heydarian (2018d).
[43] Lema and Petty (2018).
[44] Koutsoukis and Yap (2018).
[45] Ranada (2018b).
[46] Cigaral (2018).
[47] Heydarian (2018c).

inability to view itself as others view it" and fails to be "self-critical, never admits fault or error, and routinely blames others when strains emerge in its foreign relations."[48] While "China primarily remains a single-dimensional power—economic—whereas the United States brings multiple assets to bear in its relations with Southeast Asian states and societies,"[49] he adds. Far from falling into a pro-China domino, smaller powers such as the Philippines are carefully hedging their bets and engaged in robust domestic political debate on the future of their relations with Beijing, especially amid a revitalized American commitment, along with like-minded powers, to undergird the Indo-Pacific order. Contrary to conventional discussions about Asia as some straightforward battle between the United States and China, smaller powers have way more agency to shape their destiny. As David Shambaugh notes, Southeast Asian countries "pride themselves in maintaining their independence of action" and over time "could revert to their more traditional hedging positions, with a greater balance in their orientations toward Beijing and Washington."[50] Depending on their circumstances, capabilities, domestic politics, strategic culture, and levels of strategic and economic interdependence with China and other major powers, each Southeast Asian country has taken a unique approach to preserving maximum possible strategic autonomy in a highly fluid geopolitical landscape, where there is no longer an undisputed hegemon. Despite all the ballyhooed discourse over China's infrastructure investments in Southeast Asia, Japan continues to be a major, and often even leading, player in the region, a strategic trend that has gained pace, as discussed in the preceding chapter, under the Abe administration (see Map 8.1).

And the curious story of the Philippines and its fiery president serve as a good reminder of this fundamental shift in the physics of twenty-first-century geopolitics. As political scientists such as Moises Naim have perspicaciously observed, the physics of power has transformed, making it "easier to get, harder to use — and easier to lose" influence and power in our age. This is especially true in the vast and dynamic Indo-Pacific region.[51]

---

[48] Shambaugh (2018).
[49] Ibid.
[50] Ibid.
[51] Naim (2014, 2).

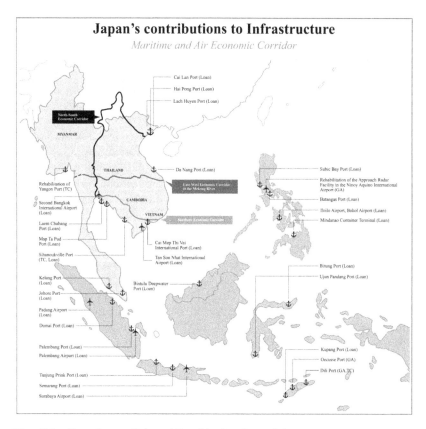

Map 8.1 Japan's own Belt and Road in Southeast Asia

THE SWING STATE

"I will be chartering [sic] a [new] course [for the Philippines] on its own and will not be dependent on the United States," Rodrigo Duterte declared shortly after his shocking electoral victory in 2016 presidential elections.[52] True to his words, over the succeeding years Duterte rapidly reconfigured Philippine foreign policy with verve and vigor. The mind-boggling shift in the country's strategic orientation is a telltale of how a charismatic and strong-willed leader can upend, almost singlehandedly,

[52] Heydarian (2016).

a century-old foreign policy tradition.[53] Almost overnight, Duterte ended his country's de facto status as an American protectorate in favor of a more transactional bilateral relationship with the Philippines' former colonial master.

Meanwhile, he began recasting China in a new light, seeking to transform a historical rival into a partner for national development.[54] To be fair, Duterte isn't the first Philippine president to reshuffle strategic relations vis-à-vis the two superpowers. Former president Gloria Macapagal Arroyo (2001–2010), currently Duterte's chief foreign policy adviser, also pursued warmer relations with China amid growing disagreement with Washington over the conduct of the Global War on Terror (GWOT).[55] By regional standards, Duterte's equilateral balancing strategy is also far from unique, closely mirroring that of other mid-sized East Asian states, ranging from South Korea to Malaysia and Vietnam, which have carefully cultivated stable relations with both China and the United States throughout the decades. This way, smaller powers have sought to preserve a measure of autonomy, avoid overdependence on any external actor, extricate themselves from Great Power rivalries in periods of conflict, and, if necessary, play bigger powers against each other for leverage and strategic benefits.[56]

What makes Duterte's case distinct is his unabashed call for a post-American order, often portraying China as the new and benign regional leader in Asia. In this sense, his foreign policy has been no less than revolutionary in, at the very least, the Philippine context. To him, Washington's decades-long hegemony in the region is a geopolitical anomaly, a contingent outcome of the Second World War that will soon fade into oblivion. Under Duterte, relations with Washington are neither sacred nor special—a remarkable break from almost all his predecessors, especially the Benigno Aquino III administration, which boosted bilateral security cooperation with the United States to counter Chinese maritime assertiveness.[57] In contrast, China, according to Duterte, is a geographical reality, which every Asian state should reckon with. He sees the Asian powerhouse as an indispensable source for development

[53] Anderson (1987).
[54] Agence France-Presse (2019a).
[55] Heydarian (2017a).
[56] Ibid.
[57] Francisco and Spetalnik (2014).

assistance as well as a stabilizing force in the region. All of a sudden, China is no longer seen as a hostile communist power by America's oldest ally in Asia.

The Philippine president has deliberately sidelined maritime disputes in the South China Sea in favor of warmer diplomatic and economic ties with Beijing.[58] Crucially, the Philippine president has also downgraded security cooperation with America and traditional partners amid the ongoing Philippine–China rapprochement. In his third year in office, Duterte remains widely popular, but he is beginning to sense the limits of his power. The festering disputes in the South China Sea have provoked widespread domestic backlash against his China-friendly diplomacy.

Despite his best efforts to cultivate a robust and enduring friendship with China, Duterte has faced stiff resistance from the defense establishment as well as prominent figures within the state, civil society, and intelligentsia, which remain wary of China. The Philippine president may be popular, but he lacks unilateral power over the country's foreign policy. Whether he wants it or not, he has had to contend with other veto players, which seek to maintain strong defense relations with Washington and limit strategic cooperation with Beijing. The Philippines' foreign policy effectively entered a twilight zone, caught between the whims of a charismatic leader, on one hand, and the traditions of the old establishment, on the other.

Duterte's Art of the Deal

There has been an ongoing debate over the origins and direction of Duterte's strategic rupture, particularly his seeming aversion toward America and, correspondingly, fascination toward China. Some critics have, without providing any concrete evidence, portrayed him as a Manchurian candidate, allegedly doing China's bidding in exchange for the former's support during the 2016 elections, when Duterte was, at least initially, a heavily underfunded candidate set against better known and established rivals from imperial Manila.[59] According to this (unsupported) narrative, China, through its proxies, namely the

---

[58] Corrales (2016).
[59] Leonen (2018).

Chinese-Filipino business community, especially in Davao, bankrolled Duterte's unlikely rise to the apex of Philippine power. The other narrative focuses on his personal attributes, with critics dismissing Duterte as an unsophisticated former provincial mayor, who has allowed his personal feelings and limited experience in high-stakes international politics to cloud his presidential judgment, much to the detriment of the country's interests. Some in the opposition view Duterte as nothing less than a "Filipino Hugo Chavez," who is supposedly bent on overturning the liberal democratic status quo in favor of a leftist-populist regime that is friendly toward China and Russia, but hostile toward the United States.[60] These quasi-cartoonish portrayals of Duterte, however, overlook important historical and geopolitical factors, which have fuelled as well as enabled his rapid transformation of Philippine foreign policy.

A more nuanced, diachronic analysis of Duterte's foreign policy, however, reveals a more complex picture, where a combination of five factors has driven his constantly evolving strategic posturing. First of all, one has to take into account how his rise to power took place within the context of right-wing populism, with Duterte, throughout his campaign rallies, portraying himself as a nationalist leader, often dramatically draping himself in the Filipino flag and promising to make the Philippine a truly "independent" nation.[61] His landslide election victory, where he comfortably trounced American-trained candidates Manuel Roxas III (Wharton) and Grace Poe (Boston College), was portrayed as a wholesale rejection of the cosmopolitan liberal establishment, which has been, according to Duterte, subservient to the West, particularly America. Duterte's campaign wasn't only about fighting drugs, but also the reassertion of the Philippines' national sovereignty after a century of alignment with Washington. Since the Philippines' formal independence (July 4, 1946), it has effectively outsourced much of its external security obligations to the United States under a package of agreements, namely Military Bases Agreement (1947), the Military Assistance Pact (1947), and the MDT of 1951, and, after the Cold War, the VFA (1998) and the EDCA (2014). Duterte promised to end the Philippines' virtual protectorate status.

---

[60]Aloc (2016).
[61]David (2016).

The second factor was Duterte's uncanny ability to colonize different branches of the state within a relatively short period of time.[62] In the first three months of his presidency, almost the entirety of the Philippine House of Representatives as well as the majority of members of the Congress defected to the new president. This was presidential bandwagoning *par excellence*, as opportunistic politicians with little party loyalty and political conviction enthusiastically tied their fate to that of the new chief executive.[63]

Duterte also had the unique privilege of appointing (without the necessity for Senate supervision as in the case of the United States) majority of the members of the Supreme Court. As one of the members of the country's highest court, who has often been critical of Duterte's policies, once told me, "It's simply a numbers game, and he got it!" In effect, Duterte managed to tighten his grip on all branches of the state without installing a formal dictatorship.[64] The rapid defection among the ranks of the ruling elite, combined with historic-high approval ratings, emboldened the Philippine president to overhaul the country's foreign policy unlike any of his predecessors.[65]

In this sense, Duterte's case mirrors that of other strongmen populists such as Vladimir Putin (Russia) and Recep Tayyip Erdoğan (Turkey), who have radically reconfigured their country's foreign relations amid a process of "authoritarianization."[66] Putin ended his predecessors' (Gorbachev and Yeltsin) *Westpolitik* within few years in office, while Erdoğan similarly reoriented his country's foreign policy toward the Near East and broader Islamic world. Both the Russian and Turkish leaders have focused on reviving of their old empires, while progressively shunning an alignment with the West. Buoyed by high approval ratings, outsized egos, and a passionate base of support, strongman populists tend to boldly challenge foreign policy dogmas with impunity. The difference, however, is that Duterte began the process of strategic rupture only a few months into office and rarely shunned from using invective-laced rhetoric to castigate traditional partners in the West. (The fast

---

[62] Cabacungan (2016).
[63] Kasuya (2009).
[64] Philstar Global (2016).
[65] Rappler (2016).
[66] Kendall-Taylor et al. (2016).

and furious pace, however, would raise its own questions on sustainability overtime, as will be discussed later in the essay.)

Yet, Duterte's strategic recalibration was also grounded in a sensible calculus, especially in light of the festering disputes in the South China Sea. For all its talk of a Pivot to Asia, the Obama administration not only failed to anticipate and constrain China's massive island-building project at the heart of the South China Sea, but also repeatedly equivocated on its alliance obligations to the Philippines. On at least two major occasions, Washington seemed less than committed to come to its treaty ally's rescue. The first one was during the months-long Scarborough Shoal standoff in 2012, which ended with China gaining effective control over the Philippine-claimed shoal. Based on conversations with senior policy-makers in all involved parties, it's clear that the Obama administration refused to provide a clear guarantee of support to the Philippines, as China deployed an armada of well-armed coast guard forces to challenge Manila's apprehension of a Chinese fisherman straddling the shoal.

The second occasion was after the Philippines' landmark arbitration award on July 12, 2016.[67] Instead of unequivocally standing by the Philippines, Obama immediately dispatched National Security Adviser Susan Rice to Beijing in order to calm down tensions, even if an arbitration body, constituted under the United Nations Convention on the Law of the Sea (UNCLOS), effectively ruled China as an outlaw in the South China Sea.[68] To many within the Philippine government, this was seen as another evidence of America trying to play good with both sides and refusing to stand firmly by its ally. As one senior Philippine defense official told me, "There was simply no firm support from Washington." No wonder then, Duterte, a month after his election, openly challenged Philip Goldberg, the then American ambassador to manila, by asking: "Are you with us [in the South China Sea]?"[69]

And this brings us to the fourth factor, which is China's unequivocal offer of a package of carrots and sticks to the Philippines. Ahead of the release of the arbitration award at The Hague, initiated by the Aquino administration to challenge Beijing's claims, the Chinese ambassador to

---

[67] Permanent Court of Arbitration (2016).

[68] Spetalnick and Brunnstrom (2016).

[69] Philstar Global (2016).

Manila Zhao Jianhua repeatedly met Duterte to negotiate a "soft-landing" on the issue.[70] Beijing made it clear that it's willing to offer large-scale infrastructure investments and mutually satisfactory arrangements, including joint development agreements, opening of Scarborough Shoal to Filipino fishermen, and establishment of marine sanctuaries in contested areas, in the South China Sea if the Duterte administration were to downplay the arbitration award, which nullified much of China's claims across the disputed waters. To make it clear that the Philippines would a pay a heavy price if it refused to do so, Beijing conducted naval drills and aerial patrols in contested areas as Manila nervously deliberated on how to leverage the arbitration award.[71] In this sense, Duterte's foreign policy recalibration was sensible and logical in light of the prevailing geopolitical circumstances in the early months of his administration. When faced with an equivocating ally and a determined adversary, Duterte opted for de-escalation and détente.

The Unraveling

In short, the tough-talking Filipino president, who has openly celebrated violence and called for mass killing of criminals and drug dealers, became an unlikely advocate for peace and pragmatism in the South China Sea.[72] As Duterte's Ambassador to Beijing, Chito Sta. Romana told the author (January 2017), "Under [Duterte's] new approach, economics, trade and commerce–and not territorial and maritime disputes–will be the key driver of Philippines–China relations. The disputes will still be subject to negotiations but they will not be at the front and center of bilateral relations [with China], nor will they [serve as] an obstacle to the improvement of bilateral ties."[73]

It didn't take long, however, for Duterte's sensible equilateral balancing strategy to come unraveling. And this is due to the final and crucial driver of his foreign policy: personal grievance and animosity.[74] Under his watch, the Philippines' external relations have often become hostage to the sentiments and historical experiences of the Filipino

[70] Ranada (2016).
[71] Corr (2016).
[72] Lim and Nawal (2018).
[73] Heydarian (2018f).
[74] Moss (2016).

president. Far from an unhinged and unmoored statesman, Duterte has approached foreign policy from the perspective of a twenty-first-century Non-Aligned Movement (NAM) leader. He has held the principle of "non-interference" as the core element of his understanding of an "independent" foreign policy. In the first months of his administration, he sought to develop a basic rapport with the West, knowing the latter's deep-seated influence among the Philippine defense establishment, intelligentsia and broader public.

As soon as the United States and other Western countries began to criticize his human rights record, however, Duterte reverted back to his age-old grievances against the United States, often denouncing them, as imperialists interfering in the domestic affairs of the Philippines. As a self-described "socialist," Duterte's ideological roots can be traced back to his college mentor, Jose Maria Sison, the founder of contemporary Philippine communist movement, and his long-term friendship with Moro nationalist leader, Nur Misuari, who has been among the most articulate critics of American imperial footprint in the southern island of Mindanao. Coming of age during the Vietnam War, Duterte has been steeped in anti-Western ideological discourse throughout his life and isolated kingdom in Davao, away from the cosmopolitan centers such as Manila. And during his long stint as a provincial mayor in Mindanao, he developed tense and often adversarial relations with Washington, particularly at the height of the GWOT.

Duterte has often mentioned the 2002 "Meiring incident,"[75] where a suspected CIA operative experimenting with explosive was escorted out of Mindanao without his permission, and the reported rejection of his visa by American authorities as just two, among many other, sources of his anger at Washington.[76] He even made the unprecedented move of blocking annual Philippine–US Balikatan exercises in his backyard, while denying Americans access to the Davao airbase for drone operations in 2013.[77] Against this adversarial background, it's no surprise that the tough-talking Filipino president would go so far as cussing at Obama and Goldberg after they criticized his human record.[78] Though

---

[75] Paddock (2016).
[76] Macas (2016).
[77] Moss (2016).
[78] Koren (2016).

the election of Donald Trump led to some thaw in bilateral relations, Duterte maintained generally tense relations with the American press, Congress, and broader government institutions. No wonder then, shortly after receiving an invitation to visit the White House in mid-2017, the Philippine president nonchalantly said, "I've seen America, and it's lousy."[79]

Unlike any of his predecessors, he snubbed the White House invitation, having, so far, shown zero interest in visiting any major Western country, including Canberra for the ASEAN-Australia Dialogue. Traditionally, Washington has been the first major foreign destination for newly elected Filipino presidents. A number of Filipino presidents visited the United States, the Philippines' sole treaty ally and former colonial master, several times during their term in office. Not for Duterte, who has instead visited China on three different occasions within first two years in office.

For Duterte, no external power should question his domestic policies, including the scorched-earth counter-narcotics campaign, which has reportedly claimed the lives of thousands of suspected drug dealers. While much of the West has regularly criticized Duterte's human rights record, China, in contrast, has expressed full support for his controversial drug war. Overtime, Duterte has been further drawn into the Chinese orbit of influence due to ideological convergence and personalization of Philippine foreign policy. In particular, he relishes Beijing's supposed commitment to the principle of non-interference in the domestic affairs of other countries. Much to his delight, China has offered full support to his drug war in multilateral fora, including at the United Nations Human Rights Council, while offering to build drug rehabilitation centers in the Philippines and large-scale infrastructure investments in Duterte's home island of Mindanao.[80]

In exchange, Duterte has refused to raise the Philippines' arbitration award in international fora, including during his chairmanship of the ASEAN, while telling external powers that the South China Sea disputes are "better left untouched."[81] He has also floated the idea of Joint Development Agreements in the South China Sea, a controversial policy

---

[79] DW (2017).
[80] Corrales (2018).
[81] Roxas (2017).

that may inadvertently legitimize China's expansive nine-dashed-line claims in the area in violation of the 2016 Arbitral Tribunal ruling at The Hague.[82] He has also given China the greenlight to expand its military access to Davao's airbase and ports in recent years, even though the two countries are yet to negotiate a formal defense agreement.[83] In effect, not only has Duterte ended the Philippines' role as the vortex of resistance against China within the ASEAN, as was the case under Aquino, but has also turned the Southeast Asian country into a potential military partner for the Asian powerhouse.

The Backlash

Amid blossoming bilateral relations, Duterte became the first Filipino president to openly express his "love" for the Chinese leadership,[84] describe the Asian powerhouse as his protector and national development partner,[85] and call on smaller nations to be "meek" and "humble" in exchange for Beijing's "mercy."[86] To top it all, Duterte has even quipped about the Philippines becoming the "province of China."[87] His quiescent policy toward China initially enjoyed public support. According to a 2017 Pew Survey, close to 7 out of 10 Filipinos supported the cultivation of stronger economic ties with China (see Fig. 8.2).[88] But Duterte's China-friendly policy only reinforced Beijing's territorial appetite and maritime expansionism. It's precisely Duterte's brazen strategic flirtation with China, which has begun to undermine his strategic realignment, unleashing widespread backlash across the country. Amid China's relentless militarization in the South China Sea and constant harassment of Filipino fishermen straddling the disputed areas, the Philippine public has openly questioned Duterte's foreign policy. No less than senior statesmen, including Vice-President Leni Robredo and acting Supreme Court Chief Justice Antonio Carpio, have been openly

---

[82] Heydarian (2018e).

[83] Mateo (2018).

[84] Mendez (2018).

[85] Legaspi (2018).

[86] Esmaquel II (2018b).

[87] Ranada (2018a).

[88] Poushter and Bishop (2017).

Fig. 8.2 Filipinos views on best policy toward China

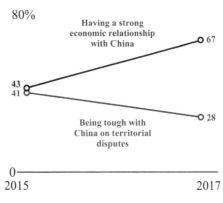

Among Filipinos, massive jump in support for strong economic relations with China at expense of being tough on territorial disputes

___ *is more important*

80%

Having a strong economic relationship with China ○ 67

43
41 ○

Being tough with China on territorial disputes ○ 28

0
2015   2017

Source: Spring 2017 Global Attitudes Survey. Q125.

critical of Duterte's soft-pedaling in the South China Sea, rallying the public against the Beijing-leaning president.[89]

Latest surveys show that vast majority of Filipinos want the president to assert the Philippines' arbitration award[90] against China and retake Scarborough Shoal and other Philippine-claimed land features under Chinese occupation (see Fig. 8.3).[91] In March 2019, former Foreign Secretary Albert Del Rosario and Ombudswoman Conchita Carpio-Morales went so far as filing an International Criminal Court (ICC) communication case against China.[92] They accused no less than Chinese President Xi Jinping of committing crimes against humanity by depriving Filipino fishermen of their rights to resources within the Philippines' exclusive economic zone (EEZ). The mainstream media and leading opinion-makers, meanwhile, have warned against welcoming large-scale

[89] Heydarian (2018b).
[90] Viray (2018c).
[91] Requejo (2018).
[92] Esmaquel II (2019).

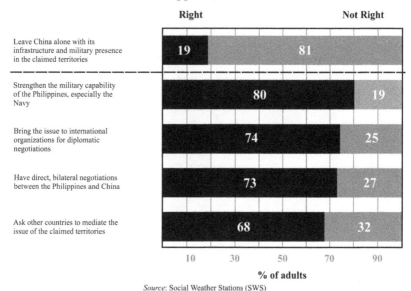

Opinion on what's right and not right for the government to do to resolve the West Philippine Sea conflict: Philippines, Jun 2018

Fig. 8.3   Philippine views on South China Sea disputes

Chinese investments to avoid possible "debt trap."[93] Justice Carpio's expose of several Chinese investment projects, which purportedly show the Philippines considered putting up its national assets as collateral in an event of debt-settlement disputes, unleashed a firestorm of criticism across the country.[94] Many worried that the Philippines could fall into the same trap as Sri Lanka and other nations that were forced into onerous debt-for-equity settlements at the expense of their national sovereignty. Under public pressure, Duterte called for review all government contracts with China.[95] But well into the third year of Duterte's

[93] Punongbayan (2018).

[94] Buan (2019).

[95] ABS-CBN News (2019, April 3).

presidency, there wasn't even a single big-ticket Chinese infrastructure investment in the country, raising concerns on whether Duterte has been taken for a ride by Beijing.[96] What made the situation even worse was the influx of hundreds of thousands of illegal Chinese workers and real estate buyers, which crowded out local workers and pushed up property prices for average Filipinos.[97] This largely undermined the foundation of Duterte's China-friendly policy, which was largely based on the promise of massive investments and trade.

Crucially, the defense establishment, particularly the Armed Forces of the Philippines (AFP), has repeatedly leaked information about Chinese threats to Philippine sovereign claims to members of the media and opposition,[98] has openly called on the government to take a tougher stance against Beijing,[99] and has openly emphasized its "constitutional duties" to protect the country's territorial integrity and sovereignty.[100] Meanwhile, the AFP has gradually restored maritime security cooperation with traditional allies. For instance, the year 2018 saw the AFP reviving joint war games with the United States in the South China Sea and expanding number of participants in the annual Balikatan joint exercises, with Australia and Japan dispatching their own warships and personnel as prominent observers.[101] The following year saw a qualitative improvement in bilateral security relations. In April, the United States' amphibious assault ship USS Wasp, with 10 F-35B stealth jets on board, participating in the annual Philippine–US Balikatan exercises close to the disputed waters.[102] The Philippine defense establishment has also been reassured by Washington's greater expression of alliance commitments.[103] As the country's top diplomat put it, they "can turn more to our only military ally" in an event of conflict with China in the South China Sea.[104] After all, a month earlier, the US Secretary of State Mike

[96] Heydarian (2018h).
[97] Heydarian (2019b).
[98] Esmaquel II (2018a).
[99] Mendez et al. (2017).
[100] Gamil (2018).
[101] Viray (2018a).
[102] Robson (2019).
[103] Ramos (2019).
[104] Ibid.

Pompeo made it clear,[105] for the first time in history,[106] that "any armed attack on Philippine forces, aircraft, or public vessels in the South China Sea would trigger mutual defense obligations under Article IV of our Mutual Defense Treaty."[107] By early 2019, bilateral tensions reached a boiling point amid a month-long siege by Chinese militia forces on the Philippine-occupied Thitu Island in the South China Sea. According to the Philippine military, there were 657 sightings of Chinese vessels, which are suspected of belonging to the formidable People's Liberation Army Maritime Militia Forces, in the first quarter of 2019.[108] As many as 275 Chinese vessels were reportedly involved in the ongoing siege,[109] which fulfilled multiple objectives simultaneously: It exposed the vulnerability of Philippine supply-lines and position in the disputed area; it allowed Beijing to monitor and restrict the Philippines' ongoing maintenance activities on the Thitu, and prevented the Philippines from fully occupying the nearby Sandy Cay and exploiting the rich fisheries resources in the area.[110] To the Philippines' further consternation, Chinese vessels were also spotted around the Kota [Loaita] Island a nearby land feature under Philippine jurisdiction.[111]

Describing China's activities as an "assault" on Philippine sovereignty, even Duterte's usually quiescent spokesman Salvador Penelo lamented: "We're supposed to be friends. As the President says, friends don't do that."[112] To the surprise of many, Duterte himself warned China, "If you touch it [Thitu Island]...I will tell my soldiers [to] 'prepare for suicide missions'."[113] The Philippine government even threatened to take the case to the United Nations General if necessary,[114] while Philippine Foreign Secretary Teddy Locsin declared he personally had "no fear of war" to resist China's actions.[115] In retrospect, the change in Duterte

[105] Taylor (2019).
[106] Batongbacal (2017).
[107] Taylor (2019).
[108] Heydarian (2019c).
[109] Gita (2019).
[110] Mangosing (2019).
[111] Colcol (2019).
[112] Merez (2019).
[113] Agence France-Presse (2019b).
[114] Parrocha (2019).
[115] ABS-CBN News (2019, April 10).

administration's tone toward China was unsurprising, though its sincerity is another question. It was precisely against the backdrop of such concerted pushback from other key sectors of the society and the broader public that the Duterte administration was compelled to issue multiple "redlines" against China in 2018,[116] warning the Asian powerhouse not to reclaim and militarize the Scarborough Shoal; refrain from coercive action against Filipino troops stationed in the disputed land features; and avoid any unilateral drilling for oil and gas exploration within the Philippines' EEZ. It's unclear how Duterte seeks to continue his rapprochement with China without undermining his position at home as well as his country's national interest. The upshot is an increasingly contested foreign policy, with varying factions jostling for the soul of Philippine foreign policy. And this largely explains the inherent contradictions and unpredictability in Manila's position toward the South China Sea issue, in particular, and relations with superpowers of China and America, in general. Though Duterte may want to cultivate a de facto alliance with China, he is facing fierce resistance from other veto players in the country's foreign policy decision-making. The future of Philippine foreign policy is uncertain, but what's clear is that Duterte is increasingly discovering the limits of his power to unilaterally shape his country's external relations. Meanwhile, in stark contrast to Duterte's China-friendly policy, another major regional leader has taken his country in a diametrically divergent position.

THE LAST TITAN OF ASIA

The electoral tsunami in Malaysia in mid-2018 not only upended the country's domestic institutions, but also the country's foreign policy, particularly toward China. Prime Minister Mohammad Mahathir's shocking return to power, at the age of 92, has precipitated a qualitative shift in Sino-Malaysian bilateral relations, as the Southeast Asian country pushes for more transparent and equitable economic deals with Beijing. By threatening to cancel big-ticket Chinese infrastructure deals, Malaysia has singlehandedly punctured the lure of Beijing's economic mega-initiatives. As a mid-sized emerging market, Malaysia's experience is also resonating among regional peers such as the Philippines, which has been reexamining its evolving relations with China.

[116]Viray (2018b).

Throughout much of his first stint in power (1981–2003), Mahathir's foreign policy largely focused on strengthening the ASEAN institutions, fostering unity among smaller Asian states, and pushing back against American unilateralism in the region.[117] While critical of Western powers, he dedicated significant diplomatic capital to augmenting ASEAN's relations with Asian powers such as Japan, India, China, and South Korea. His ultimate strategic vision was the creation of a truly 'Asia for Asians' regional security architecture, with the ASEAN at its very center.

Back then, he saw China as an indispensable counterbalance to American influence in the region, welcoming Beijing's constructive role at the height of the Asian Financial Crisis (AFC) and its then relatively subdued maritime assertiveness in the South China Sea (see Chapter 4). Against the backdrop of perceived strategic convergence, Malaysia adopted a "quiet diplomacy" vis-à-vis its territorial disputes with China in the South China Sea, while welcoming large-scale investments from the Asian powerhouse. That strategic bargain, however, has come undone since Mahathir's return to power this year.

In recent years, Mahathir has adopted a more critical view toward China, particularly under the Xi Jinping presidency, which has stepped up China's reclamation in and militarization of the South China Sea disputes. China has also begun to more openly challenge the existing global order by establishing neo-tributary relations with smaller Asian states through transcontinental infrastructure connectivity projects such as the BRI. As Mahathir told The Financial Times in early 2018, he views contemporary Chinese leadership as "inclined towards totalitarianism" and unashamed to "flex [its] muscles" in order to "increase [its] influence over many countries in Southeast Asia."[118] He characterized the new assertiveness in China's behavior as "very worrisome," particularly for smaller neighbors such as Malaysia.

Malaysia's strategic recalibration is driven by a combination of factors. In more immediate political terms, it's directly related to the new government's rejection of potentially corruption-infested bilateral deals struck by the preceding Najib Razak administration. Mahathir has accused his predecessor of selling out the nation to China in exchange for lucrative infrastructure agreements as well as financial assistance,

---

[117]Wain (2009).
[118]Anderlini (2017).

which have ballooned Malaysia's foreign debt. At the height of the 1MDB corruption scandal, with countries around the world freezing accounts of and launching investigations against senior Malaysian leaders, China provided $2.3 billion in direct assistance to bail out the embattled Razak administration. Beyond domestic politics, there was also the necessity for fiscal stabilization lest the Malaysian economy goes haywire. Confronting a $250 billion debt, some of which were hidden by the corruption-ridden Najib Razak administration through accounting wizardry, the Malaysian authorities have found it necessary to reassess big-ticket Chinese infrastructure investments. As Finance Minister Lim Guan bluntly put it, the Mahathir administration is desperate "to restore our finance and also restore our country's reputation in international financial circles," which has ben heavily damaged amid the 1MDB scandal and the country's weakening fiscal position. The Malaysian finance minister made it clear that they seek to avoid Sri Lanka's fate, "where they couldn't pay and the Chinese ended up taking over the project."[119]

The new Malaysian government has lashed out at China's major infrastructure deals for their alleged lack of transparency, questionable economic viability, and exclusion of local citizens and companies. Mahathir's warning against "new colonialism" during his recent to Beijing should be understood within this context.[120] A senior Malaysian official told the author in late 2018[121] that more than $30 billion in Chinese infrastructure deals are up for cancelation, including the $20 billion East Coast Rail Link project by China Communications Construction Company; $10 billion Melaka Gateway project co-developed with PowerChina International; and the $2.5 billion natural gas pipeline project led by a subsidiary of China National Petroleum Corporation. If China balks, Malaysia is willing to take the case to international arbitration if necessary, the official said. Mahathir has also imposed new restrictions on large-scale Chinese real estate investments such as the $100 billion Forest City, which was almost exclusively marketed to Mainland buyers. For the new Malaysian government, any major investment should be inclusive and transparent. As Senator Chin Tong Liew, currently the

---

[119] Beech (2018).

[120] Bloomberg News (2018).

[121] Partly based on the off-the-record conversations with Mahathir's senior advisers in KL in August 24 at the Parliament of Malaysia as well as senior experts on same day.

Deputy Defense Minister told the author,[122] they welcome Chinese investments so long as they create quality jobs for locals. "If investment into [a country] doesn't bring jobs, you will eventually see a domestic political problem." A renegotiation in bilateral economic relations is also affecting regional geopolitics.

Great Power Autism

"The world has always been afraid of China because of [its]...enormous size,"[123] Malaysian Prime Minister Mahathir Mohamad told me in March 2019. Thus, he highlighted an indisputable structural reality, which shapes Beijing's relations with its near neighborhood: How China's sheer size inspires not only awe but also fear among its neighbors. Thus, even "[w]hen China was poor, people were worried about China. Now that [they] have become rich they are [still] worried for other reasons,"[124] Mahathir added.

The Malaysian leader isn't only the most prominent in Southeast Asia, but also the most vocal on matters concerning Chinese economic influence in its immediate neighborhood. Since his historic return to power in 2018 after almost two decades of (partial) political retirement, which saw the former strongman constantly berating both his protégé-successors (Abdullah Badawi and Najib Razak) for their real and imagined mishaps, the Malaysian maverick has become an unlikely cheerleader for Sino-skepticism across Indo-Pacific.[125]

At the heart of Mahathir's grievance is lingering anxieties among regional states over "debt trap" under Beijing's ambitious, trillion-dollar BRI, which aims to transform the global infrastructure landscape with Chinese characteristics.[126] "If you borrow huge sums of money you [will eventually] come under the influence and direction of the lender," Mahathir told the author, underscoring the threat of involuntary "subservience" if smaller powers borrow beyond their "capacity to repay"

---

[122] Interview with the author in Malaysian Parliament last Monday, August 27, 2018.
[123] GMA News (2019).
[124] Ibid.
[125] *The Economist* (2018).
[126] Dancel (2019).

Beijing's loans. He warned recipient nations against "endangering your own freedom" due to "owing too much money to China."[127]

During his visit to Beijing in August 2018, Mahathir openly railed against "new colonialism"[128] as smaller nations such as Sri Lanka hand over strategic assets to Chinese companies after years of unsustainable borrowing.[129] He has also advocated for dialogue and cooperation with other major recipients of Chinese BRI, including Pakistan, which has been heavily indebted to Chinese companies under the $62 billion China–Pakistan Economic Corridor project.[130] "When we talk about new colonialism," Mahathir told the author, "what the Chinese are doing is not exactly that, but it has the effect of diminishing the freedom of action of other countries that are owing to much money to China." To be fair, the Malaysian leader has taken a nuanced position on Chinese investments. Far from categorically rejecting the BIR, he made it clear that "we don't mind them setting up plants to produce goods." Mahathir made it clear that, "[i]t is important for China to [also] take notice of other [countries'] views and perceptions."[131]

And here Mahathir highlights the second major concern with China among smaller neighboring nations: namely, it's inability to appreciate the worries and concerns of its geopolitical subalterns. The greatest blessing as well as curse to Chinese statecraft is the glaring historical absence of a true geopolitical peer. While this meant centuries of almost uninterrupted Chinese hegemony in East Asia, reinforcing the "Middle Kingdom" mindset, it also nurtured the perennial lack of geopolitical sensitivity on the part of the Beijing leadership throughout centuries and various regimes. The upshot is what the grand strategist Edward Luttwak notoriously termed as "great state autism."[132] In *The Rise of China vs. the Logic of Strategy*, Luttwak highlights China's "delusions of supreme strategic wisdom vouchsafed by ancient texts," which are largely irrelevant, if not counterproductive, in a modern context, where nations of immensely diverse (strategic culture) backgrounds interact as sovereign

---

[127] Interview with author, March 8, Manila.

[128] Bloomberg (2018).

[129] Schultz (2017).

[130] Sukumaran (2018).

[131] Interview with author, March 8, Manila.

[132] Luttwack and Carson (2019).

equals.[133] For Luttwak, China's "great power autism" is due to the dangerous and foolish, "misapplication of *intracultural* [among ancient Warring States] tactics, tricks, and techniques to *intercultural* conflicts, the ritualistic conduct of warfare, and the fixed Tianxia [Sino-centric regional order] presumption of superiority were all obstacles to the situational awareness of Chinese rulers, their ability to formulate realistic grand strategies and to implement them effectively by diplomatic or military means."[134]

This stands in clear contrast to other ancient powers, namely Greco-Rome and Persia (Achaemenid/Parthian/Sassanid) that experienced centuries of intense rivalry, thus brewing dynamic diplomacy and begrudging mutual respect among them. As a result, these empires sharpened and enhanced their strategic calculus overtime. The modern diplomatic astuteness of Western Europe and Iran broadly reflects this historical experience, which continues to inform the strategic culture of the modern heirs of the former empires. Malaysia's Sino-skeptic turn under no less than Mahathir is relevant for at least two major reasons. First, Malaysia has historically been among China's closest friends and top trade and investment partners, at least since Deng Xiaoping's rapprochement with Southeast Asian nations in the early 1980s.[135] And second, Malaysia is a relatively advanced, middle-sized nation, thus its experience is even more instructive to larger and more developed nations of Southeast Asia and beyond in ways that the cases of Sri Lanka, Pakistan or Laos could never be.[136] In addition, one must take into consideration the fact that more advanced Asian nations with robust credit ratings could historically rely on conventional creditors, whether international financial institutions or private investors, to raise large-scale funds for infrastructure projects. In contrast, poorer nations with weaker credit ratings had limited options, thus their reliance on the likes of China for infrastructure development. Malaysia, under the Najib Razak administration, became a cautionary tale for how even more advanced Asian nations could fall into a "debt trap" by China.

[133] Luttwack (2012).
[134] Ibid.
[135] Ng (2014).
[136] Chellaney (2017).

Careful observation of the ongoing strategic debates within and among core Southeast Asian nations only belies the myth of Chinese diplomatic astuteness as well as what can be called as the fallacy of "hegemonic inevitabilism." There is broad literature, which looks at China's expanding trading share as well as investment footprint across Southeast Asia and the broader East Asian region.[137] What the contemporary debate over China's regional role misses, however, is how the process of Chinese-driven integration is inspiring a dynamic akin to Karl Polanyi's "double-movement" in periods of rapid transformation, namely the outburst of nationalist and protectionist backlash against Beijing's growing shadow over neighboring states.[138] Beijing is running widening trade surplus with almost all of its major neighbors in Southeast Asia, with the likes of the Malaysia, Indonesia, and the Philippines largely reduced to exporters of raw materials to an industrializing China.[139] Many across the region resent the relocation of low-end manufacturing to Mainland in the past decades, while many small and medium enterprises struggle with the influx of cheap Chinese products.[140] Though China's investment in the region is expanding, its notorious reliance on Chinese workers, in addition to Chinese technology and engineering, has only exacerbated discontent among locals in recipient nations.[141]

What the conventional account of China's expanding economic ties with neighboring countries misses, thus, is the glaring asymmetry in volume and terms of trade, which has rekindled long-simmering protectionist impulses among former Third World countries, which resented Western neo-colonial economic domination in the past century. This time, however, it's China that is supplanting the position of former Western capitalist states. It's precisely within this context that one should understand Mahathir, the most prominent heir of the NAM ideology in the twenty-first century, when he speaks of "new colonialism" in Asia. What worsens China's position, and reinforces its growing tensions with more independent-minded regional states, is the country's increasingly "offensive-charm," whiplash approach in Chinese President Xi Jinping's "peripheral diplomacy."

[137] Kang (2017).
[138] Ibid.
[139] Oh (2017).
[140] See Revenhill (2006).
[141] Angaindrankumar (2018).

Mahathir's tough position seemingly paid off when, in early 2019, Malaysia managed to slash the cost of a big-ticket Chinese infrastructure project by a third and ensure greater participation by local counterparts.[142] This underscored the power and agency of smaller countries to extract concessions from China. Malaysia is also taking a tougher stance on the South China Sea disputes, with Mahathir calling for the fortification of the country's military presence in Spratlys[143] and more openly criticizing Beijing's intrusion into Malaysian waters and militarization of disputed land features.[144] Crucially, Malaysia is also gradually, yet quietly, strengthening strategic ties with China's rivals, particularly the United States. For instance, Mahathir's meeting with the US Secretary of State Mike Pompeo in early August 2018 was part of efforts to lessen Malaysia's dependence on China and explore more robust strategic ties with other external powers. He seeks to attract quality investments form both the United States and, most especially, Japan amid potential cancelation of big-ticket Chinese projects.[145] As Deputy Defense Minister Liew Chin Tong put it: "We don't want to antagonize China, but we also don't want to be seen as a client state."[146]

The Malaysian government is currently exploring a new peace formula to end militarization of the disputes and foster confidence-building measures among disputing parties.[147] Crucially, as Mr. Liew told the author, Malaysia is also interested in fostering greater strategic cooperation among ASEAN claimant states, particularly with Vietnam and the Philippines. This could come in the form of joint exercises, common diplomatic stance on the disputes, negotiation of maritime delimitation agreements in areas of overlapping claims, and reiteration of shared commitment to principles of modern international law. One proposal under consideration by involved parties is a comprehensive Code of Conduct (COC) among ASEAN claimant states himself or herself, separate from the open-ended and long-delayed one being negotiated with China. Ahead of Mahathir's visit to China for the Second Belt and Road Forum in Beijing in mid-2019, Malaysia also made it clear that it rejects

[142] Mayberry (2019).
[143] Petaling (2018).
[144] Associated Press (2018).
[145] Takenaka (2018).
[146] Interview with the author in Malaysian Parliament, August 27, 2018.
[147] Bhavan (2018).

one-on-one direct negations with China in the South China Sea in favor of a more balanced and symmetrical approach that involves all ASEAN claimant states. As Malaysian Foreign Minister Saifuddin Abdullah put it, "China is asking whether Malaysia can discuss (the South China Sea issue) on a one-on-one basis, (but) we still believe that we should enter discussion on South China Sea under an ASEAN framework rather than on a China-Malaysia framework," since "ASEAN centrality is a premium because all of us are small countries."[148]

Where Malaysia goes, the ASEAN will likely follow. The backlash against China's suffocating influence in Malaysia is reenergizing domestic opposition to Philippine President Rodrigo Duterte's China-friendly policy, while encouraging other major regional states such as Indonesia and Thailand to reconsider their growing dependence on Chinese infrastructure investments. The new Malaysian government is in a unique and privileged position to counsel its regional peers to adopt a more cautious position on China's growing influence in the region. Given Malaysia's pivotal role in the ASEAN, augmented by Mahathir's unparalleled influence as a global statesman, Putrajaya is emerging as an unlikely vortex of resistance, though not full opposition, against China's economic hegemony in the region. After all, what Mahathir is seeking is equitable, rather than hostile, relations with China, which he views as a crucial partner for development.

The Lion City-State

Malaysia's pushback has reverberated across the region, including among China-skeptic and China hawks in other neighboring states, particularly in the Philippines[149] and Indonesia,[150] but also in Singapore,[151] which is in the middle of its own increasingly open diplomatic spats with Beijing amid brewing concerns over China's interference in domestic politics. Singapore's growing frictions with China is even more astonishing than Malaysia's, especially given the city-state's Chinese-majority ethnic

[148] Channel News Asia (2019).
[149] Heydarian (2019a).
[150] Gatra (2018).
[151] Koh (2016).

background and its historically even closer diplomatic and economic ties to the Mainland. After all, the late Singaporean Prime Minister Lee Kuan Yew played a critical role in not only shaping post-Maoist China's economic policies, but also its diplomatic relations with the West.[152]

Now, even the diplomatically adroit and subtle Singapore is openly calling out China for its alleged interference in domestic affairs. As the veteran Singaporean diplomat Kausikan Bilahari put it, China is now engaged in all-out "influence operations," which seeks to rally Chinese ethnic groups across the region under the flag of the Chinese Communist Party (CCP).[153] The incorporation of the Overseas Chinese Affairs Office (OCAO) into the United Front Work Department (UFWD) in recent years signaled the birth of this new strategy, which stands in clear contrast to Beijing's "non-interference" rhetoric. The "very point of [the ongoing] united front work is to blur the distinction between the domestic and international and promote the party's interests wherever it may be, domestic or international,"[154] Bilahari said in a prominent speech on China's influence in Southeast Asian in July 2018. "In this sense, it represents a rejection or a negation of the Westphalian norm of non-interference in internal affairs, which is enshrined in Article 41 of the Vienna Convention on Diplomatic Relations," he warned.

Echoing Luttwak's observation, Bilahari highlighted China' "cultural autism" and "tendency towards self-deception" and strategic "overreach" in its relations with neighboring states. In 2017, Singapore expelled Huang Jing, a prominent China-born professor at the Lee Kuan Yew School of Public Policy, after accusing the academic of "collaboration with foreign intelligence agents [from China]" in an attempt at "subversion and foreign interference in Singapore's domestic politics."[155] Singapore has also tightened its cyber laws against Fake News and propaganda, including from hostile overseas actors. Russia's interference in American and European elections, which included systematic disinformation campaigns, likely served as a wakeup call against similar "sharp power" disruption and infiltration campaigns by China

---

[152] Gan and Zhou (2018).

[153] Yong (2018).

[154] *The Straits Times* (2018).

[155] Ibrahahim (2017).

to influence Singaporean domestic politics.[156] As Christopher Walker and Jessica Ludwig of the National Endowment for Democracy (NED) explain, "sharp power" refers to campaigns by "powerful and ambitious authoritarian regimes," which "centers on distraction and manipulation" of political affairs in foreign nations.[157] The depth of Singapore's worries over Mainland China's sharp power,[158] meanwhile, was well on display when the city-state decided to build a $110 million Singapore Chinese Cultural Center (SCCC) to assert and juxtapose its own unique Chinese cultural heritage.[159] One major worry in Singapore is Beijing's seemingly deliberate blurring of the distinction *huaren* (ethnic Chinese of all nationalities) and *huaqiao* (Chinese citizens overseas). This is particularly worrying in the context of Xi's call for "The realization of the great rejuvenation of the Chinese nation requires the joint efforts of Chinese sons and daughters at home and abroad."[160] There are as many as 60 million ethnic Chinese spread across the world, many in neighboring Southeast Asian nations.[161]

Recent years have seen heightened bilateral tensions amid Singapore's call on China to observe the UNCLOS amid a Manila-initiated arbitration against Beijing as well as closer defense and strategic cooperation between Singapore and Taiwan. In late 2016, China even impounded 9 Singaporean armored vehicles transiting via Hong Kong from military exercises in Taiwan. The episode triggered a diplomatic crisis and weeks-long negotiations over the return of Singaporean Terrex troop carriers.[162] Perturbed by China's rising maritime assertiveness, Singapore has stepped up its military cooperation with the United States, including granting permanent access to American littoral combat ships, as well as like-minded nations such as Taiwan, India, Japan, and Australia. In fact, strategic analysts are beginning to talk about the prospect of a "SQUAD," namely institutionalized strategic cooperation between Singapore and the Quad members of the United States, Australia, India,

---

[156] Parameswaran (2019).
[157] Walker and Ludwig (2017).
[158] Qin (2018).
[159] Zaccheus (2017).
[160] Xinhua (2017).
[161] Qin (2018).
[162] Jaipragas (2017).

and Japan.[163] The city-state is also rapidly expanding its military capabilities, with defense spending hitting a 12-year high in 2019 despite the economic slowdown.[164]

Yet, notwithstanding Mahathir's larger-than-life persona and influence, as well as Singapore diplomatic astuteness, allowing the city-state to punch well above its weight for decades, both countries will increasingly play in the shadow of Southeast Asia's largest and most powerful nation, which is gradually waking up to the China threat.

The Other Sleeping Giant

Perched at the crossroads of two oceans, Indonesia is the geographic heartland of the Indo-Pacific. Spanning 4700 km (3000 miles), from Aceh at the western tip of Southeast Asia to Papua in the South Pacific, the nation of 17,000 islands is perched at the intersection of the South China Sea, and the Pacific and Indian oceans. And with Indonesia's growing geopolitical heft, the Southeast Asian nation has positioned itself at the vortex of the emerging security architecture in the Indo-Pacific. As a sign of its growing strategic ambitions, Indonesia has been hosting several high-profile conferences in recent years aimed at charting the future of the region, while putting forward its own unique vision for the Indo-Pacific.

In particular, Indonesia has called for an inclusive regional order, where the ASEAN pacifist norms undergird relations among great powers, particularly the United States and China. From Indonesia's point of view, China is an indispensable regional stakeholder that has to be fully engaged. But as Jakarta begins to more proactively protect its interests, and exert influence commensurate to its size and power, it has increasingly found itself at loggerheads with an assertive China, which is challenging the maritime status quo in the region.[165]

As early as 2013, Indonesia's then Foreign Minister Marty Natalegawa advocated[166] for an Indo-Pacific order anchored by the ASEAN's core principles of non-aggression, dialogue-based management

---

[163]See Madan (2017) and Medcalf (2013).
[164]*Singapore Business Review* (2019).
[165]Cochrane (2017).
[166]Laksmana (2018).

of disputes, osmotic economic integration, and multilateral resolution of common challenges across the region.[167] At the same time, however, Japanese Prime Minister Shinzo Abe began advocating for an alternative vision of the Indo-Pacific,[168] where a "democratic security diamond" of like-minded powers, namely the Quadrilateral Alliance (Quad) of Australia, Japan, India, and the United States, collectively manage emerging challenges to the liberal international order.[169] China's rising geopolitical assertiveness and expanding economic influence, in particular, was atop the Abe concern. When the Trump administration came into power, it largely embraced Japan's vision, where Washington, in concert with key allies, keeps Beijing's ambitions in check and upholds a "Free and Open Indo-Pacific" (FOIP). Defining the Indo-Pacific as a geographical theater that stretches from "the United States to India, from Japan to Australia, and everywhere in between," US Vice-President Mike Pence warned, in a *The Washington Post* Op-Ed, that Washington and its allies "will stand up to anyone who threatens our interests and our values."[170]

Perturbed by the seeming Quad-centered, anti-Chinese conception of the Indo-Pacific, Indonesia has advocated for a more inclusive security architecture, which isn't directed against any specific power or group of nations. To this end, it has hosted a series of major multilateral fora to chart an alternative vision of the Indo-Pacific. During the Second Jakarta Geopolitical Forum (JGF) in late 2018, Foreign Minister Retno Marsudi emphasized Indonesia's role as a bridge among competing powers and an anchor for the creation of an inclusive order in the Indo-Pacific.[171] "Indonesia's humanitarian and peace diplomacy has become one of the cornerstones of foreign policy that is appreciated globally. We will continue to use this spirit to turn geopolitical competition into collaboration,"[172] Marsudi said. "Indonesia always sees cooperation [as] better than rivalry by promoting a mutually beneficial approach," the

---

[167] Partly augmented by exchanges with the author on the sidelines of the Australia-ASEAN Dialogue in Sydney, Australia, 2019.

[168] Abe (2012).

[169] Sharma (2018).

[170] Pence (2018).

[171] Yashinta (2018).

[172] Ibid.

Indonesian diplomatic chief added.[173] Her comments came against the backdrop of growing Sino-American tensions, which have raised concerns across the region over potential armed conflict and a festering trade war between the world's two largest economies. Earlier that month, during International Monetary-World Bank Annual Meeting in Bali (October 12), which was also attended by Southeast Asian heads of state and the United Nations Secretary General António Guterres, Indonesian President Joko Widodo (Jokowi) warned against Sino-American trade wars and called for greater coordination among states and international organizations to maintain a free, open, and dynamic global economic order.[174]

In fact, the Jokowi administration is exploring its own version of FOIP, which will be more inclusive, particularly toward China, and centered on the ASEAN and its values. Only two weeks after his speech at the IMF-WB meeting, Jokowi returned to Bali for the 2018 Our Ocean Conference (OOC), which brought together the world's leading marine scientists and security experts. "In the future, Indonesia would also like to enhance maritime cooperation in the Indo-Pacific region. Together with [Association of Southeast Asian Countries] and ASEAN partners, Indonesia is developing the Indo-Pacific cooperation concept by reiterating the habit of dialogue and cooperation, inclusivity and respect for international law," the Indonesian president said.[175]

Standing Up to China

Advocating a "mental revolution," Jokowi called for greater trans-regional cooperation to address "challenges facing our oceans and to manage them in a sustainable" manner, where the OOC must serve as "the driving engine" for protection of marine space and species.[176] Jokowi, however, couldn't conceal Indonesia's growing concerns over China's maritime assertiveness and its implications for regional security. "Overlapping maritime claims, if not resolved through negotiations based on international law, may pose a threat to stability.

---

[173] Ibid.
[174] Davies and Lawder (2018).
[175] *The Jakarta Post* (2018).
[176] Ibid.

International law must be a guide in the settlement of maritime affairs," the Indonesian leader warned.[177] It was a thinly veiled reference to the South China Sea disputes, where China has muscled its way through massive reclamation activities and militarization of disputed land features in defiance of international law. In broader terms, Indonesia, the only country that identifies the ASEAN as a cornerstone of its foreign policy, is worried about China's defiance of regional pacifist norms, particularly on conflict-prevention and dispute-settlement.

Back in March 2018, during the Australia-ASEAN summit in Sydney, Indonesia called for joint patrols by littoral states across the South China Sea to help de-escalate tensions and peacefully resolve overlapping maritime claims.[178] Aiming to turn his country into a "global maritime nexus," Jokowi has repeatedly reiterated Indonesia's longstanding position as a neutral arbiter among disputing parties. Yet, Jakarta is also worried about China's growing intrusion into Indonesian waters. In 2014, former Vice-Admiral Desi Albert Mamahit bluntly portrayed Beijing's growing paramilitary presence in energy-rich waters off the Natuna islands as "clearly a real threat for Indonesia."[179] In response to a growing threat from China, the Indonesian government has augmented its military presence in the area. That year (2014) saw Indonesia increasing its defense spending by a staggering 14%,[180] while exploring the deployment of an F16 as well as Apache helicopter squadron to support defensive fortifications, particularly in Pekanbaru,[181] in the Riau islands, which host one of the Asia's largest offshore gas filed exploration sites. It also stepped up joint naval exercises with the United States in the area.[182] Buoyed by a booming economy, Indonesia has been steadily increasing its defense spending.[183] As a share of the country's Gross Domestic Product (GDP), Indonesian defense spending is still modest (1.1%),[184] but it's experiencing a dramatic increase, especially in absolute terms, compared to the 2005–2014 (0.82%) and the 2000–2004

---

[177] Ibid.
[178] Jensen (2018).
[179] FlorCruz (2014).
[180] Grevatt and Caffrey (2014).
[181] *The Jakarta Post* (2017).
[182] Panda (2015).
[183] Trading Economics (l.a. 2019).
[184] Parlina (2016).

(0.78%) periods when the economy and defense spending share was much smaller. Jokowi has promised to increase defense spending from $7.2 billion in 2014 to $20 billion in 2019, and raise defense spending to 1.5% of GDP if annual growth hits the 6% threshold.[185] Troubled by China's growing paramilitary presence in its northern waters, Indonesia went so far as renaming waters off the Natuna Islands as the North Natuna Sea in 2017, reiterating its exclusive fishing and energy exploration rights amid Chinese claims of having "traditional fishing grounds" in the area.[186]

A year earlier,[187] a Chinese coast guard vessel aggressively foiled an attempt by Indonesian authorities to impound a Chinese vessel engaged in illegal fishing activities in the Natuna area.[188] Later that year, in June, Jakarta dispatched a warship to apprehend Chinese vessels that were fishing illegally. Jakarta is particularly concerned with illegal, unregulated, and unreported (IUU) fishing, which has hit the country's 2.4 million-strong fishing community pretty hard.[189] Close to half of them (45%) have been driven out of their jobs due to declining fisheries stockpiles over the past decade. According to the UN, IUU costs the country at least $1 billion in foregone marine resources every year.[190]

To address the crisis, Jokowi appointed a no-nonsense Minister of Maritime Affairs and Fisheries, Susi Pudjiastuti, who has adopted an uncompromising "Sink the Vessels" policy, which saw hundreds of impounded illegal fishing vessels blown up by Indonesian authorities.[191] This marked a dramatic departure from Indonesia's historical policy of not reporting the confiscation of foreign fishing vessels in order to maintain stable ties with neighboring countries. According to Indonesian authorities, the policy, while controversial, has led to a dramatic decline in the number of foreign illegal fishing vessels, mostly from China and Vietnam, as well as the doubling of fisheries stock in Indonesian waters. As a result of her tough policy, fishing stocks have more than doubled, while most of the 10,000 foreign illegally fishing boats, mostly from

[185] Sipahutar et al. (2018).
[186] Cochrane (2017).
[187] Beech and Suhartono (2018).
[188] Cochrane (2017).
[189] Beech and Suhartono (2018).
[190] Ibid.
[191] Ibid.

Chinese and Vietnam have disappeared.[192] Despite its best efforts to enjoy "pragmatic equidistance" with all major powers and maintain a "quiet diplomacy" vis-à-vis the South China Sea disputes, the Jokowi administration has gradually found itself on a collision course with an expansionist China.[193] It remains to be seen how Indonesia's more inclusive conception of the Indo-Pacific will be reconciled with growing Sino-Indonesian maritime tensions, which, if left unresolved, could upend bilateral relations in coming years. Though Indonesia is the largest nation in Southeast Asia, it's not necessarily the best organized against the threat of China's maritime assertiveness. Ironically, it's a communist-led nation that seems best equipped in dealing with the Asian juggernaut.

Asia's Prussian State

Vietnam is perhaps the only country in the world that is existentially defined by its centuries-old opposition to China. Its legendary resistance to superpowers, from Mongolia to France and the United States, but, most especially, China, has largely anchored the country's very national identity and historical formation. And this explains why Vietnam, more than any other Southeast Asian country, is perturbed by China's growing assertiveness, especially in the South China Sea, where Hanoi claims the Spratlys and Paracel group of islands. Vietnam is also arguably the most militarily prepared nation in the region when it comes to resisting China. In many ways, it's a fiercely organized, highly hierarchical, and heavily militarized society with few parallels in the world. As one senior former Vietnamese official put it, "If it comes to war, I am willing to sacrifice all my sons to get one of China's."[194] And Hanoi is willing to do whatever it takes, including making friends with former enemies that are enemies of its main enemy, to protect its prized national autonomy.

In a remarkable reflection of burgeoning strategic relations between former enemies, the year 2018 saw America deploying an aircraft carrier group to Vietnam for the first time in more than four decades.[195] The USS Carl Vinson, 103,000-tonne carrier, along with two other large

[192] Ibid.
[193] Laksmana (2017).
[194] Interview with author, November 2016.
[195] Head (2018).

warships, visited the Vietnamese port of Da Nang on a five-day goodwill visit. It marked the largest American military presence on Vietnamese shores since 1975, signaling the emergence of an unlikely alliance between Washington and the Southeast Asian communist regime. In its National Security Strategy (NSS) paper, released last December, the Trump administration identified Vietnam as a "cooperative maritime partner," underlining Hanoi's emergence as a key player in preserving the existing order in the East Asian seascape. "The visit marks an enormously significant milestone in our bilateral relations and demonstrates U.S. support for a strong, prosperous, and independent Vietnam," declared Daniel Kritenbrink, the US ambassador to Vietnam.[196] "Through hard work, mutual respect, and by continuing to address the past while we work toward a better future, we have gone from former enemies to close partners," he continued.[197] What lies at the heart of rapidly warming ties between the two former nemesis is the rise of China, particularly its growing military footprint across the South China Sea, which has threatened Vietnam's territorial and maritime interests as well as American's naval hegemony in Asia.

With America's traditional regional allies such as Thailand and the Philippines adopting an increasingly Beijing-leaning foreign policy, Washington has been scrambling for new and reliable strategic partners in Southeast Asia. Determined to protect its claims in the South China Sea, Hanoi has emerged as the leading—if not lone—voice of resistance against Chinese maritime assertiveness. Yet, it's far from assured if the highly symbolic visit by an American aircraft carrier will soon translate into a tangible military alliance against China. In recent years, Vietnam has consistently been at the forefront of multilateral diplomatic efforts, particularly in the ASEAN, to criticize China's massive reclamation activities across disputed land features. In response to China's rapid militarization of artificially created islands, Vietnam has embarked on limited reclamation activities of its own, accompanied by deployment of weapons systems, including precision-guided artilleries, to some of its islands in the Spratlys.[198]

[196] Minh (2018).
[197] Ibid.
[198] Gady (2016).

More broadly, Vietnam has rapidly expanded its naval capabilities, including the purchase of kilo-class submarines from Russia, and the development of its naval facilities in the highly strategic port of Da Nang. The Southeast Asian country has also opened up various gas fields within its EEZ, which is contested by China, to state-owned energy companies from Russia and India. This way, Hanoi aims to deepen the stake of other major powers in protecting its resources and maritime claims in the South China Sea. As a matter of national security doctrine, the fiercely independent Vietnam has adopted the three no's policy of non-alignment with one power bloc against the other, non-hosting of foreign military bases on its soil, and non-alliance with and dependence on any external power.

In a classic exercise of strategic diversification, however, Hanoi has reached out to major regional powers such as Russia, India, and Japan to shore up its maritime defense and domain awareness capabilities. Cognizant of its economic dependence on China, Vietnam has sought to attract large-scale investments from Japan, South Korea, Taiwan, Singapore, and Western countries. It also sought to join the Trans-Pacific Partnership Agreement (TPP), currently resuscitated as the Comprehensive and Progressive Agreement for Trans-Pacific Partnership (CPTPP),[199] in order to expand its export markets and sources of capital and technology. As a result, Hanoi has managed to develop a modicum of strategic space as well as minimum deterrence against Chinese revanchist intentions within Vietnamese waters. Nonetheless, the Southeast Asian country remains deeply insecure and constantly dreads the prospect of strategic isolation, thanks to China's growing military muscle and regional economic influence as well as the increasingly acquiescent policies of other regional claimant states such as the Philippines under President Rodrigo Duterte.

Within the ASEAN, for instance, Vietnam has often found itself as the lone voice standing up to Chinese maritime assertiveness, with many other countries region preferring strategic accommodation and continued economic engagement rather than open confrontation with the Asian powerhouse.[200] By reaching out to America, Vietnam hopes to strengthen its hands against China. Yet, this strategy not only runs the

---

[199] Suzuki (2019).
[200] Inquirer (2017).

risk of backfiring, provoking China into more aggressive action, but also faces immense structural constraints. While Vietnam is intent on holding Chinese maritime ambitions at bay, it's also highly vulnerable to Chinese economic and military reprisals. Vietnam shares extensive (land and maritime) borders not only with China, but also immediate China-leaning neighbors such as Cambodia. Meanwhile, the US Congress has been reluctant to sanction sales of more advanced weaponries to the communist regime,[201] which has been constantly accused of widespread human rights violations. To this date, there has been no major arms deal on the table. Not to mention, much of Vietnam's weaponries are of Russian origin, raising concerns over technological compatibility if the Southeast Asian country were to incorporate American weaponries. Moreover, there are broader concerns over the reliability and wherewithal of America to stand up to China, when push comes to shove. Ultimately, Hanoi deeply fears the prospect of strategic abandonment in an event of more explicit alignment with America and like-minded regional powers. No wonder, it remains doubtful if the highly promising partnership will ever translate into a full-fledged alliance against China. And this explains Hanoi's omni-balancing strategy of reaching out to as many potential partners as possible in order to keep China at bay, while ultimately relying on its own defensive capabilities and strategic will. In fairness, there is one country, in particular, that has been immensely helpful to Vietnam's minimum deterrence capability development, a vast nation that has been absent from the Asian geopolitical drama for more than two decades but is now rediscovering its purpose in its eastern shores.

RUSSIA'S OWN PIVOT

For the first time in recent memory, Russian warships docked in Manila Bay in 2017.[202] After visiting the Russian vessels, an anti-submarine ship and a sea-tanker, Duterte went so far as to call upon his guests to be "our ally to protect us," though he didn't clarify against what specific threats.[203] The two sides soon began negotiations over major trade deals

---

[201] De Luce and Johnson (2016).
[202] ABS-CBN News (2017).
[203] Salaverria (2017).

worth $2.5 billion as well as a potential military agreement to boost their historically anemic strategic interaction.[204]

The Filipino strongman's unexpectedly rapid rapprochement with Russian President Vladimir Putin, whom Duterte has described as his "favorite hero," is a reflection of both personal-ideological and pragmatic-strategic calculations.[205] It is also a byproduct of Moscow's own pivot to Asia, which has adopted greater urgency and substance in recent years, as Russia struggles with Western sanctions and aims to reclaim its Cold War-era strategic footprint in the Asia-Pacific theater.

Though a great power, and certainly a superpower in the post-Soviet space, Russia still remains largely marginal in the Indo-Pacific story. But this could change in the coming decades, as Moscow seeks its strategic destiny in the new fulcrum of global geopolitics. Russia's strategic reorientation toward Asia officially kicked off with its lavish hosting of the 2012 APEC summit in Vladivostok, which reportedly cost an estimated $21 billion.[206] The following year, during the St. Petersburg International Economic Forum, Putin expanded on Moscow's "march to the east" pronouncements, vowing to step up infrastructure investments in the neglected eastern regions of Russia, expanding trade and investment relations with energy-hungry economies of Asia, and reasserting Moscow's military presence in the Western Pacific.[207]

In fact, as part of its infrastructure buildup in the east, Russia spent $1 billion on the world's longest cable-stayed bridge, a 3600-foot span connecting Vladivostok to Russky Island, the APEC summit venue. Other major investments are expected to follow, including the trans-Siberian railway, with the ultimate aim of enmeshing Russia's eastern regions with the dynamic manufacturing and innovation networks of East Asia. With Western sanctions battering the Russian economy over the latter's annexation of Crimea and intervention in eastern Ukraine, Moscow has become even more desperate to step up its economic engagement with Asia.[208]

---

[204]Yap (2016).
[205]Gonzales (2016).
[206]*International Business Times* (2012).
[207]Hill and Lo (2013).
[208]*The Economist* (2014).

Yet, with the exception of high-profile energy deals with Beijing, namely a $400 billion agreement to transfer Russian gas to China,[209] Moscow hasn't offered much of an economic initiative to the region.[210] Nonetheless, Russia has managed to step up its strategic footprint in Asia by expanding military cooperation with and arms sales to regional states, while injecting itself into the South China Sea disputes by conducting joint drills with China.[211] Russia has astutely leveraged its status as a permanent member of the United Nations Security Council, a leading global arms exporter, and a non-claimant state in the South China Sea to once again become a regional broker. It has managed to build military cooperation with rival claimant states, particularly China and Vietnam, which have been voracious customers of Russian military technology.

Russia has been negotiating basing access to Vietnam's prized Cam Ranh Bay, where it has built a submarine base, enjoys docking rights, and supports refueling missions for Russian military assets operating across the Pacific theater.[212] Between 2010 and 2015, Russia's arms sales to ASEAN countries more than doubled. At $5 billion, Southeast Asia now accounts for around 15% of total Russian arms exports, a figure that is expected to climb as regional states upgrade their naval and air capabilities amid China's rising assertiveness.[213]

As America's staunchest ally in ASEAN, the Philippines has broadly shunned deeper military engagement with Russia for much of its history. Under Duterte, however, that is rapidly changing. Duterte has held direct meetings with both President Putin and Russian Prime Minister Dmitry Medvedev, during the APEC and ASEAN summits, respectively, and later became the first Filipino leader in recent memory to Moscow in early 2017, even while snubbing the White House. Some of the unprecedented warmth in Manila–Moscow bilateral relations can be attributed to Duterte's admiration for the authoritarian Putin, who has consolidated control over much of his country's state institutions, dominated elections and maintained high approval ratings, while constantly lashing out at alleged Western intervention in the domestic affairs of developing

---

[209] Wan and Hauslohner (2014).

[210] Putz (2016).

[211] Lendon and Hunt (2016).

[212] Snegov (2018).

[213] Otto (2016).

nations.[214] But Duterte also sees a potential protector in Putin, as the United Nations and Western allies continue to blast the Philippines' controversial war on drugs.

Due to concerns over human rights, the US State Department has frozen a shipment of firearms to the Philippine National Police[215] as well as deferring a major economic aid package.[216] In response, Duterte has waved the "Russia card" with more gusto. For Duterte, Russia—along with China—could serve as an alternative source of armaments and trade if strategic relations with the United States continue to deteriorate. Moreover, Moscow has vowed to offer, on affordable terms, sophisticated weapons systems that contrast sharply with the outdated, surplus military equipment that Washington usually provides to its oldest Asian ally and former colony.[217] There have been at least two rounds of formal discussions between Manila and Moscow on the matter,[218] with the latest one involving Philippine defense secretary Delfin Lorenzana and foreign affairs secretary Perfecto Yasay Jr., who visited Moscow in late 2016.[219] To cement its growing relevance in the South China Sea disputes, Russia is also pursuing joint naval drills with the Philippines and other ASEAN claimant states, which will require new strategic partnership agreements.[220]

Without question, a new chapter has begun in the long-stale Philippines–Russia relationship. For now, however, there is more symbolism than substance, as Manila and other Southeast Asian capitals focus more on limited arms purchase, particularly rifles and drones rather than submarines and frigates, while showing a keener interest in large-scale trade and investment deals. Ultimately, Duterte, and other Southeast Asian countries are signaling to Washington that they have alternative options, and aren't beholden to any specific power. The future of the Indo-Pacific, however, will depend on the ability of all relevant players to deal with seismic challenges that could literally imperil the existence of many nations in the mega-region. Decades from now, the ongoing Sino-American geopolitical competition will likely appear like a foolish child's

---

[214] Gonzales (2016).
[215] Zengerie (2016).
[216] Cordero (2016).
[217] Lema (2017).
[218] Delizo (2016).
[219] Pilapil (2017).
[220] Calonzo and Tweed (2017).

play compared to the scale of cataclysmic threats on the horizon. The coming anarchy, however, may unify the competing powers of the region like never before.

REFERENCES

Abe, Shinzo. "Asia's Democratic Security Diamond." *Project Syndicate.* December 27, 2012. https://www.project-syndicate.org/commentary/a-strategic-alliance-for-japan-and-india-by-shinzo-abe.

Agence France-Presse. "South China Sea: Duterte Warns Beijing of 'Suicide Missions' to Protect Disputed Island." *The Guardian.* April 5, 2019a. https://www.theguardian.com/world/2019/apr/05/south-china-sea-duterte-warns-china-of-suicide-missions-to-protect-disputed-island.

Agence France-Presse. "With Kim-Putin Summit, Moscow Eyes Role in N. Korea." *Rappler.* April 19, 2019b. https://www.rappler.com/world/global-affairs/228529-moscow-role-north-korea-kim-putin.

Aloc, Daniel. "Can Duterte Do a Hugo Chavez." *Inquirer.* June 6, 2016. https://opinion.inquirer.net/95076/can-duterte-hugo-chavez.

"An Expose of How States Manipulate Other Countries' Citizens." *The Straits Times.* July 1, 2018. https://www.straitstimes.com/asia/east-asia/an-expose-of-how-states-manipulate-other-countries-citizens.

Anderlini, Jamil. "Former Malaysian PM Mahatir Mohamad on the Rise of China." *Financial Times.* May 26, 2017. https://www.ft.com/content/b4affab0-4076-11e7-82b6-896b95f30f58?segmentid=acee4131-99c2-09d3-a635-873e61754ec6.

Anderson, Benedict. "First Filipino." *London Review of Books* 19, no. 20 (1997): 22–23. https://www.lrb.co.uk/v19/n20/benedict-anderson/first-filipino.

Anderson, Benedict. "Old Corruption." *London Review of Books* 9, no. 3 (1987): 3–6. https://www.lrb.co.uk/v09/n03/benedict-anderson/old-corruption.

Angaindrankumar, Gnanasagaran. "Chinese Labour Migration to Southeast Asia." *The ASEAN Post.* December 14, 2018. https://theaseanpost.com/article/chinese-labour-migration-southeast-asia.

Associated Press. "Mahathir Bucks Warships Stationed in South China Sea." *Inquirer.* August 14, 2018. https://newsinfo.inquirer.net/1020985/mahathir-bucks-warships-stationed-in-south-china-sea.

Batongbacal, Jay. "EDCA and the West Philippine Sea." *Rappler.* Last date modified August 9, 2017. https://www.rappler.com/thought-leaders/77823-edca-west-philippine-sea-america.

Bhavan, Jaipragas. "Forget the Warships: Malaysian PM Mahatir's Peace Formula for South China Sea." *South China Morning Post.* June 19, 2018. https://www.scmp.com/week-asia/geopolitics/article/2151403/forget-warships-malaysian-pm-mahathirs-peace-formula-south.

Beech, Hannah. "'We Cannot Afford This': Malaysia Pushes Back Against China's Vision." *The New York Times*. August 20, 2018. https://www.nytimes.com/2018/08/20/world/asia/china-malaysia.html.
Beech, Hannah, and Muktita Suhartono. "A 'Little Bit of a Nutcase' Who's Taking on China." *The New York Times*. June 8, 2018. https://www.nytimes.com/2018/06/08/world/asia/indonesia-fishing-boats-china-poaching.html.
Buan, Lian. "Carpio Warns Against Similar Waivers to China in Kaliwa Dam Project." *Rappler*. March 29, 2019. https://www.rappler.com/nation/226898-carpio-warns-against-similar-waivers-china-kaliwa-dam-project.
Cabacungan, Gil. "Most Powerful PH Leader Since Marcos." *Inquirer*. June 9, 2016. https://newsinfo.inquirer.net/789789/most-powerful-ph-leader-since-marcos.
Calonzo, Andreo, and David Tweed. "Philippines' Duterte Open to Joint Naval Drills with Russia." *Bloomberg*. January 5, 2017. https://www.bloomberg.com/news/articles/2017-01-05/philippines-duterte-open-to-joint-maritime-drills-with-russia.
"Chart of the Day: Singapore 2019 Defence Spending Hits 12-Year High." *Singapore Business Review*. February 19, 2019. https://sbr.com.sg/economy/news/chart-day-singapore-2019-defence-spending-hits-12-year-high.
Chellaney, Brahma. "China's Debt-Trap Diplomacy." *Project Syndicate*. January 23, 2017. https://www.project-syndicate.org/commentary/china-one-belt-one-road-loans-debt-by-brahma-chellaney-2017-01.
"China Took What Is 'Ours', Foreign Affairs Chief Says of West PH Sea." *ABS-CBN News*. April 10, 2019. https://news.abs-cbn.com/news/04/10/19/china-took-what-is-ours-foreign-affairs-chief-says-of-west-ph-sea.
Cigaral, Ian. "Philippine Shares Buck Regional Downswing as Xi Jinping Visit Takes Center Stage." *Philstar Global*. November 20, 2018. https://www.philstar.com/business/2018/11/20/1870232/philippine-shares-buck-regional-downswing-xi-jinping-visit-takes-center-stage.
Cochrane, Joe. "Indonesia, Long on Sidelines, Starts to Confront China's Territorial Claims." *The New York Times*. September 10, 2017. https://www.nytimes.com/2017/09/10/world/asia/indonesia-south-china-sea-military-buildup.html.
Colcol, Erwin. "Chinese Vessels Spotted Near Kota, Panata Islands—Int'l Think Tank." *GMA News*. April 17, 2019. https://www.gmanetwork.com/news/news/nation/691632/chinese-vessels-spotted-near-kota-panata-islands-int-l-think-tank/story/.
"Commentary: Historic Opportunity to Bolster China-Philippines Ties." *Xinhua*. November 20, 2018. http://www.xinhuanet.com/english/2018-11/20/c_137619809.htm.

Cordero, John Ted. "Duterte to US Aid Agency: Eat Your Money!" *GMA News*. December 17, 2016. https://www.gmanetwork.com/news/news/nation/592826/duterte-to-us-aid-agency-eat-your-money/story/.

Corr, Anders. "Chinese Bomber Buzzes Philippines' Scarborough Shoal in Latest Salvo of U.S.-China Signalling War." *Forbes*. July 17, 2016. https://www.forbes.com/sites/anderscorr/2016/07/17/chinese-bomber-buzzes-philippines-scarborough-shoal-in-latest-salvo-of-u-s-china-signalling-war/#-50ba7d2d5f7f.

Corrales, Nestor. "China Backs PH Pull Out from ICC, Urges Nations to Support 'War on Drugs'." *Inquirer*. March 30, 2018. https://globalnation.inquirer.net/165372/china-backs-ph-pull-icc-urges-nations-support-war-drugs.

Corrales, Nestor. "Duterte Says He'll 'Set Aside' Arbitral Ruling on South China Sea." *Inquirer*. December 17, 2016. https://globalnation.inquirer.net/150814/duterte-says-hell-set-aside-arbitral-ruling-on-south-china-sea.

Dancel, Raul. "Malaysian PM, on Official Visit to the Philippines, Says Manila Should Regulate or Limit Beijing Influences." *The Straits Times*. March 8, 2019. https://www.straitstimes.com/asia/beware-of-china-debt-trap-mahathir.

David, Randy. "Dutertismo." *Philippine Daily Inquirer*. May 1, 2016.

Davies, Ed, and David Lawder. "'Winter Is Coming': Indonesia Warns World Finance Leaders Over Trade War." *Reuters*. October 12, 2018. https://www.reuters.com/article/us-imf-worldbank-plenary/winter-is-coming-indonesia-warns-world-finance-leaders-over-trade-war-idUSKCN1MM0AY.

De Luce, Dan, and Keith Johnson. "U.S. Likely to Lift Ban on Arms Sales to Vietnam." *Foreign Policy*. May 9, 2016. https://foreignpolicy.com/2016/05/09/u-s-likely-to-lift-ban-on-arms-sales-to-vietnam/.

Delizo, Michael Joe. "PH, Russia Break Ice on Military Cooperation." *The Manila Times*. September 21, 2016. https://www.manilatimes.net/ph-russia-break-ice-on-military-cooperation/287145/.

"Duterte Enjoys Record-High 91% Trust Rating—Pulse Asia." *Rappler*. July 20, 2016. https://www.rappler.com/nation/140318-duterte-trust-rating-july-2016.

"Duterte: 'I've Seen America and It's Lousy'." *DW.com*. 2017. https://www.dw.com/en/duterte-ive-seen-america-and-its-lousy/av-39807340.

"Duterte to US: Are You With Us?" *Philstar Global*. May 16, 2016. https://www.philstar.com/headlines/2016/05/16/1584025/duterte-us-are-you-us.

"Duterte Visits Russian Warship." *ABS-CBN News*. January 6, 2017. https://news.abs-cbn.com/news/01/06/17/duterte-visits-russian-warship.

Esmaquel II, Paterno. "China Chopper Harasses PH Rubber Boat in Ayungin Shoal—Lawmaker." *Rappler*. May 30, 2018a. https://www.rappler.com/nation/203720-chinese-helicopter-harass-rubber-boat-ayungin-shoal-spratly-islands.

Esmaquel II, Paterno. "Duterte: 'Remain Meek', to Get 'Mercy' of China's Xi." *Rappler.* May 16, 2018b. https://www.rappler.com/nation/202674-duterte-china-xi-jinping-meek-humble-west-philippine-sea.

Esmaquel II, Paterno. "'Forces' in Gov't Pushed for PH-China Oil Deal—Locsin." *Rappler.* November 22, 2018c. https://www.rappler.com/nation/217300-push-in-government-philippines-china-oil-deal-xi-jinping-visit.

Esmaquel II, Paterno. "Wang Yi: Duterte 'the Most Respected Friend' of Xi Jinping." *Rappler.* October 29, 2018d. https://www.rappler.com/nation/215425-chinese-foreign-minister-wang-yi-duterte-friend-xi-jinping.

Esmaquel II, Paterno. "Ex-PH Officials: ICC Complaint vs China 'to Check Impunity'." *Rappler.* March 22, 2019. https://www.rappler.com/nation/226417-del-rosario-morales-say-icc-case-vs-china-check-impunity.

"EXCLUSIVE: MOU for Talks on Joint Oil Exploration 'Without Prejudice' to PH, China Legal Positions." *CNN Philippines.* November 23, 2018. http://cnnphilippines.com/news/2018/11/23/EXCLUSIVE-PH-China-MOU-joint-oil-exploration-maritime-claims.html.

"F-16 Jet Fighter Skids Off Runway in Pekanbaru." *The Jakarta Post.* March 14, 2017. https://www.thejakartapost.com/news/2017/03/14/f-16-jet-fighter-skids-off-runway-in-pekanbaru.html.

Fallows, James. "A Damaged Culture." *The Atlantic.* November 1987. https://www.theatlantic.com/magazine/archive/1987/11/a-damaged-culture/505178/.

Ferguson, Niall. *Colossus: The Rise and Fall of the American Empire.* Westminister: Penguin Books, 2005.

Fernholz, Tim. "China's 'Debt Trap' Is Even Worse Than We Thought." *Quartz.* June 29, 2018. https://qz.com/1317234/chinas-debt-trap-in-sri-lanka-is-even-worse-than-we-thought/.

FlorCruz, Michelle. "Territorial Dispute: Chinese South China Sea Occupation Is a 'Real Threat'." *International Business Time.* September 22, 2014. https://www.ibtimes.com/china-indonesia-territorial-dispute-chinese-south-china-sea-occupation-real-threat-1692916.

Francisco, Rosemarie, and Matt Spetalnik. "Philippines, U.S. to Sign New Military Pact, Part of U.S. Pivot." *Reuters.* April 27, 2014. https://www.reuters.com/article/us-philippines-usa-idUSBREA3Q05L20140427?feedType=RSS.

Gady, Franz-Stefan. "Vietnam Deploys Precision-Guided Rocket Artillery in South China Sea." *The Diplomat.* August 10, 2016. https://thediplomat.com/2016/08/vietnam-deploys-precision-guided-rocket-artillery-in-south-china-sea/.

Gamil, Jaymee. "AFP Vows to Defend Country Amid China Buildup on PH Reefs." *Inquirer.* May 19, 2018. https://globalnation.inquirer.net/167077/afp-vows-defend-country-amid-china-buildup-ph-reefs.

Gan, Nectar, and Laura Zhou. "Lee Kuan Yew Among Foreigners Honoured for Helping China to Open Up." *South China Morning Post.* December 18, 2018. https://www.scmp.com/news/china/politics/article/2178499/lee-kuan-yew-among-foreigners-honoured-helping-china-open.

Garnaut, John. "How China Interferes in Australia." *Foreign Affairs.* March 9, 2018. https://www.foreignaffairs.com/articles/china/2018-03-09/how-china-interferes-australia.

Gatra, Priyandita. "Belt and Road Investment Under Fire in Indonesia's Presidential Elections." *East Asia Forum.* November 20, 2018. https://www.eastasiaforum.org/2018/11/20/belt-and-road-investment-under-fire-in-indonesias-presidential-elections/.

GMA News. "REPLAY: FYI with Richard Heydarian: Interview with Malaysian Prime Minister Mahathir Bin Mohamad." Youtube Video, 32:31. March 8, 2019. https://www.youtube.com/watch?v=PSvBTKbpPRM&t=929s.

Gita, Ruth Abbey. "275 Chinese Vessels Sail Near Pag-asa; PH Files Diplomatic Protest." *Sunstar.* April 1, 2019. https://www.sunstar.com.ph/article/1799532.

Gonzales, Yuji Vincent. "Clinton? Trump? Duterte Says Putin 'My Favorite Hero'." *Inquirer.* October 23, 2016. https://globalnation.inquirer.net/147585/duterte-trump-airing-valid-issues-putin-my-favorite-hero.

Grevatt, Jon, and Craig Caffrey. "Indonesia Increases Defence Budget 14%." *Jane's 360.* August 18, 2014. https://www.janes.com/article/42069/indonesia-increases-defence-budget-14.

Harshaw, Tobin. "Emperor Xi's China Is Done Biding Its Time." *Belfer Center.* March 3, 2018. https://www.belfercenter.org/publication/emperor-xis-china-done-biding-its-time.

Head, Jonathan. "US Aircraft Carrier Carl Vinson in Historic Vietnam Visit." *BBC.* March 5, 2018. https://www.bbc.com/news/world-asia-43282558.

Heydarian, Richard Javad. "A Philippine Alternative to China's Takeover of Subic Shipyard." *Nikkei Asian Review.* February 20, 2019a. https://asia.nikkei.com/Opinion/A-Philippine-alternative-to-China-s-takeover-of-Subic-shipyard.

Heydarian, Richard Javad. "Chinese Migrants Spark a Backlash in the Philippines." *Asia Times.* February 26, 2019b. https://www.asiatimes.com/2019/02/article/chinese-migrants-spark-a-backlash-in-the-philippines/.

Heydarian, Richard Javad. "Is China Our 'Friend'?" *Inquirer.* April 9, 2019c. https://opinion.inquirer.net/120652/is-china-our-friend.

Heydarian, Richard Javad. "Evolving Philippines-U.S.-China Strategic Triangle: International and Domestic Drivers." *Asian Politics & Policy* 9, no. 4 (2017a). https://doi.org/10.1111/aspp.12355.

Heydarian, Richard Javad. "Philippines' Forgotten Revolution: General Luna and the Quest for Independence." *Huffington Post*. Last date modified December 6, 2017b. https://www.huffpost.com/entry/philippines-forgotten-rev_b_8199354.

Heydarian, Richard Javad. "Crossing the Rubicon: Duterte, China and Resource-Sharing in the South China Sea." October 23, 2018a. http://www.maritimeissues.com/politics/crossing-the-rubicon-duterte-china-and-re-sourcesharing-in-the-south-china-sea.html.

Heydarian, Richard Javad. "Duterte and the Philippines' Contested Foreign Policy." *Asia Maritime Transparency Initiative*. August 20, 2018b. https://amti.csis.org/duterte-philippines-contested-foreign-policy/.

Heydarian, Richard Javad. "Duterte's Efforts to Align the Philippines with China Face a Backlash." *World Politics Review*. July 19, 2018c. https://www.worldpoliticsreview.com/articles/25126/duterte-s-efforts-to-align-the-philippines-with-china-face-a-backlash.

Heydarian, Richard Javad. "Manila Quietly Pivots Back to the United States." *Asia Maritime Transparency Initiative*. November 9, 2018d. https://amti.csis.org/manila-quietly-pivots-back-to-the-united-states/.

Heydarian, Richard Javad. "The Perils of a Philippine-China Joint Development Agreement in South China Sea." *Asia Maritime Transparency Initiative*. April 27, 2018e. https://globalnation.inquirer.net/165372/china-backs-ph-pull-icc-urges-nations-support-war-drugs.

Heydarian, Richard Javad. *The Rise of Duterte: A Populist Revolt Against Elite Democracy*. London: Palgrave Macmillan, 2018f.

Heydarian, Richard Javad. "The Sino-American Cold War Is in Full Swing." *China-US Focus*. October 3, 2018g. https://www.chinausfocus.com/finance-economy/the-sino-american-cold-war-is-in-full-swing.

Heydarian, Richard Javad. "Under Duterte, Philippines Enjoying an Investment Boom, but Don't Thank China." *Forbes*. March 25, 2018h. https://www.forbes.com/sites/richardheydarian/2018/03/25/under-duterte-philippines-enjoying-an-investment-boom-but-dont-thank-china/#130f32c7393e.

Heydarian, Richard Javad. "Hide Your Strength, Bide Your Time." *Aljazeera*. November 21, 2014. https://www.aljazeera.com/indepth/opinion/2014/11/china-hide-your-strength-bide-y-201411198028498329.html.

Heydarian, Richard Javad. "Thrilla in Manila." *Foreign Affairs*. September 27, 2016. https://www.foreignaffairs.com/articles/philippines/2016-09-27/thrilla-manila.

Hill, Fiona, and Bobo Lo. "Putin's Pivot." *Foreign Affairs*. July 31, 2013. https://www.foreignaffairs.com/articles/russian-federation/2013-07-31/putins-pivot.

Ibrahim, Zuraidah. "What Singapore Is Saying by Expelling China Hand Huang Jing." *South China Morning Post.* August 12, 2017. https://www.scmp.com/week-asia/opinion/article/2106497/what-singapore-saying-expelling-china-hand-huang-jing.

Ide, Bill. "Duterte Announces Philippine 'Separation' from US." *VOA.* October 20, 2016. https://www.voanews.com/a/duterte-declares-philippine-separation-from-us/3559129.html.

"Important Speech of Xi Jinping at Peripheral Diplomacy Work Conference." *China Council for International Cooperation on Environment and Development.* October 30, 2013. http://www.cciced.net/cciceden/NEWSCENTER/LatestEnvironmentalandDevelopmentNews/201310/t20131030_82626.html.

"Indonesia Military Expenditure." *Trading Economics.* Last date accessed April 10, 2019. https://tradingeconomics.com/indonesia/military-expenditure.

"Is Russia's APEC Summit A $21 Billion Waste?" *International Business Times.* September 5, 2012. https://www.ibtimes.com/russias-apec-summit-21-billion-waste-761551.

Jaipragas, Bhavan. "Hong Kong to Return Seized Armoured Vehicles to Singapore." *South China Morning Post.* January 24, 2017. https://www.scmp.com/week-asia/geopolitics/article/2065027/hong-kong-return-singapores-seized-armoured-vehicles.

Jensen, Fergus. "Indonesia Pushes for Southeast Asian Patrols of Disputed Waters." *Reuters.* March 16, 2018. https://www.reuters.com/article/us-australia-indonesia-politics/indonesia-pushes-for-southeast-asian-patrols-of-disputed-waters-idUSKCN1GS0CL.

Kang, Daniel. *American Grand Strategy and East Asian Security in the Twenty-First Century.* Cambridge: Cambridge University Press, 2017.

Karnow, Stanley. *In Our Image: America's Empire in the Philippines,* reissue edition. New York: Ballantine Books, 1990.

Kasuya, Yuko. *Presidential Bandwagon: Parties and Party Systems in the Philippines.* Mandaluyong: Anvil Publishing, 2009.

Kendall-Taylor, Andrea, Erica Frantz, and Joseph Wright. "The New Dictators." *Foreign Affairs.* September 26, 2016. https://www.foreignaffairs.com/articles/2016-09-26/new-dictators.

Koh, Tommy. "A World Statesman." *The Straits Times.* December 27, 1990. http://leekuanyew.straitstimes.com/ST/chapter3.html.

Koh, Tommy. "China's Perception of Singapore: 4 Areas of Misunderstanding." *The Straits Times.* October 21, 2016. https://www.straitstimes.com/opinion/chinas-perception-of-singapore-4-areas-of-misunderstanding.

Koren, Marina. "The Philippine President's Vulgar Warning to Obama." *The Atlantic.* September 5, 2016. https://www.theatlantic.com/news/archive/2016/09/duterte-obama-extrajudicial-killings/498710/.

Koutsoukis, Jason, and Cecilia Yap. "China Hasn't Delivered on Its $24 Billion Philippines Promise." *Bloomberg.* July 26, 2018. https://www.bloomberg.com/news/articles/2018-07-25/china-s-24-billion-promise-to-duterte-still-hasn-t-materialized.

Kuo, Lily. "Cracks Appear in 'Invincible' Xi Jinping's Authority Over China." *The Guardian.* August 4, 2018. https://www.theguardian.com/world/2018/aug/04/cracks-appear-in-invincible-xi-jinpings-authority-over-china.

Laksmana, Evan. "An Indo-Pacific Construct with 'Indonesian Characteristics'." *Australian Strategic Policy Institute.* February 6, 2018. https://www.aspistrategist.org.au/indo-pacific-construct-indonesian-characteristics/.

Laksmana, Evan. "Pragmatic Equidistance: How Indonesia Manages Its Great Power Relations." In David Denoon (ed.), *China, the United States, and the Future of Southeast Asia,* pp. 113–135. New York: New York University Press, 2017.

Legaspi, Amita. "De Lima on Duterte's Claim That China Is PHL 'Protector': Hilarious." *GMA News.* May 8, 2018. http://www.gmanetwork.com/news/news/nation/652612/de-lima-on-duterte-s-claim-that-china-is-phl-protector-hilarious/story/.

Lema, Karen. "Russia Says It's Ready to Offer Sophisticated Weapons and Be a 'Close Friend' to the Philippines." *Business Insider.* January 4, 2017. https://www.businessinsider.com/r-russia-offers-philippines-arms-and-close-friendship-2017-1.

Lema, Karen, and Martin Petty. "Two Years After Philippines' Pivot, Duterte Still Waiting on China Dividend." *Reuters.* November 19, 2018. https://www.reuters.com/article/us-philippines-china-analysis/two-years-after-philippines-pivot-duterte-still-waiting-on-china-dividend-idUSKCN1NN0UO.

Lendon, Brad, and Katie Hunt. "China, Russia Begin Joint Exercises in South China Sea." *CNN.* September 13, 2016. https://edition.cnn.com/2016/09/12/asia/china-russia-south-china-sea-exercises/.

Lendon, Brad, and Kelly Murray. "APEC Summit Wraps with No Joint Statement Amid US-China Discord." *CNN.* November 19, 2018. https://edition-m.cnn.com/2018/11/18/world/apec-summit-us-china-tensions-no-communique/index.html.

Leonen, Julius. "De Lima Says Duterte Has Become a 'Chinese Governor'." *Inquirer.* January 17, 2018. https://globalnation.inquirer.net/163453/de-lima-duterte-china-benham-rise-foreign-affairs-cayetano-maritime.

Lim, Frinston, and Allan Nawal. "Duterte to Cops: Kill Criminals if You Have to, I'll Protect You." *Inquirer.* January 18, 2018. https://newsinfo.inquirer.net/961396/duterte-to-cops-kill-criminals-if-you-have-to-ill-protect-you.

Luttwak, Edward. *The Rise of China vs. the Logic of Strategy.* New York: Belknap Press, 2012.

316   R. J. HEYDARIAN

Luttwak, Edward, and Brad Carson. "Jaw-Jaw: China's Great Power Disease." *War on the Rocks.* February 19, 2019. https://warontherocks.com/2019/02/jaw-jaw-chinas-great-power-disease/.

Macas, Tricia. "Duterte Reveals Being Denied a US Visa in the Past." *GMA News.* October 20, 2016. http://www.gmanetwork.com/news/news/nation/585715/duterte-reveals-being-denied-a-us-visa-in-the-past/story/.

Madan, Tanvi. "The Rise, Fall, and Rebirth of the 'Quad'." *War on the Rocks.* November 16, 2017. https://warontherocks.com/2017/11/rise-fall-rebirth-quad/.

"Mahathir Warns Against New 'Colonialism' During Visit to China." *Bloomberg News.* August 20, 2018. https://www.bloomberg.com/news/articles/2018-08-20/mahathir-warns-against-new-colonialism-during-visit-to-china.

Mangosing, Frances. "Chinese Sea Militia Swarms Around Pag-asa Island—Military." *Inquirer.* March 30, 2019. https://globalnation.inquirer.net/173963/afp-notes-surge-of-chinese-fishing-vessels-around-pag-asa.

Mateo, Janvic. "Chinese Military Aircraft Lands in Davao City?" *Philstar Global.* June 10, 2018. https://www.philstar.com/headlines/2018/06/10/1823235/chinese-military-aircraft-lands-davao-city.

Mayberry, Kate. "China Signals Belt and Road Shift with Malaysia Rail Project." *Aljazeera.* April 15, 2019. https://www.aljazeera.com/news/2019/04/china-signals-belt-road-shift-malaysia-rail-project.

Medcalf, Rory. "The Indo-Pacific: What's in a Name?" *The American Interest.* October 10, 2013. https://www.the-american-interest.com/2013/10/10/the-indo-pacific-whats-in-a-name/.

Mendez, Christina. "Duterte: I Love Xi Jinping." *Philstar.com.* April 10, 2018. https://www.philstar.com/headlines/2018/04/10/1804525/duterte-i-love-xi-jinping.

Mendez, Christina, Jaime Laude, and Helen Flores. "AFP Urges Gov't: Raise Chinese Incursions in WPS." *Philstar Global.* August 18, 2017. https://www.philstar.com/headlines/2017/08/18/1730637/afp-urges-govt-raise-chinese-incursions-wps.

Merez, Arianne. "Palace: Chinese Presence in West PH Sea an 'Assault' to PH Sovereignty." *ABS-CBN News.* April 10, 2019. https://news.abs-cbn.com/news/04/10/19/palace-chinese-presence-in-west-ph-sea-an-assault-to-ph-sovereignty.

Minh, Nguyen. "U.S. Carrier Arrives in Vietnam Amid Rising Chinese Influence in Region." *Reuters.* March 5, 2018. https://ca.reuters.com/article/topNews/idCAKBN1GH0HL-OCATP.

Moss, Trefor. "Behind Duterte's Break with the U.S., a Lifetime of Resentment." *Wallstreet Journal.* October 21, 2016. https://www.wsj.com/articles/behind-philippine-leaders-break-with-the-u-s-a-lifetime-of-resentment-1477061118.

Murphy, Katharine. "America to Partner with Australia to Develop Naval Base on Manus Island." *The Guardian*. November 17, 2018. https://www.theguardian.com/australia-news/2018/nov/18/america-to-partner-with-australia-to-develop-naval-base-on-manus-island.

Naim, Moises. *The End of Power: From Boardrooms to Battlefields and Churches to States, Why Being in Charge Isn't What It Used to Be*, reprint edition. New York: Basic Books, 2014.

Ng, Fintan. "The Economic Ties That Bind Us." *The Star Online*. May 26, 2014. https://www.thestar.com.my/news/nation/2014/05/26/the-economic-ties-that-bind-us/.

"No 'One-on-One' Discussion with Beijing on South China Sea Issue: Malaysia Foreign Minister." *Channel News Asia*. April 24, 2019. https://www.channelnewsasia.com/news/asia/no-unilateral-discussion-with-china-on-south-china-sea-issue-11471154.

Office of the Spokesperson. "Advancing a Free and Open Indo-Pacific Region." *U.S. Department of State*. November 18, 2018. https://www.state.gov/r/pa/prs/ps/2018/11/287433.htm.

Oh, Yoon Ah. "China's Economic Ties with Southeast Asia." *World Economy Brief* 7, no. 18 (2017). https://think-asia.org/bitstream/handle/11540/7468/WEB%2017-18.pdf.

Otto, Ben. "The Russians Are Coming...to Southeast Asia." *The Wall Street Journal*. July 6, 2016. https://www.wsj.com/articles/the-russians-are-coming-to-southeast-asia-1467824327.

Paddock, Richard. "Mysterious Blast in Philippines Fuels Rodrigo Duterte's 'Hatred' of U.S." *New York Times*. May 14, 2016. https://www.nytimes.com/2016/05/14/world/asia/philippines-president-rodrigo-duterte.html.

Panda, Ankit. "US, Indonesian Navies Conduct Air Patrol Exercise in South China Sea." *The Diplomat*. April 11, 2015. https://thediplomat.com/2015/04/us-indonesian-navies-conduct-air-patrol-exercise-in-south-china-sea/.

Parameswaran, Prashanth. "What's in Singapore's New Anti-Fake News Bill?" *The Diplomat*. April 4, 2019. https://thediplomat.com/2019/04/whats-in-singapores-new-anti-fake-news-bill/.

Parlina, Ina. "Jokowi Pledges Ambitious Arms Spending." *The Jakarta Post*. February 24, 2016. https://www.thejakartapost.com/news/2016/02/24/jokowi-pledges-ambitious-arms-spending.html.

Parrocha, Azer. "Palace Open to Bring Arbitration Win vs. China to UN." *Philippine News Agency*. April 2, 2019. https://www.pna.gov.ph/articles/1066319.

Pence, Mike. "Mike Pence: The United States Seeks Collaboration, Not Control, in the Indo-Pacific." *The Washington Post*. November 9, 2018. https://www.washingtonpost.com/opinions/mike-pence-the-united-states-seeks-collaboration-not-control-in-the-indo-pacific/2018/11/09/.

Permanent Court of Arbitration. *In the Matter of the South China Sea Arbitration.* PCA Case No 2013-19. The Hague, Netherlands. July 12, 2016. https://pca-cpa.org/wp-content/uploads/sites/6/2016/07/PH-CN-20160712-Award.pdf.

Petaling, Jaya. "Let Malaysia Continue Occupying Islands in South China Sea: PM Mahathir." *The Straits Times.* June 20, 2018. https://www.straitstimes.com/asia/se-asia/pm-mahathir-let-malaysia-continue-occupying-islands-in-south-china-sea.

Pilapil, Jaime. "We Seek to Do Business with You." *The Manila Times.* March 22, 2017. https://www.manilatimes.net/we-seek-to-do-business-with-you/318507/.

Placido, Dharel. "Xi Wants PH as China's 'Strategic' Ally." *ABS-CBN News.* November 20, 2018. https://news.abs-cbn.com/news/11/20/18/xi-wants-ph-as-chinas-strategic-ally.

Poling, Gregory, and Conor Cronin. "The Dangers of Allowing U.S.-Philippine Defense Cooperation to Languish." *War on the Rocks.* May 17, 2018. https://warontherocks.com/2018/05/the-dangers-of-allowing-u-s-philippine-defense-cooperation-to-languish/.

Poushter, Jacob, and Caldwell Bishop. "People in the Philippines Still Favor U.S. Over China, but Gap Is Narrowing." *Pew Global Research Center.* September 21, 2017. https://www.pewglobal.org/2017/09/21/people-in-the-philippines-still-favor-u-s-over-china-but-gap-is-narrowing/.

"President Jokowi Spotlights Maritime Development at Our Ocean Conference." *The Jakarta Post.* October 30, 2018. https://www.thejakarta-post.com/news/2018/10/30/president-jokowi-spotlights-maritime-development-at-our-ocean-conference.html.

Punongbayan, J.C. "[OPINION] What Scares Me the Most About China's New, 'Friendly' Loans." *Rappler.* March 3, 2018. https://www.rappler.com/thought-leaders/197207-china-loans-philippines-fears.

Putz, Catherine. "Why Did Russia's Pivot to Asia Fail?" *The Diplomat.* April 24, 2016. https://thediplomat.com/2016/04/why-did-russias-pivot-to-asia-fail/.

Qin, Amy. "Worries Grow in Singapore Over China's Calls to Help 'Motherland'." *The New York Times.* August 5, 2018. https://www.nytimes.com/2018/08/05/world/asia/singapore-china.html.

Ramos, Christia Marie. "Locsin: PH Can Turn to US if There's a 'Clear Act of Aggression' in South China Sea." *Inquirer.* April 16, 2019. https://globalnation.inquirer.net/174518/locsin-ph-can-turn-to-us-if-theres-clear-act-of-aggression-in-south-china-sea.

Ranada, Pia. "China Envoy Visits Duterte Days Before Hague Ruling." *Rappler.* July 7, 2016. https://www.rappler.com/nation/138959-china-ambassador-duterte-hague-ruling.

Ranada, Pia. "Duterte Jokes: Why Not Make Philippines a Province of China?" *Rappler*. June 28, 2018a. https://www.rappler.com/nation/196426-duterte-philippines-province-china.

Ranada, Pia. "LIST: Deals Signed During Xi Jinping's Trip to Philippines." *Rappler*. November 20, 2018b. https://www.rappler.com/nation/217156-deals-signed-during-xi-jinping-visit-philippines.

Rappler.com. "Filipinos Like the US Even More Than Americans Do—Pew Research." *Rappler.com*. May 20, 2019. https://www.rappler.com/nation/56085-philippines-usa-pew-research.

Ravenhill, John. "Is China an Economic Threat to Southeast Asia?" *Asian Survey* 46, no. 5 (2006): 653–674.

Requejo, Rey. "Duterte Told: Assert Philippines Control of West Philippine Sea." *Manila Standard*. July 26, 2018. http://www.manilastandard.net/news/top-stories/271399/duterte-told-assert-philippines-control-of-west-philippine-sea.html.

Reuters. "Maldives Set to Pull Out of 'Lopsided' Free Trade Deal with China, Says Presidential Adviser." *South China Morning Post*. November 19, 2018. https://www.scmp.com/news/china/diplomacy/article/2174014/maldives-set-pull-out-lopsided-free-trade-deal-china-says.

Robson, Seth. "Deployment of USS Wasp, F-35Bs Shows US Commitment to Philippines, Commander Says." *Stars and Stripes*. April 9, 2019. https://www.stripes.com/news/deployment-of-uss-wasp-f-35bs-shows-us-commitment-to-philippines-commander-says-1.576274.

Rogin, Josh. "Inside China's 'Tantrum Diplomacy' at APEC." *The Washington Post*. November 20, 2018. https://www.washingtonpost.com/news/josh-rogin/wp/2018/11/20/inside-chinas-tantrum-diplomacy-at-apec/?utm_term=.13cf58299bdd.

Roxas, Patricia Ann. "Duterte: South China Sea Dispute Is 'Better Left Untouched'." *Inquirer*. November 12, 2017. https://globalnation.inquirer.net/161911/duterte-south-china-sea-dispute-china-vietnam-asean-taiwan.

Salaverria, Leila. "Duterte Asks Russia: Be PH Ally and Protector." *Inquirer*. January 7, 2017. https://globalnation.inquirer.net/151296/duterte-asks-russia-ph-ally-protector.

Santos, Matikas. "85% of Filipinos Love US—Survey." *Inquirer*. April 22, 2014. https://globalnation.inquirer.net/102487/many-filipinos-love-us-survey.

Schultz, Kai. "Sri Lanka, Struggling with Debt, Hands Over a Major Port to China." *The New York Times*. December 12, 2017. https://www.nytimes.com/2017/12/12/world/asia/sri-lanka-china-port.html.

"Senators Back Duterte Call to Review All Government Contracts." *ABS-CBN News*. April 3, 2019. https://news.abs-cbn.com/news/04/03/19/senators-back-duterte-call-to-review-all-government-contracts.

Shambaugh, David. "U.S.-China Rivalry in Southeast Asia: Power Shift or Competitive Coexistence?" *International Security* 42, no. 4 (2018). https://www.mitpressjournals.org/doi/abs/10.1162/isec_a_00314.

Sharma, Kiran. "'Quad' Seen to Discuss Ways to Curb China's Influence in Indo-Pacific." *Nikkei Asian Review.* November 14, 2018. https://asia.nikkei.com/Politics/International-relations/Quad-seen-to-discuss-ways-to-curb-China-s-influence-in-Indo-Pacific.

Sipahutar, Tassia, Viriya Singgih, and Eko Listiyorini. "Jokowi Plans Record Spending in Indonesia's Election Year." *Bloomberg.* August 16, 2018. https://www.bloomberg.com/news/articles/2018-08-16/jokowi-eyes-record-spending-to-spur-indonesia-growth-before-vote.

Snegov, Alex. "Vietnam Open to Russian Return to Cam Ranh Bay." *Russia Beyond.* May 18, 2018. https://www.rbth.com/news/2016/05/18/vietnam-open-to-russian-return-to-cam-ranh-bay_594025.

Spetalnick, Matt, and David Brunnstrom. "Exclusive: Top Obama Aide to Take Call for South China Sea Calm to Beijing." *Reuters.* July 22, 2016. https://www.reuters.com/article/us-southchinasea-usa-exclusive-idUSKCN10210Z.

Sukumaran, Tashny. "In China's Debt, Malaysia and Pakistan Pledge to Help Each Other." *South China Morning Post.* November 21, 2018. https://www.scmp.com/news/asia/diplomacy/article/2174375/chinas-debt-malaysia-and-pakistan-pledge-help-each-other.

Suzuki, Wataru. "TPP-11 Opens Doors to New Members." *Nikkei Asian Review.* January 19, 2019. https://asia.nikkei.com/Economy/TPP-11-opens-doors-to-new-members.

Takenaka, Kiyoshi. "Malaysia PM Says Japan to Consider Future Financial Support." *Reuters.* November 6, 2018. https://www.reuters.com/article/us-japan-malaysia-mahathir/malaysia-pm-says-japan-to-consider-future-financial-support.

Tang, Frank. "China's Former Chief Trade Negotiator Criticizes Beijing's 'Unwise' Tactics in US Tariff War." *South China Morning Post.* November 18, 2018. https://www.scmp.com/economy/china-economy/article/2173779/chinas-former-chief-trade-negotiator-criticises-beijings.

Taylor, Guy. "China Rivalry Hovers Over Pompeo's Manila Stop." *Washington Times.* February 28, 2019. https://www.washingtontimes.com/news/2019/feb/28/china-rivalry-hovers-over-mike-pompeos-manila-stop/.

"The Galleon Trade." *Philippine History.org.* Last date modified January 12, 2019. http://www.philippine-history.org/galleon-trade.htm.

"The Perils of China's 'Debt-Trap Diplomacy'." *The Economist.* September 6, 2018. https://www.economist.com/asia/2018/09/06/the-perils-of-chinas-debt-trap-diplomacy.

"This Is Going to Hurt." *The Economist*. August 2, 2014. https://www.econo-mist.com/europe/2014/08/02/this-is-going-to-hurt.

Vaswani, Karishma. "Apec: A Family Feud with No End in Sight." *BBC News*. November 19, 2018. https://www.bbc.com/news/business-46256123.

"Vietnam Challenges China in Asean Talks." *Inquirer*. August 6, 2017. https://globalnation.inquirer.net/159372/vietnam-challenges-china-asean-talks.

Viray, Patricia Lourdes. "Photos: 2018 Balikatan Amphibious Exercise." *Philstar*. May 11, 2018a. https://www.philstar.com/head-lines/2018/05/11/1814290/photos-2018-balikatan-amphibious-exercise.

Viray, Patricia Lourdes. "Philippines, China Draw 'Red Lines' in South China Sea Dispute." *Philstar Global*. May 29, 2018b. https://www.philstar.com/headlines/2018/05/29/1819745/philippines-china-draw-red-lines-south-china-sea-dispute.

Viray, Patricia Lourdes. "Pulse Asia: 7 in 10 Filipinos Want Duterte to Assert Rights in West Philippine Sea." *Philstar Global*. July 12, 2018c. https://www.philstar.com/headlines/2018/07/12/1832894/pulse-asia-7-10-filipinos-want-duterte-assert-rights-west-philippine-sea.

Viray, Patricia Lourdes. "Senate Minority Wants Probe into Chinese Planes in Davao, Chinese Shows on PTV." *Philstar Global*. July 9, 2018d. https://www.philstar.com/headlines/2018/07/09/1831987/senate-minority-wants-probe-chinese-planes-davao-chinese-shows-ptv.

Wain, Barry. *Malaysian Maverick: Mahathir Mohamad in Turbulent Times*. London: Palgrave Macmillan, 2009.

Walker, Christopher, and Jessica Ludwig. "The Meaning of Sharp Power." *Foreign Affairs*. November 16, 2017. https://www.foreignaffairs.com/articles/china/2017-11-16/meaning-sharp-power.

Wan, William, and Abigail Hauslohner. "China, Russia Sign $400 Billion Gas Deal." *The Washington Post*. May 21, 2014. https://www.washingtonpost.com/world/europe/china-russia-sign-400-billion-gas-deal/.

Weatherbee, Donald. *International Relations in Southeast Asia: The Struggle for Autonomy*, 2nd edition. Lanham: Rowman & Littlefield, 2010.

Wong, Catherine. "Singapore Leader Lee Hsien Loong Warns Region May Have to Choose Between China and US." *South China Morning Post*. November 15, 2018. https://www.scmp.com/news/china/diplomacy/article/2173479/singapore-leader-lee-hsien-loong-warns-region-may-have-choose.

"Xi Urges All Chinese to Contribute to National Rejuvenation." *Xinhua*. February 17, 2017. http://www.xinhuanet.com//english/2017-02/17/c_136065062.htm.

Yap, D.J. "Russia to Buy $2.5B in PH Agri Produce—DTI Chief." *Inquirer.* November 21, 2016. https://globalnation.inquirer.net/149893/russia-buy-2-5b-ph-agri-produce.

Yashinta, Difa Pramudyani. "Indonesia Puts Forward Spirit of Cooperation to Tackle Global Challenges." *Antara News.* October 24, 2018. https://en.antaranews.com/news/119839/indonesia-puts-forward-spirit-of-cooperation-to-tackle-global-challenges.

Yong, Charissa. "S'poreans Should Be Aware of China's Influence Ops: Bilahari." *The Straits Times.* June 28, 2018. https://www.straitstimes.com/singapore/sporeans-should-be-aware-of-chinas-influence-ops-bilahari.

Zaccheus, Melody. "New SCCC to Open with Cultural Festival." *The Straits Times.* April 25, 2017. https://www.straitstimes.com/singapore/new-sccc-to-open-with-cultural-festival.

Zengerie, Patricia. "Exclusive: U.S. Stopped Philippines Rifle Sale That Senator Opposed—Sources." *Reuters.* November 1, 2016. https://www.reuters.com/article/us-philippines-usa-rifles-idUSKBN12V2AM.

CHAPTER 9

The Revenge of Malthus: Pax Indo-Pacifica and Rhizomatic Order

Our choices and actions could ensure the perpetual future of life…Or in contrast, through malign intent, or through misadventure, twenty-first century technology could jeopardize life's potential, foreclosing its human and posthuman future. —Sir Martin Rees, Our Final Hour[1]

[M]an as he really [is] is, inert, sluggish, and averse from labor, unless compelled by necessity. —T.R. Malthus, An Essay on the Principle of Population[2]

[I]t is time to understand The Environment for what it is: the national-security issue of the early twenty-first century. —Robert Kaplan, The Coming Anarchy[3]

Many Indo-Pacific nations may die before they get rich. The megacity of Calcutta and the populous nation of Bangladesh may not even make it to the twilight decades of the twenty-first century, while huge parts of the mega-region will either be too hot to live in, salinized by massive flooding, or, in the case of coastal megacities, inundated by rising sea levels.[4] And this is even more tragic when one considers the boisterous optimism

[1] Rees (2004).
[2] Malthus (2007).
[3] Kaplan (2001).
[4] King (2019).

R. J. Heydarian, *The Indo-Pacific: Trump, China, and the New Struggle for Global Mastery*, https://doi.org/10.1007/978-981-13-9799-8_9

of recent past. True, the region is home to the world's most promising emerging markets, which have risen out of the ashes of poverty and conflict over the past generation or two. In economic terms, the past two decades were among the best for the rising stars of the Indo-Pacific. Between 2000 and 2005, the gross capital inflow into emerging markets such as Thailand, India, Indonesia, and the Philippines rose by 92%, almost doubling. Over the next five years, there was a whopping five-fold increase (478%), accelerating growth among the world's poorer nations. Thanks to the unprecedented surge in capital inflows, emerging markets doubled their share of global Gross Domestic Product, just as their growth rates experienced a similar boost (3.6–7.2%) compared to the preceding two decades.[5] The period marked a dramatic convergence in the global economic system, as the Global South closed its developmental gap with the North. All of a sudden, a New International Economic Order, where North–South relations are less asymmetrical and more consultative, seemed once again possible for the developing nations. The so-called "Third World" now seemed less desperate and more stridently hopeful in decades.[6] What we witnessed was a new form of globalization, where entire supply chains were outsourced from the industrialized West into the booming industrial hubs of the East. Economist Richard Baldwin termed this as "supply chain trade," whereby not only commodities and services, but also productive capacity itself was now part of the fabric of global exchange.[7] The triumphalist intoxication of turbocharged development, however, blinded many to the unsavory consequences of unfettered economic expansion. After all, as Michael Parenti, drawing on Karl Marx's observations, argued, "The essence of capitalism is to turn nature into commodities," where "[t]he live green earth is transformed into dead gold bricks…"[8] There is an indubitably dark, yet largely neglected, side to the overzealously upbeat, feel-good "Asian Century" and "Easternization[9]" narrative.[10] Many ignore the fact that such dazing prosperity has been increasingly purchased at the expense of ecological stability and, overtime, the very long-term survival of humanity. We may

[5] Sharma (2012).
[6] Prashad (2014).
[7] Baldwin (2016).
[8] Bolwell (2019).
[9] Rachman (2017).
[10] Khanna (2019).

2015 total emissions country rank	Country	2015 total carbon dioxide emissions from fuel combustion (million metric tons)	2015 per capita carbon dioxide emissions from fuel combustion (metric tons)
1	China	9040.74	6.59
2	United Sates	4997.50	15.53
3	India	2066.01	1.58
4	Russia	1468.99	10.19
5	Japan	1141.58	8.99
6	Germany	729.77	6.59
7	South Korea	585.99	11.58
8	Iran	552.40	6.98
9	Canada	549.23	15.32
10	Saudi Arabia	531.46	16.85
11	Brazil	450.79	2.17

Fig. 9.1 Top 10 countries global emissions

have achieved short-term, at least in geological terms, comfort, but at an unimaginably steep cost for our species and the planet itself.

The past three decades alone have been responsible for more than 50% of all carbon emissions in the entire human history.[11] The greatest contributors to global warming are no longer the members of the exclusive club of industrialized West, but instead the emerging giants of the East, namely China, India, Russia, the Middle East, and Sub-Saharan Africa (see Fig. 9.1).[12] China's emission levels are almost twice that of the United States, the world's largest economy. The Asian powerhouse' per capita emission levels are now above the global average, rivaling those in the developed world. If one were to take emissions from China's

[11]Wallace-Wells (2017).
[12]Friedrich et al. (2017).

China: The World's King Of Concrete

China used more concrete in 3 years than the
U.S. used in the 20th century

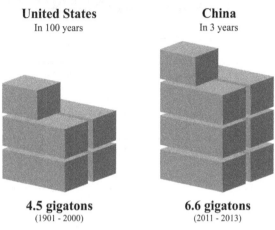

| United States | China |
| In 100 years | In 3 years |

4.5 gigatons   6.6 gigatons
(1901 - 2000)   (2011 - 2013)

Sources: Gatesnotes, USGS, Cement Statistics, USGS, Mineral Industry of China 1990-2013

Fig. 9.2 China's twenty-first-century concrete output compared to twentieth-century US

global infrastructure bonanza into consideration, namely under the BRI and the plethora of other Chinese-driven mega-projects around the world for decades to come, the overall picture would be way more asymmetrical, placing China well at the top of the emission pyramid. Just to put things into perspective: every three years, China is putting more concrete into basic infrastructure than the United States in the entire twentieth century (see Fig. 9.2).[13]

And as India and Sub-Saharan Africa move up the ladder of development, their new middle classes are expected to place even greater pressure on the global ecological balance through their increasingly private-vehicle-centric, carnivorous, and hyper-consumerist lifestyles. By imitating the mindless hedonism of the West, the far larger East is accelerating an ecological apocalypse. The rise of neo-liberal, climate change-deniers in the developing world, particularly in the case of Brazil's Jair Bolsonaro,

[13] McCarthy (2014).

who has vowed to turn the Amazon (the world's lungs) into a commercial land, will only exacerbate this precarious situation.[14] One of the biggest misconceptions about climate change is that it's an anthropogenic event that has a centuries-old genesis. The reality, however, is that the destruction of earth is a more recent phenomenon. As David Wallace-Wells, the author of *The Uninhabitable Earth*, put it, "in the length of a single generation, global warming has brought us to the brink of planetary catastrophe, and that the story of the industrial world's kamikaze mission is also the story of a single lifetime."[15] The New York Magazine editor warns, "[A]bsent a significant adjustment to how billions of humans conduct their lives, parts of the Earth will likely become close to uninhabitable, and other parts horrifically inhospitable, as soon as the end of this century."[16] The world's super-rich, including Silicon Valley tycoons, are already preparing for a socio-ecological doomsday, gobbling up precious lands in New Zealand and designing state-of-the-art private bunkers based on most fertile apocalyptic imaginations. As Even Osnos of The New Yorker observed, "Survivalism, the practice of preparing for a crackup of civilization, tends to evoke a certain picture: the woodsman in the tinfoil hat, the hysteric with the hoard of beans, the religious doomsayer. But in recent years survivalism has expanded to more affluent quarters, taking root in Silicon Valley and New York City, among technology executives, hedge-fund managers, and others in their economic cohort."[17] A sense of panic is also gaining hold over average Americans. In 2012, the National Geographic Channel launched a reality show called "Doomsday Preppers," featuring average joes preparing for the day of reckoning. The premiere drew more than four million viewers. By the end of the first season, it was the most popular show in the channel's history. Separately, the National Geographic found out in a survey that four out of ten Americans believed preparing for the Doomsday through hoarding emergency food and constructing bomb shelters was a smarter investment that than a retirement savings plan. Now that is nothing short of collective pessimism.[18]

The economic costs of climate change are expected to be staggering: Every single degree Celsius increase in global warming could reduce

[14] Leprince-Ringuet (2018).
[15] Wallace-Wells (2017).
[16] Ibid.
[17] Osnos (2017).
[18] Ibid.

global GDP by as much as 1.2%. Global warming could slash up to a quarter of per capita incomes by the end of the century. It's not only economic productivity that will suffer. For every half-degree increase in global temperatures, there will be a 10–20% increase in likelihood of conflicts. Over the next decades, the number of conflicts, largely driven by resource-competition amid ecological instability, could double. Add to this, the accelerated melting of permafrost, which will not only compound carbon emission concentration in the atmosphere, but will also release ancient diseases that will likely overwhelm modern human's immune system as well as healthcare infrastructure.[19] In our crowded plant, where hundreds of millions of individuals cross borders on a daily basis, the opportunity for global epidemic is more than abundant. The combination of economic depression, resource-driven conflict, and epidemics will likely produce and reinforce among the most demagogic forms of politics and extremist ideologies, which will make all forms of right-wing populism infesting today's democracies look like a relatively mild intimation of a far darker future. The carnage and barbarity of the ISIS and its ideology are perhaps just a flavor of things to come, especially in the less developed and more climate change-vulnerable portions of the Indo-Pacific, particularly South and Southeast Asia, where more than 2 billion people live in one of the most ethnically religiously diverse and economically unequal societies in the planet. Today's economic dynamos could very well be tomorrow's epicenter of epidemics (as global temperatures rise), urban warfare (amid collapse of public services and dwindling resources), and a mélange of extremist ideologies (as millions of distraught and emaciated people look for conceptual certainties against the backdrop of apocalyptic challenges). Using the Copernican principle, namely the likelihood of relatively short-lived peace and prosperity lasting way into the future, the odds of ecologically driven conflicts and economic dislocation are far higher than many wish.[20] Thus, the greatest cost of the ongoing Sino-American Cold War, or better described as "frozen conflict," is a shortsighted distraction from the coming anarchy. And Trump's misguided abandonment of the Paris Agreement,[21] and liminal embrace of climate change deniers,

[19] Fox-Skelly (2017).
[20] Wallace-Wells (2019a).
[21] Roberts (2018).

will likely go down as his greatest disservice to humanity.[22] Though America is no longer as central to the global order, it's role as one of the pillars of multilateral cooperation is undeniable. Thus, Trump's "Make America Great Again" could very well accelerate the true end of history. Out of the five previous mass extinctions in the earth's geological history, four were driven by climate change.[23] Two centuries of industrial revolution, and three waves of technological innovation, proved T.R. Malthus wrong. In *An Essay on the Principle of Population (1798)*, the great British thinker postulated that the exponential increase in human population would always overrun linear-arithmetic increase in food supply. This time, however, could be different, as we confront the prospect of the Sixth Extinction. After all, as the anthropologist Joseph Tainter warned, human civilizations are "fragile, impermanent things."[24] Our very conception of peace and prosperity could radically alter within this century. And the Indo-Pacific will be the center of this unfolding drama of biblical proportions.

THE COMING ANARCHY

In Roland Emmerich's epic "2012," the science fiction movie that drove countless people to the edge of apocalyptic despair, China emerges as the unlikely savior. After all, it's the Asian powerhouse that builds the twenty-first century Noah's Ark, carrying in its steely bosom humanity's best, brightest and billionaires as the rest of the world drowns in a biblical storm. The year 2012 didn't mark apocalypse, as topnotch physicists reassured with irritable tenacity, but the movie correctly highlighted the vicissitudes of nature as well as the emerging geopolitics of our times with the arrival of a new agent of history. With the twin meta-challenges of climate change and hyper-disruptive technology lurking over the near horizon, cooperation among regional powers remains immeasurably central to the preservation of global order. This is especially true in the Indo-Pacific, where much of humanity's population, economic activity, conflicts, and natural disasters are tenuously concentrated. The future of the region will be less about struggle for mastery than managing one cataclysmic disaster after the other,

[22] Friedman (2018).
[23] Kolbert (2014).
[24] Kaplan (2011a).

as individual states find themselves inundated by the scale of a myriad of evolving disasters. The magnitude of nontraditional security challenges facing humanity far surpasses the management capacity of a single power, whether the United States or China. Thus, cooperation among great and small powers will increasingly become the only game in town—the default geopolitical option in decades to come. Thus, China's buy-in will be indispensable to the efficacy and sustainability of any trouble-shooting or more institutionalized cooperative mechanism in the Indo-Pacific. The movie underscored as much the fragility of human civilization as the centrality of modern China to humanity's future.

Quite bizarrely, China, along with industrialized nations of the Indo-Pacific, has become a major source as well as possible solution to the rapid emaciation of nature and the intensifying climate change conundrum. According to a major report by the WWF, drafted by close to sixty of the world's leading scientists, the past half-century saw the extinction of 60% of all global fauna, a dizzying variety of birds, mammals, fishes, and reptiles that were around for at least millions of years.[25]

We are facing what scientists call the "sixth extinction," one that is driven by human activities rather than geological disasters, which drove, for instance, dinosaurs to extinction. Another major study showed that humans, constituting 0.01% of life on earth, have been responsible for extinction of 83% of all wild mammals and up to half of all plants throughout history.[26] The rapid, widespread extinction of non-human life on earth was accelerated with the Industrial Revolution in the West, and exacerbated by rapid industrialization of the East in recent decades. China's appetite for exotic animals and increasingly meaty diet has been a major contributor. To put things into perspective, Indo-Pacific countries of the United States, China, India, Russia, and Japan are the world's top five sources of greenhouse emissions, the primary precursor of climate change.[27] Rising global temperature and extreme weather conditions brought about by climate change will only exacerbate the ongoing natural cataclysm, placing tens of millions of people at risk. Of the top 10 countries most vulnerable to the adverse impact of climate change, according to an HSBC study, seven are from the Indo-Pacific region, namely India, Pakistan, Bangladesh,

---

[25] World Wildlife Fund (2018).
[26] Carrington (2018).
[27] CAIT (l.a. 2019).

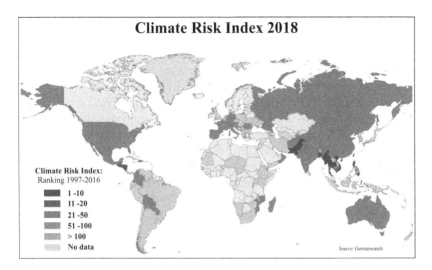

Fig. 9.3 Most vulnerable nations to climate change

the Philippines, Sri Lanka, Oman, and Kenya.[28] Nations across the mega-region have already borne the brunt of extreme weather conditions in recent years, overstretching their already limited adaptation mechanisms (see Fig. 9.3). Worryingly, most of these countries rate poorly on Fragile State Index and other measurements of state capacity to mitigate and adapt to disasters, both manmade and natural. Thus, climate change is hitting those that are least prepared for it, a perilous combination with far reaching strategic implications for the Indo-Pacific's future.

Thus, the ongoing strategic obsession over China's growing foothold in the Chittagong port in Bangladesh may seem trivial, if not distasteful, in the coming decades, since the whole country's existence would come under question were the earth's temperature to increase beyond two degrees later in this century.[29] The pristine islands of Maldives, again another nation at the heart of the ongoing geopolitical rivalry in the Indian Ocean, could very well be inundated by rising sea levels. In fact, Maldives has joined a tragic group of beleaguered island nations desperately raising funds to literally purchase a future homeland for

[28] Sieg and Takenaka (2018).
[29] He et al. (2018).

their traumatized residents.[30] And the same is true for megacities of the Indo-Pacific, from Jakarta and Manila to Mumbai and Karachi, home to tens of millions of residents living precariously close to tempestuous oceans. Many nations across the westernmost edge of the Indo-Pacific will be literally uninhabitable as temperature levels rise beyond what's humanly tolerable. The futuristic cities in the Persian Gulf, from Dubai to Doha, will have to rely on (massive carbon-emitting) mega-cooling machines or risk turning into picturesque ruins of once majestic pet-ro-empires. And regional powerhouses of Iran, Turkey, and Egypt will have to contend with tens of millions of citizens escaping biblical natural disasters. Their formidable million-strong militaries will likely be more focused on domestic stabilization amid climate-driven disasters than fighting off external threats before the end of the century.[31] The unprecedented floods across more than 500 cities and villages in Iran in early 2019 are perhaps a foreshadowing of the climactic challenges over the horizon.[32] From North Africa to Central Asia, climate change will likely congeal into an irredeemable "Arc of Instability," which will overwhelm even the most determined superpowers.[33] If current trends continue, the mega-region will not only be a graveyard of foreign empires, but also of the world's oldest continuing civilizations.

Those in the eastern and central portions of the Indo-Pacific are no safer, for they will confront their own climactic demons. Constant floods, supertyphoon, and rising sea levels will conspire against millions living in shantytowns and relying on poor public infrastructure and urban planning. Later in this century, many islands could be literally wiped off the map due to new categories of hurricanes and supertyphoon and/or increased frequency of once-every-500 years of natural disasters on a yearly basis.[34] As climactic mutation festers, certain areas could be hit by several natural disasters, ranging from droughts to typhoons and wildfires, almost simultaneously. Absent a massive and systematic reduction in global emission levels, we may see up to four feet increase in sea levels over the coming decades and up to ten feet by the end of the century. To put things into perspective: close to 600 million people live within only meters of oceans today,

[30] Ramesh (2008).
[31] Leahy (2017).
[32] Jaafari (2019).
[33] Alterman (2017).
[34] CBS News (2017).

a bulk of which resides in the Indo-Pacific. Over the next century, we may see between 100 million to 1 billion climate refugees across the world, vast majority of which will come from the climate-vulnerable Indo-Pacific nations[35] Meanwhile, the South China Sea, home to the world's marine biodiversity, is turning into an environmental catastrophe amid China's massive reclamation activities, which are devastating coral reefs, reportedly costing neighboring countries such as the Philippines $100 million annually in foregone resources; large-scale illegal, underreported, unregulated (IUU) fishing, with China again in the lead; and unrestrained plastic pollution by China, Indonesia and the Philippines. Scientists estimate that up to 70% of the coral reefs in the area have been damaged by a combination of manmade and natural factors, including a warming climate that triggers so-called "coral bleaching" (turning the millennia-old habitat of marine life into a wasteland). The question is: Do we have effective existing regional organizations to deal with these crises?[36]

As Professor David L. Fluharty, a leading environmental scientist, explains: "While the locus of sources for environmental impacts from land-based sources of pollution, for example, resides with the coastal state, fisheries management and conservation constitutes an important issue to be resolved under existing protocols ... I see it as a failure of coastal states and distant water states to mutually agree on management goals and allocation of benefits ... Best practices for environmental management generally start from agreed national boundaries and transparent data for decisions. The South China Sea lacks this ... at a minimum, the claimant countries should develop a forum where discussion can occur about the documented and prioritized environmental issues."[37] Despite the proliferation of various blueprint for environmental management regimes in the South China Sea, however, claimant countries, particularly China, seem more intent on dominating the area first before setting the environmental rules of the game. During the 2018 ASEAN Foreign Ministers Meeting (AFMM) in Singapore, China and Southeast Asian countries triumphantly announced the completion of a "Single Draft COC Negotiating Text."[38] The draft will serve as the basis for negotiation of a final document, which

---

[35] Wallace-Wells (2017).
[36] Hachigian (2015) and Wallace-Wells (2017).
[37] Interview with the author, February 9, 2015.
[38] Liang and Gomez (2018).

will operationalize the basic rules of engagement among competing claimant states in the South China Sea—namely China, the Philippines, Brunei, Vietnam, and Malaysia. The problem, however, is that China seeks to use the negotiation of a Code of Conduct as a basis to not only exclude external parties such as United States and Japan from the area, but also monopolize the marine and energy resources in the South China Sea basin. As Australian analyst Carl Thayer, who obtained the copy of the COC draft, accurately observes, China "aims to bind ASEAN members states in the COC and limit if not exclude the involvement of third parties."[39] In many ways, the ASEAN is being increasingly hijacked by China. And this has troubling implications for the region, especially in terms of prospects for effective management of shared non-traditional security concerns such as environmental crises.

As playwright Arthur Miller observed, "An era can be considered over when its basic illusions have been exhausted," In some ways, the vision of Association of Southeast Asian Nations (ASEAN) centrality in shaping the Asia-Pacific regional order is facing a similar moment of reckoning. Without a doubt, the regional body is confronting what I call the "middle institutionalization trap," namely the institutional structure, which allowed ASEAN to establish a robust security community in the twentieth century. It is now painfully insufficient to address the new challenges of the twenty-first century. The ASEAN will either have to step up to plate and embrace institutional innovation, or fast fade into irrelevance, if not subservience to its giant northern neighbor. The best way to preserve and energize a decaying yet valuable edifice is radical reform and reexamination of its basic operating principles.

The ASEAN, in its current composition and decision-making structure, is ripe for the picking by external powers, particularly China. In the past decade, the Asian powerhouse has, with mind boggling speed, transformed from an auxiliary strategic partner to a de facto veto player within the regional body. This is largely due to the self-defeating misinterpretation of the concept of consensus. In the case of ASEAN, consensus is falsely translated as unanimity, which, by its very nature, is almost impossible to attain whenever sensitive issues are on the table. Operationally, what this means is that it needs only the opposition of one country to frustrate unity and advancement on any major area of concern. External powers such as China will have to only bribe, coax, and cajole a single member nation—no

---

[39] Thayer (2018).

matter how small or remote from and unaffected by as specific crisis at hand—to undermine any collective undertaking within ASEAN.

As a result, it has almost become impossible to imagine ASEAN undertaking any major decision or initiative without taking into account either China's or its regional proxies' views into its calculus.

As the Singaporean diplomat Barry Desker rightfully points out, the main problem is the "ability of external parties to shape the positions of ASEAN members on regional issues," especially when "China exerts its influence on ASEAN members to prevent any decisions which could affect its preference for bilateral negotiations" rather than dealing with ASEAN multilaterally.[40] The upshot is an ASEAN that is paralyzed in China's shadows, incapable of acting as an independent agent of integration in the region. For years, we have feared the prospect of discord and disunity among ASEAN nations. But more recently, the situation has become even direr. Under the chairmanship of the Philippine President Rodrigo Duterte, the ASEAN effectively ceded any claim to serving as an engine of regional integration in Asia. Not only have we seen China dividing and conquering the region, but, to the astonishment of many, the ASEAN served as Beijing's shield against America and its key regional allies. Instead of standing up to China's unabated militarization of the disputes, the Philippines admonished attempts by external powers, including the United States, Japan, and Australia, to constrain Beijing's threat to regional maritime security. In Duterte's blunt language, the disputes are "better left untouched."[41] When Washington and its allies called on China to abide by a Manila-initiated landmark arbitration ruling—which invalidated China's expansive claims in the area—the Philippines effectively insisted that it's their sovereign right not to assert their sovereign rights vis-à-vis China.[42]

Without a doubt, the ASEAN should be credited for facilitating the establishment of a zone of peace and prosperity in what used to be one of the most volatile regions on earth. But to be relevant, autonomous and serve as an agent of stability (rather than subservience), it has to dispense with its cult of consensus. The regional body can revisit its decision-making structure by, for instance, more relying on the rarely,

---

[40] Heydarian (2015).
[41] Shi and Liu (2017).
[42] Mogato (2017).

but effectively, tested "ASEAN Minus X" formula, whereby unanimity isn't a prerequisite for action or even a robust joint statement.[43] Even better, the ASEAN could adopt the European Union's often-used weighted qualified majority voting modality, where the population density and geopolitical heft of member states are taken into consideration.[44]

This way, China won't be able to veto decisions within ASEAN, so long as there are enough voices of independence and reason left in the room. Moreover, like-minded and more independent nations within ASEAN, namely Indonesia, Vietnam, and Singapore, can seize the initiative and expand "minilateral" cooperation among themselves on issues of common and urgent concern. As American academic William Tow explains, "Minilateralism represents a flexible policy option for...middle powers to pursue [cooperation] re specific issue areas (hard or soft security) where common interests are readily identifiable and the costs for meeting those interests are not high."[45]

Externally, America and its allies won't have to convince and engage all of ASEAN per se, but instead only key powers within Southeast Asia, in order to constrain China's revanchist ambitions. Perhaps, the best way to save ASEAN today is to precisely transcend its broken multilateralism in favor of a more dynamic minilateralism, until the regional body gets its own institutional house in order. Astonishingly, there are even discussions of Australia and New Zealand joining ASEAN in order to save the regional body from a downward spiral of irrelevance. Desperate times call for formerly unthinkable solutions, and managing the mega-crises on the horizon requires a robust and internally coherent ASEAN.[46]

Perils of Creative Disruption

While untrammeled economic expansion is supposed to be the defining story of the mega-region, the Indo-Pacific is also highly susceptible to uneven development with potentially devastating socio-political consequences. Asia is home to almost a billion workers with "vulnerable" jobs bereft of proper compensation, benefits, and security of tenure, according

---

[43] Emmers (2017).
[44] European Council: Council of the European Union (2019).
[45] Interview with author, October 30, 2018.
[46] Dobell (2018).

to the International Labor Organization (ILO).[47] The Fourth Industrial Revolution, and advancements in Artificial Intelligence (AI), directly threatens lower skilled as well as white-collar jobs in the future. AI gurus such as Kai Fu Lee expect the full impact on jobs to be felt within less than two decades.[48] The ILO estimates that in several Southeast Asian countries, namely Cambodia, Indonesia, the Philippines, Thailand, and Vietnam, up to 137 million jobs (56%) are at risk of automation.[49] While new waves of innovation will likely create new employment opportunities, what's far more certain is the prospect of employment insecurity, which, in turn, can deepen societal fissures and grievances over rising inequality, fuel radicalization, and extremist ideologies, and push a growing number of people into transnational the underground economy. In the United States, Osnos reports, "The fears vary, but many worry that, as artificial intelligence takes away a growing share of jobs, there will be a backlash against Silicon Valley" and other centers of cutting-edge innovations.[50] Their counterparts across developing regions of the Indo-Pacific, from Shanghai to Singapore and Dubai, may face similar threats down the road. Within a generation, the very concept of lifetime career maybe forcibly replaced by constant cycles of re-employment, retraining and job insecurity. This will be devastating for hundreds of millions of individuals, especially traditionally-raised men expected to be breadwinners, across the Indo-Pacific and beyond. This is precisely what upbeat studies by International Financial Institutions such as the Asian Development Bank miss: How accelerated waves of Schumpeterian "creative destruction" and disruptive innovation will create unprecedented psychological stress and disorientation with likely perilous political ramifications.[51]

The great political theorists of the twentieth century, from Max Weber and Ferdinand Tönnies to Hannah Arendt and Karl Polanyi, were rightly obsessed about the nefarious impact of rapid modernization on previously traditional societies—and how this dynamic fuelled a Freudian "death drive" among the masses and elites. After all, the destructive wars of the early twentieth century and the rise of fascism took place on the heels of rapid modernization and its discontents. The new middle classes

---

[47] Roughneed (2018).

[48] Lee (2018).

[49] Aravindan (2016).

[50] Osnos (2017).

[51] Asian Development Bank (2018).

of the Indo-Pacific will experience, with a twenty-first-century technology flavor, the collective disorientation that far surpasses, both in breadth and quality, what their European counterparts experienced in the preceding century. Uprooted from their *Gemeinschaft*, where one could enjoy dense networks of community "life world," and thrown (Geworfenheit), in a Heideggerean sense, into *Gesellschaft*, namely anonymous and alienating "mass societies," the predominant sentiment of tomorrow's societies will likely be what Nietzsche termed as *ressentiment*, a toxic cocktail of pent-up rage, grievance, and envy.[52] We will likely witness, on the national and local levels at least, new forms of "double movement,"[53] where demagogic politics and extremist ideologies become the conventional forms of collective reaction to disruptive technological innovation.[54] As Karl Polanyi warned in *The Great Transformation*, capitalist-driven technological innovations are highly disruptive, because "[i] n disposing of a man's labor power the system would, incidentally, dispose of the physical, psychological, and moral entity of 'man' attached to the tag...human beings would perish from the effects of social exposure; they would die as the victims of acute social dislocation through vice, perversion, crime, and starvation."[55] And this dynamic could be potentially explosive on a global scale. In *The Human Condition*, Hannah Arendt observed how in a globalized world, "[e]very country has become the almost immediate neighbor of every other country, and every man feels the shock of events which take place at the other side of the globe."[56] No wonder then, events in one country, particularly of violent nature, can quickly inspire a whole wave across nations, continents, and oceans. Just when we need technocratic solutions and democratic consensus to address the most complex problems faced by humanity, a mixture of demagoguery, collective disorientation and systematic disinformation will likely gain the upper hand amid a climate of fear, grievance, and denial. At some point, political systems could collapse before we can even mobilize proper responses to challenges ahead. Thus, what the Indo-Pacific could face is a dangerous cocktail of profound

[52] Elgat (2017).

[53] See for instance Goodwin (2018) and Block (2008).

[54] See Karl Polanyi's meta-historical double-movement analysis and inner contradictions of liberal capitalism in Polanyi (2001).

[55] Harvey (1973).

[56] Mishra (2017).

economic anxieties, extreme weather conditions, and emaciation of natural resources, which will imperil our civilizations like never before. The twenty-first century may easily morph into what the Indian essayist Pankaj Mishra termed as an "Age of Anger."[57]

Even the most sober observers are pitching in. In an uncharacteristically alarmist essay, entitled *How the Enlightenment Ends*, the ever-stoic Henry Kissinger warned about the total, transformative impact of A.I. on modern politics in ways that will upend the meaning of human existence itself. After all, unlike previous waves of technological innovation, which served as human intelligence-augmentation (I.A.) mechanisms, A.I. tends to supplant human cognition and, beyond just serving a means of production, processing of societal ends.[58] In Marxist parlance, A.I. is changing the very *modes of production*—(technological) means and (capital–labor) relations of production—in twenty-first-century societies. Modern democratic politics itself could be upended by the new technological waves. Kissinger rightly warns that A.I. provides the "ability to target micro-groups" in ways that has "broken up the previous consensus on priorities by permitting a focus on specialized purposes or grievances."[59] This leaves political leaders "overwhelmed by niche pressures" and "deprived of time to think or reflect on context, contracting the space available for them to develop vision." Even more worrying is the advent of A.I.-driven "deep fake," which allows for the manufacturing of highly authentic-looking videos, images, and speeches that can be deployed for a totally new level of disinformation.[60] Thus, A.I. will change the very conduct of power. For the former American diplomat, the new technological wave allows for "mastering certain competencies more rapidly and definitively than humans" with dire consequences for humanity, since the A.I. "could over time diminish human competence and the human condition itself as it turns it into data."

And this is precisely where Sino-American tensions are a dangerous distraction, since China's buy-in is crucial to the creation of a stable, free, and open global order. Surely, China is not only a source of problem, but also a source of solutions. With its strides in green technology, tightening environmental regulations, large reserve of capital and technology,

---

[57] Ibid.
[58] See for instance Brynjolfsson and McAfee (2016).
[59] Ibid.
[60] Chesney and Citron (2019).

infrastructure development capacity, and growing naval capability, the Asian powerhouse is in a unique position to help mitigate climate change, provide humanitarian and disaster relief operations, and assist other countries to cope with the coming anarchy. In short, China can immensely contribute to the Noah's Ark of regional cooperation that will increasingly become indispensable to preserve a semblance of order and prosperity in the Indo-Pacific. Yet, China is also becoming the harbinger of another troubling development, namely the export of technological authoritarianism, amid the age of "surveillance capitalism," where data processing constitutes the ultimate nexus between profit and power.[61]

Making the World Safe for Autocracy

In an impassioned speech (April 2, 1917) before the joint session of the Congress, which effectively ended America's neutrality and age-old aloofness from the troubles of the Old World, President Woodrow Wilson emphasized the necessity to make sure the world will "be made safe for democracy."[62] This was Wilson's version of "America First," a catchphrase in his 1915 speeches.[63] Over the next hundred years, a series of presidents from across the ideological spectrum designed, implemented and justified American foreign policy along similar lines. George W. Bush and the neoconservatives prosecuted the interventions in the Middle East as a "democracy promotion" initiative, while Barack Obama and liberal hawks justified humanitarian intervention in Libya and drone operations across the Middle East as an attempt to protect the security and values of the "civilized world." President Franklin Roosevelt's patient and systematic establishment of the postwar Liberal International Order was the embodiment of what Walter Russell Mead identified as the Wilsonian streak in American foreign policy.[64] In many ways, the construction of the Bretton Woods System marked the apotheosis of Woodrow Wilson's vision of the future global order.[65] And

---

[61] The term surveillance capitalism was coined by Harvard academic Shoshana Zuboff see Zuboff (2019).

[62] History Matters (l.a. 2019).

[63] See Churchwell (2018), Illing (2018), and Snyder (2018).

[64] See Mead (2002) and Anderson (2015).

[65] Anderson (2015).

this Wilsonian impulse guided American successfully through two world wars and a decades-long Cold War with the Soviet Union.

This is important, precisely because the United States, as even prominent Western critics such as Mahathir told the author, have historically served as a beacon of freedom around the world.[66] Even worse, many see the Trump presidency as fundamentally unreliable. As the Malaysian maverick lamented, "[President] Trump is unusually aggressive and inconsistent, we don't really know what he is going to do next...He may change his mind sometimes three times a day."[67] Keep in mind that America's commitment to democratic promotion played a crucial role during the Third Wave of democratization across the world.[68] As leading democracy experts such as Samuel Huntington[69] and Larry Diamond[70] have observed, the West's material and ideological support was integral to the success of democratic transition in Eastern Europe, Asia, and Latin America. For instance, Huntington emphasized America's role as "a major promoter of democratization," which was augmented by the "unparalleled power of a seemingly successful US democratic model...a 'shining city on a hill'—to inspire admiration and emulation around the world." Echoing Huntington's argument decades earlier, Diamond underscored how Washington "provided both an end state toward which emerging democracies could move, and [the necessary] support to help them get there."[71] The Trump administration, however, is effectively abandoning America's century-old self-ascribed role as the world's primary advocate of democracy. Far from a "city on a hill," America's polarized politics, highly unequal society, poor public infrastructure, and welfare system, and structural dysfunction have collectively tarnished the country's image and authority. By electing a reality show star, with demagogic instinct and unhinged rhetoric but zero experience in executive office, American exceptionalism now seems more like a farce to much of the world.[72]

---

[66] Interview with author, March 8.

[67] Zuboff (2019).

[68] Huntington (1993).

[69] Huntington (1991).

[70] Diamond (2016).

[71] Ibid.

[72] Dutt (2016).

Prominent Asia scholars such as Amitav Acharya have argued that we are already witnessing the end of the American-led global order, or what John Ikenberry termed as liberal hegemony.[73] Instead, the world is turning into a "multiplex", where "[n]o single director or producer would monopolize" the overall system.[74] Furthermore, the international system is "more decentered...with greater scope for local and regional approaches," which, in turn, "limits the possibility for a collective hegemony of great powers over the rest..."[75] As Asia scholar Evelyn Goh explains, hegemony is anchored by the ability of a great power to set the rules and norms of interstate interaction, provide public international goods, and enforce existing rules as well as punish transgression.[76] The Trump administration is struggling on all three fronts, as it defies America's own tradition of multilateral cooperation; rejects free trade regimes, the International Criminal Court,[77] the United Nations Human Rights Council,[78] and international agreements such as the Iranian nuclear deal; and either struggles or fails to punish those that defy existing international norms and rules, including allies, which have been accused of war crimes (see Chapter 3).

In short, the "America First" Trump administration seems less interested in either making the world safe for democracy or upholding the liberal international order. Both America's commitment and wherewithal are now under question. Add to this, the American president's idiosyncratic affinity and penchant for authoritarian leaders such as Russian President Vladimir Putin and even his Chinese counterpart Xi Jinping.[79] In a way, all three leaders are committed to imperial resurgence, whether it's Trump's "making America great again" motto, Xi's "Chinese Dream" and call for "national rejuvenation," or Putin's *homo sovieticus* persona and call for Russia's return to its historical glory, a mélange of Soviet Union's military strength and Czarist Russia Orthodox, conservative imperial legacy.[80]

---

[73] Ikenberry (2018).

[74] Acharya (2014, 10).

[75] Ibid., 15.

[76] Goh (2014, 77–78).

[77] De Luce and Williams (2019).

[78] Harris (2018).

[79] Brennan (2019).

[80] See Hartog and Gudkov (2017), Kimmage (2018), and Snyder (2018).

Time and again, Trump has praised these authoritarian leaders, who oversee rival empires, which are carving out, often with coercive force, their own spheres of influence in their respective regions. America's lack or willful abdication of global leadership has provided a vacuum, which is being filled by rival authoritarian powers. As former US ambassador to NATO Ivo Daalder and Council on Foreign Relations' James Lindsay explain in *The Empty Throne: America's Abdication of Global Leadership*, "Seventy years after US President Harry Truman sketched the blueprint for a rules-based international order[81] to prevent the dog-eat-dog geopolitical competition that triggered World War II, US President Donald Trump has upended it. He has raised doubts about Washington's security commitments to its allies,[82] challenged the fundamentals of the global trading regime, abandoned the promotion of freedom and democracy as defining features of US foreign policy, and abdicated global leadership."[83] While contemporary Russia has struggled to match the strategic prowess of the Soviet Union in the Indo-Pacific, it has nonetheless developed asymmetrical means by which to exert influence well beyond its means. At the heart of Russia's foreign policy offensive is its "sharp power," namely the ability to disrupt domestic politics of rival state across oceans and continents. As Christopher Walker and Jessica Ludwig of the National Endowment for Democracy (NED) explain, Russia is primus inter pares among the "powerful and ambitious authoritarian regimes, which systematically suppress political pluralism and free expression to maintain power at home, are increasingly applying the same principles internationally."[84] Beginning in the mid-2000s, "the Kremlin launched the global television network Russia Today (since rebranded as the more unassuming RT), built up its capacity to manipulate content online, increased its support for state-affiliated policy institutes, and more generally cultivated a web of influence activities—both on and offline—designed to alter international views to its advantage."[85]

Though the much-awaited Muller Report fell short of accusing Trump and his core aides of "conspiring" with Russian elements, it nonetheless confirmed long-running suspicions of Russian interference

[81] Allison (2018).
[82] Smith and Townsend (2018).
[83] Daalder and Lindsay (2018).
[84] Walker and Ludwig (2017).
[85] Ibid.

in the 2016 American elections.[86] Sharp power serves as a force multiplier for shrinking empires such as Russia, which are in no mood to withdraw from the Indo-Pacific struggle for power. Moreover, Putin and his brand of authoritarian populism has served as a blueprint for like-minded leaders all across the world, ranging from Rodrigo Duterte in the Philippines, to whom the Russian leader is a "favorite hero," to Recep Tayyip Erdoğan in Turkey and Viktor Mihály Orbán in Hungary.[87] The challenge from China, however, is even more insidious. Combined with Russia's (and other authorities regimes') sharp power, it could radically alter the international order and usher in a global illiberal turn. To be fair, at the heart of China's global push is not only the intent to thwart efforts at exogenously-driven democratization at home, the so-called "color revolutions," but to also democratize the international system by giving greater voice to newly risen powers. While the United States spent the twentieth century to make the world safe for democracy, China is dedicating this century to make the world safe for autocracy—an impulse that was accentuated following the 2010–2011 Arab uprisings, which upended one authoritarian regime after the other.[88]

Indirectly, China is contributing to the breakdown of democratic transparency and accountability (see Chapter 5) across liberalizing autocracies and fledgling democracies by fuelling massive infrastructure projects, which lack proper regulatory oversight and transparency, fail to follow international standards followed by established creditor nations, and primarily benefit and empower a tiny elite. The cumulative impact of China's "corrosive capital" is erosion of good governance initiatives, widespread corruption, and crowding out of domestic players, especially the private sector and workers, which are essential elements of a robust civil society, which, in turn, serves as the bedrock of a mature democracy.[89] As Robert Putnam explains in *Making Democracy Work*, a key ingredient for the proper functioning of democratic institutions is a vibrant civil society, composed of an empowered working class and proactive middle class, which can hold the ruling elite accountable.[90] Venezuela most dramatically demonstrates the corrosive impact of

[86] Risen (2019).
[87] See Heydarian (2019a) and Bremmer (2018).
[88] See Johnson (2019) and Friedberg (2018).
[89] Tai and Jaques (2019).
[90] Putnam et al. (1994).

massive influx of Chinese investments and capital, which only strengthened the grip of authoritarian leaders, reduced incentives for good governance reforms and sound macro-economic policy, and eventually destroyed the middle class and undermined the civil society.[91] The same pattern held in other fledgling democracies, where large-scale Chinese investments aided and encouraged corrupt leaderships from the Arroyo administration in the Philippines and Rajapaksa regime in Sri Lanka to Najib Razak government in Malaysia. And in all three cases, China's corrosive influence became a central electoral issue that catapulted the opposition to power after leaving democratic institutions in tatters.[92]

Of greater concern, however, is Beijing's export of cutting-edge surveillance technology to fledgling and full-fledged authoritarian leaders, ranging from Venezuela to Angola and Pakistan, who are bent on monitoring and manipulating the behavior of their citizens.[93] At home, China is honing its draconian surveillance regime through the establishment of an Orwellian social credit system, which ubiquitously tracks and scores patterns of behavior of its citizens in exchange for an elaborate reward-and-punishment regime.[94] More worryingly, it has also deployed cutting-edge A.I. technology to repress, frighten, manipulate and monitor minority groups, particularly the Uighur population in Xinjiang, a far western region that has been a cauldron of separatist sentiment and pogroms over the past decade. In what some experts characterize as ethnic cleansing and crimes against humanity, China has reportedly incarcerated up to a million Uighurs in so-called "re-education" camps, forcing them to give up their way of life in exchange for unquestioned fidelity to the ruling communist party, turning ancient towns into hyper-modern prisons wired with cutting-edge surveillance technology.[95] By farming large-scale data, with almost zero considerations for the rights of millions of people, Beijing is in a position to leap ahead in A.I. technology with disturbing implications far beyond its borders. Amid the US withdrawal from its global role as a promoter of democracy, we are instead seeing the replication of the Chinese and Russian models of authoritarian governance

[91] Naím and Toro (2018).

[92] Heydarian (2018).

[93] See Chellaney (2017), Walker et al. (2018), Daalder and Lindsay (2018), and Huang (2018).

[94] Hao (2019).

[95] Kirby (2018).

across the world. Crucially, this has coincided with a global "democratic recession" in the past two decades, with 27 democracies suffering either a temporary or full breakdown.[96] As Princeton academic Aaron Friedberg observes, "Whereas fundamentalists exploited Western freedoms to sow public terror, Russia and China using influence operations to undermine institutions and elites."[97] What drives China's sense of urgency in exporting its model, Friedberg observes, is the belief "that the United States and its liberal democratic allies are implacably opposed to them on ideological grounds and that the US, in particular, seeks not only to encircle and contain China but [also] to undermine its current regime by promoting 'splitism' (that is, separatist movements in Tibet, Xinjiang and Taiwan) and 'peaceful evolution' (that is, the spread of liberal-democratic beliefs among the Chinese population)."[98] In simple terms, China sees this as an existential struggle, whereby it has to either export its cutting-edge authoritarian model of governance or risk Western-backed democratization at home. It's a fundamentally zero-sum ideological struggle. And this is the context within which one should understand China's push to dominate the global information highway and the Fourth Industrial Revolution anchored by A.I. And this time, history seems to be on the side of authoritarian regimes. The new century will be marked by the advent of "techno-tyranny," or what historian Yuval Noah Harari terms as "digital dictatorships," with China as its main harbinger. Thus, Beijing's centralized A.I. project may ultimately inundate its more spontaneously driven, private sector-centered counterpart in the West. In the twentieth century, spontaneous organization won. This century, technological tyranny will likely have the upper hand. As Harari explains:

> We tend to think about the conflict between democracy and dictatorship as a conflict between two different ethical systems, but it is actually a conflict between two different data-processing systems...Given 20th-century technology, it was inefficient to concentrate too much information and power in one place...This is one reason the Soviet Union made far worse decisions than the United States, and why the Soviet economy lagged far behind the American economy. However, artificial intelligence may soon swing the pendulum in the opposite direction. AI makes it possible

[96] Diamond (2016).
[97] Friedberg (2018).
[98] Ibid.

to process enormous amounts of information centrally. In fact, it might make centralized systems far more efficient than diffuse systems, because machine learning works better when the machine has more information to analyze. If you disregard all privacy concerns and concentrate all the information relating to a billion people in one database, you'll wind up with much better algorithms than if you respect individual privacy and have in your database only partial information on a million people.[99]

Thus, China's centralized A.I. project, which can pool together data from a billion citizens with virtually no privacy considerations, may ultimately inundate its more spontaneously driven, private sector-centered counterpart in the West. Despite vehement opposition by the Trump administration, China has also successfully pushed for the adoption of 5G networks by Chinese telecommunications giant Huawei,[100] while a growing number of Indo-Pacific nations, including Vietnam, are warming up to Chinese-style heavily regulated online platforms.[101] In coming decades, Beijing will have a unique and transformative ability to host, monitor, and even manipulate communication flows in the emerging global information network (see Fig. 9.4). Thanks to the combination of cutting-edge data processing by authoritarian regimes and a China-built global information highway, the future will likely belong to forces of illiberalism and counter-Enlightenment.

A visibly perturbed Kissinger has even called for "a presidential commission of eminent thinkers to help develop a national vision" to deal with such existential challenge[102] America is in panic, and the future of power and leadership in the Indo-Pacific is at stake. The problem, however, is that the challenges ahead far surpass both the significance of US–China rivalry as well as the individual capabilities of both superpowers, thus the necessity for a far greater collaborative and multipolar approach to establishing and preserving a durable Indo-Pacific security architecture for the twenty-first century.

[99] Harari (2018).
[100] Tobin (2019).
[101] Chen and Lee (2019).
[102] Kissinger (2018).

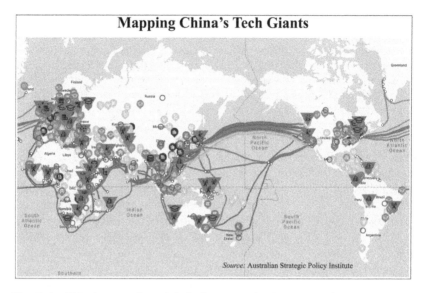

Mapping China's Tech Giants

Source: Australian Strategic Policy Institute

Fig. 9.4   China's expanding global telecommunications network

THE REAL END OF HISTORY

In *The End of History*, Francis Fukuyama, drawing on Russian émigré Alexandre Kojève's interpretation of Hegelian philosophy, warned about the dangers of boredom as the defining attitude of the twenty-first century.[103] As G.W.F. Hegel, the all-encompassing metaphysician of the eighteenth century argued, peace induces meaningless hedonistic existence while conflict evokes our greatest passions, hence highest virtues. As the German Philosopher explained in *Philosophy of History*, "[n]othing great in the world has been accomplished without passion."[104] And separately *in The Phenomenology of Mind*, he went so far as stating, "[i]t is solely by risking [ones] life that freedom is obtained…"[105] Echoing Hegel, Fukuyama posited that "in a world where [the] struggle over all of the large [ideological] issues had been largely settled, a purely formal snobbery would become the chief form of expression of megalothymia,

[103] Fukuyama (2006).
[104] Hegel (2007).
[105] Marxists.org (2019, April 30 "The Phenomenology of …").

of man's desire to be recognized as better than his fellows."[106] As scholars such as Steven Pinker and Yuval Harrari have shown, we indeed live in the most prosperous and peaceful period in human history, where more people die of suicide and obesity than homicide and hunger.[107] In the coming decades, however, the twenty-first century will likely look more Malthusian than Fukuyaman. As Robert Kaplan presciently wrote in the twilight years of the preceding century, the "future map— in a sense, the 'Last Map'—will be an ever-mutating representation of chaos," and "in places where the Western Enlightenment has not penetrated and where there has always been mass poverty, people find liberation in violence."[108] The Israeli historian Martin Levi van Creveld foresaw a twenty-first century that is no longer defined by Fukuyaman-Hegelian great struggles over ideas and best forms of social organization, but instead a gradual ossification of order on both national and international level. In *The Transformation of War*, Creveld foresaw religious fanaticism and extremist ideologies playing "a larger role in the motivation of armed conflict" than any time "for the last 300 years."[109] He argues "[a]rmed conflict will be waged by men on earth, not robots in space. It will have more in common with the struggles of primitive tribes than with large-scale conventional war."[110] For the Israeli scholar, "Once the legal monopoly of armed force, long claimed by the state, is wrested out of its hands, existing distinctions between war and crime will break down."[111]

The rise of transnational terror groups such as the so-called Islamic State (IS) has, so far, provided a foreshadowing of this possible future. Early 2019 saw the defeat of the terror group, which utilizes state-of-the-art communication technology and art, as a state-building enterprise. But the group has quickly morphed into a global terror network with frightening implications across the Indo-Pacific, where ethnic-religious faultlines are deepest. Huntington famously discussed the so-called "fault line wars," where conflicts of the twenty-first century could be

---

[106]Fukuyama (2006).
[107]See Harari (2015) and Pinker (2012).
[108]Kaplan (1994).
[109]Creveld (1991).
[110]Ibid.
[111]Ibid.

most pronounced. For him, these "identity wars[112]" are highly fluid and unpredictable, because they "bubble up from below."[113] As Huntington explains, the world will confront a "hate dynamic," in which "mutual fears, distrust, and hatred feed on each other. Each side dramatizes and magnifies the distinction between the forces of virtue and the forces of evil and eventually attempts to transform this distinction into the ultimate distinction between the quick and the dead."[114] In these emerging wars, Huntington argued, "the identity most meaningful in relation to the conflict [that] comes to dominate" is "almost always...defined by religion."[115]

Huntington thesis on the macro-geopolitical landscape of inter-civilizational conflict was highly questionable, given the strength of nationalism and intra-civilizational conflicts. But he correctly foresaw the meso/micro-geopolitics of anarchy, terror and small-scale wars, which could inundate many nations across the Indo-Pacific. This dynamic has been patently in display in the highly populous and dynamic nations of South and Southeast Asia, which are also cauldrons of religious-ethnic conflicts.[116] The Philippines, a Catholic-majority nation, experienced the far-reaching tentacles of the IS in 2017, when a group of IS-affiliated fighters laid a months-long siege on the country's Muslim-majority city of Marawi in the deep south. It took the combined efforts of the Armed Forces of the Philippines, together with direct and continuous assistance from the United States, Australia, China, and a number of Southeast Asian nations, to prevent the IS from gaining a foothold and establishing a *Wilayat* (governorate) in East Asia. Given southern Philippines' porous borders, long history of religious-ethnic conflict as well as widespread poverty and underdevelopment, it was always, and will continue to be, considered as the strategic depth of the IS and other transnational Jihadist groups. By the end of the siege in October 2017, much of the city was reduced to ashes after months of bombardment and heavy clashes between the military and terror group. And more than a year later, there was hardly any rehabilitation and reconstruction effort underway, which will create a new wave of grievance that could serve as

[112] Huntington (2011, 266).

[113] Ibid., 298.

[114] Ibid., 266.

[115] Ibid., 267.

[116] D'Souza (2019).

a potential source of radicalization in the near future. The episode awakened the world to IS' own pivot to Asia after its progressive defeats in the Middle East following the entry of major powers, including Russia, the United States, and Iran, into the disparate anti-IS alliance in 2015.[117] Far from being discouraged by its failure to establish a foothold in Marawi, IS and its affiliates upped the ante in recent years, engaging in brutal attacks on Christian communities across the Indo-Pacific. On Palm Sunday in 2017, IS affiliates launched attacks on two Coptic churches in Egypt killing 49 individuals.[118] In May 2018, IS affiliates launched terror attacks against three Christian churches in Indonesia, killing 12 individuals and injuring dozens more.[119] Few months later, they attacked a Catholic Church during a Sunday mass in southern Philippines, killing at least 20 individuals.[120] In April 2019, during the Easter Sunday, IS-affiliated groups launched the deadliest terror attack since 9/11 attacks in New York. This took place, almost simultaneously, across various locations in Sri Lanka, targeting worshipers as well as tourists in Negombo, Batticaloa, and Colombo. The bombing, carried by a South Asian IS-affiliated group, killed 290 individuals and injured at least 500 others.[121]

In the Philippines, the siege on Marawi took place amid decades of neglect by the Christian majority national government exacerbated by stalled peace negotiations between the government and Muslim rebels.[122] In Sri Lanka, where Muslims also constitute around 10% of the population, it was the result of complete and total government paralysis amid a vicious power struggle between President Maithripala Sirisena and Prime Minister Ranil Wickremesinghe. As a result, the authorities failed to act on actionable and reliable intelligence relayed by Indian intelligence services days ahead of the attacks.[123] The perturbing ossification of political institutions across the region will only increase the probability of new waves of terror attacks, disintegration of political order, and festering of ethnic-religious conflicts across the Indo-Pacific.

[117] Heydarian (2019b).

[118] Michaelson (2017).

[119] Otto and Sentana (2018).

[120] CNN Newsource (2019).

[121] McKirdy et al. (2019).

[122] Heydarian (2017).

[123] Francis (2019).

The advent of climate change, which will bring about more natural disasters, will likely further feed on the "hate dynamics" that is driving fault line wars. In the case of Indonesia, the 2004 Tsunami upended collective mindsets in heavily devastated areas such as Banda Aceh, which turned increasingly austere and radicalized in recent years. What Muslim-majority nations such as Indonesia face is the prospect of ultra-conservative Salafist-Wahhabist Islam supplanting the traditionally more moderate, tolerant and syncretic form of Islam that dominated archipelagic Southeast Asia for centuries. Thus, we may soon witness the end of Southeast Asia's "Islamic exceptionalism," or what Robert Kaplan termed as "tropical Islam," an age-old thesis built on the (false) assumption that Arab-Middle East radical and ultra-conservative interpretations of Islam would never gain ground in the region.[124] In fact, recent years have already seen the erosion of secular "Pancasila" values in Indonesia, as even supposedly progressive leaders such as President Joko Widodo cuddled ultra-conservatives for electoral gain and political survival. As Indonesian novelist Eka Kurniawan wrote ahead of the 2019 Indonesian presidential elections, where Islamism was a major theme, "No matter who ends up being president, conservative Islamic groups, backed by radical groups, will win — have already won — the election."[125] In a sense, we are entering Hegel's "slaughter bench" of history,[126] where reactionary politics supplants utopian ideological struggles, which defined the twentieth century. In another sense, we may enter the real end of history, namely the irredeemable defeat of our centuries-old quest for order and prosperity in the material world, as opposed to the world of collective conscious (*Geist*) and ideological apotheosis that obsessed Hegel and his disciples like Alexandre Kojève and Fukuyama.

In *Collapse*, Jared Diamond explains the extinction of societies across the world throughout history due to either their inability to detect and appreciate impending crisis or failure to devise feasible solutions and, accordingly, mobilize necessary response in time. Climate change and environmental degradation played a crucial part in extinction of various societies, but even more important was their inability to mobilize urgent and effective response in cooperation with friendly neighbors and

[124] Kaplan (2011b).
[125] Kurniawan (2019).
[126] Marxists.org (2019, April 30 "Hegel's Philosophy ...").

based on a democratic pact between the ruling elite and the masses. In a globalized world, Diamond warns: "The problems of... environmentally devastated, overpopulated, distant countries [will] become our own problems..."[127] Thus, to stave off the worst effects of climate change, what's needed is the mobilization of collective resources comparable to World War II preparations by the allied forces, though on a far larger scale and across an extended time frame.[128] In this vortex of chaos, order will be pursued, and could only be achieved, through increasingly networked rather than hierarchical modes of cooperation. Or, to use the terminology of philosophers Gilles Deleuze and Felix Guattar, the future of the Indo-Pacific will have to be anchored by a "rhizomatic," namely flexible, decentered, and fluid modes of interaction and cooperation, as opposed to an arborescent/hierarchical order led by either the US or China. The upshot will be likely be a Pax Indo-Pacifica, rather than a Pax Sinica, as the scale, frequency, and intensity of spoke-to-spoke cooperation among US allies and like-minded nations increases in tandem with emerging challenges in coming decades. Instead of Washington or China singlehandedly dictating terms of the regional order, what we will likely witness are multifarious, multidirectional, horizontal, and dynamic "rhizomatic" networks of issue-driven "minilateral" cooperation. With the dissolution of defined and definite hierarchies, however, comes greater uncertainty of sustained cooperation commensurate to the magnitude of challenges at hand. As Naim Moises explains in *The End of Power*, we live in a "world where [too many] players have enough power to block everyone else's initiatives, but no one has the power to impose its preferred course of action is a world where decisions are not taken, taken too late, or watered down to the point of ineffectiveness."[129] The Indo-Pacific will either have to move toward a stable, rhizomatic order or risk falling into a "G-Zero" anarchy.[130] In the wise words of Malthus, which are poignantly relevant to our Indo-Pacific age: "Evil exists in the world not to create despair but activity. We are not to patiently submit to it, but to exert ourselves to avoid it."[131]

[127] Diamond (2011, 517).
[128] Wallace-Wells (2019b).
[129] Naím (2014).
[130] Bremmer and Roubini (2011).
[131] Malthus (1959).

For the past 100 thousand years, our species has not only survived against the greatest odds, but also thrived and became the dominant force on earth through its unique ability for adaptive and large-scale cooperation.[132] The question now is whether nations, as the largest aggregation of human collectives, can come together and overcome the cocktail of challenges on the horizon. All regional players, from smaller nations such as the Philippines, Vietnam, and Indonesia to middle powers of Australia, India, and Japan, all the way up to great powers of China and United States, will have to pitch in and collectively manage the existential conundrum facing the mega-region. A world state may not be inevitable,[133] contrary to the argument of creative scholars, but some form of institutionalized cooperation among all key players will become indispensable. The Indo-Pacific will either become the anchor of global order or, alternatively, the cauldron of humanity's darkest instincts. To avoid the latter scenario, the mega-region should shun zero-sum rivalry in favor of "coopetition" (cooperative competition). The Indo-Pacific security architecture stands at a crossroads: either we transition to sustained cooperation or collapse into barbarism.[134] It's a clear choice between enlightened coopetition and apocalyptic anarchy.

References

"'500-Year' Rain Events Are Happening More Often Than You Think." *CBS News*. September 8, 2017. https://www.cbsnews.com/news/what-does-500-year-flood-really-mean/.

"A Warning Sign from Our Planet: Nature Needs Life Support." *World Wildlife Fund*. October 30, 2018. https://www.wwf.org.uk/updates/living-planet-report-2018.

Acharya, Amitav. *The End of American World Order*. Cambridge: Polity, 2014.

Allison, Graham. "The Myth of the Liberal Order." *Foreign Affairs*. June 14, 2018. https://www.foreignaffairs.com/articles/2018-06-14/myth-liberal-order.

Alterman, Jon. "Militancy and the Arc of Instability in the Middle East and North Africa." *Center for Strategic & International Studies*. April 5, 2017.

---

[132] Harari (2015).

[133] Wendt (2003).

[134] Paraphrasing of Rosa Luxemburg's "Junius Pamphlet" in 1916, where the communist ideologue argued, "Bourgeois society stands at the crossroads, either transition to Socialism or regression into Barbarism."

https://www.csis.org/programs/transnational-threats-project/past-projects/militancy-and-arc-instability/militancy-and-arc.

Anderson, Perry. *American Foreign Policy and Its Thinkers*. New York: Verso, 2015.

Aravindan, Aradhana. "Millions of SE Asian Jobs May Be Lost to Automation in Next Two Decades: ILO." *Reuters*. July 7, 2016. https://www.reuters.com/article/us-southeast-asia-jobs-millions-of-se-asian-jobs-may-be-lost-to-automation-in-next-two-decades-ilo-idUSKCN0ZN0HP.

Baldwin, Richard. *The Great Convergence: Information Technology and the New Globalization*. Cambridge: Belknap Press; New York: W. W. Norton, 2016.

Block, Fred. "Polanyi's Double Movement and the Reconstruction of Critical Theory." *Revue Interventions économiques*. December 1, 2008. https://doi.org/10.4000/interventionseconomiques.274.

Bolwell, Dain. *Governing Technology in the Quest for Sustainability on Earth*. Abingdon: Routledge, 2019.

Bremmer, Ian. "The 'Strongmen Era' Is Here. Here's What It Means for You." *Time Magazine*. May 3, 2018. time.com/5264170/the-strongmen-era-is-here-heres-what-it-means-for-you/.

Bremmer, Ian, and Nouriel Roubini. "A G-Zero World." *Foreign Affairs*. January 31, 2011. https://www.foreignaffairs.com/articles/2011-01-31/g-zero-world.

Brennan, David. "Donald Trump's Indulgence of Putin, Xi and Kim Seen as 'Weakness and Manipulability' by World's Dictators: Veteran Diplomat." *Newsweek*. April 8, 2019. https://www.newsweek.com/donald-trump-dictators-weak-manipulate-vladimir-putin-xi-jinping-kim-jong-un-1388617.

Brynjolfsson, Erik, and Andrew McAfee. *The Second Machine Age: Work, Progress, and Prosperity in a Time of Brilliant Technologies*. New York: W. W. Norton, 2016.

Carrington, Damian. "Humans Just 0.01% of All Life but Have Destroyed 83% of Wild Mammals—Study." *The Guardian*. May 21, 2018. https://www.theguardian.com/environment/2018/may/21/human-race-just-001-of-all-life-but-has-destroyed-over-80-of-wild-mammals-study.

Chellaney, Brahma. "China's Creditor Imperialism." *Project Syndicate*. December 20, 2017. https://www.project-syndicate.org/commentary/china-sri-lanka-hambantota-port-debt-by-brahma-chellaney-2017-12.

Chen, Lulu Yilun, and Yoolim Lee. "The U.S. Is Losing a Major Front to China in the New Cold War." *Bloomberg*. April 15, 2019. https://www.bloomberg.com/news/articles/2019-04-14/china-wins-allies-for-web-vision-in-ideological-battle-with-u-s.

Chesney, Robert, and Danielle Citron. "Deepfakes and the New Disinformation War: The Coming Age of Post-Truth Geopolitics." *Foreign Affairs*. January/February 2019 Issue.

Churchwell, Sarah. *Behold, America: The Entangled History of "America First" and "the American Dream".* New York: Basic Books, 2018.

"Climate Watch Overview." *CAIT Climate Data Explorer.* April 19, 2019. http://cait2.wri.org/.

CNN Newsource. "Sri Lanka Suspects International Terror Link to Easter Sunday Atrocities." *The Denver Channel.* April 22, 2019. https://www.thedenver-channel.com/news/national/sri-lanka-bombings-death-toll-rises-to-290-in-brand-new-type-of-terrorism.

Creveld, Martin Van. *The Transformation of War: The Most Radical Reinterpretation of Armed Conflict Since Clausewitz.* New York: Free Press, 1991.

Daalder, Ivo, and James Lindsay. "The Committee to Save the World Order." *Foreign Affairs.* November/December 2018. https://www.foreignaffairs.com/articles/2018-09-30/committee-save-world-order.

De Luce, Dan, and Abigail Williams. "Trump Admin to Ban Entry of International Criminal Court Investigators." *NBC News.* March 16, 2019. https://www.nbcnews.com/politics/white-house/trump-admin-ban-entry-international-criminal-court-investigators-n983766.

Diamond, Jared. *Collapse: How Societies Choose to Fail or Succeed,* revised edition. Westminster: Penguin, 2011.

Diamond, Larry. "Democracy After Trump: Can a Populist Stop Democratic Decline?" *Foreign Affairs.* November 14, 2016. https://www.foreignaffairs.com/articles/world/2016-11-14/democracy-after-trump.

Dobell, Graeme. "Australia as an ASEAN Community Partner." *Australian Strategic Policy Institute.* February 20, 2018. https://www.aspi.org.au/report/australia-asean-community-partner.

D'Souza, Shanthie Mariet (eds.). *Countering Insurgencies and Violent Extremism in South and South East Asia.* Abingdon: Routledge, 2019.

Dutt, Barkha. "Is This the End of American Exceptionalism?" *Washington Post.* November 30, 2016. https://www.washingtonpost.com/news/global-opinions/wp/2016/11/30/is-this-the-end-of-american-exceptionalism/?utm_term=.249518066c5f.

Elgat, Guy. *Nietzsche's Psychology of Ressentiment: Revenge and Justice in "On the Genealogy of Morals".* Abingdon: Routledge, 2017.

Emmers, Ralf. "ASEAN Minus X: Should This Formula Be Extended?" *RSiS.* October 24, 2017. https://www.rsis.edu.sg/rsis-publication/cms/co17199-asean-minus-x-should-this-formula-be-extended/#.XNEWoo4zbIU.

Fox-Skelly, Jasmin. "There Are Diseases Hidden in Ice, and They Are Waking Up." *BBC.* May 4, 2017. http://www.bbc.com/earth/story/20170504-there-are-diseases-hidden-in-ice-and-they-are-waking-up.

Francis, Krishan. "Sri Lanka Political Rivalry Seen as Factor in Easter Blasts." *Associated Press.* April 26, 2019. https://www.apnews.com/43544291d0ac4d678e29c4c19c43bbff.

Friedberg, Aaron. "Competing with China." *Global Politics and Strategy* 60, no. 3 (2018): 7–64. https://doi.org/10.1080/00396338.2018.1470755.

Friedman, Lisa. "'I Don't Know That It's Man-Made' Trump Says of Climate Change. It Is." *The New York Times*. October 15, 2018. https://www.nytimes.com/2018/10/15/climate/trump-climate-change-fact-check.html.

Friedrich, Johannes, Mengpin Ge, and Andrew Pickens. "This Interactive Chart Explains World's Top 10 Emitters, and How They've Changed." *World Resource Institute*. April 11, 2017. https://www.wri.org/blog/2017/04/interactive-chart-explains-worlds-top-10-emitters-and-how-theyve-changed.

Fukuyama, Francis. *The End of History and the Last Man*. Michigan: Free Press, 2006.

Goh, Evelyn. *The Struggle for Order: Hegemony, Hierarchy, and Transition in Post-Cold War East Asia*. Oxford: Oxford University Press, 2014.

Goodwin, Geoff. "Rethinking the Double Movement: Expanding the Frontiers of Polanyian Analysis in the Global South." *Development and Change* 49, no. 5 (2018). https://doi.org/10.1111/dech.12419.

Hachigian, Nina. "The Other Problem in the South China Sea." *The Diplomat*. April 8, 2015. https://thediplomat.com/2015/04/the-other-problem-in-the-south-china-sea/.

Hao, Karen. "Is China's Social Credit System as Orwellian as It Sounds?" *MIT Technology Review*. February 26, 2019. https://www.technologyreview.com/f/613027/chinas-social-credit-system-isnt-as-orwellian-as-it-sounds/.

Harari, Yuval Noah. *Sapiens: A Brief History of Humankind*, reprint edition. New York: Harper Perennial, 2015.

Harari, Yuval Noah. "Why Technology Favors Tyranny." *The Atlantic*. October 2018. https://www.theatlantic.com/magazine/archive/2018/10/yuval-noah-harari-technology-tyranny/568330/.

Harris, Gardiner. "Trump Administration Withdraws U.S. from U.N. Human Rights Council." *The New York Times*. June 19, 2018. https://www.nytimes.com/2018/06/19/us/politics/trump-israel-palestinians-human-rights.html.

Hartog, Eva, and Lev Gudkov. "The Evolution of Homo Sovieticus to Putin's Man." *The Moscow Times*. October 13, 2017. https://themoscowtimes.com/articles/the-evolution-of-homo-sovieticus-to-putins-man-59189.

Harvey, David. *Social Justice and the City*. University of Georgia Press, 1973. http://www.jstor.org/stable/j.ctt46nm9v.

He, Hongmei, Jiao Nie, and Yao Wang. "China's Assistance for Chittagong Port Development, Not a Military Conspiracy." *The Daily Star*. June 26, 2018. https://www.thedailystar.net/opinion/perspective/chinas-assistance-chittagong-port-development-not-military-conspiracy-1595092.

Hegel, Georg W.F. *The Philosophy of History*. New York: Cosimo, Inc, 2007.

"Hegel's Philosophy of History." *Marxists.org*. Last date accessed April 30, 2019. https://www.marxists.org/reference/archive/hegel/works/hi/history3.htm.

Heydarian, Richard Javad. "Crisis in Mindanao: Duterte and the Islamic State's Pivot to Asia." *Aljazeera*. August 6, 2017. http://studies.aljazeera. net/en/reports/2017/08/crisis-mindanao-duterte-islamic-states-pivot-asia-170806101544864.html.

Heydarian, Richard Javad. "Duterte Is the Putin of Asia. Maria Ressa Is the Proof." *South China Morning Post*. March 4, 2019a. https://www.scmp. com/week-asia/opinion/article/2188183/duterte-putin-asia-maria-ressa-proof.

Heydarian, Richard Javad, "The Philippines' Counter-Terror Conundrum: Marawi and Duterte's Battle Against the Islamic State." In Shanthie Mariet D'Souza (ed.), *Countering Insurgencies and Violent Extremism in South and South East Asia*. Abingdon: Routledge, 2019b.

Heydarian, Richard Javad. "Hooking Up with Najib, Arroyo and Rajapaksa: The Risk of China's Attachment to Discredited Leaders." *South China Morning Post*. July 1, 2018. https://www.scmp.com/news/china/diplomacy-defence/article/2153194/hooking-razak-arroyo-andrajapaksa-risks-chinas.

Heydarian, Richard Javad. "Is ASEAN Still Relevant." *The Diplomat*. March 26, 2015. https://thediplomat.com/2015/03/is-asean-still-relevant/.

Huang, Zheping. "Xi Jinping Says China's Authoritarian System Can Be a Model for the World." *Quartz*. March, 2018. https://qz.com/1225347/xi-jinping-says-chinas-one-party-authoritarian-system-can-be-a-model-for-the-world/.

Huntington, Samuel. "Democracy's Third Wave." *Journal of Democracy* 2, no. 2 (1991): 12–34. https://doi.org/10.1353/jod.1991.0016.

Huntington, Samuel. *The Clash of Civilizations and the Remaking of World Order*. New York: Simon & Schuster, 2011.

Huntington, Samuel. *The Third Wave: Democratization in the Late 20th Century*. Norman: University of Oklahoma Press, 1993.

Ikenberry, G. John. "The End of Liberal International Order." *International Affairs* 94, no. 1 (2018): 7–23. https://doi.org/10.1093/ia/iix241.

Illing, Sean. "How 'America First' Ruined the 'American Dream'." *Vox*. October 22, 2018. https://www.vox.com/2018/10/22/17940964/america-first-trump-sarah-churchwell-american-dream.

Jaafari, Shirin. "Iran Wasn't Ready for These Huge Floods: But They Should Get Ready for More in the Future." *PRI*. April 29, 2019. https://www.pri.org/stories/2019-04-29/unprecedented-floods-iran-have-brought-people-together.

Johnson, Ian. "A Specter Is Haunting Xi's China: 'Mr. Democracy'." *The New York Review of Books Daily*. April 19, 2019. https://www.nybooks.com/daily/2019/04/19/a-specter-is-haunting-xis-china-mr-democracy/.

Kaplan, Robert. *Monsoon: The Indian Ocean and the Future of American Power*. New York: Random House Trade Paperbacks, 2011a.

Kaplan, Robert. "13: Indonesia's Tropical Islam." In *Monsoon: The Indian Ocean and the Future of American Power.* New York: Random House Trade Paperbacks, 2011b.

Kaplan, Robert. "The Coming Anarchy." *The Atlantic.* February 1994. https://www.theatlantic.com/ideastour/archive/kaplan.html.

Kaplan, Robert. *The Coming Anarchy: Shattering the Dreams of the Post Cold War.* New York: Vintage, 2001.

Khanna, Parag. *The Future Is Asian.* New York: Simon & Schuster, 2019.

Kimmage, Michael. "The People's Authoritarian." *Foreign Affairs.* July/August 2018. https://www.foreignaffairs.com/reviews/review-essay/2018-06-14/peoples-authoritarian.

King, David. "David King on Climate Repair." *Talking Politics.* Podcast Audio. April 27, 2019. https://www.talkingpoliticspodcast.com/blog/2019/160-david-king-on-climate-repair.

Kirby, Jen. "China's Brutal Crackdown on the Uighur Muslim Minority, Explained." *Vox.* November 6, 2018. https://www.vox.com/2018/8/15/17684226/uighur-china-camps-united-nations.

Kissinger, Henry. "How the Enlightenment Ends." *The Atlantic.* June 2018. https://www.theatlantic.com/magazine/archive/2018/06/henry-kissinger-ai-could-mean-the-end-of-human-history/559124/.

Kolbert, Elizabeth. *The Sixth Extinction: An Unnatural History.* New York: Henry Holt, 2014.

Kurniawan, Eka. "Indonesia's Next Election Is in April: The Islamists Have Already Won." *The New York Times.* February 14, 2019. https://www.nytimes.com/2019/02/14/opinion/indonesia-election-religion-islam-islamists.html.

Leahy, Stephen. "Parts of Asia May Be Too Hot for People by 2100." *National Geographic.* August 2, 2017. https://news.nationalgeographic.com/2017/08/south-asia-heat-waves-temperature-rise-global-warming-climate-change/.

Lee, Kai-Fu. "10 Jobs That Are Safe in an AI World." *Medium.* October 1, 2018. https://medium.com/@kaifulee/10-jobs-that-are-safe-in-an-ai-world-ec-4c45523f4f.

Leprince-Ringuet. "The Brazilian Election Could Be a Disaster for the Amazon Rainforest." *Wired.* October 28, 2018. https://www.wired.co.uk/article/brazil-election-runoff-bolsonaro-amazon.

Liang, Annabelle, and Jim Gomez. "China Calls Draft Pact on Territorial Feud a 'Breakthrough'." *Associated Press.* August 2, 2018. https://apnews.com/bb4ae083f10d45f292520a6a5cd296fd.

"Making the World "Safe for Democracy": Woodrow Wilson Asks for War." *History Matters.* Last date accessed April 19, 2019. http://historymatters.gmu.edu/d/4943/.

Malthus, Thomas Robert. *An Essay on the Principle of Population.* New York: Dover Publications, 2007.

Malthus, Thomas. *Population: The First Essay.* Michigan: Ann Arbor Paperbacks, 1959.

McCarthy, Niall. "China Used More Concrete in 3 Years Than the U.S. Used in the Entire 20th Century [Infographic]." *Forbes.* December 5, 2014. https://www.forbes.com/sites/niallmccarthy/2014/12/05/china-used-more-concrete-in-3-years-than-the-u-s-used-in-the-entire-20th-century-infographic/#ff5df644131a.

McKirdy, Eaun, Sheena McKenzie, Caitlin Hu, Lauren Said-Moorhouse, Harmeet Kaur, Jessie Yeung, and Meg Wagner. "Sri Lanka Attack Death Toll Rises to 290." *CNN World.* April 24, 2019. https://edition.cnn.com/asia/live-news/sri-lanka-easter-sunday-explosions-dle-intl/index.html.

Mead, Walter Russel. *Special Providence: American Foreign Policy and How It Changed the World,* 1st edition. Abingdon: Routledge, 2002.

Michaelson, Ruth. "Egypt: Isis Claims Responsibility for Coptic Church Bombings." *The Guardian.* April 9, 2017. https://www.theguardian.com/world/2017/apr/09/egypt-coptic-church-bombing-death-toll-rises-tanta-cairo.

Mishra, Pankaj. *Age of Anger: A History of the Present.* New York: Farrar, Straus and Giroux, 2017.

Mogato, Manuel. "Philippines Says China Wanted Non-legally Binding South China Sea Code." *Reuters.* August 8, 2017. https://www.reuters.com/article/us-asean-philippines-southchinasea-idUSKBN1AO1LW.

"Multilateral Development Banks Present Study on Technology's Impact on Jobs." *Asian Development Bank.* April 19, 2018. https://www.adb.org/news/multilateral-development-banks-present-study-technologys-impact-jobs.

Naím, Moisés. *The End of Power: From Boardrooms to Battlefields and Churches to States, Why Being in Charge Isn't What It Used to Be,* reprint edition. New York: Basic Books, 2014.

Naím, Moisés, and Francisco Toro. "Venezuela's Suicide." *Foreign Affairs.* October 15, 2018. https://www.foreignaffairs.com/articles/south-america/2018-10-15/venezuelas-suicide.

Osnos, Evan. "Doomsday Prep for the Super-Rich." *The New Yorker.* January 22, 2017. https://www.newyorker.com/magazine/2017/01/30/doomsday-prep-for-the-super-rich.

Otto, Ben, and I Made Sentana. "Family of Suicide Bombers Attacks Churches in Indonesia." *The Wall Street Journal.* May 13, 2018. https://www.wsj.com/articles/bomb-attacks-rock-three-indonesia-churches-1526177568.

Pinker, Steven. *The Better Angels of Our Nature: Why Violence Has Declined.* Westminster: Penguin Books, 2012.

Polanyi, Karl. *The Great Transformation: The Political and Economic Origins of Our Time,* 2nd edition. Boston: Beacon Press, 2001.

Prashad, Vijay. *The Poorer Nations: A Possible History of the Global South.* Brooklyn: Verso, 2014.

Putnam, Robert, Robert Leonardo, and Raffaella Nanetti. *Making Democracy Work: Civic Traditions in Modern Italy.* Princeton: Princeton University Press, 1994.

Rachman, Gideon. *Easternization: Asia's Rise and America's Decline from Obama to Trump and Beyond.* New York: Other Press, 2017.

Ramesh, Randeep. "Paradise Almost Lost: Maldives Seek to Buy a New Homeland." *The Guardian.* November 10, 2008. https://www.theguardian.com/environment/2008/nov/10/maldives-climate-change.

Rees, Martin. *Our Final Hour: A Scientist's Warning.* New York: Basic Books, 2004.

Risen, James. "Unanswered Questions in the Mueller Report Point to a Sprawling Russian Spy Game." *The Intercept.* April 28, 2019. https://theintercept.com/2019/04/28/mueller-report-trump-russia-questions/.

Roberts, Timmons. "One Year Since Trump's Withdrawal from the Paris Climate Agreement." *Brookings.edu.* June 1, 2018. https://www.brookings.edu/blog/planetpolicy/2018/06/01/one-year-since-trumps-withdrawal-from-the-paris-climate-agreement/.

Roughneed, Simon. "Nearly One Billion Asians in Vulnerable Jobs, Says ILO." *Nikkei Asian Review.* January 23, 2018. https://asia.nikkei.com/Economy/Nearly-one-billion-Asians-in-vulnerable-jobs-says-ILO.

Sharma, Ruchir. "Breakout Nations: In Pursuit of the Next Economic Miracles." New York: W. W. Norton, 2012.

Shi, Jiangtao, and Zhen Liu. "'Better Left Untouched': Philippines and Vietnam Wary of Trump Offer to Media South China Sea Disputes." November 12, 2017. https://www.scmp.com/news/china/diplomacy-defence/article/2119551/better-left-untouched-philippines-and-vietnam-wary.

Sieg, Linda, and Kiyoshi Takenaka. "Japan to Resume Commercial Whaling After Pulling Out of IWC." *Reuters.* December 26, 2018. https://www.reuters.com/article/us-japan-whaling/japan-to-withdraw-from-international-whaling-commission-idUSKCN1OP03O.

Smith, Julianne, and Jim Townsend. "NATO in the Age of Trump." *Foreign Affairs.* July 9, 2018. https://www.foreignaffairs.com/articles/europe/2018-07-09/nato-age-trump.

Snyder, Timothy. *The Road to Unfreedom: Russia, Europe, America.* Manhattan: Tim Duggan Books, 2018.

Tai, Catherine, and Ken Jacques. "Democracy That Delivers #141: The Belt and Road Initiative's Impact on Chinese Corrosive Capital." *Center for International Private Enterprise.* January 23, 2019. https://www.cipe.org/blog/2019/01/23/democracy-that-delivers-141-the-belt-and-road-initiatives-impact-on-chinese-corrosive-capital/.

Thayer, Carl. "A Closer Look at the ASEAN-China Single Draft South China Sea Code of Conduct." *The Diplomat*. August 3, 2018. https://thediplomat.com/2018/08/a-closer-look-at-the-asean-china-single-draft-south-china-sea-code-of-conduct/.

"The Phenomenology of the Mind: Self Consciousness." *Marxists.org*. Last date accessed April 30, 2019b. https://www.marxists.org/reference/archive/hegel/works/ph/phba.htm.

Tobin, Meaghan. "My Way or the Huawei: How US Ultimatum Over China's 5G Giant Fell Flat in Southeast Asia." *South China Morning Post*. April 20, 2019. https://www.scmp.com/week-asia/geopolitics/article/3006961/my-way-or-huawei-how-us-ultimatum-over-chinas-5g-giant-fell.

"Voting System: Simple Majority." *European Council: Council of the European Union*. Last date accessed May 6, 2019. https://www.consilium.europa.eu/en/council-eu/voting-system/qualified-majority/.

Walker, Christopher, and Jessica Ludwig. "The Meaning of Sharp Power." *Foreign Affairs*. November 16, 2017. https://www.foreignaffairs.com/articles/china/2017-11-16/meaning-sharp-power.

Walker, Christopher, Shanthi Kalathil, and Jessica Ludwig. "How Democracies Can Fight Authoritarian Sharp Power." *Foreign Affairs*. August 16, 2018. https://www.foreignaffairs.com/articles/china/2018-08-16/how-democracies-can-fight-authoritarian-sharp-power.

Wallace-Wells, David. "The Copernican Principle." *Talking Politics*. Podcast Audio. April 18, 2019a. https://player.fm/series/talking-politics-1423621/the-copernican-principle.

Wallace-Wells, David. *The Uninhabitable Earth: Life After Warming*. New York: Tim Duggan Books, 2019b.

Wallace-Wells, David. "When Will the Planet Be Too Hot for Humans? Much, Much Sooner Than You Imagine. *New York Magazine*. July 9, 2017. http://nymag.com/intelligencer/2017/07/climate-change-earth-too-hot-for-humans.html.

Wendt, Alexander. "Why a World State Is Inevitable." *European Journal of International Relations* 9, no. 4 (2003): 491–542. https://doi.org/10.1177/135406610394001.

Zuboff, Shoshana. *The Age of Surveillance Capitalism: The Fight for a Human Future at the New Frontier of Power*. New York: Public Affairs, 2019.

CPSIA information can be obtained
at www.ICGtesting.com
Printed in the USA
LVHW011926150822
725987LV00002B/90